MW01089395

Racial Battle Fatigue

Racial Battle Fatigue

Insights from the Front Lines of Social Justice Advocacy

Jennifer L. Martin, Editor

Foreword by H. Richard Milner IV

 PRAEGER

AN IMPRINT OF ABC-CLIO, LLC
Santa Barbara, California • Denver, Colorado • Oxford, England

Library of Congress Cataloging-in-Publication Data
Racial battle fatigue : insights from the front lines of social justice
advocacy / Jennifer L. Martin, editor ; foreword by H. Richard Milner IV.
     pages cm
   Includes bibliographical references and index.
   ISBN 978-1-4408-3209-3 (print : alk. paper) — ISBN 978-1-4408-3210-9 (e-book)
1. Discrimination in education—United States.   2. Racism—United States.   3. Racism—
United States—Study and teaching.   4. Social justice—United States.   5. Social justice—
United States—Study and teaching.   I. Martin, Jennifer L. (Professor of education)
   LC212.2.R325   2015
   371.829′96073—dc23   2014029036

ISBN: 978-1-4408-3209-3
EISBN: 978-1-4408-3210-9

19 18 17 16 15   1 2 3 4 5

This book is also available on the World Wide Web as an eBook.
Visit www.abc-clio.com for details.

Praeger
An Imprint of ABC-CLIO, LLC

ABC-CLIO, LLC
130 Cremona Drive, P.O. Box 1911
Santa Barbara, California 93116-1911

This book is printed on acid-free paper ∞

Manufactured in the United States of America

Contents

PART III: PEDAGOGY AND PRACTICE

Foreword

H. Richard Milner IV

In 1964, Fannie Lou Hamer delivered a provocative speech at the Williams Institutional CME Church in Harlem, New York. The title of her lecture was "I'm Sick and Tired of Being Sick and Tired." Hamer, a Black woman born in 1916 in Montgomery County, Mississippi, was a civil rights leader and worked tirelessly for voting rights for Black people and other marginalized groups. In her speech, she talked about racist and sexist experiences she encountered in Mississippi and also stressed that some in other cities across the United States still dealt with relentless discrimination against Black people and women in particular. A central point of her lecture was that some people were not "free" at all and that current conditions caused some to experience life in society in slave-like ways, even though federal mandates had begun to support rights among all citizenry in the United States. She provided poignant stories of resilience of her family as they worked and fought through phobias and isms both in their personal interactions in the south and in the workforce. The title of Hamer's speech metaphorically connects with the theme and message of this book. Like Hamer, the authors of this volume are *sick and tired of being sick and tired* of racist, sexist, homophobic, xenophobic, hegemonic, and inequitable structures and systems both inside and outside of education.

Racial Battle Fatigue: Insights from the Front Lines of Social Justice Advocacy is a powerfully important volume that brings together a diverse range of scholars committed to social justice. The stories shared in this book provide empirical, analytical, and conceptual sites of nuance that allow consumers of the text to critically examine how oppressive conditions can foster psychological, socio-emotional and cognitive strain as social justice advocates work to expose and dismantle inequity. Although much of the empirical and theoretical scholarship related to microaggression has shepherded the field into more deeply examining, measuring, and understanding race and racism, this book extends this dialogue—not ignoring the salience and permanence of racism—by including other forms of marginalization such as gender discrimination and the intersecting nature of oppressive structures such as racism and gender discrimination.

Although some still believe and advance conversations that would suggest that we currently live in a postracial U.S. society—mainly because of the election of our nation's first Black president—this book disputes this notion by providing compelling examples of the ways in which microaggressions *still* manifest in people's everyday lives. Unlike some edited volumes, here are consistent and provocative stories between and among the different chapters that draw a logical story line, which allows the book to tackle common themes from diverse perspectives. Thus, readers of this text will learn about how the micro can result in macro outcomes. As institutions of higher education (and beyond) slowly and incrementally undermine the very essence and existence of particular individuals and groups of people, they almost methodically ensure that these people continue to be negatively influenced personally. Moreover, the slow (and what might be seen as small) actions that undermine some by those in power work to ensure that the perspectives, contributions, and actions of those committed to social justice and equity remain on the margins. In this way, readers are invited to think about and deepen their insights about how racial battle fatigue can exist and why. This book makes the case for why it is critical that social justice workers are not bullied away from emancipatory work that can make a difference for those within and outside of traditional institutions of education.

Across the chapters, the stories shared about the challenges these social justice educators face indeed provide insights into what the editor Jennifer Martin calls a *pedagogy of vulnerability*. And while her explanation of this pedagogy is shaped by her untenured status, such vulnerability likely will not end post-tenure. For instance, as a scholar committed to social justice but also one who experiences microaggressions, even as an endowed chair and full professor at a research-intensive-institution, the sad reality is that even after one earns tenure, microaggressions persist and racial battle fatigue can intensify. They may falter a bit—become somewhat less noticeable or occur less frequently—but microaggressions and the fatigue they cause continue.

Just a few weeks ago, as an African American male, I sat in a meeting and offered my perspective to the group about ways to increase the number of doctoral applications to our program. People in the room ignored my suggestions—moving on by offering others. Then, a few minutes later, a white colleague at my same rank offered the *exact same* suggestion I made minutes prior. This time, the suggestion was accepted, and this full professor was "lauded" for such an outstanding idea. But the idea was mine, and I offered it just minutes earlier. However, the white colleagues in the room either did not hear me or did not *want* to hear me. But I, like Fannie Lou Hamer and the authors of this book, am *sick and tired of being sick and tired*. Revealing these microaggressions is only part of a much more complex task we face. We must do something about them. This book is not only a compelling example of how an edited volume can bring together a set of collective voices to expose readers to the persistence of racism and other forms of discrimination, it is also a call to action to actually do something to end these toxic (individual and institutional) practices! Exposing microaggressions; calling them out when they occur; and demanding individual, structural, and systemic shifts are but a few ways we can redress their deleterious effects. But as the authors of this book query, is it possible for microaggressions—especially related to race—to ever completely end in a society in which race and racism are at the very core of our work and lives? Certainly our physical, mental, physiological, psychological, and emotional humanity are at stake and deserve better! Fortunately, this book takes us one step forward in the arduous task for social justice.

REFERENCE

Hamer, F. L. (1964). I'm sick and tired of being sick and tired. [Speech delivered with Malcolm X at the Williams Institutional CME Church, Harlem, New York, December 20, 1964.] Accessible at http://www.crmvet.org/docs/flh64.htm

H. Richard Milner IV
University of Pittsburgh, Pittsburgh, PA

Acknowledgments

There is no greater agony than bearing an untold story inside you.
—Maya Angelou

I dedicate this volume to two public intellectuals who lived their lives as allies for social justice: Dr. Maya Angelou and Dr. Maxine Greene. Although we lost two of our heroes in the year of this writing, 2014, their ideas will continue to challenge us, just as their lives will continue to inspire us. They were open in telling the stories of their lives. We would do well to do the same.

I could neither do what I do, nor be where I am today without the support of great mentors, and I have many. I wish to thank Dr. Michele Paludi, Dr. Julia Smith, Dr. Nancy Brown, and Dr. Michelle Collins-Sibley for providing me with endless guidance and support throughout the years. Your lives and your work have been a model for the person I hope to one day become.

I thank my institution, The University of Mount Union, for supporting this work. I thank my students, past and present, for challenging me to do a better job every single day. I am grateful to be able to share my story in this space and to welcome new and old friends and colleagues to share theirs.

I thank my friends and my family for understanding my need to do social justice work, despite the repercussions that undoubtedly impact them. They have been unwavering in their support of me, and crucial in reading drafts. Thank you to Peter Midtgard, Martina Sharp-Grier, Julia Persky, and Ken Vanderworp.

I would like to extend an extra special thanks to Dr. H. Richard Milner IV for his support of this project and for agreeing to write the Foreword. I contacted Dr. Milner, never having met him in person, because I admired and was inspired by his work. He immediately agreed to contribute. Soon thereafter, I had the opportunity to meet Dr. Milner at the American Educational Research Association Annual Meeting in Philadelphia, in early 2014. He was most gracious and mentored a group of novice scholars, myself included, for an extended period of time. Dr. Milner openly shared his knowledge with us, and I am immensely grateful for his guidance.

I also thank Debbie Carvalko at Praeger for believing in this project from the beginning.

REFERENCE

Angelou, M. (n.d.). *Maya Angelou quotes.* Retrieved June 1, 2014, from http://www.brainyquote.com/quotes/authors/m/maya_angelou.html

Introduction

Jennifer L. Martin

What the best and wisest parent wants for his own child, that must the community want for all of its children. Any other ideal for our schools is narrow and unlovely; acted upon, it destroys our democracy. All that society has accomplished for itself is put, through the agency of the school, at the disposal of its future members. All its better thoughts of itself it hopes to realize through the new possibilities [are] thus opened to its future itself.

—John Dewey

All our silences in the face of racist assault are acts of complicity.

—bell hooks

Racial Battle Fatigue: Insights from the Front Lines of Social Justice Advocacy brings together a collection of personal stories and critical reflections on the repercussions of doing social justice work in the field and in the university. In this volume, activists, scholars, activist scholars, and public intellectuals share experiences of microaggressions, racial battle fatigue, and retaliation because of their identities, the people for whom they advocate, and what they study. The term racial battle fatigue (RBF) is used to describe three major stress responses—physiological, psychological, and behavioral—and involves the energy expended on coping with and fighting racism that is exacted on racially marginalized and stigmatized groups (Smith, 2008); dealing with daily microaggressions is but one example of dealing with everyday racism.

According to Sue, Capodilupo, Torino, Bucceri, Holder, Nadal, and Esquilin (2007), "Racial microaggressions are brief and commonplace daily verbal, behavioral, or environmental indignities, whether intentional or unintentional, that communicate hostile, derogatory, or negative racial slights and insults toward people of color. Perpetrators of microaggressions are often unaware that they engage in such communications when they interact with racial/ethnic minorities" (p. 271). Sue et al. conceptualized a classification system of racial microaggressions in 2007, thereby noting three types of racial transgressions: micro-assaults, micro-insults, and micro-invalidations. Micro-assaults involve "conscious and intentional actions or slurs" (p. 274), such as racist speech, a display of racist symbols (swastikas, confederate flags), or performing racism through showing preference to a white person over a person of color. Micro-insults involve communication, verbal or nonverbal, that either invalidates or demeans one's racial heritage or identity; for example, asking whether a person of color was hired because of affirmative action policies, thereby questioning her or his qualifications (Sue et al., 2007). Micro-invalidations are overt or covert nullifications of the feelings and experiences of people of color who experience the aforementioned transgressions; it is common for people possessing privilege to deny the existence of racial transgressions (Sue et al., 2007).

Experiencing racial microaggressions often leaves the person of color "in question" caught in a double bind; this is the classic "Catch-22": If a victim of racial transgressions confronts the perpetrator, commonly, the perpetrator will deny it, minimize it, or dismiss it (Sue et al., 2007, p. 279). Thus, the person of color questions what actually happened—and even her own sanity; these experiences can be exhausting and emotionally taxing (Sue et al., 2007). I would also argue that micro-assaults, micro-insults, and micro-invalidations can be perpetrated against persons who possess any identities that deviate from the hegemonic norm, such as nondominant gender or sexual identities, particularly those possessing multiple minority statuses.

Persons possessing dominant identities often do not see their own societal privilege (Milner, 2013), often deny the existence of structural inequalities, and instead attribute success to hard work. These insights set the stage for my entrance to the tenure track: I work at a PWI (Predominantly White Institution) and have experienced a variety of microaggressions, including resistance from students when asking them to examine the status quo, privilege, racism, and white supremacy in our schools and society. I deem my examination of this journey "a pedagogy of vulnerability." These feelings of vulnerability led me to ask the question: Do educators who engage in social justice work face heightened challenges in comparison to their colleagues, and, if so, how does this impact them professionally? This question then led me to conceptualize this volume in general, but I first must acknowledge my own privilege as a white woman and state that although I am seeking to tell my own story in this space, I am interested in diverse perspectives in investigating and interrogating this question. As a white woman, I do not claim racial battle fatigue, but I seek to learn what my colleagues of color face in their classroom and institutional spaces.

Brene Brown (2010) tells us that "what makes us vulnerable makes us beautiful" (n.p.), but despite the fact that I agree with Brown's assessment of the concept of vulnerability in general, the topics that will be addressed in this volume critique the implications of this vulnerability; working for social justice, thereby making ourselves vulnerable, can cause those who engage in this work great personal and professional consequences. It would be much easier for us to teach traditional, noncontroversial content, but something stops us from doing so. We are moved and inspired by our heroes to create a more just world. We are troubled by the business model of education, a model that cares more for the bottom line than for the hearts and minds of students, and, consequently, for those who teach them. Teaching for the hearts and minds of our students is more difficult than teaching with an eye to the bottom line. As Deresiewicz (2008) reminds us, "Being an intellectual means thinking your way toward a vision of the good society and then trying to realize that vision by speaking truth to power. It means going into spiritual exile" (para. 27). This is necessary work, but one laden with challenges. As educators, we are demonized by politicians and the media and demoralized by claims that our schools and universities are broken. This is an elaborate ruse.

When the smoke clears, if we allow our eyes to adjust to the harsh and painful realities, we realize that schools and universities are the battlegrounds of cultural wars and hegemonic fears that our country is changing. The banning of ethnic studies in Arizona is but one illustration of this fact. We must continue to tell our stories so that the truth of this work, this vulnerability, may be revealed. Finding support from colleagues also speaking truth to power can give us the strength to continue to fight for our ideas and our ideals, and for the hearts and minds of our students. In a live chat (Nieto, 2014) with Dr. Sonia Nieto on June 5, 2014, I had the opportunity to ask this question, "How do you deal with the pain of doing anti-oppression work with resistant students, or dominant students who deny inequality?" Dr. Nieto replied, "Make sure the rest of your life is in order, have good strong relationships with people who you love, make sure you do things that bring happiness to your life so this is not the only thing you do all the time. Some people have left the field because it is so painful. But I understand. There is a psychic cost to it" (n.p.). Because this work is so personally taxing, we must do other things to nurture our spirit. I would also argue that we must share our stories, for much can be learned from this telling; one such lesson is that structural inequality is still a disturbing reality in the United States, which often plays out in our schools and universities.

At the time of this writing, summer 2014, we celebrate the 60th anniversary of *Brown v. Board of Education* (1954), the U.S. Supreme Court case declaring separate public schools for Black and white students unconstitutional, overturning *Plessy v. Ferguson* (1896), which upheld state-sponsored segregation in public education. The *Brown* decision made de jure racial segregation a violation of the Equal Protection Clause of the 14th Amendment. A major factor in the *Brown* case was the work of Kenneth and Mamie Clark. Psychologists at Columbia University, the Clarks' "doll experiments" of the 1940s illustrated how children were impacted by segregation. In these experiments, children were presented with two identical dolls, but for skin and hair color: one with brown skin and black hair, the other with white skin and blonde hair. The children participants were asked which doll they preferred and various other questions, such as which one looks "bad," and which has the "nicer color." The participants showed an overall preference for the white doll, which illustrated internalized racism among African American children. Such feelings of self-hatred were more pronounced in children who attended segregated schools (American Psychological Association, 2014). As Kenneth Clark stated, "The Negro child accepts as early as six, seven, or eight the negative stereotypes about his own group. . . . These children . . . like other human beings who are subjected to an obviously inferior status in the society in which they live, have been definitely harmed in the development of their personalities" (Clark, as cited in Beggs, 1995, n.p.).

In fact, new data from the U.S. Department of Education's Office for Civil Rights (2014) illustrates how racism and structural inequalities impact schools today. Some of the most startling findings from these data include: although African American students account for only 18 percent of U.S. pre-K enrollment, they account for 48 percent of *preschoolers* [emphasis mine] with multiple suspensions; African American students are expelled three times more than their white counterparts; African American and Latina/o students account for 40 percent of enrollment at schools offering gifted programs, but only 26 percent of students in said programs; African American, Latina/o, students and Native American students attend schools with higher percentages of first-year teachers (3 to 4 percent) than their white counterparts (1 percent); and African American students are more than three times as likely to attend schools where less than 60 percent of teachers meet all state requirements for certification and licensure. The above findings have great implications for our K–12 schools, for higher education, and for society in general. The issue of financial and resource equity in education continues to be a crucial issue. Can the heart of our nation be judged by the allocation of their resources? Tellingly, more resources are allocated to incarceration than to education. Despite the fact that the United States is one of the wealthiest nations, it comprises 5 percent of the world's population and 25 percent of the world's inmates (Darling-Hammond, 2010). As Kozol (2005) argues, the discrepancy in funding for public schools in the United States disproportionately impacts the poor and people of color, leading to an intractable opportunity gap. The question that remains is, how far are we from *Brown*?

Although we are decades away from *Brown*, we are not metaphorically far from the above-mentioned feelings of students of color illustrated by the Clarks' experiments, trapped in segregated schools and reduced to feelings of inferiority; their surroundings teach them this. According to Chanel Smith, current Philadelphia public school student and advocate for Youth United for Change, "We don't have support at all. We have lack of books, resources, anything you can think of, but when we go in contact with these white children, or as some say Caucasian, they don't know how to act because they believe that they're better than us, and we don't know how to act because we believe that they're better than us" (quoted from Harris Perry, 2014, n.p.). This issue is not only relevant to those students attending these schools, but to society in general. We cannot sustain the social bargain if we do nothing about inequality. The cultural workers and public intellectuals who point out these truths require institutional support in order to continue to engage in this work, for although it is often taxing, thankless, and disheartening, it is crucial. This volume, *Racial Battle Fatigue: Insights from the Front Lines of Social Justice Advocacy* is necessary in sharing the difficulties of doing anti-oppression work.

Banks (2013) argues that what is necessary in today's schools is "transformative citizenship education," which includes: challenging mainstream knowledge for the purpose of improving the human condition, recognizing and valuing diversity and social/community activism with the goal of producing a multicultural democracy, and developing cosmopolitan values. In our current era of accountability, the exact opposite of what Banks advocates is occurring in schools today. Darling-Hammond (2013) argues that to meet the demands of the 21st century, we must establish equitable schools in order to prepare our students for this knowledge-based, global, and multicultural world economy. In order to do this, we must view diversity as a strength and not as a deficit (Apple, 2013). We must develop and nurture all students with the intention of embracing the ideal of global citizenship, and it begins in schools.

The 19th-century Common Schools were created to build and sustain democracy, teach children to live and work together, and teach the skills and knowledge necessary to fully participate within a democratic society. Cronon (1998) reminds us that education should celebrate and nurture human freedom, with the goal that "everyone might someday be liberated by an education that stands in the service of human freedom" (p. 2). Collectively, we must do more as a society to heed the advice of Dewey

(1899): to educate our children in a democratic and equitable manner. Cultural workers and public intellectuals must advocate for: an investment in early childhood education; rich and varied curriculums, including the arts, in all schools; the measurement of knowledge and skills with care (not standardized tests); the democratic control of public schools; the recognition of education as a public good; reduced segregation; equitable and fair resource allocation (adapted from Ravitch, 2013); and the heightening of education as a profession, both in K–12 and the professorate. Educators must be empowered to speak the truth of the reality of schooling, and their institutions must support them in these endeavors. If these needs are not met, we must ask the questions: what is the purpose of schools? And what is the purpose of education in a democratic society? The acknowledgment that inequities exist is a fundamental part of this process; if we do not sound our voices, we are complicit, as hooks (1996) suggests, in the inequities that abound around us. It is my hope that this volume, *Racial Battle Fatigue: Insights from the Front Lines of Social Justice Advocacy*, can play some part in bringing to light some of the issues we face when teaching about issues of racism and other forms of oppression in today's classrooms. We are raising our collective voices in the hope that many will listen.

REFERENCES

American Psychological Association. (2014). *Featured psychologists: Mamie Phipps Clark, Ph.D. and Kenneth Clark, Ph.D.* Retrieved May 1, 2014, from http://www.apa.org/pi/oema/resources/ethnicity-health/psychologists/clark.aspx

Apple, M. (2013). Thinking internationally and paying our debts: Critical thoughts on diversity, globalization, and education. *Kappa Delta Pi Record, 49*(3), 118–120.

Banks, J. (2013). Group identity and citizenship education in global times. *Kappa Delta Pi Record, 49*(3), 108–112.

Beggs, G. (1995, October). Novel expert evidence in federal civil rights litigation. *The American University Law Review, 45*. Retrieved May 1, 2014, from http://www.wcl.american.edu/journal/lawrev/45/beggstxt.html

Brown, B. (2010, June). *The power of vulnerability.* TEDxHouston. Retrieved May 1, 2014, from https://www.ted.com/talks/brene_brown_on_vulnerability

Cronon, W. (1998). "Only connect . . .": The goals of a liberal education. *The American Scholar, 67*(4). Retrieved June 1, 2014, from http://www.williamcronon.net/writing/Cronon_Only_Connect.pdf

Darling-Hammond, L. (2010). *The flat world and education: How America's commitment to equity will determine our future.* New York, NY: Teachers College Press.

Darling-Hammond, L. (2013). Diversity, equity, and education in a globalized world. *Kappa Delta Pi Record, 49*(3), 113–115.

Deresiewicz, W. (2008, Summer). The disadvantages of an elite education. *The American Scholar*. Retrieved June 1, 2014, from http://theamericanscholar.org/the-disadvantages-of-an-elite-education/#.U5_BDi8skco

Dewey, J. (1899). *The school and society*. Chicago, IL: The University of Chicago Press.

Feistritzer, C. E. (2011, July). *Profiles of Teachers in the U.S. 2011*. National Center for Education Information. Retrieved April 8, 2013, from pot2011final-blog.pdf

Harris Perry, M. (2014, May). *Segregation 60 years after Brown v. Board of Education*. Retrieved June 1, 2014, from http://www.msnbc.com/melissa-harris-perry/watch/segregation-in-americas-birthplace-258512963619

hooks, b. (1996). *Killing rage: Ending racism*. New York, NY: Holt.

Kozol, J. (2005). *The shame of the nation: The restoration of apartheid schooling in America*. New York, NY: Random House.

Milner, H. R. (2013). *Start where you are, but don't stay there: Understanding diversity, opportunity gas, and teaching in today's classrooms*. Cambridge, MA: Harvard Education Press.

Nieto, S. (2014, June 5). *KDP Laureate Fireside Chat*. Webinar.

Ravitch, D. (2013). *Reign of error: The hoax of the privatization movement and the danger to America's public schools*. New York, NY: Alfred A. Knopf.

Smith, W. A. (2008). Campuswide climate: Implications for African American students. In L. Tillman (Ed.), *A handbook of African American education*. Thousand Oaks, CA: Sage.

Sue, D. W., Capodilupo, C. M., Torino, G. C., Bucceri, J. M., Holder, A. M. B., Nadal, K. L., & Esquilin, M. (2007). Racial microaggressions in everyday life: Implications for clinical practice. *American Psychologist, 62*(4), 271–286.

U.S. Department of Education Office for Civil Rights. (2014, March). *Civil rights data collection, data snapshot: School discipline*. Retrieved May 1, 2014, from http://www2.ed.gov/about/offices/list/ocr/docs/crdc-discipline-snapshot.pdf

Part I

Theory and Narrative

Chapter 1

Self-Study of Social Justice Teaching on the Tenure Track: A Pedagogy of Vulnerability

Jennifer L. Martin

[T]he political struggle for freedom and equality must first of all be a struggle within each person.

—Marta Nussbaum

THE FAMILIAR *IS* STRANGE

Making ourselves vulnerable is to reveal the chinks in the armor; in this revelation one exposes the places where one is weakest. Is this bravery or something else? Nussbaum (2010) encourages us to engage in intellectual struggle with ourselves, for only then are we able to engage in political battles for equality both inside and outside of our classrooms. But do we need to make our personal struggles public? If we decide to do so, are there benefits: lessons to be learned and strategies to share—both personal and political? Are they one and the same? Although slightly terrifying, I believe in such endeavors, which is why I decided it was crucial to write this chapter and to publish this volume about the difficulties in doing social justice work in academe. In this chapter, I share my personal struggles in teaching "unsafe content": topics that destabilize students or make them uncomfortable. Asking students to grow, often when they are disinclined to do so, can make professors who ask students to do this work vulnerable in their own right. This is my work. This is my story.

To engage in this struggle within us there must be a method; my chosen approach is currere. According to Pinar (2012), *currere,* literally curriculum as a verb, or "the course to be run" (p. 43), is a form of criticism where one's understanding stems from a personal analysis of how culture shapes one's own consciousness; moreover, it is a process of examination where one stories how academic knowledge influences one's lived experiences and vice versa. Through the practice of self-study using currere as the vehicle, the major existential crisis of my transition to life on the tenure track was my heightened vulnerability to microaggressions because I asked my students to do the hard work: to examine their biases, to think about discriminatory practices, to challenge their thinking—exactly what I thought higher education was supposed to be, or so I thought. I had no idea how wrong I was, or how difficult this proposition would be.

When I first moved about four hours south from my urban/suburban home—where I had lived and worked into my early 40s, I noticed immediately there was a change in climate, not meteorologically speaking, but metaphorically: Something in the air was different, and the change was palpable. My initial experiences upon moving were over the top: My friends who came to visit in those initial weeks were shocked at the behavior of wait staff, bartenders, and store clerks, going out of their way to gush at the newcomers, to offer advice, local wisdom, and suggesting places to eat, drink, and shop. I was immediately recognized when walking into a place that I had been only once before, remembered, and welcomed. I thought that I was from the Midwest, but I had never experienced that stereotype of the "culture of niceness"—the stereotype of midwestern values. However, this culture played out very differently within the university. Pittard and Butler (2008) define the "culture of niceness" as:

> school culture (including external factors such as school structure, community culture and nature of the profession in general) characterized by conformity and professional interactions wherein the expectation for teachers is to not be confrontational or critical of the school structure, but to accept it or at the very least to work within it without outward resistance. In other words, the expectation is for teachers to "play nice" within the system of schooling, accepting the status quo and modeling it for their students. We see this as part of the "hidden curriculum" of schools and, as such, it is pervasive and invisible at times. (p. 72)

I found a very similar culture in my new institutional home.

This was a predominantly white institution (PWI), and coming from a very diverse area, I was shocked at the homogeneity of my students. In fact, it was difficult for me to tell many of them apart, as there appeared to be a uniform right down to the accessories. When, on the first day of class, I asked my students to tell me an interesting fact about themselves, something to set them apart in my mind so that I could connect a face to a name, many of the young women stated they were in a sorority, the men indicated they were athletes. My new career home was a football school in a football town; I questioned whether I would fit in.

My charge has always been to move my students from their comfort zones. But in this predominantly white institutional space, this was a more difficult endeavor than what I was accustomed to, as my first year coincided with a new multicultural education course, which I taught, to complete the licensure program in education. Prior to this, students were not required to take a course in multicultural education; previous social foundations courses did not deal explicitly with issues of diversity. Thus, I knew that I would face resistance, but I had experience teaching these courses. Student resistance is to be expected when one delves into the dangerous waters of asking students to move beyond their own experience and to engage in thinking that is uncomfortable, particularly for students from dominant groups (Sleeter, 2011). In predominantly white institutions, multicultural education is often seen as unnecessary (Milner, 2005a), but, as Milner reminds us, "The idea that racial discrimination and cultural misunderstandings do not exist in predominantly White institutions is a fallacy" (p. 394). All of our students will eventually engage in a multicultural society, and they need to have the knowledge and skills necessary in order to do this effectively without relying on stereotypes or models of deficit thinking. I was a bit unprepared, however, for the invisible wall that I faced on a daily basis. I learned of the existence of this wall when I read my first semester's evaluations.

One particular evaluation from a graduate student disturbed me greatly; this student indicated that I "did not understand the institution or know how it worked." Essentially, this student viewed me as an outsider, as someone who was challenging the status quo—which many of my students found unacceptable. Many were troubled by the content of my courses, as evidenced by student evaluations, but most never expressed this to me openly so that I could deal with their anger or discomfort and assuage their fears. It typically only came out after the fact. Now, at this particular institution, several professors attended as undergraduates. My institution is considered a teaching institution, and student evaluations are the primary tool for determining tenure. So, I could play it safe and teach safer courses or be who I am and take my chances. Of course, I chose the latter, but not without fear and great trepidation.

METHODOLOGY AS A SELF-REFLEXIVE PROCESS

Reflective practice begins where practitioners are problematizing their practice and learning afresh about both the knowledge and skills and attitudes that their practice demands.

—Peter Jarvis

My approach to this chapter is a methodological bricolage, or an inter-weaving of story (Lincoln & Denzin, 2003). I incorporate aspects of Pinar's concept of currere (2012), or the manner in which to understand the self through reflection filtered through the lens of academic knowledge as well as Milner's approach to narrative inquiry (2005a; 2008) and Brown's theory of using narrative as a form of resistance (2008) in order to examine and make sense of my experiences doing social justice work in academe. Self-study involves critical reflection with the goal of changing the curriculum and the world (Schon, 1991). Pinar's method of currere involves thinking and writing to understand ourselves in this manner, "Reactivating the past reconstructs the present so we can find the future" (p. xv) because it is "Through academic self-study [that] we reconstruct ourselves and the world we inhabit" (p. 2). My telling is inspired by thinkers such as Ives who contends that "we do not write about things as they are or were or will be, we write about these things as *we* are" (as cited in Nash, 2004, p. 130), and Richard Rorty, who theorizes, "truth is made, not discovered" (as cited in Nash, 2004, p. 7). Sharing one's vulnerability and struggles and then problematizing them is key to social justice work, to our own survival—this is the truth we attempt to create and to share. According to Brown (2008) currere involves three steps: delving into our pasts and restorying our educational journeys, forging into the future to an imagined reality of what is possible, and finally, analyzing ourselves as texts in order to gain knowledge of practice and potential practice. However, I have reconfigured Brown's steps in this telling; I will first delve into my past, problematizing my current educational dilemmas; second, contextualize my story as text to be analyzed; and then, third and finally, imagine a future utilizing story as lessons learned for an informed praxis. It must here be noted that not only can the telling of our own stories assist in sharing effective classroom prac-tice, but sharing ourselves can also help us to connect with our students.

According to Pinar (2012), currere is an autobiographical method, which tells one's lived experience and provides a strategy for self-study. This work is crucial in creating classrooms and curriculums that are attuned to ourselves and to our students: to the knowledge that is not only shared but also coconstructed. According to Berry (2014), "Such understandings have expanded curriculum through experiences, past, present, and future, in terms of what we know, what we need to know, and who determines what we need to know. Curriculum, from a reconceptualist stance, bears the question of what knowledge is worth knowing . . ." (p. 4). In this telling, one will examine one's own beliefs about education by examining the relationship between academic knowledge and one's life history in order to gain self-understanding and social transformation. These endeavors necessitate what Pinar describes as complicated conversation with the self with the goal of some form of pedagogical action. According to Pinar (2012), channeling Virginia Woolf, "Only after that room of one's own becomes quiet enough to hear oneself think, then one can initiate conversation, first with oneself, then with others, others who are also occupants of rooms of their own" (p. 6). Essentially, we work from within in order to move into transformational classroom spaces. We must know what we love and what we fear, what inspires us and inhibits us, in order to find pedagogical freedom in the classroom and peace in our lives.

My process during my two years as an assistant professor is both complex and intertwined between the study of the self and developing effective practices to inspire culturally responsive teachers and leaders and studying the evolution of students to this end. This telling is informed by the following: my personal currere, personal field notes detailing my classroom experiences and reflections on interactions with students, and course evaluations.

DANGEROUS WATERS: DOING THE WORK

In general, although the pre-K–12 student population in the United States is becoming increasingly diverse, the teaching force is increasingly homogeneous (Milner, 2005b). According to the National Center for Education Information (Feistritzer, 2011), 84 percent of the teaching force in the United States is white.[1] To compound this problem, there are many current challenges to political correctness and the demonization of inclusive diversity programs, the dismantling of affirmative action, anti-immigration legislation and attitudes, and less academic freedom for educators. This atmosphere contributes to the challenges of being a teacher educator today. Although difficult, it is critical that teacher educators assist in the development of competencies for future teachers to effectively work in diverse schools (Milner, 2005b), but it simultaneously makes the educators who work to dismantle white supremacy and patriarchy more vulnerable to microaggressions and racial battle fatigue, particularly if these educators work in predominantly white institutions (Milner, 2005a, 2005b).

At both the undergraduate and graduate levels, most of my students (82% of whom are white) had little exposure to ethnic and racial diversity. Often they would confuse diversity with individuality: "Everyone is

---

[1] In comparison, according to census data, the white, non-Hispanic/Latina/Latino population is 63 percent.

different." Most could not talk about diversity, let alone race. They con-
fessed that talking about racism made them uncomfortable, and, in fact,
"guilty." Additionally, when asked to reflect on questions of racism in the
United States, many communicated that the problems are over: simultaneously believing that we live in a postracial America, while also sharing memories of nooses hung in the lockers of the lone African American
student in their high schools. But, for them, that was a long time ago, and
everything is okay now because, as many stated, "We have a Black president!" Teaching multicultural education provided students with a venue
to discuss issues of race, gender, sexuality, and the like, and largely, the
only time they were asked to do this work, but conversations about white
privilege were often met with resistance and denial. I learned that most of
my students felt that their predominantly white institution (PWI) was in
fact diverse. And, for most of them, it was. White students often tend not
to be critical of issues of race and racism in their lives for various reasons:
They do not have to deal with the issue on a daily basis or even confront
their own privilege; some view racism in terms of binaries (e.g., this person is a racist and that person is not), but this is not an either-or situation;
as Trepagnier (2006) argues, some view racism only in terms of derogatory words and de jure discrimination, but the unconscious engagement
in behaviors that serve to reinforce the status quo *is* silent racism.

Most of my undergraduate students, on entering the multicultural
course, in general communicated a "colorblind" ideology, as realized in
statements such as, "I do not see color." This is a privileged viewpoint
to possess because it delegitimizes the experiences of others who do not
share a dominant identity and/or racial identification; in effect, it justifies
the perpetuation of the status quo. To simplify, according to colorblind/
genderblind ideology, if you talk about race you are racist; if you talk about
sexism or feminism, you are sexist (Ludlow, Rodgers, & Wrighton, 2005).
Adopting colorblind and "other-blind" ideologies makes it difficult to recognize systemic and institutional policies and practices; instead, teachers
may tend to blame the students for their failure to conform to dominant
ideologies, which contributes to cultural mismatch and the disproportionate percentage of students of color referred for special education services
and subject to heightened discipline policies (Carter & Welner, 2013; Kohl,
1994). According to Milner (2013), "By adopting color-blind ideologies,
practices, and mind-sets that ignore the importance of race, educators
can contribute to and actually exacerbate the persistence of opportunity
gaps" (p. 23). The widespread adoption of colorblind ideology throughout
the United States is not only a political neoliberal consequence, but also
implicated are curricular choices that impact our students. Pinar (2012)
details the systemic removal of the history of American racism from U.S.
textbooks, which is a situation that contributes to the problem of colorblindness; this curricular assault cannot be ignored and must be rectified.

In essence, it is not uncommon for white preservice teachers to engage in the aforementioned denials of inequality and a general questioning of the need for multicultural education, both in their own educations and in their future classrooms (Milner, 2013). Many of these white future teachers, and mine are no exception, believe that they will go on to teach in schools much like they were educated in: small, rural, and all-white, and thus feel that multicultural education is neither relevant to them nor to their students. As Milner (2013) states, many of these educators "gloss over race" for various reasons:

> (1) They are uncomfortable talking about it, (2) they find it irrelevant to do so, (3) race is sometimes considered a taboo subject due to its horrific history for some in U.S. society, and (4) race is misunderstood by so many, both within and outside of education. (p. 7)

However, Gay (2010) reminds us that students can feel ashamed, embarrassed, and angry when their ethnic or racial group is either portrayed only negatively through the curriculum or not at all. It is thus necessary for teacher educators to push to create culturally responsive educators and educational leaders.

Although I had a difficult time teaching multicultural education to undergraduates in a PWI, I had an even more challenging experience with my graduate students, many of whom were alumni, and thus did not benefit from the multicultural course requirement during their undergraduate careers; these challenges were exacerbated by the online delivery of much of our Master's program.[2] I saw much more growth in my undergraduate students than in my graduate students through the course of a semester. Delivering content dealing with issues of diversity is demanding in and of itself; attempting to do so online in an asynchronous format is even more difficult because one does not have the benefit of the "teachable moment." In the two-year cohort-based Master's program, I taught two curriculum courses: one in year one and one in year two. My philosophy of teaching courses in curriculum involves teaching everything as text: the school and society, politics and policy impacting education, the larger culture, popular culture, social media, and so on. Because my graduate students were unaccustomed to dealing with the complex issues of oppression and educational inequities on a variety of levels, I made this my focus. Colorblind ideology revealed itself when one of my graduate students indicated that at her "all-white" elementary school, her principal did not see the need for multicultural education, that there is no need for change; in white suburban schools with majority white populations, this attitude is not uncommon (Milner, 2005b).

---

[2] This program was a Master of Arts in Educational leadership. Our graduate students were teachers with aspirations of becoming principals or educational leaders in another capacity.

In general, I noticed a disturbing notion in many of my graduate students, particularly at the start of the program; I refer to this phenomenon as hegemonic arrogance: many communicated the precept that "all opinions are created equal." More specifically, despite evidence-based conclusions, "an opinion is an opinion," and thus it cannot be "wrong." When grappling with issues of racial disparity in schools, many of my graduate students would deny that such inequities existed, despite extensive evidence. Some implicitly indicated that if they had not experienced it, that means it does not exist. Thus, particularly at the start of the program, most of my students denied structural inequality, the notion of privilege in general, and failed to move beyond their experience and comfort zones. Again, although they were upset about having to engage with these issues, most did not explicitly communicate their discomfort in the form of anger toward me. They kept their true feelings hidden from me in this "culture of niceness."

I have also seen colorblindness in the extreme, when another one of my graduate students, a social studies teacher, proclaimed that he has experienced "the opposite," as he deemed it, of the educational inequities we discussed in class: "reverse racism"; he taught in a diverse school where he viewed himself as the minority, and thus a victim of racism perpetrated by his students. He asked the question, "Why isn't there a *white* history[3] month?" He also protested the feasibility of adding multicultural content or reframing his curriculum to that end altogether because "we can't possibly cover everything." The implications here are, do nothing because it is easier, and that multicultural education is not important enough to make a priority. This may very well have been a coping mechanism, a self-protective resistance to shield one's self from the guilt of the privileges of white supremacy. As Wise (2010) argues, "The first rule of white supremacy [is]: do not talk about white supremacy"; the fact is, we cannot solve race specific injury with race neutral or colorblind rhetoric on policy.

At the time of this writing, I am in my second year as an assistant professor. Prior to entering the tenure track, I taught high school for 17 years—15 of those at an alternative high school for students labeled at-risk for school failure. Additionally, I taught graduate courses in research methods and multicultural education and undergraduate courses in women's and gender studies for approximately eight years. With all of my experience dealing with high conflict and "unsafe content," I thought that this transition would be pretty straightforward. However, I was naive

---

[3] A way to teach about the non-parallelness of Black history month with "White history month" may include the notion that we do not deem "White power" to be equivalent with Black power. White power connotes racism and white supremacy; Black power connotes liberation. One is about taking, the other about giving.

to the implications of my students' lack of exposure to cultures and people different from them.

Because, as previously indicated, I had more difficulty delivering "unsafe content" to my graduate students, I will share some of their thoughts and my analysis of these experiences in general. Prior to their first course and again at the semester's end, I surveyed students to gauge their perceptions of multicultural education and culturally responsive pedagogy. I asked my first group of graduate students to respond to the question, "What have you done to incorporate diversity into your classroom or school?" The following responses capture of essence of the group:

- *"I have tried to incorporate more literature from perspectives of people from other nationalities, race, religion. Admittedly, I have not done enough of this as the majority of the literature in our books is that of white males!"*
- *"I'm very aware of the different learning styles of my students as well as their different backgrounds. Because of this, I make certain to be sensitive to each student and try to get to know them and find what makes them tick."*

In this first cohort, all of my students had grown up in homogenous environments with a traditional hegemonic curriculum. Beyond the notion of "everyone is different," diversity for them meant learning styles and personal preferences: valid notions, but not adequate knowledge for a teacher working in a school with real students who may possess stereotypes of people they may not yet have had the chance to meet.

I also asked students to describe their own experiences or backgrounds with multicultural education; the following statements are generally representative of the group:

- *"Other than my college observations and playing sports with many different types of people, I haven't had much of an educational background with multicultural students."*
- *"None."*
- *"I have had minimal experience with multicultural education with school-aged children. I have worked in schools that do not focus on multicultural education. It is rarely discussed, and I am rarely held accountable for providing multicultural education."*
- *"It is very limited. Even in college, I tended to gravitate toward the classes that taught literature from the perspective I was most used to and that was mainly the canonized literature."*

Clearly, I knew that I had a lot of work to do. I was grateful for the honesty of my students and for the institutional support I received to conduct this research. These responses gave me an indication of what I needed to focus on in my courses, and a clue as to the potential resistance I may face regarding said content. I found that relaying my own personal stories and stories of my former students of color who had worked in predominantly white schools and the inequitable treatment they faced were instrumental in the growth of my students.

When I asked what reasons (if any) would prevent them from being more culturally responsive, student responses included:

- *"Knowledge and application."*
- *"Lack of knowledge; fear of the unknown."*
- *"Lack of experience, lack of knowledge about other cultures."*
- *"I may need more knowledge about it, especially when I advance to an administrative position so that I can better help everyone."*
- *"I am not around various cultures very often."*
- *"It is not something that is asked of me."*
- *"I don't have a diverse classroom of students."*
- *"I have never been placed into a situation that really needed it."*

I found the above responses to be the most revealing. I deem them as falling into two categories: (1) ignorance of the importance of the issue and/or knowledge of how to implement issues of diversity in the classroom and (2) the notion that because one does not work in a diverse school setting, multicultural education is not a pressing need. Again, such responses are not uncommon for white preservice students to express (Milner, 2013).

In my first class with this cohort of students, I asked them to complete a curriculum project where they created a unit based on best practices, global relevancy, and multicultural education. I had a student, a kindergarten teacher, submit a project about pumpkins, including texts about pumpkins. Not having any experience with early childhood education, I was confused. I asked him, "What do pumpkins have to do with multicultural education?" He replied, "All pumpkins are different." I advised that he incorporate multicultural texts and even provided him with a list, and he responded with, "My principal is okay with this, so I do not feel the need to revise my project." I was flabbergasted, both about this particular curricular approach and about the student's defensiveness about revising his project to be more culturally responsive. I have paid close attention to this student throughout my two years with him, and have seen tremendous growth; however, in my second cohort of students, another student submitted a similar curriculum project about pumpkins for kindergarteners, a disturbing trend, to say the least.

Toward the end of the first semester, when I asked students to describe their reactions to multicultural education, they replied with the following:

- *"I would like to expose students to more elements of culture that is not theirs. I am not sure how to integrate this authentically."*
- *"It has been my experience that we teach all kids as though they are middle-class white Christians. It disappoints me even though I am a middle-class white Christian."*
- *"I need to learn more about it. I didn't realize the extent in which we try to make others conform to the one idea that success is equal to that of the white experience. I have had little diversity in the classes I took through school and college and have had even less as a teacher."*
- *"I am very open to learning more about multicultural education but also have concerns about the challenges that may be displayed."*
- *"I think it can be more challenging on the educator since you have to be more aware of the backgrounds of your students as well as the fact that we as the educator usually can't relate to a lot of what kids are going through today."*

In general, I saw tremendous growth in my graduate students as they ended their first course and even more so when they ended their second year. However, this growth came with great struggle. Some of the most negative student comments included on the first semester's course evaluations included, "Not everything is about race," "This professor is very opinionated," and "Sometimes she talks down to us." Undoubtedly, the worst comment I ever received on a student evaluation was from a student in the second cohort of graduate students: "The climate of [my] questions were always as if the person were not doing what they should. I felt the questions were delivered in a mean spirited way rather than a constructive way. Her delivery method is often gruff and makes you feel like nothing you do will ever be good enough. This is the kind of teacher that we all strive not to be." Student evaluations were much more mean spirited from my graduate students than from my undergraduate students during the first year and a half. I attribute this to the online delivery of the courses, which is supported by research (Bonanno & Brocat, 2012); it is difficult to communicate one's personality and sense of caring in an online format.

However, at the time of this writing, at the end of year two, in comparing my evaluations of this first cohort of graduate students with my two undergraduate courses, the graduate students' evaluations were the best. In fact, they were outstanding. Perhaps this difference involves both my students and I taking the time to get to know one another and retooling our approaches toward a coconstruction of knowledge.

I have heard professors at other institutions indicate that they do not read their evaluations; that is how they survive. I strive to always improve

my practice, and reading course evaluations is part of this process. I strive
to be nice (while also critical), available to my students, and funny as a
way to compensate for asking students to go to places they do not want
to go, to think about things that make them uncomfortable. Although
I was criticized by some undergraduate students for focusing too much
on diversity (and on race and gender specifically), despite the fact that this
was a course in multicultural education, the comments were not as scath-
ing as were the graduate student comments in their first course with me.

Interestingly, I faced even more resistance from my second cohort of
graduate students in relation to course content. When asked, "What have
you done to incorporate diversity into your classroom or school?" some of
the most telling responses from the second cohort included:

- *"I do believe I was given some formal multicultural education in school;
  however, it generally came from parents, grandparents, great-grand-parents,
  pictures, and African Americans that address such issues. I believe multicultural education has diminished. African American students do not
  identify themselves as being worthy of education unless the educational
  structure that they are a part of makes them understand its importance. I do
  not feel students are being educated about multicultural education at home,
  which is where education begins."*
- *"I do not have experience with multicultural education."*

I found the first comment to be particularly offensive because this student
specifically views African American students as operating from deficit
models. In this group in general, my students tended to operate by viewing
racial and socioeconomic groups of which they were not members, including their students, from deficit models. There were many times that I had
to be very firm with this group and openly correct offensive statements.
I had to call one student to ask him to remove his homophobic and racist
posts from Twitter; his students and their parents are among his followers.

When asked to describe their own experiences or background with
multicultural education, some of the responses from my second cohort of
students included:

- *"I am not quite sure how I feel about 'multicultural education' and if it
  truly exists. It we are still struggling to implement it, or if it's just an educational phase! There are so many dynamics at so many levels. It also has
  to do with introducing students to a 'realistic' perspective of the world and
  education when a school is 99% white or 99% black."*
- *"I would personally find it difficult since I don't have any experience."*

The resistance is clear, but the question remains: How does one break
through this? Persistence may in fact be the key to dismantling resistance.

At the time of this writing, I have not yet had this second cohort for their second course; my hope is that they will progress in similar ways as my first cohort of graduate students.

When I asked this group of students what reasons (if any) prevent them from being more culturally responsive, they replied as follows:

- *"I believe I try to be culturally responsive but I also know that my past personal experiences and the feelings that stem from those things I have to continually work through."*

- *"The limitations of my curriculum. It's hard to achieve multiculturalism plurality when there are precious few resources published. I suppose I could write and publish them, but as this point in time, this doesn't seem to be a reality."*

It appears that some students are attempting to work through their resistance, but I found this last comment to be particularly revealing. No resources published on multicultural education? This is clearly not the case, as I have provided many resources and suggested venues where students may find more. This final comment seems to be a convenient dismissal of the ease in finding and implementing multicultural education, for such an endeavor may conflict with this particular student's world view and prior educational experience.

Being a woman and asking critical and difficult questions of students in an environment where female professors, particularly in the education department, are expected to be "nice" and "nurturing" makes my job a bit more difficult than the white male across the hall who, admittedly, does not ask the tough questions or assign difficult reading because he needs to be "liked." Typically I experienced indirect anger, such as retaliation on course evaluations; although uncommon, I was infrequently exposed to direct anger in the classroom. During a unit on critical media studies with undergraduate students, I asked students critical questions during a discussion, such as "who is 'we?'" and "what do you mean by . . . ?" in an attempt to move them beyond dichotomous thinking. A student, in front of the entire class, stated, "I do not think your questions are appropriate." When I spoke with him privately after class he informed me that he "did not appreciate my sassy comments." The next day I felt the need to discuss with the class the nature of microaggressions, and what my purpose had been in asking them critical questions. I shared with them the idea that professors who teach "unsafe content" often have more difficult experiences because of student resistance and anger. I asked students to imagine I was a man asking those same questions and if they would have had a different response. I waited. The room was silent. I could feel them thinking. A male student replied, "Yes. If I have a male professor who comes on like a drill sergeant, not saying you do, I would be like, cool, that's how

he is. He's in charge. But, if a woman acts like that I think, 'what a bitch.'"
A corner was turned with the entire class that day.

The good news is, after spending a considerable amount of time with the aforementioned student who did not appreciate my "sassy comments" during office hours, he sent me a personal e-mail a few weeks after the course ended and the grades were in:

> *I can't thank you enough for getting my mind prepared and ready to study and think critically. Thanks to you, I wouldn't of [sic] known were [sic] to start if not for you making us question and challenge what we already knew.*

> *I know that I was not the best student and was downright disrespectful to you and questioned everything you taught us, but now I see why. And I wanted to let you know that I now see why. Finally, I wanted to say again how much you helped me grow as a person and as a student. I truly appreciate everything you have done and how everything was completely worth it.*

As a white woman, I do not possess racial battle fatigue; this is not a term that I feel comfortable claiming as a person possessing middle-class and white privilege. However, I will state that I feel stress and fear in terms of my career success because of certain comments on my course evaluations that deal directly with asking primarily white students at a historically white and private institution to think about race, gender, and other forms of oppression. On a midterm evaluation that I gave to students in my freshman Introduction to the Teaching Profession course, a student wrote, "I hate this class. You talk about diversity too much." Although these disheartening comments represent a small percentage of student responses, they are not less hurtful because they are few in number.

Several of the professors at my current institution are home grown; the institution hires its own, and this leads to a very homogeneous teaching faculty. This may impact how students view me, because I do not come from a rural background; I do not share those experiences. There are definitely regional differences in verbal and nonverbal communication styles that set me apart. For example, I initially found it difficult to operate in this "culture of niceness," for my intellectual and academic background and tradition were geared toward a continual questioning; some students and colleagues often viewed such questioning as confrontational. I have found that meeting with other professors who teach similar content can help tremendously.

INFORMING PRAXIS

> *Conflict is the gadfly of thought. It stirs us to observation and memory. It instigates to invention. It shocks us out of sheep-like passivity,*

and sets us at noting and contriving . . . conflict is a "sine qua non"
of reflection and ingenuity.

—John Dewey

The curriculum we create and the pedagogy we utilize are both inherently political. As Pinar (2012) argues, "The school curriculum communicates what we choose to remember about our past, what we believe about the present, what we hope for the future. Curriculum debates—such as those over multiculturalism and the canon—are also debates over the American national identity" (p. 30). To illustrate Pinar's point, much of the traditional curriculum in the United States constitutes the eraser of systematic violence against and oppression of indigenous peoples, people of color, and women of color and white women, sexual minorities, and the disabled, by the white male heterosexual hegemony (Pinar, 2012). As a professor of education it is my charge to unearth these graves, instill a sense of questioning in my students, and address the issue that all curriculum choices are political choices. And, as Pinar argues, "This is the moment when self-study becomes reconstituted as public service" (p. 47). This is rough terrain in a PWI—and potentially dangerous ground to cover by a new faculty member without tenure. But one does the work one is called to do.

Although, as Dewey (1922) reminds us, we should not fear conflict or controversy in the classroom, as a junior faculty member I am compared equally with my peers who teach innocuous courses such as educational technology, despite decades of research on student resistance to content pertaining to diversity and multiculturalism (Ludlow et al., 2005). Fear of controversy is not the issue; the issue is fear of the implications of doing this work. To not do this work is also a political choice, a choice to maintain the status quo. The choice to maintain the status quo is a dangerous one because it ignores the teaching of the histories of educational inequities in this country that have disproportionately disadvantaged students of color through heightened placement into special education programs and lower-tracked classes, stricter discipline policies, and various educational policies that ignore a myriad of societal and political issues that lead to opportunity gaps for students of color, for low-income students, and in particular for low-income students of color (Carter & Welner, 2013; Milner, 2013). Despite the controversy in broaching these complicated conversations, such curricular choices are necessary in dismantling and problematizing this inequitable status quo. If we, as teacher educators, do not make these issues a priority in our classrooms, who will? If we do not dare to do this dangerous work the cycle will perpetuate.

If our institutions and our departments do not value our work, then we are left standing alone, pushing our largely white population of teacher candidates into rough terrain, terrain that may have largely been unexamined by them. If my students are upset at having to examine their biases, will they take their anger out on me in student evaluations? Sometimes the answer to this question is a definite yes. Will I eventually be denied tenure because I chose to take this risk by volunteering to teach these courses? Currently, I am unsure how to answer this question. What I can say is that privilege is often correlated with student resistance (Ludlow et al., 2005). The implicit institutional norm is for junior faculty to avoid teaching such classes, because it is easier and safer not to. According to Patton, Shahjahan, and Osei-Kofi (2010), "to critically engage with social justice scholarship and practice is not at the top of the list when it comes to advice for new faculty members on how to be successful in higher education today" (p. 265). The implicit question raised by the work of Patton, Shahjahan, and Osei-Kofi is, "should we wait until we achieve tenure to do this work?" And, "in the meantime, who will carry these burdens?"

I acknowledge that I possess a great amount of privilege, and that I have a lot of work to do to dismantle or unlearn the damaging ideas that I have been taught, and that I can do more to move beyond my own experience. I consider myself to be an ally on many fronts, working in various ways to undermine oppression, and working to undo the potential assaults that may be perpetrated in our future classrooms by teachers who are untrained in cultural responsiveness: or, to complicate the conversations of those students who feel that being "nice" is enough to deal with any "–ism" that may enter her or his classroom (Nieto, 2008).

Although I am committed to teaching "unsafe content," I understand that not only is achieving tenure more difficult for women and faculty of color because of organizational cultures that do not support their work or their identities (Jones, Taylor, & Coward, 2013; Smith, 2007), but also, this work is further complicated when teaching courses with "unsafe content"; according to Ludlow, Rodgers, and Wrighton (2005), "resistant White/male heterosexual/mainstream students respond to diversity courses by inverting the dominant/subordinate paradigm: the White student perceives himself/herself to be subordinated by the discourse of diversity and resists it as if she/he were the marginalized group" (p. 8). Additionally, the more dominant identity the instructor possesses, the least likely s/he is to face student resistance on evaluations; the more distant the instructor's identities are from dominant identities, the more "intense, abusive," and discrediting the resistance can become (Ludlow et al., 2005, p. 8). According to Sandler (1991), "When women's issues are introduced as part of the curriculum [and, I would argue, issues of multiculturalism], these issues may also be devalued and not seen as 'real' issues. Students may indicate their displeasure with overt comments, hissing or booing, negative body language, and inattention or yawning" (p. 11).

Professors who violate students' expectations by, for instance, stepping out of students' proscribed gender [or racialized] role expectations can face consequences (Bachen, McLoughlin, & Garcia, 1999). In fact, when women professors are perceived to be "nonnurturing," they can be criticized as arrogant or as having something "to prove," particularly by male students (Bachen et al. 1999, p. 208). Sheryl Sandberg (2013) relays a conversation with Professor of Leadership Deborah Gruenfeld, "'We believe not only that women are nurturing, but that they should be nurturing above all else. When a woman does anything that signals she might not be nice first and foremost, it creates a negative impression and makes us uncomfortable'" (p. 43). Sandberg's concern is a great one, for it impacts both our lived experiences as women and the trajectory of our careers. Students often expect women faculty to be more "maternal": personable, supportive, and open to providing special treatment; but despite reporting receiving more attention from women professors, students often rate them less favorably (Sandler, 1991). Women who are outspoken tend to receive more negative repercussions for their behavior (Takiff, Sanchez, & Stewart, 2001).

Sandberg's concern is my concern. I feel as if there is resistance to being a strong woman in my current institutional space. According to Takiff, Sanchez, and Stewart (2001), "Female professors, like other women in the workplace, may often have to decide whether to conform to traditional gender-role norms or to demand the status and success they deserve at the cost of likability" (p. 143). It is as though my students expect a maternal figure, someone who is perpetually nice: someone who is not too challenging, someone who does not ask too many questions, for, as Sandler (1991) reminds us, gender can impact how students evaluate a faculty member's competence. According to Baker and Copp (1997), "students may hold contradictory and unrealistic expectations of them [women]. These contradictions may make it hard for women faculty members to receive outstanding teaching evaluations, because students judge women by their gender performance" (p. 29). Attribution plays a part here too, as women's successes are often attributed to luck, while men's to talent (Sandler, 1991). Just as possessing nondominant gender identities can result in lower teaching evaluations, the same can be said for nondominant racial identities. White instructors' course evaluations tend to be higher than their counterparts of color; the same phenomenon exists for sexual identities (Ludlow et al., 2005). But student evaluations are not the only concern; teaching classes covering issues of diversity can result in overt or thinly veiled resistance on the part of students. As Brown (2004) argues, "Resentment is frequently reflected on teacher evaluations, whereas resistance is apparent in inadequate preclass preparation, reluctance to engage in class discussions and activities, and a lack of commitment to required cross-cultural

interactions and research" (p. 326). This fact becomes even more complicated when women professors teach feminist or other "unsafe content"
(Baker & Copp, 1997; Ludlow et al., 2005). In sum, professors who teach
"unsafe content," particularly if they possess nondominant identities, can
receive consequences from students: anger, resistance, negative evaluations, and, potentially, negative consequences from administration and
tenure and promotion committees.

Despite these difficulties, we must work to change the curriculum to
be more inclusive and to work to engage our colleagues in supporting
us in these endeavors. I have made the conscious choice to do this work,
despite its risks. To wit, it is important to me to teach my students about
issues of race, class, gender, and sexuality despite the difficulty, despite
the discomfort, and these struggles are not uncommon among professors
who teach such content (Milner, 2005a, 2005b). According to an African
American teacher working in a predominantly white high school, "You
teach what you know; you teach what you've experienced; you teach who
you are. And when we have White teachers who don't deal with race and
culture and difference, it's really a handicap to the students because they
are not teaching reality" (as cited in Milner, 2005a, pp. 391–392). The reality for that particular African American teacher was that her ninth-grade
students reported her to the principal for racism, because she broached
the uncomfortable issue of racism with her all-white students. An additional consequence for this particular African American teacher was that
she was no longer allowed to teach ninth-grade classes (Milner, 2005a).
In sum, the consequences for challenging majoritarian discourses can be
great, particularly for those teachers and professors living in the margins
who may be accused of playing race or gender cards.

Although often difficult to broach, it is important for educators to
address inequities in the school, classroom, and curriculum; otherwise,
only "majoritarian" discourses will be perpetuated, and students with
counternarratives to share may be marginalized. As Chaisson (2004) states,
"Subverting discourses on race functions to perpetuate the racial system
that advantages Whites for being white and oppresses racial minorities"
(p. 346). Initially, the dismantling and problematizing of white privilege
can cause anger and defensiveness in majority populations, which speaks
to the necessity of such an undertaking, especially in predominantly white
schools (Chaisson, 2004). According to Delpit (1995), those who possess
power and privilege are often the least likely to acknowledge their existence. Thus, it is crucial to not only teach multicultural education courses,
but also critical whiteness studies within those courses. According to
Sleeter (2011), "Critical whiteness studies focuses on invisibility of racial
power to whites, social privileges associated with whiteness, and interpretations of race and ethnicity through which people of European descent
minimize the significance of race" (p. 424). Critical whiteness studies

attempts to make racial power and its corresponding ideology visible, and to assist whites to learn how to work against racial oppression and white supremacy within institutions and within their lives as opposed to simply dismissing it (Sleeter, 2011).

In general, "unsafe content" makes us vulnerable in "unsafe courses." There are too many hills, and one would argue that one should pick her battles. So what should one do? Milner (2013) argues that teachers from any background can be successful in teaching diverse students; it is about what they know and have the skills to acquire. As previously stated, if a professor or a teacher acknowledges the racial background of her or his students, she or he may be considered a racist. I too, have found this to be true. But, I think we need to work harder to help to create preservice allies, most of whom are white, in our classrooms. We need to popularize the notion that not talking about race, class, gender, sexuality, and other forms of oppression, will not make them go away. We need to make these issues visible in our classrooms and in the minds of our students.

CONSEQUENCES FOR WHISTLE BLOWERS

When freedom is the question, it is always time to begin.
—Maxine Greene

Around the time of this writing, Jill Abramson, the first female executive editor of *The New York Times*, was fired after she broached issues of inequity in the workplace. She was also deemed "hard to work with" and "brusque" (Auletta, 2014). As Abramson was made to look extreme, as a woman doing a traditionally male job, no one batted an eye when her male colleague, Dean Baquet, punched holes in walls in an anger that was justified (Byers, 2013). A woman's anger is never justified. As Gloria Steinem once stated, "Whoever has power takes over the noun—and the norm—while the less powerful get an adjective" (as cited in Sandberg, p. 140). The noun is boss; the adjective is aggressive, and that adjective is just unacceptable if one is a woman.

I share the above anecdotes because after almost two decades of doing social justice work, initially as a classroom teacher and part-time feminist activist, and now as a professor, I am still surprised, as I am sure Jill Abramson was, when I am faced with systemic or institutional harassment and discrimination, or when I "become the adjective": aggressive. This should never surprise me, but for some reason it always does. I know that those who speak up and speak out are highly susceptible to negative consequences for their actions: retaliation, harassment, microaggressions, even termination. And, true to form, in my second year, in an attempt to point out the inequitable division of labor based on gender in my

department, I was painted as aggressive, overly emotional, and unpro-
fessional. Despite years of activist work and publications dealing with
equity in its many forms on my vitae, a colleague constructed lies about
me in an attempt to assassinate my character and ultimately sabotage my
career. I suspect he did so because I was unwilling to perpetuate the status
quo: Our department ran on an institutional norm of sexism, including an
inequitable division of labor based on gender, the silencing of dissenting
voices (particularly if they were female), and threatening and retaliatory
behavior with the above goal of silencing dissenting voices (particularly if
they were female). This person perpetuated a pattern of hiring young and
untenured women to positions of power so that he could control them.
In fact, to many colleagues he admitted to hiring young women because
"they work harder." I was unwilling to keep silent about these inequities, despite the fact that I was a junior faculty member without tenure.
Instead, I kept a journal of what I had been experiencing.

The literature supports what I have faced, which includes social isolation from key information, personal attacks, verbal threats and criticism, and rumor spreading/attacks on one's reputation (Frazier, 2011).
According to Frazier (2011), for workplace bullying to occur, the following
three condition must be met: "(1) a power imbalance, (2) systemic nature
of behaviors occurring over time, and (3) victims must find it difficult
to defend themselves against the bullying behavior" (p. 2). I would also
argue that victims of bullying and harassment need time to reflect on their
experiences; they need time to talk about them, to contextualize them, in
order to come to terms with the fact they are, in fact, being bullied and/
or harassed. The simple acknowledgment that a colleague is attempting
to cause intentional harm, in fact that one is being bullied or harassed,
is often hard to accept. The nature of self-protection often causes us to
minimize such behavior or to make excuses for it. People in positions of
subordination are often not entitled to the full gamut of emotions; in fact,
"getting angry" is often seen as a justification for termination (Gruber &
Morgan, 2004). "Not getting angry" is a privileged point of view to have;
such retaliatory behavior is a common tactic to get those in positions of
vulnerability (or lack of power) angry so that they may be framed as an
unreasonable, uncollegial. Women, particularly feminist women, commonly face this phenomenon (Webber, 2005), which represents the classic double bind. What should the reasonable response be to bullying and
harassment if not anger?

The above is undoubtedly the most serious consequence I have faced
for doing social justice work. This work does not end when one leaves
the classroom, but extends into our lives: to interactions with colleagues
and institutional policies and practices. I could not very well teach my
students to become advocates for their students and their future schools
without doing the same myself.

MAIEUTIC METHOD: ENVISIONING AN IDEAL, THE IMAGINED FUTURAL

Remember, the entrance door to the sanctuary is inside you.

—Rumi

I conceptualized this volume by asking, "Do teachers/professors who engage in social justice work face challenges that their colleagues do not face? And how does this impact them personally? Professionally?" After two years engaging in this work at a PWI, I feel it is safe to say that yes, we do face heightened challenges, challenges that are terrifying, the consequences of which can threaten to end careers. Despite this, I can imagine a better future.

The lesson that I learned in my department and from my students is that it is easier not to challenge, not to question; but I do not believe that the easiest work is the best or the most important work. I want to work in a place that values me for who I am and what I can contribute. Although I know that I am doing important work in my current institutional space, it remains to be seen whether my work is truly valued. Through the process of currere, Pinar (2012) inspires us to engage in the imagined futural: to envision and then to work toward a better educational project. During these two years, in addition to teaching and writing, I made many friends and allies across campus, developed a respectable contingent of loyal students, volunteered, and went to as many campus events as I could. I was elected to the campus diversity steering committee in my first year and named chair at the end of my second. I won two diversity awards in my second year: one a women's award selected by faculty, the other a faculty of the year for diversity award selected by students. I wanted to make myself bulletproof: beyond reproach in my teaching, scholarship, and service, so that I could be free to be me. I imagined a future where I would be accepted for who I am, and respected for my work on issues of equity and social justice.

But this work does not come without consequences. One must be brave because this work can be too much: Although I possess a majority identity (white) as well as a minority identity (feminist woman), I taught largely "unsafe content," which becomes taxing in and of itself, but when compounded by student resistance in a PMI and departmental harassment, it all becomes too much. When we have made ourselves vulnerable by teaching "unsafe content," and this is compounded by a lack of support from colleagues, the environment can become unbearable, affecting one's emotional, psychological, and physical health. I have often asked my trusted confidants, "Am I crazy?" and, "Can you believe what just happened?"

I often have night terrors; such is the reality of working in a metaphorical battlefield for nearly 20 years. During this past year, after a particularly taxing day, I awakened myself and my husband with the loudest and longest blood-curdling scream that ever left my lungs—it was a scream of self-protection as someone in my dream was trying to forcefully enter my home, my sanctuary; such is one of my consequences for teaching from a place of vulnerability in an often overt hostile environment. But teaching is always an exercise in vulnerability, where one is center stage: exposing us to doubt, critique, and sometimes abuse in the pursuit of cocreating knowledge between teacher and student. Compound that with my past of working with students in trouble and constant conflict, night terrors are the result. In my current space, teaching "unsafe content" in a hostile environment with overt saboteurs, the terrors at night continue. Teaching "unsafe content" can cause literal pain to those who attempt to deliver it. This work has serious implications for our health; this speaks to the necessity of institutional and departmental support. An institution cannot claim that it values diversity without providing institutional supports for those who actually do the work.

Yet I still imagine a future where professors engaging in "unsafe content" will be protected by their universities, where research on the difficulties in doing this work are taken into consideration when determining tenure and promotion, and where colleagues embrace the work and are not threatened by it. Gilroy (2007) argues that evaluations should be used with caution. I, and others, have argued that evaluations should be considered while using other measures; tenure and promotion committees must also take into consideration the possibility of student bias (Lazos, 2011). But, some questions remain: "How can we make this happen?" "How can we protect ourselves?" "What are the compensatory strategies that will not only keep us safe but also keep us sane?" "How can we keep ourselves safe and healthy while doing the taxing work of challenging the status quo and making ourselves potentially vulnerable to microaggressions, retaliation, and potential termination?"

Although I am a novice scholar, I have found some strategies that work for me. I have found that writing helps. Writing can be a vehicle for sharing ourselves with our students and to expose the reality of what this work is like. It is beneficial to our profession to share this. We must write through our anger, and write through our fear; and there will be both anger and fear caused by doing this work, and this must be acknowledged. To deny that we experience anger when we are treated inequitably will only make the situation worse. Another answer involves coalition building. It is crucial to get involved and to build ally relationships with others across campus. We must also find mentors and trusted confidants. Sometimes we need those networks. Attending affirmative conferences and occasionally preaching to the choir rejuvenates the soul. We must find the joie de vivre: find what makes us happy and pursue this; otherwise, the work will be the end of us. And, in viewing the landscape realistically, we must know the facts, know our rights, and be able to stand up for ourselves, for some will be threatened by our endeavors. We must know what to do to protect ourselves.

In the imagined futural, we hope that our mentors and our departments and institutions will advocate for our work; this includes how our institutions will deem our evaluations in teaching "unsafe content." According to Baker and Copp (1997), "To prevent this kind of injustice, faculty members in tenure and promotion decisions need to consider students' gendered [and, I would argue, racialized] expectations of women and men professors. They also need to consider how classroom conditions constrain a professor's ability to fulfill students' expectations" (p. 41). In teaching courageously we may experience exile; we must find solidarity with others in exile so we do not feel so alone.

According to Ludlow et al. (2005), in order for campuses and mentors to be allies in this work, they should adhere to the following precepts:

1. Educate themselves about bias in student evaluations of faculty.
2. Train deans, department heads, and faculty to recognize the difference between students' critiques of, and biases against, faculty.
3. Institute procedures for effective peer evaluation of faculty teaching.
4. Provide alternative methods for determining merit, tenure, and promotion when bias is evident in student evaluations of a faculty member. (p. 12)

In general, academe has embraced the notion of diversity. Most institutions require at least one course in diversity. But this has come at a cost, for most institutions do not provide the necessary institutional and administrative support for professors delivering said curriculum (Ludlow et al., 2005); to wit, "People at the frontlines in the war against inequality need someone at their back" (p. 12).

I have found that giving students the opportunity to evaluate the course halfway through the semester (anonymously) provides me with the chance to retool the class to better meet students' needs and to address any issues that may be in play. I work tirelessly to be ever-present for my students through text, e-mail, and phone with any questions or concerns they may have in order to compensate for the potential discomfort they may feel with the content that troubles them. Humor is also helpful, although humor can be difficult to deliver in an online environment. Additionally, I got the following advice from a mentor who suggested that before students complete their course evaluations, the professor, particularly those who deliver "unsafe content," should ask the following questions of their students in an anonymous survey: "Do you think I care about you?" "Have I done my best to facilitate your learning in this course?" "What can I do differently to assist you in your learning in this course?" She argues that this informal evaluation allows students, who may be harboring anger toward a professor who has forced them from their comfort zones, the chance to release this anger before delivering a more unbiased formal course evaluation.

In conclusion, as Pinar (2012) and Brown (2008) remind us, there is power in story. When one tells a story the listener can be inspired and perhaps transformed. It is my hope on hearing my story that others will be inspired to tell theirs. Making one's self vulnerable through self-study and revealing the consequences of asking students to do the difficult work, or attempting to truly prepare them to work with diverse student populations, is crucial to education as a field because it reveals the dangers of this job. In our work to transform the field, we must first transform ourselves and then share our struggles in this exercise of vulnerability.

REFERENCES

Auletta, K. (2014, May 14). Why Jill Abramson was fired. *The New Yorker*. Retrieved May 15, 2014 from http://www.newyorker.com/online/blogs/currency/2014/05/why-jill-abramson-was-fired.html

Bachen, C. M., McLoughlin, M. M., & Garcia, S. S. (1999, July). Assessing the role of gender in college students' evaluations of faculty. *Communication Education, 48*, 193–210.

Baker, P., & Copp, M. (1997, January). Gender matters most: The interaction of gendered expectations, feminist course content, and pregnancy in student course evaluations. *Teaching Sociology, 25*, 29–43.

Banks, J. A. (2007). *Educating citizens in a multicultural society* (2d ed.). New York, NY: Teachers College Press.

Berry, T. R. (2014). Internationalization, internalization, and intersectionality of identity: A critical race feminist re-images curriculum. *Journal of Curriculum Theorizing, 30*(1), 4–13.

Bonanno, A., & Brocat, B. (2012). Issues related to IDEA evaluation in online classes. Retrieved June 1, 2014 from http://www.shsu.edu/dept/faculty-senate/minutes/4-19-12/UA-Report-OnlineCourses-4-19-12.pdf

Brown, D. (2008). Restorying ourselves: Using currere to examine teachers' careers. Saarbucken, Germany: VDM Verlag.

Brown, E. L. (2004). What precipitates change in cultural diversity awareness during a multicultural course: The message of the method? *Journal of Teacher Education, 55*(4), 325–340.

Byers, D. (2013, April 23). Turbulence at The Times. *Politico*. Retrieved May 25, 2014 from http://www.politico.com/story/2013/04/new-york-times-turbulence-90544.html

Carter, P. L., & Welner, K. G. (Eds.). (2013). *Closing the opportunity gap: What America must do to give every child an even chance*. New York, NY: Oxford University Press.

Chaisson, R. L. (2004, October). A crack in the door: Critical race theory in practice at a predominantly white institution. *Teaching Sociology, 32*, 345–357.

Delpit, L. (1995). *Other people's children: Cultural conflict in the classroom*. New York, NY: The New Press.

Dewey, J. (1922). Morals are human. In *Human nature and conduct: An introduction to social psychology* (pp. 295–302). New York, NY: Modern Library.

Feistritzer, C. E. (2011, July). *Profiles of Teachers in the U.S. 2011*. National Center for Education Information. Retrieved April 8, 2013, from http://www.edweek.org/media/pot2011final-blog.pdf

Frazier, K. N. (2001). Academic bullying: A barrier to tenure and promotion for African-American faculty. *Florida Journal of Educational Administration and Policy, 5*(1), 1–13.

Gay, G. (2010). *Culturally responsive teaching: Theory, research, and practice* (2nd ed.). New York, NY: Teachers College Press.

Gilroy, M. (2007). Bias in student evaluations of faculty? *The Hispanic Outlook in Higher Education, 17*(19), 26–27.

Greene, M. (1998). *A light in dark times: Maxine Greene and the unfinished conversation*. W. Ayers & J. L. Miller (Eds.). New York, NY: Teachers College Press.

Gruber, J. E., & Morgan, P. (Eds.). (2004). *In the company of men: Male dominance and sexual harassment*. Richmond, VA: Maple Press.

Jarvis, P. (1999). *The practitioner-researcher: Developing theory from practice*. San Francisco, CA: Jossey-Bass.

Jones, S. J., Taylor, C. M., & Coward, F. (2013). Through the looking glass: An autoethnographic view of the perceptions of race and institutional support in the tenure process. *The Qualitative Report, 18*(58), 1–16.

Kohl, H. (1994). *I won't learn from you and other thoughts on creative maladjustment*. New York, NY: The New Press.

Lazos, S. R. (2011). Are student teaching evaluations holding back women and minorities? The perils of "doing" gender and race in the classroom. In G. Gutierrez y Muhs, Y. Flores Niemann, C. G. Gonzalez, & A. P. Harris (Eds.), *Presumed incompetent: The intersections of race and class for women in academia*. Boulder, CO: University Press of Colorado.

Lincoln, Y. S., & Denzin, N. K. (2003). *Turning points in qualitative research: Tying knots in a handkerchief*. Walnut Creek, CA: AltaMira Press.

Ludlow, J., Rodgers, L. A., & Wrighton, M. G. (2005). Students' perceptions of instructors' identities: Effects and interventions. *Academic Exchange Extra*. Retrieved May 20, 2014 from http://www.unco.edu/ae-extra/2005/3/Art-2.html

Milner, H. R. (2005a). Developing a multicultural curriculum in a predominantly white teaching context: Lessons from an African American teacher in a suburban English classroom. *Curriculum Inquiry, 35*(4), 391–427.

Milner, H. R. (2005b). Stability and change in U.S. prospective teachers' beliefs and decisions about diversity and learning to teach. *Teaching and Teacher Education, 21*, 767–786.

Milner, H. R. (2006). Preservice teachers' learning about cultural and racial diversity: Implications for urban education. *Urban Education, 41*(4), 343–375.

Milner, H. R. (2008). Disrupting deficit notions of difference: Counter-narratives of teachers and community in urban education. *Teaching and Teacher Education, 24*, 1573–1598.

Milner, H. R. (2013). *Start where you are, but don't stay there: Understanding diversity, opportunity gas, and teaching in today's classrooms*. Cambridge, MA: Harvard Education Press.

Nash, R. J. (2004). *Liberating scholarly writing: The power of personal narrative.* New York, NY: Teachers College Press.

Nieto, S. (2008). Go beyond niceness: Think critically about what it means to "care" for students of color. In Mica Pollock (Ed.), *Everyday antiracism: Concrete ways to successfully navigate the relevance of race in school* (pp. 28–31). New York, NY: The New Press.

Nussbaum, M. C. (2010). *Not for profit: Why democracy needs the humanities.* Princeton, NJ: Princeton University Press.

Patton, L. D., Shahjahan, R. A., & Osei-Kofi, N. (2010). Introduction to the emergent approaches to diversity and social justice in higher education special issue. *Equity and Excellence in Education, 43*(3), 265–278.

Pinar, W. F. (2012). *What is curriculum theory?* (2d ed.). New York, NY: Routledge.

Pittard, M., & Butler, D. (2008). Liberally educated teachers and the culture of niceness: Findings from a qualitative study in liberal arts and secondary teaching. In M. Pittard, D. Butler, & J. McDowell (Eds.), *Liberal arts education and teacher education: A lasting relationship* (pp. 69–90). Retrieved June 1, 2014 from http://www.ailacte.org/images/uploads/general/monograph_opt.pdf

Rumi. (n.d.). Rumi quotes. Retrieved May 1, 2014 from http://www.quoteswave.com/picture-quotes/371252

Sandberg, S. (2013). *Lean in: Women, work, and the will to lead.* New York, NY: Knopf.

Sandler, B. R. (1991). Women faculty at work in the classroom, or, why it still hurts to be a woman in labor. *Communication Education, 40,* 1–15.

Schon, D. A. (Ed.). (1991). *The reflective turn: Case studies in and on educational practice.* New York, NY: Teachers College Press.

Sleeter, C. E. (2011). Becoming white: Reinterpreting a family story by putting race back into the picture. *Race and Ethnicity in Education, 14*(4), 421–433.

Smith, B. (2007). Student ratings of teaching effectiveness: An analysis of end-of-course faculty evaluations. *College Student Journal, 41*(4), 788–800.

Takiff, H. A., Sanchez, D. T., & Stewart, T. L. (2001). What's in a name? The status implications of students' terms of address for male and female professors. *Psychology of Women Quarterly, 25,* 134–144.

Trepagnier, B. (2006). *Silent racism: How well-meaning white people perpetuate the racial divide.* Boulder, CO: Paradigm.

Webber, M. (2005). "Don't be so feminist": Exploring student resistance to feminist approaches in a Canadian university. *Women's Studies International Forum, 28*(2), 181–194.

Wise, T. (2010). *Colorblind: The rise of post-racial politics and the retreat from racial equity.* San Francisco, CA: City Lights Books.

Chapter 2

"She Was More Intelligent Than I Thought She'd Be!": Status, Stigma, and Microaggressions in the Academy

M. L. Sharp-Grier

"Nuh-uhhh! . . . Seriously?" I sat staring blankly at the computer screen that taunted me with the results of my student observations from the semester that I'd just completed. I had (and still do) always loathed getting them. The process, in my estimation, was unnerving. The idea that someone—anyone—had the authority to judge me made me feel somewhat powerless. Logically, I completely understood the reasoning behind evidence-based practice (EBP) (McKibbon, 1998); after all, I'd worked in criminal justice and mental health for seventeen years, and had no qualms about being held accountable for my professional performance and outcomes. Hell, for four years, I was in charge of compiling and analyzing the EBP data of an organization for which I previously worked; but, this process seemed different—almost punitive. The knowledge that my professional career hinged upon the very subjective opinions of the students whom I may or may not have inadvertently pissed off during the course of their semester-long immersion into sociological thought just seemed suspicious to me. Moreover, the idea that education itself—the process of imparting knowledge and information to students—could somehow be

quantitatively analyzed was (and still is) a bit confusing to me. I didn't
know if I bought into that process. But, I digress. . . .

I motioned to my office mate, summoning—"Look at this! Am I reading this right? This doesn't say what I think it does, right?" My office
mate of four years walked over and took a peek at the offending screen.
"Noooooooo! Are you serious? Someone actually WROTE that?" I confirmed the observations, "Yep, unfrigginbelievable. What the hell am
I supposed to do with this? Is this supposed to be FLATTERING?"
I could feel the tears—those of anger, helplessness, and utter and complete
humiliation—forming in my eyes. I fought them back. There was no way
that I could allow myself the privilege of becoming outwardly emotionally vulnerable—not in this venue or for this reason. So, I pinched the back
of my thigh (my personal method of emotion management) and sent them
back from whence they came. "I dunno, dude," my office mate said, seeing my frustration (and the burgeoning tears). "That's just mean."

I turned back to my computer. The words taunted me. *"She was more
intelligent about the subject than I thought she would be."* I stared at the
screen and vacillated between hurt and anger. I realized that my office
mate was right—it *was* mean. It was also professionally offensive. It was
unconscionable to me that a student would evaluate his or her instructor's
intelligence—not their organization, conveyance of subject matter, acces-
sibility, or any of the other "objective" variables that our organization used
to measure one's efficacy in the classroom, but their INTELLECT. In my
world, my professors' intelligence was never up for debate. *"The unmiti-
gated GALL,"* I thought. Of course, during the sequence of my undergraduate and graduate careers, I had questioned whether or not some of the
profs that I had studied under were aptly suited for the classroom; but,
never would I question their knowledge base—their *aptitude.* My mind
swirled, and I couldn't concentrate. As a sociologist, I was acutely aware
of the processes associated with stereotyping and labeling. I also understood that as a woman of color who taught sociology in a Midwest collegiate venue, I was subject to increased scrutiny of the subject matter that
I taught, and that, according to Turner, González, and Wood (2008), in
their investigation of the state of minority faculty within the academy, I
would receive challenges to my credentials at a rate higher than my nonminority contemporaries. I was similarly cognizant of the reality that
often, consistent with findings by Hamermesh and Parker (2005), the presentation of my ascribed status would result in lower course evaluations as
triggered by my sex, race, and sexuality, rather than as indicated by my
actual classroom performance. I had already been told that I was a racist
with a gay agenda. I thought about introducing that particular student to
my white, Jewish girlfriend, but I figured that would be overkill. The intellectual operationalization of these truths was not the problem. I mean,
contextualizing the real-world manifestations of privilege and oppression

was something that I did for a living—daily. This, however, *"She was more intelligent about the subject than I thought she would be,"* cut me to the white meat—down to my core. I was devastated.

I felt the same way as I had in 1986, as a nineteen-year-old undergrad walking past a men's dorm on the campus of my private Midwestern university and hearing a faceless voice angrily scream ". . . nigger BITCH" from behind the windows. Then, too, I was stunned. *"Wait, I'm at college—aren't folks supposed to be different, more educated?"* I stopped dead in my tracks, my paradigm of the intellectual college campus having been shattered. I couldn't believe what I had just heard. *"Seriously?"* I thought. *"Someone really just called me a nigger in broad daylight, at college?"* I couldn't wrap my mind around what I'd just heard. I would have understood this type of behavior if it had happened at home, but not *here* . . . this place was supposed to be better.

I had been raised in a pseudo-suburban mill town just northeast of Pittsburgh during the '70s and '80s and was (by virtue of repeated exposure) relatively immune to the racial slurs and epithets that were not yet taboo to use in public—words and sentiments that aptly reflected the collective ideology surrounding just how "Black folk" were perceived and sometimes treated. Even when those overt labels (daggers) weren't used, people—well-meaning individuals who would have never considered themselves even remotely bigoted—made seemingly benign comments referencing my race. I later found, during my review of research conducted by multiple authors on the subtleties of racism, that such expressions—my very favorite being "You're so ARTICULATE!"—are not uncommon (Sue 2010; Sue et al., 2007; Yosso, Smith, Ceja, & Solorzano, 2009). These types of statements are meant as compliments but amount to nothing other than watered-down insults and, in my case, served to mask the not-quite-obsolete racist sentiment that had been a normal part of my life in western Pennsylvania. During the course of my childhood, I had developed a relatively thick skin and came to anticipate—really, to expect—being subjected to the indirect and oftentimes knee-jerk digs, jabs, and attacks aimed at minorities that I later understood to be racial microaggressions, as iterated by Pierce (1970) and Sue (2010). I was an honor student, had played in the band (first flute, second chair from seventh to twelfth grades—I just couldn't get past my biggest competition), and had been the first and last Black cheerleader captain at my junior high school. Each of these accomplishments, I eventually learned, was a source of confusion for folks who weren't used to seeing Black children in roles that were in direct opposition to the lower-class culture defined by Braithwaite (1981) and Fukurai (1996). Parents of my classmates seemed simultaneously confused and tickled pink by the little Black girl who had a sophisticated vocabulary and who loved world and classical music, British Literature, and Greek Mythology. My contemporaries (depending on their racial and ethnic backgrounds) were vocal in the way that only youth can get away with. I was, depending on the audience, an Oreo who was trying to be white, or just another Black girl whose physical appearance was somehow reflective of her character. Suffice it to say that I knew how to handle myself, and I was always armed with a pithy comeback just in case I needed to verbally check someone who—with or without malice aforethought—insulted my race by juxtaposing it with my intelligence. The guy in the dorm window had no idea with whom he had chosen to tango. I was ready for him.

And so, standing on the sidewalk that ran adjacent to one of two men's dormitories on campus, I dropped my book bag (I was heading to the student union to grab a quick bite before trekking off to the library to study for finals), faced the looming brick building, and screamed back, "That's all you got? C'mon! You're in college; can't you find better adjectives than that? If not, you need to go back to elementary school!" I stood, with clenched fists, waiting for a response from the individual who didn't have the decency to show his face to me—someone whom he did not know—as he took the liberty of impugning two of the most treasured aspects of myself—my race and my sex. I stood with the audience that had gathered when I yelled at the empty windows, waiting—hoping that the coward would respond, but knowing that he would not. After a minute or so, I laughed, unclenched my fists, picked up my book bag, and headed on. I had won. I had used my wit to stop this individual's attempt at shaming me. My cache of pithy comebacks had served me well. As I walked to the student union, I remembered my mother's words, "They can never take your intelligence from you." Those were words that I lived (live) by. No matter what, because I was smart, I had a way to hold onto myself—onto my race, my sex, and as I would later realize, my sexuality. The proverbial "they" as warned by my mother, often seemed poised to take my definitions of self away, through both interpersonal and institutionalized means. If I could just hold onto my faculties, I could hold onto me. That time, I stood my ground and fought. This time, *She was more intelligent about the subject than I thought she would be.* I couldn't fight back. There was no one in the window to yell at—there was only a cold, bright, computer screen.

"Hey, you OK?" My office mate was still standing there, watching me watch the screen. "Yeah, I'm good. I'm just shocked, is all." I lied. I wasn't OK, and I didn't know if I would be. "Anyone questioning your smarts?" I asked. I chuckled a bit in an unsuccessful effort to let my office mate know that I was OK. It didn't work. "Nope"—was the reply, and the point was taken. My office mate sat down and returned to whatever task I had interrupted. I turned around, faced my Dell, and thought—hard.

That thinking process—the one that started when I turned back to my computer and attempted to resume some semblance of a normal afternoon—lasted quite some time. As I packed and headed home,

I continued to muse on both the comment and the sentiment that it elicited. I was confused. What was the big deal? Why did this seemingly benign statement drive me to such a visceral response? After all, I was pretty good at sublimating and then analyzing my emotions, which is why I had ended up studying within the field and concentration that I had (sociological social psychology); and I most certainly had, over the course of my eight years of collegiate teaching, thirteen years as a probation/parole officer, and four years as a mental health social worker, been the target of remarks that were much more derogatory than the one in question. Managing nasty comments was not unusual, and I was pretty good at it. This *particular* comment, however, stuck in my craw. Why? What in the world had just happened to me? Ostensibly, I knew that I had experienced a slur. That cold feeling, *"You are so ARTICULATE!"* had reared its head and brought me back to my adolescent self. I knew a backhanded compliment when I heard it; but, I needed more—I needed to understand the words *and* the phenomenon surrounding their use—contextually.

First and foremost, I had to decide if something actually *had* happened, or whether or not I was just being overly sensitive. Sue (2010) was correct when he surmised that oftentimes, the subjects of microaggressive commentary are left bewildered—trying to determine whether or not they have, in fact, been abused. Personally, I knew that I had been slighted, but I was unsure of whether or not it was purposeful. I couldn't figure it out. Did the student actually diss me, or was he or she trying to sing my praises? I already knew the answer, but I hoped I was wrong, *"Wait, I'm at college—aren't folks supposed to be different, more educated?"* Why did I interpret the comment as racist, when the student could have just as easily been referencing my sex, my age, or the venue within which I taught? The idea that I questioned whether or not my intersectional self—that point where my race, my sex, my sexuality, and my class converge to create a multilayered, multifaceted individual (Crenshaw, 1989; Hill-Collins, 1999; Powell, 1996)—was linked to this comment sparked my sociological imagination. It heightened what Mills (2000) suggested was my awareness of myself at the intersection of my personal experiences and knowledge, and the institutional and interpersonal mechanisms of the greater social realm. This awareness challenged me to attempt to disentangle my hurt feelings and racial apprehension from the larger social context of not only the statement itself, but why the student felt free to make it. My analytical self kicked in, and I needed to find out more. The incident smacked of Critical Race Theory (CRT), which, Ladson-Billings (1998) proposed, acknowledges that race, having been dismissed as a valid biological model, remains a culturally and institutionally salient social construct that shapes our interpersonal experiences and structural realities. CRT analyzes the intersection of citizenship and race, and my student's words, *"She was more intelligent about the subject than I thought she would be,"* were ripe for such investigation. Over the next few days, I determined that I would attempt to understand just why I was so upset about this singular comment. My grad-school prof was right: we *do* research what is salient to us.

I waited for the initial sting of the comment to subside before I delved into what would become quite the reflective process. On a sunny afternoon, weeks later, I grabbed a cup of coffee and several packages of fruit snacks, settled in behind my home office desk, and retreated to my books—one of the spaces that had always been safe for me. When I was a kid, I would cope with stress and disappointment through reading— incessant reading. Generally it mattered not what kind of books I picked up, I just read voraciously or played music. My rented Artley flute got quite a workout between the second and twelfth grades whenever I was anxious or sad. When I was 12, muddling through junior high school was not an easy process for me, such as I'm sure was the case for most kids my age. To soothe my adolescent angst during the school year, when I wasn't driving my mother mad with my attempts at playing anything by Stevie Wonder by ear, I read *The Autobiography of Malcolm X*, followed up promptly with both Stephen King's *Salem's Lot* (1975) and *Night Shift* (1978). Again—genre be damned. The books provided an escape from my youthful problems and allowed me to feel powerful and—well—smart. I learned quickly that through books, I could both escape the melee that was my teenage life and bolster my self-esteem. Now, 34 years later, I still felt (feel) the pull of the read. This time, however, I steered clear of Black history and horror, and dove right into research. After all, this problem fit squarely within the realm of sociology, and what kind of sociologist would I be if I did not endeavor to understand the social praxis of how I interpreted what I inferred as being catalogued by my student?

What I found in the literature was simultaneously disheartening and illuminating. As I examined racism, its variants, and its subsequent manifestations, I realized that my student's comment, *"She was more intelligent about the subject than I thought she would be,"* and my reaction to it were, taken together, reflective of a differential reality—a disconnect in how we perceived our worlds and each other. Because our habitus (Bourdieu & Wacquant, 1992; Sue, 2010) was different—individually and historically we had not experienced the social realm similarly—it was highly probable that we interpreted the statement and the meaning behind it (objectively and subjectively) differently. My student may have truly believed that positively commenting on an African American woman's intellect was a high compliment, regardless of the social and occupational position of said woman. Through that statement, my student may have been attempting to articulate that his or her initial paradigm regarding persons of color had been shattered, and that he or she now saw minorities in a different light. In short, he or she was most likely not attuned to the microaggressive tenor (Sue, 2010; Sue et al., 2007) of the evaluation, and was unaware that declaring *"She was more intelligent about the subject than I thought she would be"* blatantly reinforced enmeshed stereotypes regarding Blacks. That student may have earnestly supposed that the statement was wholly positive, and that I would be pleased by this assessment. Moreover, he or she most likely did not see him- or herself as perpetuating racism.

I, however, as many African Americans are, was attuned to the social construction of Blackness, which included, in part, our being defined as unintelligent (Penner & Saperstein, 2013; Solorzano, Ceja, & Yosso, 2001; Steele & Aronson, 1995; Sue et al., 2007). I was aware that the label of limited intellectual aptitude operates to maintain a system of stratification in the social realm and forces us to be hypervigilant in our ideology construction and presentation of self. Oftentimes this hypervigilance operates to the detriment of our professional and academic performance and self-esteem (Steele & Aronson, 1995; Sue, 2010). The label of "unintelligent"— *"She was more intelligent about the subject than I thought she would be"*—acts as a stigmatizing marker and necessitates an attempt by the one labeled to mitigate the effects of the diminished status that accompanies it (Davis, 1988).

Most often, as was in my case, individuals attempt to minimize the label through impression management and facework (Goffman, 1959)— by managing their public (front-stage) image through the presentation of a carefully constructed social performance that reflects the perception of themselves that they want others to have (Davis, 1988; Goffman, 1959; Steele & Aronson, 1995). Interestingly, over time, even as majority attitudes regarding Black Americans have changed somewhat, the label—the diminished status and social stigma associated with "Blackness"—has remained (Crenshaw, 1989; Davis, 1988) but is understood differently (Penner & Saperstein, 2013). Race markers are more fluid than they were in the past and can be ascribed regardless of physical race presentation. Yet, an inverse relationship still exists between the assignment of Blackness and the ascribing of status, regardless of who exhibits it (Penner & Saperstein, 2013). In other words, certain behaviors, achievements, and statuses are understood as "Black," while others are not. What is perceived as "Black" is stigmatized *"She was more intelligent about the subject than I thought she would be,"* while the reverse is also true—what is seen as "white" is accepted and understood as positive and desirable behavior. To be "less Black" means to have more status. Part of my personal impression management and facework system was (is) the adoption and maintenance of my front-stage, socially accepted (Goffman, 1959), less-Black role of being intelligent. My student had done nothing more than reinforce the concept that "Black folk just ain't smart," and had deconstructed the image of my statused (intelligent) self that I had carefully fabricated through years of education and professional achievement. This individual forced me to question my own impression management, something that I had been encouraged to maintain since I could remember.

I recalled my mother's admonition to me as I prepared to leave for Fort Jackson, South Carolina. I'd enlisted in the U.S. Army Reserve to take advantage of the GI Bill as a way to pay for college. During the course of the three months between my high school graduation and my boarding a plane to head away from home, she embarked on a deliberate and somewhat stealthy campaign to prepare me for what lay ahead in the immediate future, and beyond. "You have to be twice as good as they are to get ahead in this world, Martina." Now, in a sense, I had already learned and internalized that lesson. After all, Mum had told me this more than once during my young life, and I had made sure to do everything that I possibly could to be "better." In other words, I'd learned to hustle—to, as defined by Whitehead, Peterson, and Kaljee (1994) and Dalla (2006), engage in nonconventional and nontraditional methods to survive. I'd learned to do what I had to do to get things done. For me, "doing what I had to do" meant putting on the face (Oreo) of someone who, according to the outside world, didn't look like me—someone who was "better" than the socially constructed understanding of the symbol that was (is) the color of my skin. With my mother's guidance, I learned to comprehend the narrowly defined and expected (and wholly incorrect) role of a working-class Black girl in 1970s and 1980s America, and made a conscious decision to exert concerted effort not to play it. In its place, I internalized and played the opposite—non-Black, nonstigmatized character. Externally, I did just that: played a role. Internally, however, I was being true to my core self—I did everything in my power not to be seen as Black or white; rather, I desperately tried to carve out an identity for myself that was not linked to race—one that screamed "MARTINA is twice as good" rather than "THIS BLACK GIRL is twice as good." My student unwittingly brought back into vivid view that my master status oftentimes speaks for me before I can speak for myself. I had been judged as inferior (Black) before I could illustrate that I was not. That hurt.

I pushed away from the pile of papers and books that had amassed atop my home office desk and clenched my teeth. "Yeah, yeah, yeah, OK," I thought. I tried to stop my analytical self from quelling my anger. I was offended and indignant, and I was on a mission. I wanted to bask in my self-righteous state. I *wanted* to be angry. After all, my personal and professional standing had been attacked. Somehow, however, I felt myself becoming less irate and more willing to attempt to see the situation outside of the frame within which I had placed it. *"So, maybe this individual doesn't see the world in the same way that I do. So what? This person was my student! We discussed systems of privilege and oppression all semester long. How could they not have considered that saying something like this was—at least symbolically—not OK?"* The idea that my student had no idea that his or her statement and the belief system tacitly expressed by it reinforced racial stereotypes exasperated me. I had spent an entire term engaging this person in a reflexive discussion regarding the structural formations and interpersonal realities of the American social environment. While I had no idea who the student in question was, I knew within which of the six sections that I taught he or she had been enrolled. It was a good one. Students in that section had actively engaged in discussion and asked honest questions. They had appeared to really be interested in dissecting what they saw as their "Truth," and learning the "Truths" of others. At this juncture, given the statement in question, *"She was more intelligent about the subject than I thought she would be,"* I wondered whether or not I had actually impacted this person in the way that I thought I had. *"We discussed racism, and we acknowledged that it still exists. How in the WORLD could they not GET that?"* I was disappointed and miffed. I turned back to my pile and half-heartedly picked up another article. I was frustrated but was hell bent on gaining as much insight as possible into why this student felt comfortable making what I perceived to be a racist comment. I read on.

Whites often believe that minorities are less affected by prejudice and discrimination than they were in the past (Sue et al., 2007). Many also believe that because they do not perceive themselves as racist, they are incapable of being discriminatory. They don't see themselves as harboring negative racial beliefs (Solorzano et al., 2001; Sue, 2010; Sue et al., 2007), despite being socialized into structural and interpersonal processes that both reinforce and promote racism (Abelson, Dasgupta, Park, & Banaji, 1998; Davis, 1988; Sue et al., 2007). Because they believe that they see the world through colorblind eyes, they don't recognize their behaviors, verbal and nonverbal, as reinforcing bias (Sue, 2010; Sue et al., 2007). Blacks, on the other hand, are acutely aware of the attitudes and processes associated with racism and racial stereotypes (Harris & Khanna, 2010; Waters, 2009). We are confronted with them daily and are attuned to the social places within which they lie. We know and recognize the language, imagery, and patterns of stratified racial interaction embedded within the fabric of the American social realm, and we understand that they provide context to our ascribed racial status and subsequent interactive experiences (Penner & Saperstein, 2013). This context shapes not only our individual constructions and presentations of self (Goffman, 1959) but also the interpersonal and institutional connections that we exact and navigate within the social milieu—those connections that shape status achievement and the acquisition of social capital (Penner & Saperstein, 2013; Steele & Aronson, 1995). My student may have believed himself or herself to be past the point of being racist. Maybe this individual felt that because he or she had taken my course, they had learned how not to be racist. *"Yeah . . . maybe THAT was it."* I put the article down and chuckled a bit at my own sarcasm. I was being snarky, but maybe that *was* it. Had my student, through privileged lenses, gleaned what he or she believed to be sufficient knowledge about the systems and applications of racism that they really thought that they had arrived? Did this person believe that he or she couldn't be racist—or at least, that they wouldn't reinforce racist ideology? I didn't know, and I had hit the wall. I was done trying to figure it out.

I began cleaning up the flurry of papers and books that covered every open space—floor and desk—of my home office. I told myself that I was finished analyzing what had happened. I'd devoted more time, effort, and emotional energy toward this endeavor than I had planned, and I realized that I would never really know what that student intended without actually speaking to him or her, and that wasn't an option for a variety of reasons. I haphazardly slid a pile of articles into my briefcase (out of sight, out of mind). For me, cleaning up usually entailed the systematic rearrangement of items to achieve the image, but not quite the state, of order. My partner came around the corner as I did, and I looked up at her, sheepishly. She was a relative neat freak (opposites really do attract), and I braced myself for the onslaught of impending mockery regarding my filthy office. It didn't come. "How ya doin', Martha?" Martha was a nickname that she had adopted for me after I told her about an unfortunate incident that occurred during high school, where my name was incorrectly displayed on local television. My high school cheerleading squad was told that we would be acknowledged in the credits of a televised basketball game, just as the ball players usually were. This was big. We were generally overlooked (we were only cheerleaders) but our recent ascent to relative stardom (we had subbed for a major university squad at a college game and had done very well) prompted our high school and the local media to recognize us. I remember sitting in front of the TV one cold Saturday morning, positively giddy—waiting for my name, Martina Sharp, to flash across the screen. I watched as the rest of the squad's names appeared in alphabetical order. One by one, the list of western, southern, and eastern European names materialized, each clearly and correctly listed. Then, it was my turn. I sat up on the couch and held onto the cereal bowl in my lap. *"Ok, I'm next!"* I thought after the "R's" flashed by. The moment had arrived, and I waited impatiently to see Martina Sharp flash across the screen. "Martha Shoip" is what appeared in its place. *"Huh? Seriously?"* I was flabbergasted at how my name—the simplest one in the bunch (my last name was Sharp, for goodness sake) could have been butchered. The fact that I was the only little brown face on the squad didn't escape me, and I wondered if that fact played a role in the mishap.

"Ok. I still haven't figured it out, but I'm finished." She looked at me warily. "Finished for the day, or finished, period?" *"Good question,"* I thought. "I don't know, but I'm not doing any more today." I kept my promise and let go of the day's mission. Try as I might, however, over the next few weeks, I wasn't able to completely shirk the gnawing restlessness that I felt about the comment. I went back to work and got ready for a new semester. I drafted syllabi, formulated schedules, and updated lectures. I was eager to welcome a new group of students to sit in my classes. Something was different though. I didn't feel the excitement that I normally felt during start-up week. I felt disconnected and a bit apathetic. I was nervous—something that I never felt going into a semester—about how my students would perceive me. Would they see "Professor" or, would they see "Black professor?" I was afraid of the stereotypes associated with the racial marker, and I felt that no matter what I did—whether or not I lived up to them—I would be sanctioned. In my mind, it seemed easier (and smarter) to numb myself, alienate myself from my work (Pierce, 2011; Steele & Aronson, 1995), and let the chips fall where they may. I gave thought to divesting myself from everything that I believed that a good professor should be, and to presenting sociological theory and concepts in the most basic way, without engaging my students in dialogue or critical, analytical thought. *"Just do your job and go home,"* I thought. *"It doesn't matter how well you do, anyway. You'll be judged whether or not you do well. You're damned if you do, and damned if you don't. Why even try?"* I did give serious consideration to tapping out. The stereotype threat, defined by Steele and Aronson (1995) as being at risk of corroborating, through one's own actions, a negative stereotype or label about a group or category to which one is associated, was real. I didn't want to risk making myself (or my race) look bad, and I didn't want to confirm—through inadvertent action . . . like walking into the classroom—a stigma associated with my race. I wanted to give up. I couldn't do that, though. My mother's advice and admonitions were in the forefront of my mind. "They can never take your intelligence from you. You have to be twice as good as they are to get ahead in this world, Martina." She was right. I couldn't let my guard down. As a Black, gay woman, I didn't have the luxury of crumbling.

And so, I didn't crumble. I did what I had always done—what was expected of me—not only by virtue of me being my mother's daughter, but what was expected of me because of my race and sex. As an African American woman, part of my impression management and facework process included (includes) the Strong Black Woman persona—being strong, resilient, and tenacious (Sharp-Grier, 2013)—and it was my responsibility to live up to that uniquely cultural and historical image. As much as I wanted to "let go," I felt as though doing so would have been disrespectful to not only myself and my family, but also to my forebearers, and I couldn't do that. Suffice to say, I sucked it up and carried on. I didn't let "them" see me sweat (another of my mother's tidbits). I paid a price for both the comment and the perseverance, though. I caught myself changing my approaches in the classroom—being a little less "Martina" than I would have been, had that comment not been made. I didn't change my rigor, but I certainly was less "professorial" (Pittman, 2012), something that I'd prided myself on. I wasn't as direct in discussions, and I found myself hesitant to play devil's advocate during the analysis of social phenomenon, a technique that had consistently proven robust in encouraging critical thought among my students. I tried not to be self-conscious—to not let the student's evaluation get the better of me, but I couldn't erase the smear of the comment, *"She was more intelligent about the subject than I thought she'd be."* Ultimately, this student had done more than he or she had intended to impact my teaching. I don't think that this individual anticipated that they would influence me in the way that they had, but they did. And that was sad.

Such is the insidious nature of microaggressions. Such is the nature of our social realm, and as a microcosm of it, the academy. Embedded in a system of history and routine is an academic structure that was at face value designed to promote meritocracy but inherently serves to diminish talented minorities and women and often stifles the voices of persons who identify as queer (Toombs, 2013). Not only are voices frequently hushed by stereotype threat (Steele & Aronson, 1995), minority, women, and queer faculty are burdened with the understanding that when their performance is critiqued for the purposes of evaluation and subsequent promotion, as mine was, they are consistently rated negatively compared to their hegemonic nonminority counterparts (Henderson-King & Nisbett, 1996; Lambert, Cronen, Chasteen, & Lickel, 1996). This system of adverse evaluation often results in the reinforcement of negative ideology regarding Black professors (Black people in general) and serves to truncate the career trajectory that so many in the academy strive to achieve (Toombs, 2013). Unfortunately, despite longitudinal and interdisciplinary research that illustrates and reinforces the negative effects of microaggressions on minority, women, and queer faculty, the reality is that consistently, nonmajority faculty are relegated to working within the very paradigm that they (and the academy) know is ineffective for them (Hamermesh & Parker, 2005; Pittman, 2012; Toombs, 2013; Turner et al., 2008). It will not be until the academy at large simultaneously acknowledges that this phenomenon—subtle racism through microaggressions within institutional constructs—exists, and determines that minority, women, and queer faculty deserve the opportunity to be evaluated fairly and without systematized bias, that progress can be made toward leveling the playing field for all faculty. Until then, we (I) carry on, saddling ourselves with the professional risk of managing poor student evaluations and negative evaluations of performance of both nonminority and (ironically) minority faculty who are oftentimes unaware of the pitfalls of both being minority in the academy and teaching what is oftentimes seen as superfluous and contradictory material—a risk that often results in being overlooked for promotion or tenure (Hamermesh & Parker, 2005; Turner et al., 2008).

I try to be a good professor. I care about my students, and I take my profession seriously. I strive to make a difference in the social realm—to "do good" by those with whom I share physical and metaphysical space. I believe that these are the goals of most who enter the academy. We seek to share and learn. To do this as a queer woman of color, however, I've had to develop the skills that my mother taught me—a drive to be the best, a sense of strength and resilience, and most important, an intelligence and wit that keeps me one step ahead of those who choose to label and stigmatize me. I relish the idea of proving wrong those who hold negative ideology about minorities, women, and persons identifying as queer. When I achieve that goal—proving them wrong—I don't mind someone saying, "Wow. She was more intelligent than I thought she'd be."

REFERENCES

Abelson, R. P., Dasgupta, N., Park, J., & Banaji, M. R. (1998). Perceptions of the collective other. *Personality and Social Psychology Review, 2*(4), 243–250.

Bourdieu, P., & Wacquant, L. J. (Eds.). (1992). *An invitation to reflexive sociology.* Chicago, IL: University of Chicago Press.

Braithwaite, J. (1981). The myth of social class and criminality reconsidered. *American Sociological Review, 46*(1), 36–57.

Crenshaw, K. (1989). Demarginalizing the intersection of race and sex: A Black feminist critique of antidiscrimination doctrine, feminist theory, and antiracist politics. *University of Chicago Legal Forum,* 139–167.

Dalla, R. L. (2006). You can't hustle all your life: An exploratory investigation of the exit process among street-level prostituted women. *Psychology of Women Quarterly, 30*(3), 276–290.

Davis, P. C. (1988). Law as microaggression. *Yale Law Journal, 98*(8), 1559–1577.

Fukurai, H. (1996). Race, social class, and jury participation: New dimensions for evaluating discrimination in jury service and jury selection. *Journal of Criminal Justice, 24*(1), 71–88.

Goffman, E. (1959). *The presentation of self in everyday life.* Garden City, NY: Doubleday.

Hamermesh, D. S., & Parker, A. (2005). Beauty in the classroom: Instructors' pulchritude and putative pedagogical productivity. *Economics of Education Review, 24*(4), 369–376.

Harris, C. A., & Khanna, N. (2010). Black is, black ain't: Biracials, middle-class blacks, and the social construction of blackness. *Sociological Spectrum, 30*(6), 639–670.

Henderson-King, E. I., & Nisbett, R. E. (1996). Anti-Black prejudice as a function of exposure to the negative behavior of a single Black person. *Journal of Personality and Social Psychology, 71*(4), 654–664.

Hill-Collins, P. (1999) *Black feminist thought: Knowledge, consciousness, and the politics of empowerment.* London, UK: Routledge.

King, S. (1975). *Salem's lot.* New York, NY: Anchor Books.

King, S. (1978). *Night shift.* New York, NY: Doubleday.

Ladson-Billings, G. (1998). Just what is critical race theory and what's it doing in a nice field like education? *International Journal of Qualitative Studies in Education, 11*(1), 7–24.

Lambert, A. J., Cronen, S., Chasteen, A. L., & Lickel, B. (1996). Private vs public expressions of racial prejudice. *Journal of Experimental Social Psychology, 32*(5), 437–459.

McKibbon, K. A. (1998). Evidence-based practice. *Bulletin of the Medical Library Association, 86*(3), 396–401.

Mills, C. W. (2000). *The sociological imagination.* Oxford, England: Oxford University Press.

Penner, A. M., & Saperstein, A. (2013). Engendering racial perceptions: An intersectional analysis of how social status shapes race. *Gender & Society, 27*(3), 319–344.

Pierce, C. M. (1970). *Offensive mechanisms.* In F. Barbour (Ed.), *The black seventies* (pp. 265–282). Boston, MA: Porter Sargent.

Pierce, M. A. (2011). *Microaggressions across the great divide: High-stakes written assessments, the threat of stereotype and hidden curriculum.* Pittsburgh, PA: Rosedog Books.

Pittman, C. T. (2012). Racial microaggressions: The narratives of African American faculty at a predominantly white university. *The Journal of Negro Education, 81*(1), 82–92.

Powell, J. A. (1996). The multiple self: Exploring between and beyond modernity and postmodernity. *Minnesota Law Review, 81*(6), 1481–1520.

Sharp-Grier, M. L. (2013). Ain't no pity party here! African American women's socialization into the SBW. Presented at the Ninth Annual International Congress of Qualitative Inquiry, The University of Illinois, Champaign-Urbana, Champaign, IL.

Solorzano, D., Ceja, M., & Yosso, T. (2001). Critical race theory, racial microaggressions, and campus racial climate: The experiences of African American college students. *Journal of Negro Education, 69*(1/2), 60–73.

Steele, C. M., & Aronson, J. (1995). Stereotype threat and the intellectual test performance of African Americans. *Journal of personality and social psychology, 69*(5), 797–811.

Sue, D. W. (2010). *Microaggressions in everyday life: Race, gender, and sexual orientation.* Hoboken, NJ: Wiley.

Sue, D. W., Capodilupo, C. M., Torino, G. C., Bucceri, J. M., Holder, A. M. B., Nadal, K. L., & Esquilin, M. (2007). Racial microaggressions in everyday life: Implications for clinical practice. *American Psychologist, 62*(4), 271–286.

Toombs, C. (2013). Diverse faculty: The collision of academic freedom, course content/subject. Presented at the American Association of University Professors Summer Institute, The University of Washington, Seattle, WA.

Turner, C. S. V., González, J. C., & Wood, J. L. (2008). Faculty of color in academe: What 20 years of literature tells us. *Journal of Diversity in Higher Education, 1*(3), 139–168.

Waters, M. C. (2009). *Black identities.* Cambridge, MA: Harvard University Press.

Whitehead, T. L., Peterson, J., & Kaljee, L. (1994). The "hustle": Socioeconomic deprivation, urban drug trafficking, and low-income, African-American male gender identity. *Pediatrics, 93*(6), 1050–1054.

X, Malcolm, & Haley, A. (1973). *The autobiography of Malcolm X*. New York, NY: Ballantine Books.

Yosso, T. J., Smith, W. A., Ceja, M., & Solorzano, D. G. (2009). Critical race theory, racial microaggressions, and campus racial climate for Latina/o undergraduates. *Harvard Educational Review, 79*(4), 659–691.

Chapter 3

Shocked into Silence No More

Linda Prieto

This chapter serves as a *testimonio* of my experiences of racial battle fatigue (RBF) and microaggressions as a new faculty hire at a predominantly white institution (PWI) of higher education. Here, testimonio serves as a method and political tool that conveys my story in the academy. According to Prieto and Villenas (2012):

> *Testimonio* then, names the workings and abuses of institutional power, the human costs, and our collective *sobrevivencia* (survival and beyond). Latina and women of color creative writers, artists, intellectuals, and scholar/activists make the case for the intensely political nature of our creative and professional work. Through our stories, we bear witness to our unique and collective experiences as racialized/ethnicized women in the United States. Different from the traditional genre of *testimonio*, Latina/Chicana feminist *testimoniantes* bear witness to each other as interlocutors through our own voice and authoring. (p. 415)

The quote above appears in an article coauthored with a mentor prior to my employment at the PWI that I discuss here. At that time I did not expect that I would return to writing about my challenges as a woman of color faculty in PWIs (Vargas, 2002). Perhaps naively, I hoped microaggressions would be easier to handle with time, less potent in some way. Instead I am reminded as we wrote then, "Latina educators' *testimonios* and Latina/ Chicana feminist perspectives can rearticulate pedagogies of *nepantla*—a space of frustration, discomfort, and always improvised visionary modes of teaching and learning" (p. 412). The following is my account of the frustrations and discomforts I encountered in the profession and specific moments that shocked me into silence and how collectively these incidents continue to inform my world view.

Not only was I a first-generation undergraduate and graduate student but also the first in my family to pursue a doctoral degree and later secure a tenure-track faculty position in higher education. Growing up poor, it was essential that my siblings and I contribute to the household by working in the fields alongside our parents in the central San Joaquin Valley of California. Thus, while I have experienced racial battle fatigue in various forms throughout my personal and professional life, for the scope of this chapter I focus on my experiences at my former place of employment. I will leave it up to you, the reader, to determine if these experiences can be classified as microaggressions or, if perhaps, as a Chicano/Latino colleague mentioned to me, "These aggressions are not *micro*," that indeed they are macro—a reality that institutions of power such as universities in the United States seem unwilling or too slow to recognize.

EMPTY PROMISES

After two years of employment in my first tenure-track position at a PWI in northern Texas, I accepted a tenure-track position that would take me back to my home state of California. My new position sounded dynamic; I would continue to work in my area of expertise—bilingual education—so although I would be the only faculty in the school of education in the area of bilingual education, it was presented as a great opportunity to develop a Spanish/English bilingual authorization program with the office of teacher credentialing. What I did not realize until I began employment in the fall of 2012 was that I would also be the only faculty of color in the school of education. At the time of my campus visit I was introduced to other people of color who I naively believed to also be faculty in the school of education only to later learn they either were not faculty or they were faculty in another department on campus. When I later mentioned the gap this presented in philosophical approaches toward teaching, research, and service to my supervisor, he rationalized that that was why I was there. As it turned out I was the quota.

At a new faculty welcome hosted at the university president's home on campus, our college dean approached me individually and said that he hoped I would be with the university for quite some time. He explained that in the past five years a number of Latina faculty had left the university. I quickly thought, "Who are these women and how can I speak with them to learn why they left?" As if somewhat reading my mind, the dean provided his rationale for their departure. He shared that these women's husbands had not been able to find adequate employment in the area, "You know how your culture is; the women follow the men." I was shocked into silence by all the assumptions implicit in his statement. He assumed we were all in heterosexual relationships, and married at that, he assumed we all followed our "men" wherever their employment might take us, and that married women of other ethnic backgrounds never follow their spouses. I would wonder, and continue to wonder about these other Latina faculty, and why they left the university . . . not knowing their names I have had no contact with them.

Prior to receiving or accepting that job offer, I explicitly shared with the search committee, including the person who would serve as my direct supervisor, that as a single parent of a toddler, it would prove quite challenging for me, to teach evening classes and secure care for my child after hours. Teaching evening hours had already proved a challenge at my last place of employment with such a young child, and I was very clear about my needs before accepting the offer. I was repeatedly reassured during my interview that it was not necessary for me to teach evening classes. This commitment from my prospective colleagues and employer played a major role in my accepting this particular offer. While teaching the evening course the first term, I approached my supervisor again and reminded him of the difficulty of teaching evenings and the prior understanding we had that I would not be assigned to evening courses. In the end, I was the one who established a relationship with the then-director of secondary English language development in the school district, invited her to guest lecture in my class, asked if she would be interested in teaching the course, and recommended that she be hired on as an adjunct to teach that evening class the following term. However, I was still bothered by how my supervisor initially responded to my request. He retaliated by writing an e-mail and copying the dean of the school of education on the message. In it he expressed his concern over my decision; that it was a shame that I would choose to "deprive over 60 students of my expertise." Never a mention was made about the other over 60 students I was forced to teach in an area outside of my expertise. Additional rationale I was presented with for teaching the social studies course was that since the bilingual education program did not yet exist, I needed to teach this course to fulfill my full-time equivalent (FTE). It was a shame that there was not a more creative and inclusive approach to my FTE assignments. Had I been considered before these decisions were made I would have suggested thinking beyond the school of education and/or the teaching of courses exclusively to fulfill my FTE. For example, I could have taught courses in ethnic studies, women's studies, and/or Spanish or served in an advisory role on issues pertaining to Chicana/Latino education to our school or college deans. Yet, I was never consulted; instead I was mandated to teach the courses my supervisor found most convenient for him.

VICTORIES—AT WHAT COST?

In the summer of 2012, as I arrived in what would serve as my family's place of residence for the following year, I contacted my supervisor via e-mail and offered to meet with whom he had shared could inform the process of applying for bilingual authorization with the California Commission on Teacher Credentialing. I was informed of the following: those colleagues were away for the summer and that the application for bilingual authorization had actually already been submitted to the state and was awaiting review. A non-tenured-track colleague, and veteran bilingual education teacher, became the person I worked most closely with on the bilingual authorization. It was not until the fall and after much digging around on our part that we learned that the application had been sitting on someone's desk for months and never submitted to the state— apparently as a result of a personal grudge with the former bilingual education faculty member.

The veteran bilingual education teacher and I took the lead in reviewing and extensively revising the application and submitting it to the state for consideration. Although the process was lengthy and involved reiterations of revisions and amendments, I was never recognized by the dean as the point of contact for these efforts, which was very frustrating. Any time we had a school of education meeting, he always listed one of the credentialing officers on the agenda to be the one who reported out on the progress of the bilingual authorization. In November of 2013 I heard from my former colleague—the veteran bilingual education teacher—that the application was successful. It was rewarding to receive her e-mail, even as I was no longer connected to that institution. However, do others in that school of education, wider college, or university recall or realize the efforts involved in bringing about the program? Will the program be appropriately supported, implemented, and sustained? Even though I no longer work there I am still concerned with these questions as they undoubtedly impact the experiences of many Chicana/Latino K–12 students in that area.

Perhaps it should not have been so surprising that neither my supervisor nor the dean had questioned whether or not the application had really been submitted in the summer. My supervisor even mentioned to me that I should not be concerned if the bilingual authorization was not approved, as there would always be work for me to do there. He did not seem to value the field of education or the difference between teaching any course(s) versus teaching those in which we have specialized. As for the dean, at one of my first meetings with him, he shared with me his concern for working with the almost exclusively Chicana/Latino populations some 30 miles south of the university. When I asked him if the populations were bi- or trilingual, he responded that some did also speak "Nahuatl or some damn thing." When I raised this concern with other colleagues the dean's linguicism was brushed aside as just representative of his generation. Somehow the fact that he was well into his senior years excused his behavior and language.

WOMEN FACULTY OF COLOR AS PAWNS

The first methods course I was required to teach was outside my area of expertise. I was told I had to teach this course due to personnel shortage. I was assured that once the bilingual authorization program was approved I would be able to focus on my actual job description—the reason why I had been hired and had accepted the position. I could not afford to be without a job; as such, I felt my hands were tied. Please note that no other tenured or tenure-track faculty member in the school of education was teaching outside their areas of expertise.

I later learned that having me teach that methods course was also a way to get rid of a non-tenure-track instructor who was perceived as having shortcomings in her pedagogical techniques. My colleagues perceived her approach to the course as antiquated and lacking a social justice perspective. I was both eager to see how I might improve the course and uncertain about the position in which I now found myself. Here, my supervisor and the dean, two white males—with no professional or academic background in education—were using a new Latina faculty member to oust an elderly white woman. Somehow they did not find this problematic, or if they did, it was not shared. So in the name of inserting social justice pedagogy into this course, I was being used without dignity to remove someone from her job. Although it was very difficult to live through this experience of manipulation, I was able to have a respectful relationship with the instructor I was used to remove and at the end of my time there, she was the only one who formally recognized my contributions to the school of education.

As the academic year progressed, I learned former students enjoyed her class, while on my course evaluations I had students share that I focused too much on multicultural education and LGBTQ (lesbian, gay, bisexual, transgender, queer) issues in particular. In preparing teacher candidates to teach a culturally and linguistically diverse population, how can we not approach our teaching through a social justice lens? I quickly learned that the students in my classes, and in the wider university population, were from middle- to upper-class backgrounds, highly entitled, and did not want to be asked to question issues of social dominance and inequality or any other topic that might make them feel uneasy. As my first-year review unfolded I was very disappointed that neither the tenured faculty on my review team, my supervisor, nor the dean addressed these narrow comments from students or that including social justice pedagogy in courses is particularly difficult for the mostly white mainstream students enrolled. I followed another colleague's recommendation and included a detailed written response to my first periodic review. I wanted to be certain my colleagues and deans were aware of the available research articulating that faculty of color and faculty who teach university courses that explicitly address culturally responsive teaching, multicultural perspectives, differences and privilege, notions of social justice, and/or the need to empower historically underrepresented communities in PWIs have lower end-of-term evaluations that reflect the students' discomfort with having their feelings stirred up or world views challenged and being uncomfortable with those feelings (Berry & Mizelle, 2006; Martin, 2010; Nast, 1999; Vargas, 2002). However, I never received a response to my comments.

COMMUNITY RESPONSIBILITY

My contributions to the school of education and the larger university extended beyond the campus walls. During the fall semester, I met with my supervisor to share with him the efforts I was working on beyond my assigned courses. As I met with him it became clear that the very collaborations that were serving to sustain me at the university were perceived as extraneous, as he informed me that they would not have as much value in the retention, tenure, and promotion process as compared to my colleagues who did work directly in school classrooms with teachers and students.

Some of my service work included serving as a member of the Chicana/Latino Faculty Staff Association on campus, as a countywide Title III/English learner (EL) advocacy committee member, conducting EL parent trainings on the importance of developing biliteracy skills, and as the MEChA (Movimiento Estudiantil Chicano de Aztlán) faculty advisor—a cultural and political student organization I belonged to as an undergraduate student at Stanford, and one that was instrumental in informing my world view, social justice approach, and my retention as a first-generation college student from a poor working-class background. So my work with the Chicana/Latino community and English learner populations on- and off-campus was work that I was choosing to engage in, but my supervisor insisted that I understand that it was more important that I participate on department, college, and university committees as part of my service commitment. He also told me not to apply to too many external research grants because I was there "to teach," and yet other colleagues were touted for pursuing external grant awards.

Although the university devalued my service, on more than one occasion I was called on to represent the university in front of the external Chicana/Latino community. For example, when the school of education wanted to formally establish a working relationship with a predominantly Chicana/Latino high school south of the university, I was invited to attend the meeting. I agreed thinking that I was also being invited to participate in the collaboration. I arrived at the meeting and this is what unfolded. It was like a mirrored quandary. The university team consisted of one Chicana/Latino (or person of color)—myself—and the high school team was all Chicana/Latino with the exception of one white male teacher. The dean opened the meeting and quickly introduced me as the newly hired Latina faculty. We went around the room and each took a turn introducing ourselves. Then the dean said that we would now move on to the "important stuff" and that I could leave. I was shocked into silence, gathered my materials, and excused myself from the meeting.

Later in the year, there was a community event hosted at the local middle school where the topic of discussion focused on the educational experiences of Chicana/Latino students. The dean called on me to attend. He indicated that there was no one from the president's office who could attend, and neither could he, so he needed me to be there to represent the university. He also said he would pass my name along so it was clear who would be there to represent the university. I attended the event, and showed up early, as my parents taught me to always try to do. As I saw parents gathering at the cafeteria, I went around shaking hands and introducing myself in Spanish as I am accustomed to doing with family. As the event began, the organizer thanked a number of attendees, including staff from the superintendent's office and the local community college (all of whom were white). Since he did not mention me I was left to assume that no one had informed him of my attendance on behalf of the university, but wait, I had actually introduced myself to him prior to the event. Some of the parents I was sitting next to asked me, "*¿Por qué a usted no la presentan?*" ("Why don't they introduce you?"). I shrugged my shoulders, smiled awkwardly, and said it was okay, although inside, I, like the parents, felt disrespected, ignored, and invisible.

As the year progressed, I continued with my commitments to Chicana/Latino students, staff, and faculty on campus and English-learner populations off-campus, and met the gatekeeper responsibilities of service on-campus. As part of my department, college, and university obligations, I volunteered to serve on a hiring committee for a faculty position within the school of education. At the end of that process, I was reminded how the majority of my colleagues were more concerned with how this new person would (or would not) positively contribute to their own retention, tenure, and promotion process than the potential benefits to our teacher candidates and the larger community beyond the university walls. Two white female faculty cried during a meeting, and the search was tabled. No offer was extended that year with the understanding that a new search would be pursued the coming year. I could not help feel that the entire process had been a waste of time.

Perhaps symbolically, on the day of the César Chávez commemoration, I walked out of the school of education to support the event, and as I saw Chicana/Latino colleagues from across campus I was so overwhelmed with all that had unfolded over the past seven months, I found it necessary to share with them. I was overcome by emotion and appreciative for the safe space among these colleagues where I could truly share my experiences without judgment or retaliation. This began my journey of healing. But in the immediate I was to return to the school of education and teach class where, when I asked students what they knew about César Chávez, they reported that they either knew nothing, assumed he had lived long long ago or that he was still living. Maybe I should not be as surprised as I was but again these students were all future teachers in the state of California where César Chávez Day is an official state holiday.

COMMUNITY SUPPORT

After the April 4 César Chávez event I began engaging more formally with my Chicana/Latino colleagues across campus about my experiences of micro/macroaggressions and racial and linguistic battle fatigue. When I shared that I was leaving the university altogether and had accepted a job out of state, they expressed great sadness to see me go but wished me well as I needed to do what was best for my child and myself. I hated the idea of going home with poison after such negative experiences at work and having my toddler somehow exposed to that toxicity. The poison was born from having my areas of expertise in bilingual education and cultural studies undervalued; my contributions to the school, university, and larger community unrecognized; and myself unappreciated in the process. So I came to realize that there was no more for me to do there. Although I am a champion of social justice, I would no longer risk my family as collateral damage of the physiological and psychological stressors I was facing.

My colleagues in the Chicana/Latino faculty/staff association encouraged that I request an exit interview with the employment equity director on campus so that my experiences would be documented and shared anonymously with the university president. I met with her and also called for a meeting with the university president and executive director of the newly created office of diversity and inclusivity. Since our schedules did not coincide before my departure, I only met with the employment equity director so that there would still be documentation for the president to determine how, if at all, he would work to improve the university climate.

Another factor that also impacted my decision to originally accept this offer for employment was that when I visited the campus, I had lunch with two other Chicana/Latino faculty on campus and when I asked if a Chicana/Latino faculty association existed, I was informed that indeed, a Chicana/Latino faculty/staff association was active on campus, and I was invited to join. This organization proved to serve as my strongest ally and form of retention in the coming year. I learned so much through this experience, including not to trust people, their kind words, or offers, but rather, to require that every agreement be followed up in writing—although we cannot ignore that the United States has a rich history of breaking written promises with underprivileged communities.

CONCLUSION/LESSONS LEARNED

The experiences I share in this chapter are painful to relive, yet it is politically urgent that I do so. I must recall them as a process of healing and closure and as a way to share with others my experiences as a Latina professor and scholar in academia. And for the other feminist activists, scholars, students, and researchers who will also come across this work, perhaps the testimonio presented here can serve as a cautionary reminder of the inequities in society, inequities that remain prevalent in higher education, specifically at PWIs, and also, to be reminded that allies can be forged across cultural and linguistic differences. At my former institution those allies included white lesbian colleagues who, given their sexual orientation, were not immune to micro/macroaggressions.

Currently, I serve as tenure-track faculty at a Hispanic-serving institution (HSI) where critical scholars of various cultural and linguistic backgrounds all concerned with the educational needs and strengths of traditionally underserved populations surround me. Granted, this is not the case across the university, nor is the fact that we are an HSI openly celebrated, but it is a significant and much recognized improvement from where I have been. My biggest challenge now is to carve out my research agenda in a space where I no longer have to be everything for everybody. Now I can focus on research that explores teacher formation across the continuum from teacher candidates to teacher educators. I am supported in examining my work from a critical perspective using life her/histories and testimonios informed by Chicana feminist thought. But even now as I make my words publically available I wonder about possible retaliation and repercussions. However, I know I must share my experiences with the hope that doing so might help others expand their knowledge and understanding of these topics or feel validated in their own experiences of micro/macroaggressions, racial and linguistic battle fatigue, and retaliation and still move forward.

REFERENCES

Berry, T. R., & Mizelle, M. (Eds.). (2006). *From oppression to grace: Women of color and their dilemmas within the academy*. Sterling, VA: Stylus.

Martin, K. (2010). Student attitudes and the teaching and learning of race, culture, and politics. *Teaching and Teacher Education, 26,* 530–539.

Nast, H. (1999). 'Sex,' 'Race' and Multiculturalism: Critical consumptions and the politics of course evaluations. *Journal of Geography in Higher Education, 23*(1), 102–115.

Prieto, L., & Villenas, S. (2012). Pedagogies from Nepantla: Testimonio, Chicana/Latina feminisms and teacher education classrooms. *Equity and Excellence in Education, 45*(3), 411–429.

Vargas, L. (Ed.). (2002). *Women faculty of color in the white classroom*. New York, NY: Lang.

Chapter 4

Being Tall Isn't Exactly the Same Thing as Being Black: The Challenges of Critical Perspective-Taking in a Nearly All-White Classroom

Sherry L. Deckman and Beatriz M. Montilla

It seemed an innocuous enough task: have students respond to various quotes and ideas from *Affirming Diversity* (Nieto, 2004) and *Why Are All the Black Kids Sitting Together in the Cafeteria?* (Tatum, 1997). The context was our Social and Cultural Foundations of Education class in which we were the professor (Dr. Sherry, as my students refer to me) and a student (Beatriz). The course, which aimed to provide preparation for critically reflective decision making and for working effectively with diverse students and communities, was required for all undergraduates in our Ithaca College teacher education programs. Aligning very much with national trends (Feistritzer, 2011), all but 3 of 21 students and the instructor identified as white—Dr. Sherry identifies as biracial (Black/white), Beatriz as Latina/Black, one male student as African American, and another female student as biracial (Asian American/white). For this activity, students circulated around the room engaging in a "silent conversation," writing thoughts on large sheets of chart paper. I (Dr. Sherry) had supplied several prompts to get them started that included questions or quotes from the texts meant to elicit deeper thinking. One poster included this quote: "For those readers who are in the dominant racial category, it may sometimes be difficult to take in what is being said by and about those who are targeted by racism" (Tatum, 1997, p. 27).

I had chosen this quote deliberately to provoke reflection from some of the students who had asked why we were spending so much time in the course focused on issues of racial inequality in education. A number of students in this class section as well as the others I was teaching were incredulous that acts of overt discrimination were still occurring in the United States, at least in the Northeast. They found evidence of racial injustice difficult to assimilate into their perception of the world, wanting to believe that they were fair, nondiscriminatory people who had grown up in fair, nondiscriminatory communities in a fair, nondiscriminatory country. To demonstrate otherwise might implicate them and their loved ones as the beneficiaries of unearned privileges and as perpetrators of injustices. Consequently, the images and counterstories (Yosso, 2006) of various marginalized communities that they were being exposed to in our class threatened the very core of their self-views. This was especially apparent when watching present-day updates of the Clark doll experiments of the 1940s.

In an effort to demonstrate the negative psychological effects of segregation, Dr. Kenneth Clark and his wife Mamie showed that when asked, young Black children expressed a preference for white dolls and attributed negative characteristics to black dolls (see Library of Congress, n.d.). Decades later, researchers and journalists find similar results (CNN, 2010; Davis, 2007; Williams, 2008). My students argued that the research was poorly executed and asked what region of the United States the current experiments were conducted in. Though I showed them three different contemporary examples of the experiment, many could or would not entertain the possibility of the truth of persistent societal racism revealed in them. Therefore, my hope for this silent conversation was that students might understand that their inability or refusal to witness racism could be related to their social position rather than the absence of racism.

A couple of posters were left blank so that student volunteers could fill in their own question or salient quote. One white, male student offered, "What is racism?" This turned into a heated whole-group conversation, after which students jotted down lingering thoughts representing a range of takeaways from those who felt they had a new perspective on the topic, to those who felt resentful of the discussion. Three quotes from three different students[1]—the first two of whom identify as white—inform the motivation for this chapter:

---

[1]Identifying characteristics have been obscured to protect student confidentiality. In instances where this is impossible, students have given permission for us to write about our shared experience.

"I think people are still failing to see how people often use their minority status to get what they want. Some people totally ignore every part of their background that may not give them an advantage of a minority."

"The use of hyperbole [referring to claims about the genocide of Native Americans] *to elicit guilt and emotional responses is the least effective form of social justice rhetoric. I hate that any comment that disagrees with violent liberalism is met by huffs and grunts."*

The final quote is from Beatriz: *"I am frustrated because I feel like my point is constantly being demeaned in subtle ways. For example, saying that not all people of color 'feel like that' doesn't mean that the statement is not valid."*

These quotes illuminate the potential difficulty inherent in being one of very few students of color in a class that tackles issues of race, feeling simultaneously expected to speak for and represent your "group," but then having your individual experiences denied as idiosyncratic.

Currently in the field of higher education, "diversity" is regularly discussed as an unproblematic ideal. However, what is often left unexplored is exactly what diversity means and how it is experienced by the faculty and students of color who are viewed as the "diversifiers" (Kramer, 2008) on predominantly white campuses. In the service of the institution and greater good we may be daily subjected to microinequalities and microaggressions (Sue, 2010), such as being told explicitly, or through furtive eye rolls, that our views are dismissible, as Beatriz reveals when she writes, "I feel like my point is constantly being demeaned in subtle ways."

Thus, in this chapter, we offer a counterstory to the dominant diversity narrative by exploring the personal and professional challenges encountered as we—2 of only 4 people of color in a 22-person class—attempted to engage white members of our one-semester course in critical perspective-taking related to race and oppression. For the purposes of the chapter, we define critical perspective-taking as the act of analyzing the root of each of our perspectives and understanding the ways in which our personal standpoint impacts our perception of the world. Perspective-taking is a key activity when working for social justice (see Silverstein, 2013) and involves recognizing the views of those we consider "other" and acknowledging the role of power dynamics in shaping one's views. However, we argue that and demonstrate how this can be a fairly fraught process for the professor and student who are among the only non-white members of the class, particularly a class that tackles issues of race and social justice as ours did.

Throughout this chapter, we uniquely intertwine our voices as professor and student, illuminating how each of us felt the difficulties of asking other members of the class to interrogate their privilege and how we grew in the process. Our point here is not to vilify the white students or even to position them as ignorant and us as all knowing. Rather, we hope to provide a counterstory that challenges notions of campus racial diversity as unproblematic and demonstrates how discussions about race in higher education are complicated and can be exhausting and especially so in classroom settings designed to focus on social inequality that are overwhelmingly white and overwhelmingly privileged.

We tell our story/ies using three salient moments in the course: the silent conversation described above, a discussion in which a white, male student equates racial oppression with "sizeism," and the viewing of the civil rights documentary *Eyes on the Prize* (Hampton & Vecchione, 1987). We begin by describing how we came to work together as professor and student processing our experiences in the class, with Beatriz's voice appearing in italics.

UNITING VOICES

In retrospect, my (Dr. Sherry's) shock at the whiteness of our campus and the town in which our college is located seems naive. I knew the statistics indicated an overwhelmingly white majority for the city and institution—around/over 70 percent white population and less than 10 percent Black population. Having attended elite, predominantly white institutions of higher learning for both my undergraduate and graduate studies, I assumed moving to Ithaca, New York, would be much the same. The past times I had been "the only" Black person or even the only nonwhite person in the room were too numerous to count. I reasoned, "How could this next experience be any different?" Yet, I was unprepared for what it would feel like to live and work in such a place on a daily basis.

My freshman year of high school I (Beatriz) attended an elite boarding school where I was part of a very small minority of people of color. At my middle school I was considered one of the high-achieving students and because it was a very small school, I was friends with pretty much everyone; being social was always my strong suit. It became clear from the beginning that at the boarding school being popular was not just a given. There were summer homes to be accounted for and ski trips to Vail that were a far cry from my winters in the Bronx in our small apartment. For a twelve-year-old, being different can often be translated into a traumatic experience, and I made every effort to distance myself from being that poor girl from the Bronx who had never seen a snowboard a day in her life. Eventually I became so invested in trying to make friends and keep up appearances that my grades suffered horribly and I left the school for good that May. When I returned to the city I attended a public school in the Lower East Side and graduated at the top of my class from a high school where people of color were in the majority. In fact the only white people who I came into contact with in school were my teachers and administrators.

Because of my experience at the boarding school, Ithaca College was not much of a culture shock, although it took me a while to grasp the concept of once again being the only person of color in my classes. Instead of trying my hardest to fit into the dominant white culture, I began to make it a point of sharing my perspective in all the classes where I felt as if it were one of the few times when my white peers would be exposed to the way that I saw the world. My experience at boarding school was instrumental in helping me get over my initial fear when I was 12 to be seen as an outcast in an environment where my presence was a novelty.

What quickly became apparent in this new context was how limited my (Dr. Sherry's) students' perspectives were in terms of having come from mostly white and affluent or comfortably middle-class communities. They were eager for examples that illustrated experiences that challenged their own, which they sometimes rejected as impossible realities. The needs of my white and affluent students regularly came into conflict with what I felt was my responsibility to the students in the class who might feel marginalized by those examples. *I (Beatriz) brought this up in a weekly feedback form where I expressed my frustration at feeling like my peers weren't taking my points seriously in our class discussion or that I had to represent extreme points of view—that I didn't necessarily agree with—because otherwise my peers might never have the opportunity to consider these views, ones which I know people in my community in the Bronx, for example, take seriously.*

When I (Dr. Sherry) read Beatriz's comments, I was both grateful and taken aback. I was grateful that she was willing to put herself out there in such a way as to be open to her peers' critiques for the sake of our joint learning and ultimately the learning of the young people our class members would be responsible for as K-12 educators. But, I was troubled that our classroom environment was such that Beatriz felt like this potentially demeaning position was one she *had* to take for our joint learning. In an e-mail exchange early in the semester I shared with Beatriz, "I wanted to let you know that a few of your classmates mentioned specifically [on the class feedback survey] being impacted by your words in class today. You managed to change some hearts and minds. I hate that it seems like a responsibility you have as one of the very, very few students of color in the class. But, I am not sorry that it did have an impact on students today. I am grateful for your sacrifice, and I think about the future students of your classmates who might also be beneficiaries." Writing this chapter together became our opportunity to disrupt the tormenting silence about how we experienced our roles as the only people of color in conversations about race in a predominately white setting.

THE "WHO IS MORE OPPRESSED" GAME (BEATRIZ'S VOICE)

It was a Monday afternoon, and our task for the weekend was to read various articles that discussed media representations of marginalized groups in our society. We had been asked to submit responses to the readings and participate in an online discussion, which allowed me to digest the information presented, so I was particularly excited to share my thoughts in class. The class discussion was especially vibrant that afternoon; it is not every day that we are asked to think critically about the movies we fondly remember from our youth.

Having grown up watching children's movies and wondering why there were few people of color represented, who often completely filled a stereotype, I found the readings to be a breath of fresh air. I was struck by the examples from popular media that one chapter (Kellner & Share, 2007) cited as problematic and limited at best and as harmful and racist at worst. For example, Princess Tianna from *The Princess and the Frog* (Clements & Musker, 2009) is frequently celebrated as the first African American Disney princess, but as one of my classmates noted she was an animal for nearly the entire film, which in many ways takes away from the fact that she could be considered a pioneer in the world of Disney Princesses. Finally, my feelings regarding how I saw myself on a TV screen were being acknowledged by the world of academia.

As this class session progressed, I began to feel a lot more comfortable sharing my feelings regarding the texts from a perspective that I knew some of my classmates had rarely been exposed to. Although there were certainly moments within this course where I felt as if I was alone in my ideas, I was grateful that my classmates seemed to be receiving my thoughts in an open-minded and respectful manner. Being a minority in a predominantly white institution led me to have a particular appreciation of classes like this one, especially knowing that I would not always have the privilege of sharing a space with individuals who would make me feel comfortable when sharing my views.

However, as I was finally feeling heard by my peers about the portrayal of people of color in the media, a white male drew on his point of view to make a point about media representation. He protested, "There are very few people who look like me in the media. I am often self-conscious of my size and never stand up straight." His central idea, as I interpreted it, was that he felt marginalized due to reactions to his tallness, as well as a general lack of representation for tall, full-figured males in the media. I could tell from his tone of voice that this was something that had bothered him for a while, and had his comment been introduced in a context that was not comparing his struggle to that of people of color in the media, it is very likely that I would have had a completely different reaction. But in this instance, his comment drew attention away from our discussion of race and oppression as other white classmates chimed in with how they too felt disregarded by the media for whatever reason.

It was a difficult conversation for me to process; how could my classmate equate my feelings of invisibility in white culture with feeling like there weren't enough tall people on TV? As a woman I could connect with my classmate's struggles regarding body image and his frustration with the way media portrayed people who weren't necessarily considered thin. However, as a person of color I was outraged. While Hollywood might not be very accepting of actors with different body types, I was confused by the connection my classmate was making between being tall and under-represented and the way people of color are portrayed in media. As a future teacher who might work with racially marginalized students, what would it mean that he saw the social injustices they faced as being equitable with the inconveniences of being tall? In fact, tallness is often privileged in our society, for instance with taller people documenting higher earnings than shorter peers (Donohue, 2007).

In the week that followed I shared the story of the class discussion with pretty much all of my close friends who were of color. In my process of becoming a person who is respectful and understanding of varying perspectives, it was important to me that my friends also took issue with the comments made in the class. Looking back, I am interested in who I chose to tell the story to. Although I have close friends who are white, I did not tell them about this. In sharing the story with my friends I was seeking a certain sense of validation. I wanted to know if my reaction was appropriate and specifically chose to tell this story to friends who would process the situation in a way that was similar to me. Aside from this particular incident, I find myself hesitating to share stories where the racial implications could be ambiguous to white friends. I attribute this to not wanting to have a heated conversation about race when I am trying to enjoy time with my friends. There is also always a lingering fear of discovering that my friends are not as open minded as I thought they were.

The discussion with my friends led me to see that by sharing his story, my classmate was merely trying to make a personal connection to the course material. It speaks to a greater issue of race being something that we rarely discuss in K–12 education, leaving students who do not have conversations about race at home to base their ideas about race on what they are exposed to in the media, which oftentimes is a stereotype. At the same time, this type of interaction can lead to the very unproductive state of comparing our plight to others in a game of "who is more oppressed." In this particular scenario the student failed to consider his tallness as a part of his identity that is not systematically, institutionally, or historically oppressed, even though it may have felt like a burden in daily life.

As a minority student in an institution that is primarily white, I often labeled my status among the dominant race as misunderstood. Even with discussions in courses and on a personal level with white people about race, I never left those conversations feeling like my point of view was completely accepted. There was a definite frustration in knowing that this was completely out of my control. I knew that my experiences as a Black Latina woman were something that I could never describe within a few minutes of any discussion. The fact that I was among three students of color in this class led me to take on the role of sharing my experiences regularly in order to compensate for there not being many other people who could do the same.

VISUAL(IZED) VIOLENCE (DR. SHERRY'S VOICE)

"I start out by asking them, 'Who has heard of Mose Wright or Emmett Till?' Some of them have, but many haven't. I say, 'By the end of this class, you won't be able to forget those names.'" A colleague of mine was describing how transformative it has been having her classes watch segments from the documentary series, *Eyes on the Prize* (Hampton & Vecchione, 1987). The series recounts the history of the U.S. civil rights movement, and I had watched episodes as an undergraduate student and remember how moving they were. The specific segment my colleague was describing tells the story of Emmett Till, a young man from Chicago, and his uncle Mose Wright, who Till was visiting in Mississippi. It was certainly one story I couldn't forget. I never understood how anyone could justify brutally murdering a 14-year-old boy—even in Mississippi in the 1950s—for "flirting" with a white woman.

As I considered showing the one clip from *Eyes on the Prize* that had been permanently seared into my memory from my first viewing almost two decades before, I nearly became physically sick. I was kept up at night thinking about it. It seemed like one thing for a white woman who has been a longstanding faculty member at our school to show the clip to our practically all-white classes than for me, a new faculty member and younger woman of color to do so. That aside, I remembered the personal trauma I felt viewing that clip and was not eager to do so again even for the benefit of learning.

Despite my hesitance at including *Eyes on the Prize* as one of my course texts, I respected my colleague's advice and didn't want my classes to miss out on a potentially transformative experience because of my own fear. The week prior to the class in which we were set to watch the clip, I consulted a number of other faculty members regarding what they might do in my position. Most of them happened to be white, consistent with the demographics of the professorate in the United States (U.S. Department of Education, 2013). These trusted friends and mentors encouraged me and offered advice on how I might introduce the video. One tenured faculty member sagely said, "Just because something is hard doesn't mean you shouldn't do it. I know you'll make the right decision for your class."

In teacher education, the "right decision for [my] class" also bears the moral responsibility of the "right decision" for my students' future students. It is not my students' fault—and I don't want to think in those terms—that many of them have not had the opportunity to "see" the experiences of "others" with whom they have had little to no personal experience. We live in a society so rampant with residential (Massey & Denton, 2001) and K-12 schooling segregation (Orfield & Lee, 2005) that students come to college hoping for and often proclaiming that it is the most diverse context they have ever been in (Espenshade, Radford, & Chung, 2009) and this may be even more so for white students who are the most racially isolated of all groups (Sidanius, Levin, & Van Laar, 2008). In many cases they hope and expect to encounter people and views different from themselves and what they have known before. And for future classroom teachers, this might be the first and one of the only opportunities they have to learn about "diversity" before beginning to teach young people from backgrounds different than their own. If I wasn't going to accept some responsibility for this, my students might not have the chance to engage as deeply with issues of race and racism in any of their other undergraduate coursework.

I steeled myself for possible revolt and anger on the part of my students—of all backgrounds—as I asked them to watch what I found to be a deeply painful moment in American history. Over a period of two days, given that I taught multiple sections of this course, I watched again and again as Emmett Till's open casket flashed on the screen. His disfigured face, barely recognizable as a face, paused in front of us. I wanted to avert my eyes as the scene appeared, and I certainly didn't make eye contact with students at this point. Their attention was fixed on the image.

In the end, students said they were moved by the clip, including one who left the class astonished that he had never heard of the *Brown v. Board* Supreme Court case. I accepted that to open up learning opportunities for my students, I would have to endure the personal violence of engaging with traumatic historical memories. Nonetheless, I remained conflicted about what this meant for the students of color in my class who did not have the same professional obligations. Making oppression visible to white students—helping them see something that to them is typically otherwise invisible—requires that students of color be subjected to images of oppression that are already lived, familiar, and deeply painful.

RECONCILING THE COST OF EMPATHY

Research has linked racial disparities in society to a lack of empathy between whites and people of color. Put quite simply, we can't feel each other's pain. If we don't learn to breach this "racial empathy gap" (Silverstein, 2013), we will likely continue seeing extensive social disparities. Courses such as ours are directly poised to address this gap through the practice of critical perspective-taking. Through witnessing the accounts of those who experience the brunt of racism and inequality, white students may come to better understand these experiences and commit to working as partners and allies in the struggle for justice. This seemed to be the case with students in our class who reflected on the course at the end of the semester:

"Made me think in ways I never have."
"I thought this was one of the most beneficial courses I have taken at Ithaca College."

One student wrote "Being the fish that sees the water," referring to a metaphor invoked in the class and attributed to Margaret Mead: "If a fish were an anthropologist, the last thing it would discover would be water." But, the emotional burden of making the water of white privilege and racism visible uniquely fell on the shoulders of the people of color in the class.

In engaging in critical perspective-taking, we endured assaults to our self-worth and well-being. We had to persist through denials of the truth of our experiences of racism, the demeaning of our views through counterclaims of oppression by those with privilege, and through the self-imposed psychic violence experienced when repeatedly viewing and reliving traumatic historical and contemporary moments. Despite the difficulty of this endeavor, we maintain that it is crucial to provide students with the ability to explore the implications of race on their lives. As one recent student of color in reflected, "Discussing race in a predominantly White class can be difficult, but this is part of the fight to end racism . . . [White students] need to see the segregation and racism we [people of color] experience today because many of them are going to be the ones teaching our children."[2] We endure so that others might not have to.

REFERENCES

Clements, R., & Musker, J. (Directors). (2009). *The princess and the frog* [Animated film]. United States: Disney.

CNN. (2010). *Study: White and black children biased toward lighter skin*. Retrieved from http://www.cnn.com/2010/US/05/13/doll.study/

Davis, K. (director) (2007). *A girl like me*. Produced by Reel Works Teen Filmmaking. Retrieved from http://www.youtube.com/watch?v=YWyI77Yh1Gg

Donohue, M. (2007). *Why tall people make more money*. Retrieved from http://www.cnn.com/2007/US/Careers/02/02/cb.tall.people/index.html

Espenshade, T. J., Radford, A. W., & Chung, C. Y. (2009). *No longer separate, not yet equal: Race and class in elite college admission and campus life*. Princeton, NJ: Princeton University Press.

Feistritzer, C. E. (2011). *Profile of teachers in the U.S. 2011*. Washington, DC: National Center for Education Information.

---

[2]Thanks to Joel Hilario for offering this insight.

Hampton, H. (Creator and executive producer), & Vecchione, J. (Producer and director). (1987). *Eyes on the prize* [Documentary]. United States: Blackside, Inc.

Kellner, D., & Share, J. (2007). Critical media literacy, democracy, and the reconstruction of education. In D. Macedo & S. R. Steinberg (Eds.), *Media literacy: A reader* (pp. 3–23). New York, NY: Peter Lang.

Kramer, R. (2008). Diversifiers at elite schools. *Du Bois Review, 5*(2), 287–307.

Library of Congress. (n.d.) "With an even hand": *Brown v. Board* at fifty. Retrieved from http://www.loc.gov/exhibits/brown

Massey, D., & Denton, N. (2001). American apartheid: Segregation and the making of the underclass. In D. B. Grusky (Ed.), *Social stratification: Class, race, and gender in sociological perspective* (2nd ed., pp. 660–670). Boulder, CO: Westview.

Nieto, S. (2004). *Affirming diversity: The sociopolitical context of multicultural education* (4th ed.). Boston, MA: Pearson.

Orfield, G., & Lee, C. (2005). *Why segregation matters: Poverty and educational inequality.* Cambridge, MA: The Civil Rights Project at Harvard University.

Sidanius, J., Levin, S., & Van Laar, C. (2008). *The diversity challenge: Social identity and intergroup relations on the college campus.* New York, NY: Russell Sage Foundation.

Silverstein, J. (2013, June 27). I don't feel your pain: A failure of empathy perpetuates racial disparities. *Slate.* Retrieved from http://www.slate.com/articles/health_and_science/science/2013/06/racial_empathy_gap_people_don_t_perceive_pain_in_other_races.1.html

Sue, D. W. (2010). *Microaggressions in everyday life: Race, gender, and sexual orientation.* Hoboken, NJ: Wiley.

Tatum, B. D. (1997). *"Why are all the black kids sitting together in the cafeteria?" And other conversations about race.* New York, NY: Basic Books.

U.S. Department of Education, National Center for Education Statistics. (2013). *The condition of education 2013* (NCES 2013-037), Characteristics of Post-secondary Faculty. Retrieved from https://nces.ed.gov/fastfacts/display.asp?id=61

Williams, B. (2008). *A conversation about race.* MSNBC. Retrieved from http://www.nbcnews.com/id/24165209/ns/msnbc-documentaries/t/conversation-about-race/#.UzAsnKhdWSo

Yosso, T. J. (2006). *Critical race counterstories along the Chicana/Chicano educational pipeline.* New York, NY: Taylor & Francis.

Many thanks to the members of our class for making themselves vulnerable in sharing this experience with us and giving us permission to process and share this story with others. We also thank Ellie Fitts-Fulmer, Joel Hilario, Sheeba Jacob, Nia Makepeace, and Carla Shalaby for their feedback on drafts of this work.

Chapter 5

"Alien" Troublemakers and Nonthreatening Pets at a Predominantly White University

Yukari Takimoto Amos

Studies found that instructors' race, gender, and language seemed to impact the ratings of student evaluations at college. However, do they matter only in the classroom? Or do they also matter at the workplace in higher education? Several studies found that most faculty of color experience racial and ethnic bias in the workplace (Astin, Antonio, Cress, & Astin, 1997; Turner & Meyers, 1999). Padilla and Chávez (1995) revealed that white colleagues either ignore faculty of color or make subtly racist comments about aspects such as appearance or linguistic skills. Ling et al. (2004) reported that white colleagues stereotype female faculty of color as unsmiling, angry, and sulky, and these images silence and subordinate their voices. Bronstein (1993) found that those who combined several "differentness" factors (such as female, ethnic minority, and homosexual) experienced the greatest amount of hostility from white colleagues and/or the administration. In summary, Laden and Hagedorn (2000) conclude that "faculty of color often face issues and barriers, such as low to nonexistent social and emotional support and heightened feelings of loneliness and isolation at a level much higher than that experienced by their white counterparts" (p. 58).

Relationships among faculty within a college or university range from vigorously congenial and collegial to dangerously competitive and hostile. It seems that faculty of color's experiences in the workplace are more toward the latter. This seems to be caused by their minority status as the more different people are, in comparison with the mainstream model, the more difficult time those different people face (Bronstein, 1993) in the relationships with the majority mainstream colleagues. The purpose of this chapter is to explore in detail a step-by-step process in which a dangerously competitive and hostile work environment is formed at a university, using my case as an Asian female faculty member who speaks nonnative English.

ASIAN CRITICAL RACE THEORY AND ASIAN AMERICAN FACULTY MEMBERS IN U.S. HIGHER EDUCATION

In the United States, the image of Asians being a successful model minority is prevalent. The model minority thesis attributes the success of Asian Americans to their adherence to traditional Asian cultural values and family structures. There are images attached to this thesis: Asians are "more obedient to authority, respectful of teachers, smart, and good at math and science, hardworking, cooperative, well behaved, and quiet" (Kwon & Au, 2010, p. 221). These images are reflected not only at K–12 but also in the higher education environment. Ng, Lee, and Park (2007) observe that Asian American faculty members are perceived as "model minorities who are passive, hard-working, and non-confrontational" (p. 117).

These images associated with the educational and economic success of Asian Americans have produced several misconceptions about this minority group, such as Asian Americans are all the same and Asian Americans are well-represented in college faculties and key administrative positions. The most dangerous misconception, however, is a viewpoint that Asian Americans do not face discriminatory and unfair treatment because of their race. This particular misconception derives from a simple-minded assumption that the success of Asian Americans means that they are fully accepted in the white mainstream, and thus "they no longer encounter either overt or covert racial discrimination that might limit their opportunities for social and professional advancement" (Nakanishi, 1993, pp. 53–54). Surprisingly, some professionals in higher education institutions, whom many of us view as more tolerant, objective, enlightened, and open to new ideas and perspectives openly reject the notion that Asian Americans suffer from discrimination (Museus & Kiang, 2009, p. 9). Instead of addressing the issue of discrimination against Asian Americans, they divert "the conversation to challenges low-income white students face" (Museus & Kiang, 2009, p. 9). I encountered a similar case at my university. At a committee meeting where we discussed which racial and ethnic minority group should be the focus for the next symposium on diversity after Native Americans, African Americans, and Latinos, a white female colleague of mine asserted, "Muslims should be the focus. Asians are doing okay and don't seem to have any problems."

Several studies have revealed that racial realities do shape the conditions and experiences of Asian peoples in society and in the education system in particular. Sue and others (2007) identified eight microaggressive themes toward Asian Americans: alien in own land, ascription of intelligence, exoticization of Asian women, invalidation of interethnic differences, denial of racial reality, pathologizing cultural values/communication styles, second-class citizenship, and invisibility. Their participants described feelings of belittlement, anger, rage, frustration, alienation, and of constantly being invalidated. In academia, according to Wu and Jing (2013), just 42 percent of Asian men are tenured, compared with 58 percent of white men, 49 percent of Black men, and 50 percent of Hispanic men; and just 21 percent of Asian women in academia are tenured, the lowest proportion for any ethnicity or gender. They are also least likely to be promoted to full professor. Nakanishi (1993) described that the university administrators referred to him with a racial slur, such as a "dumb jap" and a "fat jap" in their attempt to deny him tenure.

Although discrimination and unfair treatment are experienced by many groups, the types of racism, both covert and overt, directed at Asian Americans may be qualitatively and quantitatively different from other marginalized groups (Sue, Bucceri, et al., 2007). For these reasons Asian critical race theory (AsianCrit) provides a necessary structure in which to explore how a hostile work environment develops with regard to an Asian female faculty member. AsianCrit is a branch of critical race theory (CRT). CRT is a theoretical approach to the study of race that originally emerged in the field of law (Delgado & Stefancic, 2001). It privileges the experience of people of color in opposition to normative white standards (Liu, 2009) and generally speaks to the following six primary tenets: (1) racism is commonplace rather than out of the ordinary, (2) the dominant ideology promotes the interest convergence or material determinism of whites over people of color, (3) race is socially constructed, (4) minorities are differentially racialized as a matter of convenience, (5) it is important to understand the intersectionality and anti-essentialism of identity, and (6) to recognize voices-of-color (Delgado & Stefancic, 2001). In summary, CRT is "a framework or set of basic insights, perspectives, methods, and pedagogy that seeks to identify, analyze, and transform those structural and cultural aspects of education that maintain subordinate and dominant racial positions" (Solorzano & Yosso, 2009, p. 132).

AsianCrit, in particular, emphasizes and critiques stereotypes, language, and immigration as it pertains to Asian people in the United States.

One way to critically examine the issues Asian people face in the United States is to contest model minority stereotype. Although the model minority stereotype views Asian Americans as competent and diligent, thus is seemingly positive, there is also evidence of negative attitudes and emotions toward Asian Americans (Johnson, Terry, & Louis., 2005; Lin et al., 2005). For example, Leslie, Constantine, and Fiske (2001) found that Chinese and Japanese were seen as especially intelligent, industrious, and scientifically minded (highly competent) but also loyal to family ties and reserved (still not sociable with the dominant group). Negativity in sociability also appeared in Ho and Jackson's (2001) study in which they found that Asian Americans were perceived as intelligent but also antisocial, non-English speaking, and unassimilated. In other words, the stereotype carries a mixed feeling of respect and resentment. There is a contradiction among the majority whites in labeling Asian Americans as smart and diligent, while maintaining negative attitudes toward them. Why does this contradiction occur?

Feelings of threat seem to play a role in why the contradiction occurs. Johnson and others (2005) revealed that white Australians who perceived that their higher social status was unstable showed increasing prejudice toward Asian Australians. In contrast, white Australians who perceived that their high-status position was stable did not show increased prejudice. Further, Lin and others (2005) explain that the Asian outgroup's presumed competence could engender group competition, given the tendency for positive attributes to be appreciated as assets only when they reflect well on oneself and the in-group. Lin and others (2005) conclude, "Mixed feelings about the perceived competence of Asian Americans emerges specifically within the context of positive attributes being regarded as negative when the outgroup is believed to possess them" (p. 35). In summary, when Asian Americans' positive characteristics are perceived to be *too* good, they stir feelings of jealousy and envy among the dominant group, and are seen as competitors who might threaten the status quo. Glick and Fiske (2001) argue that one function of viewing Asians as competent yet unsociable is to justify a system whereby competence is rewarded but some competent groups are rejected on other grounds, such as lack of social skills.

The fact that Asians are viewed both positively and negatively indicates that they are strategically positioned by the dominant group in a racial hierarchy with two axes—superior/inferior and insider/foreigner (Kim, 1999). Thus, Asian Americans are racialized both as model minorities and as non-Americans (Ancheta, 2000), and this racial construction extends to the view of Asian Americans as "forever foreigners" (Tuan, 1998). Lin and others (2005) state, "the dimensions of competence and sociability operate together to determine the stereotypic content that is the source of prejudice and discrimination against Asian Americans" (pp. 35–36).

The dominant group uses language as a particular weapon to further the image of Asian Americans as perpetual foreigners. Hune (1998) contends that language bias and accent discrimination are significant obstacles to Asian Americans in both the larger society and academia. Cultural bias in U.S. society accepts and even privileges English spoken with European accents, while is generally intolerant of English spoken with Asian accents. When this cultural bias is intertwined with race, it creates a false conception that anyone who is physically identified with Asians is regarded as a "foreigner," leading to another false expectation that she/he is English deficient regardless of her/his English proficiency.

MY BACKGROUND

This chapter portrays a self-study conducted by a Japanese female professor who is a nonnative English speaker and teaches a multicultural education course and TESL courses in a predominantly white university in a rural area of the Pacific Northwest. I came to the United States for my graduate studies, obtained a doctoral degree in multicultural education from a prestigious research institution, am now married to a bilingual (Chinese and English) white American male social scientist, have a bilingual (Japanese and English) daughter, a bilingual (Chinese and English) step-daughter, and live in the United States as a permanent resident. I am a citizen of Japan, speak Japanese as a native language, learned English as a foreign language, and speak and write English as a nonnative. The university at which I work is a state university with a strong emphasis on teaching, not research. I joined the university in the fall of 2005 after teaching ESL and social studies at public schools for three years.

CRT legitimizes "narratives and storytelling that present a different interpretation" (Parker & Lynn, 2009, p. 150). These assembled stories from the participants' subjective perspectives became a valid research procedure because it openly acknowledges that "perceptions of truth, fairness, and justice reflect the mindset of the knower" (Taylor, 2009, p. 8). Thus, this chapter employs my personal stories and reflections from AsianCrit's perspectives.

THE HOSTILE WORKPLACE

The competitive and hostile work environment did not exist from the beginning. It emerged gradually as a result of my white colleagues attempting to confine me into the image of a helpless foreigner, and finding themselves unable to do so. There were four stages in which the workplace at my university, particularly with regard to the relationships with white colleagues, gradually became competitive and hostile. Each stage was not independent. Rather they overlapped and coexisted.

Stage I: The Missionary Attitudes

My accented English became a constant and easy target at the beginning. A white female colleague offered her help in a condescending tone, "Let me be of help. I'm sure your students are having difficulty understanding your English. Honestly speaking, I myself sometimes can't understand what you're saying." This comment is based on the assumption that foreign faculty with an accented English struggle with American students' evaluation of their teaching. I am not a native speaker of English and as result I speak English with an accent. However, my nonnative English is competent, and sometimes strangers mistake me for a native speaker of English. My colleagues' comment on my English being deficient, therefore, seems to be perceptional and derived from the intersection between my foreign accent with my Asian face. In reality, my student evaluations were higher than the department average, and much higher than the white woman who offered me help.

My small stature and youthful appearance aggravated the white colleagues' missionary attitudes because they implied that I was childlike; thus I needed to be protected and given proper guidance by someone superior.

My accented English also triggered foreignness, and foreignness automatically created an assumption that I did not know much about customs, traditions, history, and society of the United States. I am indeed a foreigner in terms of a legal status, but have learned about historical events and participated in cultural practices due to the marriage to my American husband. My colleagues frequently asked me, "You don't know this, do you? Let me teach you . . ." Whenever I responded, "I know it already," I could tell that they were disappointed.

Stage II: Microaggressions

When they found me neither helpless nor completely culturally foreign, the second stage of intentional putdowns began. These putdowns were manifested in the form of microaggressions. Sue, Capodilupo, et al. (2007) define microaggressions as "brief and commonplace daily verbal, behavioral, or environmental indignities, whether intentional or unintentional, that communicate hostile, derogatory, or negative racial slights and insults toward people of color" (p. 271).

Again, my accented English received an immediate attack. A white female colleague said with a concerned look, "Don't your students complain about your English?" Microaggressions could be nonverbal. Several colleagues still make a perplexed face with one ear leaning toward me when they talk to me. "How can she teach with an infant baby?" was sarcastically uttered by a white female colleague when she heard about my high student evaluation scores. The fact that I defy the stereotype of Asian women being shy and submissive invited a comment such as, "You're not quiet at all! Are you a real Asian?" Sometimes my physical appearance itself became a target of casual attack with a comment such as, "You're so petite!" while laughing. One time at a meeting where two senior white female colleagues and I were present, the following conversation took place:

> WF1: "I heard that the Kenyan woman we just hired this year hates whites."
> I: "I don't think so. She doesn't talk to me either, and I'm not white."
> WF2: "You're pale." (*grinned*)

The implication I gathered from the second white female colleague was that my fair skin is a good attribute, which would allow me to ally with the white club, but not to join.

Because of the antisocial Asian stereotype associated with the lack of interpersonal skills seems to produce the assumption that Asians are "foreigners whose cultural differences are so great they are incapable of leadership" (Ng et al., 2007, p. 117). When I was appointed the Bilingual/ TESL program coordinator by a department chair, a senior white female colleague reminded me, "You were appointed, not elected," subtly but clearly indicating her nonsupport of my leadership. Later I learned that this same faculty member had told other faculty members to elect a different faculty as the coordinator.

The above comments were irritating and offensive, but putdowns related to my scholarship were vicious in nature. My university is a teaching university which places less emphasis on scholarship. We are required to produce one peer-reviewed journal article in a five-year tenure/promotion cycle. With a heavy teaching load, many colleagues struggle to find time to meet the minimal requirement. Therefore, my constantly producing both quantity and quality of scholarship invited jealousy. When my paper was accepted for presentation at a prestigious national conference, a white male colleague questioned with suspicion: "But your paper was accepted for a round-table session, not a paper session, right?" When I was awarded a merit award by the university, a white female colleague said with a genuinely surprised look: "Why you?" When I was awarded the outstanding scholarship award by the college, another white female colleague reiterated this question with a serious look: "You? You?"

The image of an Asian woman being socially and academically competent started to bother some of my colleagues. I did not need their help and had made my own accomplishments. This aroused some jealous feelings within their souls. The fact that white colleagues casually and openly used microaggressions to express their jealousy means that there was an unequal power relation between me and them, with me lower in the hierarchy.

Stage III: Discrimination

Allport (1979) states that prejudiced people start verbally rejecting a person in out-groups and may resort to discrimination when negative attitudes intensify. When jealous people are in positions of power they can retaliate against members of out-groups who "don't know their place." The third stage began where verbal microaggressions changed to acts of discrimination.

My department chair, a white male, turned down my early tenure and promotion, stating that my scholarly work lacked variety because I wrote only on social justice, and he felt that the topic of social justice was not academic at all. Ironically, I found out later that this chair had neither produced any publications nor had he presented at conferences ever since he became tenured. Another time, without evidence or cause, I was reprimanded by other department cochairs (a white female and a white male) for supposedly sabotaging a white colleague's study-abroad plan. They threatened that they would put a letter in my personnel file regarding the sabotage. My request for evidence was followed by a repeated comment, "We know you did it." When I consulted with the university's equal opportunity office, I was bluntly told, "You will never win over the chairs." When I consulted with the dean, she was not sympathetic at all and instead chastised my behavior: "Because you talked back to them!" Another time for no justifiable reason, a white female chair made an elaborate effort to transfer me to another department regardless of my seniority over other faculty members. This was the first time when I officially used the term "discrimination" in my grievance letter to the university. The letter surprised and even alarmed the chair, perhaps because a nonconfrontational Asian stereotype operated in her mind. She subsequently resigned.

Stage IV: Ostracization

Since I joined the current university, a Native American male colleague, "Jack," (a pseudonym) has been supportive of my university career. However, the fact that he openly discusses the problems of whiteness invites disdain, disrespect, and distance among white colleagues. In my first year at the university, I overheard a white male colleague talking to a secretary, "Did you see that new Asian hire talking to Jack? Is she gonna be like him? What a shame!" The shame took place: Jack and I are political and scholarly allies.

A friendship between Jack and me, however, triggered an unanticipated reaction among some minority colleagues. At a predominantly white university, the presence of a very few minority faculty provides us with a chance to unite and see ourselves "as part of a larger group from which one can draw support" (Tatum, 1997, p. 70). This union took place only at the beginning and eventually became nonexistent. In other words, many minority colleagues began to distance themselves from me. Some made subtle moves. When I asked for a letter of recommendation to a Native American female colleague, she e-mailed me back, "I don't know you enough. I can't write one for you." I had substituted her class with no compensation before, and we used to go to a charity luncheon together. An Asian male colleague proudly declared: "Racism occurs only to those minority who think about it. I've never experienced racism." A middle-eastern male colleague followed this line of thinking and stated, "I have a doubt about critical race theory. Minorities are given more opportunities than whites." A newly hired Latina colleague timidly and frequently says, "I don't want to make enemies." Some minority colleagues were more overt in distancing themselves from me. An Asian female colleague has been openly hostile and abruptly severed her friendship with me. An African American male colleague warned me: "If you want a tenure/promotion, you had better not hang around with Jack. Whites have no respect of him at all."

Their effort to distance themselves yielded a good result. Except for the African American male colleague who left the university and the newly hired Latina, all of the minority faculty members mentioned above were granted tenure/promotion either early and/or with special accommodations and seem to have collegial relationships with white colleagues. In contrast, I feel ostracized not only from my white colleagues but also from my fellow minority colleagues (except for Jack). A sense of being on the periphery at the workplace—alone, indifferent, invisible, unheard, and nonexistent—always follows me now.

AN "ALIEN" TROUBLEMAKER AND THREATS TO THE STATUS QUO

Several factors seem to have contributed to the development of the hostile workplace I have been experiencing. At Stage I, my colleagues seemed to be irritated with my not being a "helpless foreigner." Their comments regarding my accented English illustrate not only my English being perceived as deficient, but also my inferiority and their superiority. My white colleagues' comments convey their "the white-as-savior mind-set" (Marx, 2006). Using a metaphor of the missionary, Warren and Hytten (2004) explain this attitude:

They see themselves as information providers ready to spread their vision of how the world should be. This intense investment with

self is coupled with a belief that they have "answers" and therefore
should be out helping others to see the light. (p. 327)

The missionaries go to foreign cultures to civilize foreign people. If those
foreign people are already civilized, there is no room for the missionaries,
which is a disappointment.

At Stage II, if, as Kim (1999) contends, Asians are racially positioned
with two axes, superior/inferior and insider/foreigner, the combination
of my competence in teaching and scholarship regardless of my nonnative English and my degree of acculturation in U.S. culture stirred a sense
of competition and threat among my white colleagues. When I was perceived to be "too" good and "too" acculturated, it seems that the competitive and threatening relationship between us emerged and gave white
colleagues a motivation to disparage, fear, and discriminate against me.

At Stage III, my white colleagues seem to have acted on their Asian
stereotypes. Nakanishi (1993) noted that the image of Asian educators as
passive and permissive has invited intimidation and aggression from students, colleagues, and administrators. Chou and Feagin (2008), for example, quote an Asian American saying, "black/Latino folks are 'feared'
because of the strong political connections and faculty/staff support"
(p. 87), while Asian American faculty/staff tend to "participate in the
'don't rock the boat' ideology, and with little political support outside"
(p. 87). The nonconfrontational Asian stereotype seems to have escalated
my white colleagues' aggressiveness because they did not expect counter-
responses from me, an Asian woman of small stature.

Two factors intersected with each other to create Stage IV. First, it seems
that my scholarly focus on social justice was perceived to be dangerous
to the dominant group. Discussing oppression and injustice necessarily
leads to the examination of power relations in a racial hierarchy, which
is discomforting to members of the dominant group. Instead, the dominant group endorses multiculturalism and diversity celebration. Sullivan
(2006) explains this point:

> Appeals to multiculturalism and diversity likewise can operate as a
> related mechanism for protecting the white "soul." If those who are
> (allegedly) colorblind have gone beyond race, then it is easy for them
> to think that racism no longer exists. In that case, the unequal power
> relations evoked by the language of race are flattened out into a mere
> multiplicity of diverse cultures to be celebrated and affirmed. (p. 127)

Obviously, my scholarly focus on social justice and whiteness was not
approved, but rather denounced, by white colleagues.

Coalitions among social, cultural, and ethnic minority groups are dangerous to majority groups because they threaten the status quo. The best

way to avoid the formation of coalitions is to segregate minority groups and individuals by rewarding those minority individuals who do not form coalitions among themselves. This untold and unwritten strategy was effectively used to ostracize me and Jack. The fact that the minority colleagues of mine not only avoided us but also took the attitude that racism no longer exists suggests how powerful the strategy was to untenured minority colleagues at the university.

The fact that minority faculty were deliberately separated into two categories, pets and troublemakers, indicates how threatening it is for the dominant group to witness minority individuals working toward social justice. Pets will continue to be rewarded because they are neither dangerous nor threatening. To liberal-minded whites who are highly motivated to maintain an image of themselves as egalitarian individuals who are neither prejudiced nor discriminate against others on the basis of race (Gaertner & Dovidio, 2005), the presence and the cooperation of minority faculty who are willing to approve flattened multiculturalism and participate in cultural celebration is not only comforting but also desperately needed. This accomplishes two purposes simultaneously: going through the motions of eagerly working toward cultural diversity while sustaining the status quo. On the other hand, troublemakers will continue to be discriminated and ostracized because they challenge the existing racial hierarchy without giving the dominant group any comfort. In this harsh structure of reward and punishment at my university, minority faculty are vulnerable to being manipulated and used by the dominant group in order to maintain the hierarchy that has served the latter better than others.

CONCLUSION

It is easy to predict that the workplace would be more congenial and collegial for me if I were not who I am. However, it is difficult to change myself. I do not wish to unwittingly participate in my "own subordination by taking on the dominant group's hegemonic devices of racial and gender stereotypes" (Shrake, 2006, p. 193). I cannot accept living a schizophrenic life. Even with subtle and overt exclusion, intimidation, and coercion, I would rather not accept "the rules of the game played by white America" (West, 1994, p. 42).

Teaching for social justice has lately become a buzz word in the field of education. Numerous articles and books have been written on this topic. "The Diversity Education Center" at my university has recently changed its name to "The Center for Diversity and Social Justice." This is a good trend. However, real teaching for social justice is difficult or even impossible when an institutional culture does not support this concept within its structures and does not provide progressive minority faculty with social justice.

REFERENCES

Allport, G. W. (1979). *The nature of prejudice* (25th anniversary ed.). Reading, MA: Addison-Wesley.

Ancheta, A. (2000). *Race, rights, and the Asian American experience*. New Brunswick, NJ: Rutgers University Press.

Astin, H. S., Antonio, A. L., Cress, C. M., & Astin, A. W. (1997). *Race and ethnicity in the American professoriate, 1995–96*. Los Angeles, CA: Higher Education Research Institute, University of California.

Bronstein, P. (1993). Challenges, rewards, and costs for feminist and ethnic minority scholars. *New Directions for Teaching and Learning, 53,* 61–70.

Chou, R. S., & Feagin, J. R. (2008). *The myth of the model minority: Asian Americans racing racism*. Boulder, CO: Paradigm.

Delgado, R., & Stefancic, J. (2001). *Critical race theory: An introduction*. New York, NY: New York University Press.

Gaertner, S. L., & Dovidio, J. F. (2005). Understanding and addressing contemporary racism: From aversive racism to the common ingroup identity model. *Journal of Social Issues, 61*(3), 615–639.

Glick, P., & Fiske, S. T. (2001). Ambivalent stereotypes as legitimizing ideologies: Differentiating paternalistic and envious prejudice. In J. T. Jost & B. Major (Eds.), *The psychology of legitimacy: Ideology, justice, and intergroup relations* (pp. 278–306). New York, NY: Cambridge University Press.

Ho, C., & Jackson, J. W. (2001). Attitudes toward Asian Americans: Theory and measurement. *Journal of Applied Social Psychology, 31*(8), 1553–1581.

Hune, S. (1998). *Asian Pacific American women in higher education: Claiming visibility and voice*. Washington, DC: Association of American Colleges and Universities.

Johnson, D., Terry, D. J., & Louis, W. R. (2005). Perceptions of the Intergroup structure and anti-Asian prejudice among white Australians. *Group Processes Intergroup Relations, 8*(1), 53–71.

Kim, C. (1999). The racial triangulation of Asian Americans. *Politics and Society, 27*(1), 105–138.

Kwon, H., & Au, W. (2010). Model minority myth. In W.-C. Chen & G. J. Yoo (Eds.), *Encyclopedia of Asian America issues today* (Vol. I, pp. 221–230). Santa Barbara, CA: Greenwood.

Laden, B. V., & Hagedorn, L. S. (2000). Job satisfaction among faculty of color in academe: Individual survivors or institutional transformers? *New Directions for Institutional Research, 105,* 57–66.

Leslie, L., Constantine, V., & Fiske, S. T. (2001). *The Princeton quartet: How are stereotypes changing?* Unpublished manuscript, Princeton University.

Lin, M. H., Kwan, V. S. Y., Cheung, A., & Fiske, S. T. (2005). Stereotype content model explains prejudice for an envied outgroup: Scale of anti–Asian American stereotypes. *Personality and Social Psychology Bulletin, 31*(1), 34–37.

Ling, A., Grant, R., Kubota, R., Motha, S., Sachs, G. T., Vandrick, S., & Wong, S. (2004). Women faculty of color in TESOL: Theorizing our lived experiences. *TESOL Quarterly, 38*(3), 487–503.

Liu, A. (2009). Critical race theory, Asian Americans, and higher education: A review of research. *InterActions: UCLA Journal of Education and Information Studies, 5*(2), 1–12.

Marx, S. (2006). *Revealing the invisible: Confronting passive racism in teacher education.* New York, NY: Routledge.

Museus, S. D., & Kiang, P. N. (2009). Deconstructing the model minority myth and how it contributes to the invisible minority reality in higher education research. *New Directions for Institutional Research, 142,* 5–15.

Nakanishi, D. T. (1993). Asian Pacific Americans in higher education: Faculty and administrative representation and tenure. *New Directions for Teaching and Learning, 53,* 51–59.

Ng, J. C., Lee, S. S., & Park, Y. (2007). Contesting the model minority and perpetual foreigner stereotype: A critical review of literature on Asian Americans in education. *Review of Research in Education, 31,* 95–130.

Padilla, R. V., & Chavez, R. C. (1995). *The leaning ivory tower: Latino professors in American universities.* New York, NY: SUNY Press.

Parker, L., & Lynn, M. (2009). What's race got to do with it?: Critical race theory's conflicts with and connections to qualitative research methodology and epistemology. In D. Taylor, D. Gillborn, & G. Ladson-Billings (Eds.), *Foundations of critical race theory in education* (pp. 148–160). New York, NY: Routledge.

Shrake, E. K. (2006). Struggling with the model minority stereotype and lotus blossom image. In G. Li & G. H. Beckett (Eds.), *"Strangers" of the academy: Asian women scholars in higher education* (pp. 178–194). Sterling, VA: Stylus.

Solorzano, D. G., & Yosso, T. J. (2009). Critical race methodology: Counter-storytelling as an analytical framework for educational research. In E. Taylor, D. Gilborn, & G. Ladson-Billings (Eds.), *Foundations of critical race theory in education* (pp. 131–147). New York, NY: Routledge.

Sue, D. W., Bucceri, J., Lin, A. I., Nadal, K. L., & Torino, G. C. (2007). Racial microaggressions and the Asian American experience. *Cultural Diversity and Ethnic Minority Psychology, 13*(1), 72–81.

Sue, D. W., Capodilupo, C. M., Torino, G. C., Bucceri, J. M., Holder, A. M. B., Nadal, K. L., & Esquilin, M. (2007). Racial microaggressions in everyday life. *American Psychologist, 62*(4), 271–286.

Sullivan, S. (2006). *Revealing whiteness: The unconscious habits of racial privilege.* Bloomington, IN: Indiana University Press.

Tatum, B. D. (1997). *"Why are all the Black kids sitting together in the cafeteria?" And other conversations about race.* New York, NY: Basic Books.

Taylor, E. (2009). The foundations of critical race theory in education: An introduction. In E. Taylor, D. Gilborn, & G. Ladson-Billings (Eds.), *Foundations of critical race theory in education* (pp. 1–13). New York, NY: Routledge.

Tuan, M. (1998). *Forever foreigners or honorary whites? The Asian ethnic experience today.* New Brunswick, NJ: Rutgers University Press.

Turner, C. S. V., & Myers, S. L., Jr. (1999). *Faculty of color in academe: Bittersweet success.* Needham Heights, MA: Allyn & Bacon.

Warren, J. T., & Hytten, K. (2004). The faces of whiteness: Pitfalls and the critical democrat. *Communication Education, 53*(4), 321–339.

West, C. (1994). *Race matters.* New York, NY: Vintage Books.

Wu, L. G., & Jing, W. (2013). Leadership hurdles. *Nature, 493,* 125–126.

Chapter 6

"Becoming the Bear": A Meditation on Racial Battle Fatigue, Resistance, and Grace in Academia

G. Michelle Collins-Sibley

I returned to my office after class one afternoon this past fall semester to find Joy Harjo's (1990) poem, "Transformations," taped to my office door. Attached to it was a sticky note bearing the distinctive handwriting of a colleague in the English Department, someone whom I've known and with whom I've worked in a more-or-less collegial fashion over the last 20 years at a small university with liberal arts inclinations in northeastern Ohio. The poem was the latest in an escalating campaign of harassment—public and private—directed at me since I'd taken on a half-time administrative position as director of the university's new general education curriculum. The transition from the old to the new "Gen Ed" curriculum hadn't been without controversy; indeed, I was the third program director appointed to oversee its implementation in the last three years, so I was expecting and fully prepared to have a target pinned to my back from the moment the dean called to offer me the position in August. Attempts at curriculum transformation at the university had been not only professionally divisive but often had featured highly personal attacks for as far back as institutional memory could reach. I had been hired just as a failed effort to change the curriculum was pulling the faculty into factions and had been part of still another task force whose efforts had been derailed, reduced to cosmetic renaming and reorganization. So this was par for the course, right?

Not quite. While many of the players were still the same, this time the result had been different. This time the faculty—by a narrow margin—had passed a curriculum that was significantly, some might even say radically, different from the "Old Gen Ed." And this time the faculty on the "losing side of the proposition" had decided that nothing was over until the proverbial fat lady had sung, and she wasn't singing just yet; or if she was, she couldn't be heard above the cacophony of protests that the new curriculum, although streamlined, was too labor intensive, demanded too many resources, and would mark the death knell of the liberal arts tradition at the university. But what has any of this to do with the question of racial battle fatigue? The first program director appointed had been an untenured white women. The second director had been a tenured white man. This time the director of the "New Gen Ed"—The Core—is an African American woman, a tenured full professor, who despite her deep and broad experience in interdisciplinary and integrative teaching, learning, and scholarship, had been passed over twice for the job. My moment of triumph, personal and professional? Or permission to launch an all-out attack, with a Black woman as scapegoat not just for the new curriculum but for a litany of other discontents, at a moment when not only the liberal arts but also the very notion of higher education is under attack not only on our beautiful campus but also in the world at large?

MOST OF THE WOMEN ARE *STILL* WHITE, MOST OF THE BLACKS ARE *STILL* MEN, *BUT* ...

Inspired by Gloria T. Hull, Patricia Bell Scott, and Barbara Smith's groundbreaking critique of feminism in academia, *this* was the original title of my essay. I am standing at a crossroad in both my career and my personal life, a moment at which while some of us—myself included—are still brave, we are also tired. Very, very tired. I didn't start out to be a peace and social justice activist in the classroom or in the academy; I was a shy, introverted undergraduate with an AB in Comparative Literature from Stanford University, a newly minted MA in Intercultural Communication/ Translation & Interpretation from the Monterey Institute of International Studies, a deep and abiding love for language and literature, and a relatively recent but well-established passion for literary theory. The idea that I could construct a life around reading, researching, writing about, and— to my surprise and delight—teaching literature seemed like a dream come true. Little did I know that upon my acceptance into a doctoral program in Comparative Literature and move to the East Coast, I was entering not an academic meritocracy, but a wilderness of microaggressions, stereotype threat, and structural violence. And after a nomadic childhood spent on marine corps bases, I was primed to join an intentional community of seekers of knowledge and truth.

And so it began: the program director who began our first advising session with the statement, "I don't know why you're here"; a conversation overheard while hard at work preparing a forum women's issues, "So who's our audience? You know, local activists, feminist, and black women like Michelle who are interested in feminism"; a greeting from a fellow graduate student on the first day of a seminar on philosophy of language, "So you're our token woman!"; a word of warning from a Black male friend, "you know that feminist shit is just for white women"; a phone conversation with someone who'd been told I'd be a good speaker for Black History Month who prefaces her formal request with, "But, you'll laugh when you hear this—they told me you were black!" only to be dismayed by my response, "But I *am* black" (at least she didn't ask if I was sure); a dialog with freshmen in my first college composition class, "Students: We've figured you out! You're British! Me: No I'm not, in fact never been to England. Students: Are you sure?" Then there's the colleague who says, "We'd really like it if you'd join this committee," and when I respond, "Thanks, I'd love to but I've set that time aside to work on my dissertation (or my next publication, or the paper I'm presenting next month)," replies, "But it's *really* important that we have a black woman on the committee." A friend who cheerfully and triumphantly informs me that when she looks at me she doesn't see a Black person, she just sees a person; her smile turns to anger when I ask her what it is about my Blackness that makes it impossible to see me as a person. The student who announces in a discussion that she knows that slavery is a bad thing, but she really can't say she regrets it because without the Atlantic Slave Trade she'd never had had the chance to read all the cool Black women writers featured in our class. The standard request that I explain how Black people feel about an issue that turns into anger when I respond that I don't know all Black people but I'd be happy to explain my position on the issue. And of course the perennial, "I'm not just saying this because you're black . . ." I could go on but the pattern is unmistakable.

W. E. B. DuBois said it best in "Of Our Spiritual Strivings," when he explained that these and so many other variations on the same theme are all versions of the same question: How does it feel to be a problem? Or still worse than a problem, a token. None of these comments are malicious. All of the people who made and continue to make them are well meaning. And yet each and every one of them communicates a variation on the same theme: You are not a subject but an object; not a friend or an ally but an accessory, a mirror in which we *should be able* to see reflected our own better selves, best selves, nonracist selves, nonsexist selves. There's the

colorblind trap—perhaps it's a genderblind trap as well—in which negative racial or gender experiences are denied, and the unique perspectives
of women and racial minorities in the academy are invalidated as expressions of oversensitivity, being thin-skinned, or simply making excuses for
one's own failure to work hard enough. To be "colorblind" or "genderblind" is to turn institutional conflicts into personal conflicts rather than
examining the larger institutional picture at the intersection of stereotypes
and cultural values placed in appropriate context. And it is, by extension,
to ignore harassment and personal attacks when deployed as part of an
institution-wide conflict. Which brings me back to the "literary assault,"
the copy of "Transformations" taped to my office door.

FROM MICROAGRESSIONS TO ... HARASSMENT

As I said initially, the poem and accompanying personal note taped
to my door marked an escalation in the pattern of harassment that had
formed my professional life at the university since the day I was appointed
as director of "The Core." The colleague—I'll call him M—had strolled
into my office in August to announce that he planned to "go to war with
the liberal arts" that semester. In the previous academic year, he had led
a faculty insurrection over the Board of Trustees' denial of tenure to two
white, male probationary faculty; that insurrection against the board's
interference had morphed into an attack on the current university president and academic dean. This new phase of his plan, he explained glee-
fully, could save the liberal arts from the danger of "The Core"—about
which he'd been uncharacteristically silent during the planning, discussion, and debate phases—and might even bring down the current administration. Our conversation had been cut short, partly by my objection to
the idea of "going to war," and partly by an opportune telephone call, but
M completed his pitch in the form of an e-mail message to me later that
same day. It was a message in which he outlined the role he had assigned
to me in his campaign and just how I was to carry it out thanks to my new
position as director of the Core.

I was wary of any engagement with M, much less one that had the
whiff of personal vendetta—I had been the object of a series of harassing
e-mails and office intrusions some years before, when I was a newly tenured associate professor, and he, as acting Academic Dean, had attempted
to block my efforts to submit a National Endowment for the Humanities
grant. I knew from that past experience that any response would be taken
as agreement to his plan and later confirmation of his accusations; I was
doubly wary because at that time I had forwarded all of his harassing communications to my department chair, feeling the need to establish a record
of his communications should the situation escalate. When it did, I went
to the that same department chair to ask what the next steps in responding

to his harassment should take only to be told that the chair had deleted all the e-mailed correspondence I had forwarded; the chair didn't like to think about "things like that" and was confident that M and I would be able to resolve this personal disagreement on our own. This time while I chose not to engage with M—I took the precaution of retaining every piece of electronic correspondence, including mysterious anonymous personal attacks from an e-mail listserv forwarded to me by concerned colleagues, to fully document the extent and degree of his harassment.

What is perhaps the most disturbing aspect of this semester-long experience of ever-escalating harassment was the fact that it unfolded, by and large, in public. M and fellow white male colleagues regularly challenged me in personal and at times highly condescending language during faculty meetings, in weekly, some sometimes daily, e-mails—some anonymous and some signed—circulated throughout the campus. Special meetings of the full faculty were called at their insistence—during the month of November the faculty met every Monday until Thanksgiving, and there were plans afoot for a special faculty meeting during the last week of classes that December so that "colleagues could reach consensus about curricular issues." I was repeatedly accused of aggressive and uncollegial behavior; everyone, the messages read, was wondering why I hated M so much, why I was so hostile to him, when M was just trying to help the faculty reach clarity about the new curriculum and the dangers it represented to our limited faculty resources; I was accused of misrepresenting the source of policies about the Core, of having and pursuing a private agenda. Besides, he continually asserted, nobody understood what interdisciplinarity or integrative teaching and learning were about, or how the next phase of the Core could or would work! Michelle just needed to explain it better! And this despite my presentation of an impressive array of resources, primary and secondary materials, and national discussions of just those subjects in a variety of forms and venues. While this unfolded in the public eye, the academic deans held meetings with M in private, when I was out of state; they arranged and invited him to strategy sessions after which he would publically contradict the statements he had made in those meetings, misrepresent the gist of the discussions, and denounce the very deans who had extended to him such special consideration. And me, of course, as I had single-handedly blocked the thoughtful compromise he had offered. I learned the visceral truth behind Stuart Hall's comment at the 1991 Black Popular Culture Conference that "what replaces invisibility is a kind of carefully regulated, segregated visibility" (as cited in Wallace, 1994, p. 3).

But this public harassment although deeply disturbing—largely because it went unchallenged by the majority of my colleagues—was ultimately a blessing in disguise. Just as public as his assault was, so too was my response to it a public one. Colleagues, male and female, privately spoke of my courage in standing up faculty meeting after faculty meeting facing such condescension—the president of the university even remarked on it—and I challenged them to speak up, as M consistently maintained that he was doing this in their names and for their benefit. He represented the "literary assault" as a conciliatory gesture on his part; I shared the specific contents of the poem—by then I had obsessed over it sufficiently that I could recite long passages from memory—to any and all who asked. Women coworkers began asking me if I had security's emergency number programmed into my phone and counseled that I should never again meet with M without a third party present. I spoke to my department chair, the Title IX officer, and the deans about M's continued harassment and raised the specter of a hostile work environment suit.

Inadvertently, M had done me a tremendous service; by the virulence of his ever-escalating attack he had made visible the invisible structure of gender violence in the patriarchal and racialized yet color- and genderblind institution that is academia. In her critique of tokenism and the question of the Black female gaze, Michelle Wallace (1994) observes that

> although the white male "gaze" (or the gaze of the dominant culture) objectifies and, therefore, dehumanizes the white woman, in fact, that objectification also implicitly verifies the crucial role white women play in the process of or circuit of spectatorship. In other words, the process of objectification also inadvertently humanizes as well a built-in advantage that is them denied to women of color in general, but to the despised or (desired) black woman in particular. (p. 14)

In this passage, she could have been speaking of our current situation. M, during this same period, and for a time preceding his harassment of me, had harassed a white female colleague who had herself gone public with his harassment. My "segregated visibility" in conjunction with the paradoxical humanization of my white female colleague, had rendered me visibly human undoing the dehumanization of this tactic and, perhaps, simultaneously revealed the foundation of M's trademark strategy whenever he didn't get his way. As a new colleague in the Psychology Department observed over drinks one evening, "M's tactic seemed to be making himself irritating to the point that people gave in just to make him go away; in the past that had been primarily an invisible, passive aggressive tactic to which any effort at counter-narrative was effectively characterized as uncollegial behavior and as such, dismissed." "And then," she smiled, "he tried again on you. And you wouldn't back down." Despite the fact that I refused to back down, in public or in private, M kept on escalating, until what he was doing could no longer be ignored or dismissed as merely a "personal matter."

When the prospect of yet another special faculty meeting to be scheduled during the final week of classes was broached, my colleagues protested. I reminded those present that M continued to maintain that he was doing what he was doing in their names and for their benefit. And I declared, before those same witnesses, that my days of servicing as "scapegoat" for the Integrative Core had come to an end. I would not attend another special faculty meeting. I would consider the possibility that a Title IX complaint remained my only recourse. The onslaught came to an end, for the most part.

Perhaps the attack is harassment, or perhaps the spring semester has been but a long intermission. M and his most reliable male ally behind the scenes have both been on sabbatical. While others have continued the effort to subvert or derail the next stages in implementing the Core, those efforts have clearly been made in the service of personal and, to put it bluntly, selfish agendas. Work has continued on the implementation of the Core and quite a bit has been accomplished. But I remain very conscious of the reality that this fall, as we work to implement the final—and perhaps most challenging and resource intensive—phase of the Core, M and his comrade will be back from sabbatical leave presumably reenergized and renewed. After all, the fat lady has yet to sing.

BECOMING THE BEAR . . . AND BATTLING RBF

Aha, at last she's going to explain what "becoming the bear" has to do with racial battle fatigue in academia. Yes, I am.

M's other strategic mistake was his choice of the poem to tape to my door and the note he attached to it. As if to make perfectly clear that I was the "you" indicted for hatred in the poem, he'd attached to the print out a sticky note on which he had written, "and you are a wonderfully imaginative woman" in reference to Harjo's (1990) lines, "hatred can be turned into something/else, if you have the right works, the right meanings" (lines 19–20). Not only did his appropriation of a powerful piece of writing by a woman of color addressing the colonization and cultural genocide of her people make me angry, it turned my RBF—my exhaustion—into righteous and transformative rage while at the same time offering me the path to and language for that transformation as referenced in those verses.

A recurrent theme in Joy Harjo's poetry—and in much contemporary Native American writing—is that of transformation, specifically the transformation of human into animal and the story of the boy who became a bear; "[B]ecoming bear" for Harjo and others represents an "aesthetically channeled choice resisting assimilation into a mainstream American culture that undervalues respected creatures of nature like the bear" (Haseltine, 2006, p. 87). Harjo's evocation (or invocation) of the bear precedes her assertion that "hatred can be turned into something else," not the hatred attributed to me by M and victimizing him, but his hatred directed not only toward me but to other women, people of color in the academy. By taping Harjo's poem to my door, M reminded me not only of the power of poetry and my commitment to it, but ironically enough reminded me of why I had accepted what I knew might well be a thankless appointment. In an interview with Laura Cotelli, Harjo speaks eloquently of what it means to be an American Indian woman in this culture; it

> means that you are a survivor. [. . .] It means you carry with you a certain unique perception . . . I believe there is a common dream, a common thread between us, mostly unspoken . . . I realize that being born an American Indian woman in this time and place is with a certain reason, a certain purpose. These are seeds of dreams I hold, and responsibility, that go with being born someone, especially a woman of my tribe, who is also part of this invading other culture, and the larger globe. (as cited in Haseltine, 2006, p. 85)

I am no Joy Harjo, nor am I a Native American woman, but as an African-American woman who has earned not only advanced degrees but also tenure, promotion, and an administrative place at the university, I share the dreams common to all of us on the margins, the "seeds dreams" of which Harjo speaks in the above-cited passage. I also feel that double sense of responsibility—dare I call it "double-consciousness"—to which Harjo alludes. I *am* part of "this invading other culture" *and* at the same time part of "the larger globe" that has been invaded. M's "literary assault" did violence not just to me, but also to the poem itself—to Harjo's voice and language. The assault made me angry and that anger—righteous rage—was empowering. Through his efforts to silence me by appropriating and deforming the words of a woman of color, M paradoxically reminded me of my own commitment to transformation in the classroom and in the academy, not to mention the unique *opportunity* and *responsibility* I have as an administrator—even if only a half-time administrator—to speak truth to power.

I take that hatred directed toward me and others like me and transform it, per the lesson found in another favorite poem by another woman of color, Alice Walker (1973), to "[t]ake the contradictions . . . [a]nd wrap them around" (l. 1, 3) myself as both shield and solace. Or at least I'm trying to. To stay warm and to remember that since we were never meant to survive, survival and healing are ultimately the best revenge. I'm still that girl with the new degrees, the love of language and literature, and a by now well-established love of literary theory. And I'm a peace and social justice activist in the classroom and in the academy. And I'm not quite so tired anymore.

REFERENCES

Harjo, J. (1990.) Transformations. *In mad love and war* (p. 59). Middletown, CT: Wesleyan University Press.

Haseltine, P. (2006, January). Becoming bear: Transposing the animal other in N. Scott Momaday and Joy Harjo. *Concentric: Literary and Cultural Studies, 32.1*, 81–106.

Walker, A. (1973). Be nobody's darling. *Revolutionary petunias & other poems* (pp. 21–32). New York, NY: Harcourt Brace Jovanovich.

Wallace, M. (1994). Black female spectatorship and the dilemma of tokenism. In D. Looser and E. A. Kaplan (Eds.), *Generations: Academic feminists in dialogue* (pp. 81–101). Minneapolis, MN: University of Minnesota Press. Retrieved from http://www.lorraineograby.com/sites/default/files/Michelle-Wallace_Generations-Academic-Feminists-in-Dialogue_Black-Female-Spectatorship-and-the-Dilemma-of-Tokenism_0.pdf

Chapter 7

Difficult Dialogues: A Story of Relationship as a Strategy for Racial Battle Fatigue

Melissa Payne and Victoria Pruin DeFrancisco

For us, the phrase "Racial Battle Fatigue" spoke to our experiences of trying to create a more inclusive campus in a predominantly white institution of higher education. It reminded us of our partnership and the shared challenges of implementing a diversity inclusion program on campus, called the National Coalition Building Institute (NCBI, n.d.). But the phrase also brought up different pains and experiences for each of us because of our differing social positions and life experiences. Let us introduce ourselves:

(Melissa) "I am an African American woman, 33-year-old heterosexual wife, mother, and higher education professional from Iowa."

The authors wish to thank O.J. Payne and David Pruin for their love and support through an emotional process; Reanae McNeal, April Chatham-Carpenter, and Harry Brod for their writing recommendations; and Chris Neuhaus, Marjean Clemons, and Cindi Sweedler for their research assistance. We also thank Robert Dungey, Joyce Shabazz, and Cherie Brown, leaders of the National Coalition Building Institute; and UNI Executive Vice President and Provost Gloria Gibson and the members of the UNI-National Coalition Building Institute for their leadership and for believing in us.

(Victoria) "I am an Italian American, white heterosexual, 59-year-old, feminist professor, married with stepchildren and grandchildren."

This is a story about how a common ground of seeking social justice helped forge our biracial friendship and how our relationship developed through continued difficult dialogues about racism, which has itself become a reward, a strategy, and a solution for coping with "racial battle fatigue." One of the many things we have learned from NCBI is that "One-on-one relationship building is at the heart of effective intergroup coalitions. . . . We [as social justice activists] don't change institutions, we change the people who set policies for institutions" (Brown, Mazza, & The National Coalition Building Institute, 2005, p. 85).

OUR NARRATIVE METHOD

To tell this story in a way that honors our attempts toward genuine racial dialogue and relationship, and hopefully to model it for others, we embrace a conversational style of story-telling, where our unique voices are marked. This is meant to recognize the places in which we cannot speak as one voice even though the paper is coauthored. In doing so, we harken back to the writing style of feminist scholars who showed us how this might be done. María Lugones and Elizabeth Spelman (1983) wrote their influential piece, "Have We Got a Theory for You! Feminist Theory, Cultural Imperialism and the Demand for 'The Woman's Voice,'" speaking alternatively in Spanish (Lugones's Hispana woman's voice) and English (Spelman's Anglo woman's voice). Similarly, Karma Chavez and Cindy Griffin (2009) wrote "Power, Feminisms, and Coalitional Agency: Inviting and Enacting Difficult Dialogues," in English, but using a narrative form where they as individual speakers were identified to clarify how each one's different personal backgrounds became political as they attempted to forge a discussion of their individual and shared feminist standpoints. Without these points of distinction the reader could conclude from our chapter that we have been successful in developing a unified voice. We reject such a simplistic conclusion because we recognize our relationship and our identities do not exist in a political vacuum. Instead, our challenge is to stay honest. It is the honesty that keeps our relationship dynamic and that makes it rewarding both personally and as a tool to fight racial battle fatigue.

LOCATING OURSELVES

We begin by further describing our individual intersectional identities (Crenshaw, 1989) to provide a better understanding of the backgrounds most pertinent to our relational journey.

(Victoria) A friend encouraged me to write about my ethnic and class background as Melissa and I weave our stories and think about how our backgrounds impacted the relationship. Oddly, I didn't want to. I would have normally jumped at the chance to do this because I take great pride in my Italian immigrant heritage. I think I hesitated out of white guilt. However, my work with NCBI has taught me that letting go of guilt is a key step in moving forward. As long as I hold on to the guilt of what members of my group, whites, have done to people of color, I cannot be an effective ally to move social justice forward. I need to return to the pride of my identity so I can better respect and support others' identities. And so I wrote.

I have a deeply ingrained identity as a second-generation Italian American working-class kid that grew up in little Italy on the south side of Des Moines, Iowa, during the 1950s and 1960s. I grew up in a pretty sheltered community where ethnic pride was possible. I attended Catholic schools and almost everyone in my grade school was Italian, Irish, or Mexican American. There was definitely a class and ethnic hierarchy, and for the most part, I benefited from both. However, I was not blind to privilege or discrimination. I knew my parents didn't teach my siblings and me to speak Italian for a very practical reason. They did not want us to experience the discrimination they and their parents had faced. Holding up our ethnic pride was a way to deflect the discrimination we knew existed outside our community. I still believe my childhood planted the seed for me to be a social activist.

My first realization on being white did not come until high school with my first African American friend, Robin. I was trying to suggest we had something in common, I said "We are paesans," meaning to me, "we are the same," we are not "Amedicanas," (white Americans). She straightened me out right away, "Girl," she said, "You are white." Her words hung in the air and hurt my heart. It was the first time I really understood I was white, not a person of color. It was also the first time my white privilege had been called out. I thought she was telling me we could not be friends because I was white and she was Black. It took a colleague reading this chapter 44 years later, to help me realize what I was really saying to her and what she was likely saying back (H. Brod, personal communication, April 14, 2014). "Paesan" is a term reserved for people of Italian heritage to identify with each other. When I said this, I was not calling attention to our similarities, I was asking her to assimilate to my identity. Her response was likely a declaration that if she had to assimilate (once again) to my culture, she was not interested in the friendship.

While likely painful for both of us, that moment of realizing privilege has stayed with me. It led me to take classes about other cultures and social justice issues in undergraduate school and eventually led me to feminist studies and social activism in graduate school. I'd like Robin to know the lesson she taught me was a contributing factor in my lifelong self-reflection on race and my work now with Melissa and others to create a more inclusive campus climate.

(Melissa) I am an African American 30-something woman from Davenport, Iowa. Not only that, I am proud to be from Iowa. I am proud to place a high value on hard physical work, and to place integrity and honesty above all values except love. I am polite and professional, even when I am expressing my disdain or anger. I have perfected the "Iowa nice" way to tell a person just about anything. Although some have written about the ways that Midwestern niceness limits the ability of white students to engage in meaningful social justice work (Marshall & Theoharis, 2007), as a Black woman, this part of Midwestern culture has been important to my upbringing. Marshall and Theoharis describe the ways that doing social justice work with white Midwestern students was challenged by a cultural expectation that the students remain nice. It was not considered nice to even reflect critically on the ways that race or racism impacted their upbringing or their current experience, so moving from noticing to confronting or addressing it in some way was a difficult leap. As an African American woman raised with these same values of niceness, I feel I got a different message than my white peers.

My parents raised me to function well in a predominantly white institution exactly like the one where I worked. I learned as a young child that I would do my best work if I came in to an organization and learned the language. From there, I could use that language to impact the organization. The people in this institution of higher education were all very nice on the surface. They lived a colorblind existence, comfortably oblivious to their own racism. As an advocate for social justice, I did my best work underneath that surface. When I had concerns about racism, sexism (or any other -ism for that matter), I did not confront my colleagues, or even name the behavior in terms of an -ism. Instead, I came up with an entirely different (and reasonable) explanation for why we should change our behavior. I have perfected the art of talking about one thing as a way of talking about another. I learned this as a survival skill. I have excelled in traditional institutions (like higher education) because I can feel good about accomplishing modest social justice goals without offending (or even creating dissonance) within my colleagues. I learned by the example of many other Black women in my field, young and old, who can no longer get colleagues to hear what they have to say about anything because they are considered to be the people always "crying discrimination." Finding other ways to accomplish my social justice goals was challenging, but it allowed me to maintain relationships.

I enjoyed my role of straddling the fence between being considered an authentic member of the African American community while not appearing "too angry" for my white colleagues. I must confess, though, that the daily, persistent racism in my work space left me stressed. After experiencing tingling and numbness on my right side off and on for several weeks, I found myself visiting a neurologist. This appointment with the neurologist was my wake-up call. "Are you experiencing a lot of stress?" she asked. I thought of the constant juggling I did to advocate for social justice in my job on a predominantly white campus. Constantly holding back what I was really feeling until I could rephrase it in a way that was more comfortable to my white colleagues wasn't just an annoyance, it was impacting my health.

OUR RELATIONAL BEGINNING

(Shared voices) We met in a professional setting. Victoria was coordinating a newly developed NCBI program on campus. As the program went campuswide the advisory committee expanded to include individuals representing the different divisions on campus.

(Melissa) I thought I had located the perfect opportunity for support and an outlet for the stress when I was asked to be involved in a new diversity inclusion model on campus. This model, NCBI, focused on relationship building as the key to social justice change. It challenged people to learn affectively and to connect in very deep and personal ways. Although I knew Victoria prior to doing this work, the advisory committee she led was the place where a relationship actually began to develop.

(Victoria) It is hard to recall the first time Melissa and I met. Her reputation as a smart, collaborative campus leader for social justice preceded her. I sought her out to join the NCBI advisory committee. She seemed to know what steps we should take next much more clearly than I did and so I knew I needed her leadership.

(Shared voices) What we did not realize at the time was that Melissa, in particular, was walking into an insider-outsider dynamic. The NCBI program was initiated by the Provost in academic affairs and included an informal advisory committee consisting of Victoria and two other faculty members. One was Victoria's good friend (Karen), also white Italian American second generation, and the other was a white Jewish man (Harry) whose parents had survived the Holocaust. He was also Karen's relational partner. The three were all full professors in their late 50s/early 60s with established reputations for their leadership in social justice work. In the summer of 2012, Melissa and another staff person, Michelle, were selected to represent their respective divisions. Michelle, white identified and in her 40s, was an upper level administrator. Melissa, a midlevel administrator in her 30s, was developing a reputation for her contributions to social

justice, even though she had only been working at the university for three
years.

The advisory committee oversaw the activities of a team of 40-plus
campus volunteers that included students, faculty, and staff. Our first
significant step as the new advisory committee was to attend a five-day
national leadership training institute with NCBI. It was an opportunity for
the committee to get to know one another in a deeper way and to build
coalition.

(Victoria) Melissa and I shared a room at the leadership institute. We got
to talk on a more personal level and process the day's activities together.
I fell in love with her children just through the stories and got to see how
she was raising them with her spouse to have cultural pride and respect
for others. As a stepmom and grandma, I have struggled with learning
such parenting skills so I tried to learn from a good model.

(Melissa) I am a person who has always enjoyed and needed close relationships with other women. Developing close relationships with white
women has always presented some unique challenges, though. The constant translating that I find myself doing to be able to function within a
predominantly white institution has often left me too tired to risk my own
emotions (and job security) in a personal relationship. From my introduction into Victoria's work and the specific diversity program, however, I realized that this was different. This model was not about creating awareness of
issues or advocating for some platform or specific political change. Instead,
it was about asking people with courage to share some personal story of
how they had been dehumanized by racism (or another -ism). In return for
taking the risk, those people could expect to be listened to and respected.
I was eager to put in the energy necessary to make the program a success.

(Victoria) For me, the leadership development time was sorely needed.
I was struggling more than I realized with self-confidence as I tried to lead
the program and coauthor a book with increasingly severe writing anxiety. The NCBI leaders must have known I was insecure about my leadership abilities as they singled me out to work on letting go of my past
and embracing my strengths. I thought the institute experience bonded
the five of us on the advisory committee as the leaders of our campus
program. We challenged each other to do our best thinking and began to
weave our ideas together in planning monthly meetings for our team of 40
that were engaging, community-building, and rewarding.

(Shared voices) Over the course of the fall 2012 semester, the advisory
committee continued to meet weekly, so there was a great deal of connection between the two of us. What wasn't entirely clear to us at the time,
however, was that the two of us were feeling differently about how things
were going on the advisory committee. Victoria, clearly an insider among
friends, was feeling affirmed and empowered by this group while Melissa
felt increasingly alienated as a younger, Black newcomer.

A PIVOTAL MOMENT

(Shared voices) In November 2012, the advisory committee, along with some other members of the NCBI program on campus, attended the NCBI annual conference. The conference was a time for connecting with colleagues from other campuses, learning new skills, and strengthening bonds on the campus teams.

(Melissa) Unfortunately, after seeing my younger, Black voice silenced or ignored within our older, whiter advisory committee, I felt there was a duplicity about the way we were working as a team that distressed me. I was spending time, several times a month, telling people about the importance of opening up and communicating about identity. However, in the face of the racism of my diversity team, I attempted to ignore it. My Iowa nice skills came back to me quickly, and I found myself arguing against racism without actually identifying how it was playing out on the advisory committee.

At the annual conference, I realized that this unique diversity inclusion program had changed me. As we worked through the activities at the conference, I was struck by the genuine bonds that existed between the team members on other campuses. During a series of team-building activities with participants from other campuses, I shared the following example with a white woman from another campus.

"I was just brainstorming with my campus team. I mentioned a new idea and everyone just sort of moved on. When one of my white colleagues mentioned it, the whole group erupted in applause. Can you believe this just happened?" "Right here, just right now?" she steamed. "I'm sorry this happened. I want to come alongside you, however you feel comfortable. Would you like me to go with you for support while to you talk to them about this?" I quickly shook my head "no," but her response got me thinking. I began to realize that not saying anything about how I was feeling on our team was not only making me feel bad; it was stunting the growth of the entire team.

I finally decided that I needed to do something about my schizophrenic approach to diversity work. Spending three intense days with my university's team, surrounded by other teams, made me recognize just how much the racism within our team bothered me, and it also made me realize that every other team seemed not to function in quite the same way. After I shared my concerns with the national leadership, I was so honored to hear them say that they wanted to ally with me to create space for a Black voice in the midst of the racism of my team. I spent an entire 24 hours gathering my thoughts, recalling events that ranged from microaggressions (Sue, 2010) to blatant disrespect for me and my identity. I sat down with my team and our NCBI consultants, who led the discussion to share my concerns.

(Victoria) This was one of the hardest conversations I have ever had. I can't recall the order Melissa followed in voicing her concerns about my leadership, but I realized that for her it was the first time she probably felt safe enough to say them. She had two of the national leaders who are African American on each side of the table, something she never gets working and living in a predominantly white Midwestern state. Melissa described for the group examples of me not listening to her. I had recognized the white members of the advisory committee for ideas she had already suggested.

I thought to myself, "How many times have I taught about this problem in my classes? It's Peggy McIntosh, 101." As a white woman antiracist, she was among the first to write about white privilege in a way that whites could no longer deny. She described it as being like an invisible knapsack because white privilege is like "an invisible package of unearned assets which I can count on cashing in each day, but about which I am meant to remain oblivious" (1988, p. 1). In her essay she identified 46 daily life advantages based on her white skin. White privilege includes everyday entitlements, such as being accepted into a new neighborhood, using a credit card without suspicion, or offering one's views without those opinions being generalized to all members of one's race. These are "unearned white privileges taken for granted as neutral, normal, and universally available to everybody" (McIntosh, 1988, p. 10). I've shared McIntosh's list of 46 privileges in my classes for at least 20 years and challenged students to come up with more, which they are always able to do. Yet, I was being racist toward Melissa and other members of color on the campus team every time I maintained the white status quo of how to run meetings, make decisions, and respect individuals.

Further, Melissa shared that I had not respected the national office consultant's guidelines as to how we used the organization's materials. The other representative from the national office chimed in that indeed I had gone over our consultant's head and attempted to contact the white founder of the organization. I responded in complete denial. I could not recall doing so. I can remember Melissa saying through tears and utter frustration, "For heaven's sake Victoria, take some responsibility."

(Melissa) With support from my colleagues in the national leadership, I was able to express my concern to my colleagues: this group, with an antiracist goal, had perpetrated racism against me. My voice shook as I began. I hesitated to make eye contact with my colleagues as I explained, "I wouldn't have requested this meeting if I didn't believe in our work. This work is all about our relationships. This is my attempt to reach out for an authentic relationship with you." I looked down at my notes for support and read my first specific example directly from the screen of my phone. Although I was trying not to directly accuse my friends, I knew that sharing specific examples would convict individuals. We were all there. We all knew the "who" even though I didn't mention any names. I continued with increasing strength in my voice, "I shared a story about racism perpetrated against me at the team meeting last month. The response I got from the team was an expression of sympathy for the person who hurt me, rather than concern for me."

This conversation was difficult for me. It was counter to my upbringing as a child of my parents, and as an Iowan. Although I was very emotional about the pain I was experiencing because of the choices of my colleagues, there was only one person at the table with the privilege to do what she did from the first sentence of my presentation: she cried. She didn't cry a subtle, one tear at a time kind of cry that one might expect to see (if there were tears at all) in a professional setting. Victoria's eyes welled up immediately. She shook at times because she was crying so hard. She looked up occasionally, but most of the time her face was hidden behind tissues and tears. Before I could complete my first sentence, she interrupted me, "That wasn't what I meant. I think this is just a misunderstanding." The NCBI leadership rallied around me, though, and I got to say all that I wanted to say.

Although it was a risk, I shared my perspectives about the team for myself, not so much for the team. My stress over all aspects of my job, not just my work on the team, had become uncontrollable, and it was taking its toll on my health. If I was to move forward as a member of the team, I would do so free of the duplicity of every other aspect of my professional life. I would no longer spend energy translating the needs of my community from honest, authentic language into something that was more palatable for my colleagues. Instead, I would stand up for myself and for future African American team members. After Victoria's insistence in arguing that what I was saying was not true, the NCBI leadership insisted that I deserved to be heard. I felt real freedom when they supported me by saying, "Be quiet, Victoria." For the first time, I felt my team knew that I, a young African American woman, was there to be heard.

So, I took a risk. I trusted a group of white-identified people with the honest truth about how I understood their behavior and treatment of me. Ignoring me when I present an idea? Racism. Restating the same idea and having the group accept it when it came from a white person? Racism. Describing some Black men on our team as intimidating and difficult to get along with when nothing could be further from the truth? Also racism. I explained why I tried to talk to them about it without mentioning racism and I committed to maintaining an honest and open posture with them into the future. I was done tiptoeing around the issue of racism with folks who professed to be committed to social justice. This was an extremely empowering experience. Although it impacted my colleagues, I had to do this for myself. If I was going to sincerely encourage others to approach their social justice work with authenticity, then I had to do the same. At that time, I thought this event was a powerful sign that I was coming into my own as an authentic leader. It turned out that this event marked the beginning of my journey. As challenging as it was to share how I had experienced the past few months, it was even more difficult to try to maintain a relationship that remained open, instead of reverting to the ways I had been taught to survive racism in my life.

(Victoria) First came tears of mortification, then deep denial, then tears about the hurt I had inflicted on the very person I had come to love, respect, and value so much. What got me through was I kept telling myself to forget about my loss of face, it was nothing compared to who I had revictimized. I kept repeating to myself Melissa's first words, "I wouldn't have requested this meeting if I didn't believe in our work. . . . This is my attempt to reach out for an authentic relationship with you." She was willing to hold on to this broken relationship. This biracial, honest relationship is one I had never had and most needed.

MOVING FORWARD

(Victoria) During and certainly after the annual NCBI conference I realized for the first time in my life that my crying in this situation was itself a privilege. At the meeting I tried to stop crying but I could not. I've since realized that by crying so heavily I was not respecting who was the victim in this situation. It was not me. While this may not be true for others, I'm learning that sometimes, even emotion, which seems beyond my control, is not beyond my control. If I really want to listen, I need to set aside my pain and focus on hers. In a culture where emotion is seen as weakness, I have felt weak in my uncontrolled tears. I am now learning that portraying weakness can be a white woman's privilege. That realization has helped me think about crying as more multifaceted. There are healthy tears of healing that I might shed, but in this moment, my tears were not healing—not for me or for Melissa.

This was a new-found realization for me personally, but it harkened back to Ruth Frankenberg's (1993) study of 30 white U.S. feminist women in an effort to discover if they saw themselves as racially or ethnically "identified beings" (p. 26). She did so because of her own frustration with white feminists' responses to charges of racism in the 1980s, "At worst—and it appeared from where I was standing that 'worst' was much of the time—it seemed as though we white feminists had a limited repertoire of responses when we were charged with racism: confusion over accusations of racism; guilt over racism; anger over repeated criticism; dismissal; stasis" (p. 2), and I would add, crying. I understood that by crying in such difficult dialogues, the subject of attention turns from women of color to taking care of white women in the room, much like what happened historically when Black women slaves and servants had to stuff their pain to care for white women's tears. I have since found that little research exists on this matter.

Sociologist Sarita Srivastava (2005, 2006) is among the few making this racially gendered emotion privilege visible. In her qualitative study, she interviewed 15 feminists, white women and women of color (which included identifiers such as Muslim, lesbians of color, etc.) who were members of women's organizations in Toronto, about their experiences in discussing racism. She also observed feminists in 12 antiracist workshops or workshop series. She found patterns of white women crying and women of color feeling they had to stop the discussion and take care of their white sisters, "Vijaya, one of the activists I interviewed echoed a common sentiment that white women's tears flow more openly in these discussions: 'White women cry all the fucking time, and women of colour never cry'" (Srivastava, 2006, p. 61). Srivastava found this reaction among the white women not only shut down individual conversations on racism, it became a barrier to organizational progress. The researcher suggested tears may tend to have different meanings for women of color and white women, "Tears for white women may offer a place of comfort and even distraction, while emotional disclosure can be a place of vulnerability for women of colour, and a diversion from anti-racist change" (p. 78). The problem has been assuming a universal interpretation of women's tears based on a white-woman model. In an interracial dialogue, when white women cry in response to charges that they are being racist, they may be making a claim of innocence (see also Fellows & Razack, 1998). When I cried so hard in that meeting with Melissa and allies, I was proclaiming an innocence I didn't have the right to do.

I asked Melissa if we could meet the Monday following the conference, which had become a pivotal moment in my life. Not that I am once and for all done with being racist, but it has become a moment that continues to ground me in the work and remind me of how far I have to go. I was nervous about meeting but I knew the previous experience was so emotional, I had not listened well, and if I wanted to change, which I deeply wanted to do, I knew I needed to stay in relationship with Melissa and listen. I was surprised that she so readily accepted my invitation. I would have felt it was not my job to fix the other person or to put more emotional time into this relationship, but I'm so grateful she did. More than the content of what was said, what I recall is sitting at a small table in the middle of the busy student union where everything around us became a blur while I listened. At the end, I apologized deeply and asked her if we could meet once a week for lunch; she concurred.

(Melissa) I received some refreshingly sensitive and supportive responses from several of my colleagues regarding my sharing at the conference. Not all of my colleagues appreciated me baring my soul the way I did, though, and I got to endure the wonderful excuses that are often created to explain away racism. I expected to have to endure more of this type of conversation when Victoria asked me to have lunch with her.

Instead, I was pleasantly surprised. We sat down to chat, and she thanked me for sharing at the conference. Then, she said, "I was pretty emotional when you shared before and I feel like I missed some of the things you said. Would you mind telling me more about your experiences on our advisory committee?" This was the beginning of the development of a true ally relationship with Victoria.

We were connected by our shared interest in the work of social justice and diversity on our campus, but it went beyond that. Chatting about the ways we were challenged by that work led naturally to a deep personal relationship. Slowly, the struggles I was having in other aspects of my job didn't need to be hidden from everyone. I could share them with Victoria and be validated in a way that was new to me. She didn't make excuses for the university, and she didn't apologize for her race. Instead, she shared my anger and sadness, and she appreciated the difficult situation I found myself in.

Even though Victoria had become a wonderful friend, my overall work environment was taking a toll on my health. When an opportunity to join the faculty at another college came along in July of 2013, I decided to leave the institution. I started my new role in August of 2013.

WRITING OURSELVES INTO TRUST

(Shared voices) As we began to write this chapter in the fall of 2013, we were challenged to articulate the unique aspects of this relationship that provided an outlet for the stressors of racial battle fatigue. Further, we realized a part of this chapter necessarily had to be about the decision processes and thoughts we went through to negotiate the methods we would use to write this piece—the format and content. Making these decisions a part of the chapter became clear when Melissa called to check on how Victoria's writing was going. After the call Victoria wrote:

(Victoria) Melissa called me last night, January 18, 2014. I am always thrilled to hear her voice because I miss her. It is an honor to feel she thinks of me as a friend although I honestly still feel I don't deserve her friendship. I am still struggling with my racism, guilt, awkwardness, and heightened awareness that my family has no friends of color. I have lived most of my life in a predominantly white Iowa where the way I raised my status was to basically turn my back on my ethnic identity as Italian American. I embrace it in times where I seek ethnic pride and to demonstrate possible empathy with persons of color. But, unlike Melissa, I can choose when I identify my ethnicity. I have not taken many opportunities to build close personal relations with a person of color, and in my mind, if I don't reach for that now, I really will never develop a culturally inclusive world view.

When Melissa called, I also felt guilt about not writing. I have always struggled with writing anxiety by procrastinating, but this seems a little different or has an added dimension. I realized I am afraid of sharing my preliminary writing with Melissa. I know I need to be honest with myself as I write, but should I then share that honesty if it is racist with my friend? Will this writing process risk hurting her again and hurting our relationship? After all, a part of why we decided to write the chapter was as a way to maintain genuine relationship. I know she has survived much worse and that she is an exceptionally strong person, but it seems like she never gets to choose to let her guard down. On the other hand, this writing demands, and she deserves my honesty. Writing collaboratively and sharing our feelings demands trust, and I'm realizing I am, and maybe we, are not quite there yet. I am afraid of letting my half-developed ideas go. It may just be that we have not written together before, it may not all be about racism, but I feel in my heart it is also about racism. I know I feel vulnerable and I'm guessing she might, too. I did not want to see any of her writing until I had something to share at the same time—why? I said I didn't want to be influenced, but isn't that what relationships and coauthorship are about? Similarly, when I suggested we interview each other, Melissa was quick to reject the idea. She feared my questions might overly frame what she had to say. What I am realizing is the only way one builds trust is to just push through—to take risks.

(Melissa) So Victoria brought up this point about trust. A part of writing this chapter was realizing that maybe we didn't know (or trust) one another as much as we initially thought we did. I was really struck by her insights, particularly her thought that trust involves continuing to push through our own hesitations, to continue to dig deeper. This left me trying to push deeper, to share more of the layers hidden by years of niceness. My attempt to do so follows.

I explained to Victoria in our last call that my issues related to trust are not really about her. Trust issues between Black and white women in the United States are as old as the first Europeans and Africans who found themselves on this piece of the Earth. I believe, however, that the first seeds of this mistrust were actually sown in sexism and heterosexism. Aida Hurtado (1989) describes the ways that white women and women of color, although they are both subordinated by sexism, tend to experience that sexism very differently. White women are subordinated primarily through seduction. They are cajoled into maintaining a sexist system where they will find acceptance and affirmation as long as they are willing to continue to do so. Hurtado makes clear that failure to comply is met with harsh and significant consequences. Women of color, whose racial and class positions have worked historically with sexism, learn a woman's place in the world through rejection and exclusion. Through social, emotional, and physical sanctions and rejection, women of color experience a type of racialized sexism that is perpetrated not only by men, but also by white women themselves. As I try to reflect on my own

challenges with trust, I hear my voice join the symphony of Black wom-
en's voices throughout history.

The first low sounds that come from my heart were written anonymously in the *Independent* in 1902. A woman who identified herself only
as "a colored woman, wife and mother" describes her challenges of living
in the Southern United States at the time, "A colored woman, however
respectable, is lower than a white prostitute," she says (as cited in Lerner,
1973, p. 167). I can almost hear her pain in the timbre of her words as she
describes the ways that she has lived a respectable life, and that she is not
alone in being Black, and female, and full of morals and character. Even
then, in 1902, my sister saw the contributions that white women were making to maintain a system of racism in the United States. She calls out in a
melodic tone, harmonizing with my own tenuous voice, the one I am only
now recognizing in the symphony of history, "Is it surprising that feelings
grow more bitter, when the white mother teaches her boy to hate my boy,
not because he is mean, but because his skin is dark?"(Anonymous, 1902,
as cited in Lerner, 1973, p. 168). How many times have I found myself
disappointed by other mothers in my life, white women who are teaching their children a 21st century version of this exact thing? How many
times have I wondered, much like my anonymous sister, "Why are we
forgotten?"

Time has moved on, and the challenges that exist in the collective
understanding about who we are as Black women has changed, but has
also remained a clear theme that is woven through the song of our voices.
As the slow, deep strumming of the pain in my heart diminishes, I hear
my own emotionally charged questions coming in a quick staccato.

What is rational about a culture where white women's values are
assumed to be more pure than the values of other women based solely on
race? Since white women are assumed honest, it must be mental illness
when they lie. Since they are assumed to have noble intentions, it must
be a misunderstanding when they do something intentionally mean or
manipulative. They are part of an oppressed group, women. Yet somehow, the cultural values of the United States leave us all assuming that
this status leaves them incapable of perpetrating racism as a regular practice, both personally and professionally. Why doesn't that status leave us
holding them to a higher standard? Shouldn't they not only notice and
acknowledge, but also be agents for change?

Mary Church Terrell, an activist and scholar, enters the tune with a
more moderate tempo. Her eloquent legato smooths over my not fully
formed staccato and illuminates the unspoken angst down in the hearts
of so many Black women, "But what a tremendous influence for law and
order, and what a mighty foe to mob violence Southern white women
might be, if they would arise in the purity and power of their woman-
hood . . . !" (Terrell, 1904, as cited in Lerner 1973, p. 210).

As women subordinated through rejection and exclusion, we ask white women what is it like to walk in your shoes? How does the seduction of sexism blind you to the relative power that you possess that women of color do not? Bell and Nkomo (2001), two Black women academics interested in the careers of Black women executives, interviewed 80 Black and 40 white women professionals about their experiences with race throughout their careers. As a part of their study, they heard a recurring theme among the white women they interviewed. White women recounted memorable childhood experiences that reinforced the notion that Black people's values were inferior to their own. How does it feel to be a part of a group whose moral character has been historically perceived to be higher than others? How does it feel to be a part of a group of women who are assumed to be less capable of doing wrong than other groups? Although these are just questions, they must ring with the dissonance of accusation in the ears of white women.

And all of this, this symphony of rejection and pain, question and accusation, is the tune ringing in my ears when I enter a relationship with a white woman. Unfortunately, I am usually the only one of the two of us who hears it. As we wrote, I tried to share some of my perspective with Victoria. I wanted her to understand that even though women were expressing these ideas in the early 1900s, that the same musical strains can be heard in the voices of Black women today. My voice was singing this same tune, but I was not alone.

It was actually Victoria who introduced me to the voice of Audre Lorde. It got me thinking that even though Victoria may not have had a Black woman share this kind of information with her directly before, she was also familiar with this tune. She had heard the voice of Audre Lorde (1997) observing that white women continued to see no need, even in 1981, to further examine the "contradictions of self, woman, as oppressor" (p. 283). She also heard Lorde, when she explained that there is power in turning our anger, the anger of Black women, toward usefulness. Lorde entered the symphony of Black women to say that we will no longer apologize for or be consumed by our hidden anger. Instead, we will put it into action. I was so affirmed by this deep canorous theme in the symphony that I had never heard before. I was very nervous about sharing with Victoria, not only out of compassion for her, but also because, as a white woman, she had the right to be more sensitive to anything I would say about race than I could be. Talking this out with Victoria was really difficult. But it was also so real, so refreshingly real to be raw. I was able to share my pain and my struggle and, in the midst of contemplating trust, I reached for Victoria in trust. The writing of this chapter is an example of what we are writing about: reaching for each other in trust, even when it is difficult.

(Victoria) Melissa said in our society Black women and white women's hearts and intentions are not seen as the same. She asked, "What is it like to be a part of a group that is assumed to not hurt others?" Her question nearly knocked me off my feet. I do have this privilege. As a white woman, I can always blame others. I am the nurturer, the well-intentioned, the kind, the meek, and sometimes the helpless one who needs to be cared for. What I've learned is that not only the concept of femininity, but feminist moral identity itself has been historically framed as benevolent innocence (Sriastava, 2005). Mariana Valverde (1992) found the historical standard of moral purity in colonial settings as well as the U.S. and Canadian feminist movements in the late 19th and 20th centuries was a benevolent Anglo-Saxon bourgeois woman. When Melissa shared why she struggled to trust white women, she said the depth of her pain in having to say this was so strong she cried and shook as she spoke. I struggled to listen instead of cry. After I hung up the phone in my office I did just that.

(Shared voices) Our challenge has been to acknowledge racism but not let it define our relationship. We are constantly connecting through our shared identities; they are a key reason why we are friends. However, even when we are focused on our commonalities in faith, family, gender, and education or sharing the joys and pains of rural life, it is critical for us to both validate and accept one another as individuals without ignoring the role that race plays in our lives. We have been through a lot in our friendship, which has been relatively brief (a few years). It has not been easy to maintain our authenticity. Our primary goal is not to teach one another about racism. It is much more than that. We have grown to truly love one another. As much as race matters, our relationship would not flourish without more in common. Our relationship is as much about our willingness and interest in connecting across the boundaries created by societal racism as it is about our connection because of personality and common values.

(Victoria) Melissa and I just finished with our February 2014 check-in call regarding writing. I knew I missed her as a friend—her laughter, her constant insights, her standing beside me, but I really also miss the excitement I felt from working together in the diversity inclusion program on campus. I was so relieved and exhilarated to hear her say, "When we were working together with NCBI we had a synergy that not only kept us both focused, working hard, being creative problem-solvers, but that it was an energy others could see." I think it "infected" the entire team—or at least those who were active in the program. Until this moment, I thought it was just me as the white woman in our relationship who felt this so strongly.

(Shared voices) This relationship, which has continued to grow and develop over time and distance, consistently serves as a source of support in the midst of racial battle fatigue. The distance makes it difficult to maintain relationship, and we sometimes go long periods of time without much interaction. However, when we do interact, the intimacy of the relationship and the trust that has developed has helped us to pick up where we left off. We intentionally disclose about our daily lives. More than "how was your day?" we share what is going on in our hearts in the midst of our daily lives. In closing, we felt the following story about a recent meeting particularly depicts where our relationship is today.

HOW WE CAME TO REALIZE HOW FAR WE HAD COME:
NOVEMBER 2013–MARCH 2014

(Victoria) People often realize major relational change through socially significant events such as graduations, weddings, deaths, or intense conflicts. But our moment came in the seemingly mundane, simple effort to move about with agency in our day. We went to a local café for lunch at my suggestion. That restaurant had nostalgia for me, which I shared while we waited to order. The first time I went there was in about 1969 when my brother was playing football for a local college on scholarship. My dad took the whole family and some of my brother's teammates there to eat. It is the only time I remember eating out as a family. With six kids, mom a full-time homemaker, and dad working construction, there just was not much opportunity for eating out. So I wanted to share this nostalgic moment with my friend.

(Melissa) I don't visit this restaurant unless I am in the company of white people. My family and I have never gotten good service at this restaurant, and we are typically treated better when we have at least one white person with us. Ironically, a restaurant that I didn't feel comfortable visiting without a white escort is the same restaurant that brought Victoria so much joy as a kid. True to form, the service at the restaurant was awful.

(Victoria) Melissa had ordered a homemade salad dressing with her meal. After some time the server came back to say they were out of the dressing. It took several returns to our table before the server understood that Melissa wanted to change her order completely—merely changing the dressing was not acceptable. I had several questions about what was in the soup I ordered, but that didn't seem to shake the server. She looked me in the eye each time, her body was even oriented toward me, but she only engaged Melissa by looking to the side. I first attributed it to my gray hair—looking older, but Melissa is an adult. So why did this happen? Melissa's order took what seemed like an inordinate amount of time, and so we basically ate separately with me finishing my soup long before she was able to finish.

(Melissa) After we received our food, I told Victoria about my experiences with the restaurant, and I explained why I never go without a white escort. I knew we had come a long way in our relationship because she didn't apologize and she didn't pity me. She was indignant, but she didn't act as if this was the first time she had ever witnessed racism. It was complicated to experience the contradictory emotions this restaurant brought up for the two of us. And yet, in spite of different history and different experience, our negative restaurant encounter brought us closer.

(Victoria) After we exited the building Melissa said, "Can I just say that one thing I hate about racism is I can't reward for bad service. If I do, I'll just contribute to the stereotype that black people are cheap and impolite." Her statement struck me with a reality I had not considered before. I have always exercised that right—no, the privilege—that I can reward for effort in tipping and use my money for good. I mumbled something back, "yes it sucks!" But in truth, if Melissa had not shared this with me, I think I would have failed to think about that part of the racism she had just experienced. Not only was she treated poorly, but she did not have the ability in this white small town to even convey nonverbally the injustice she felt. As I reflected on the event, I realized I was creating an extension of Peggy McIntosh's 1988 classic knapsack list of white privilege awareness: Item number 47, "I can choose when to tip or not to tip for bad service and the amount won't be taken as a reflection of my racial identity."

(Melissa): If this event had happened at another time or with another friend, this is how it would have played out. I would have been questioning in the back of my mind whether the restaurant treated me that way because of racism. I would have considered whether I had a responsibility or an interest to respond in some way. I would have tried to consider the ways that I could satisfy my own need to share my anger, indignance, and pain with someone else without being perceived as that ugly person who always cries race. Eventually, I would have forced myself to tamp down the emotions, unresolved. According to my neurologist, these stressors seem like they are buried, but they actually find their way out in physical ways. This is not just my experience. This is the story of racial battle fatigue. African Americans like me are battling to go to work, pursue careers, and provide for their families. The stressors of racism on my community are contributing to serious health problems (e.g., Carty, Kruger, Turner, Campbell, DeLoney, & Lewis, 2011; Brondolo, Brady, Pencille, Beatty, & Contrada, 2012). Burying stressful emotions is necessary to avoid anger that can quickly lead to unemployment. However, the cost of functioning in the midst of racism without relief and release is the negative impact on my health.

Because of my relationship with Victoria, I was able to experience a racist event, share it, and find peace in a matter of hours, not days or weeks. Our relationship did not replace the pain of the racism, the anger that I still have to deal with it, or the shock that it could happen in my community. However, I never questioned myself. I wasn't wondering whether I was paranoid or insane. In spite of the racism, I was validated by a friend.

(Shared voices) When we reflected on this encounter, it seemed to be a perfect example of the ways that this relationship serves as an outlet for the stressors of racial battle fatigue. Fighting for social justice, no, living a life for social justice will always involve stress and challenge. We will find ourselves with pain, anger, and frustration. Developing an authentic interracial relationship has allowed us to thrive in spite of those emotions because it breaks the isolation. When we left that restaurant, we realized the power of being together physically, but also the power of experiencing the difficult world we live in free of isolation.

(Melissa) The most powerful thing about this experience for me was that I had a bad experience around racism and I looked into the eyes of my friend, my white friend, and I saw her say, "You are not paranoid or overreacting. I saw it too."

WHAT WE'VE LEARNED

(Shared voices) Our purpose for writing and sharing our relational journey was to offer it as an illustration of how individuals can survive and even thrive inside institutions that are not changing as quickly as people need them to. The slow process of pushing for change and the continued setbacks are part of the reason for battle fatigue.

Our method for this chapter and for surviving racial battle fatigue is one and the same. It is our written and oral conversations with each other. Our method is not just reflecting, however; it is dynamic, it is this living breathing relationship we are constructing. We are risking, forging, and hopefully growing our relationship through a great deal of work. Not the traditional academic work of researching a topic and reporting it, but the work of peeling back layers of ourselves to each other and the potential audience beyond who might benefit from reading about our process. It is the most immediately rewarding academic writing we have done. We don't have to wait to see what our colleagues or the editor, or the readers think. It is rewarding right now, and that reward is not self-indulgent. It is social justice work through self and relationship.

(Victoria) I asked Melissa, "So now that our story is written, are there other insights we have gained?" One thing I have noticed is that my chronic writing anxiety has dissipated. I am writing! I am excited to write, something I have not felt for a long time as an academic for whom writing (and publishing) are expected. The excitement is about more than the writing. It's the engaging and honest conversation. Being together exhilarates me. Regarding my anxieties around being in a leadership role, I know I am now being more honest about my leadership shortcomings with members of the NCBI team. We are working even more collaboratively to lead. This is a much more sustainable model for the program and one I had not realized I was preventing through my defensive stance as the coordinator.

How are the headaches, Melissa?

(Melissa) Headaches? Did I not mention that I am not even seeing a neurologist anymore? I have moved into a new institution, but it is still a

predominantly white institution. Some things about my work life remain
the same. I have actually shared many of them with Victoria already.
Thankfully, I am working hard to cultivate a relationship that is not only
about giving out, but about having an amazing opportunity to be affirmed
as a woman: a whole, 30-something African American Melissa who is finding other places to be more authentic about how race and racism impact
my life. Writing has been about shedding light on a part of my experience
that has been in the shadows for generations in my family. The stress of
racism will not go away soon, but I have another tool to help me manage
so that I can focus most of my energy on living life to the fullest.

(Victoria) I feel honored and affirmed that you did not give up on me,
Melissa. You were willing to stay in relationship with me, as did the leaders of NCBI who served as your allies in that important meeting, and the
African American provost of UNI when I told her about my struggle with
racism. The meeting was a wakeup call to my own racism particularly
tied to leadership and why it's even more important as a leader in this
diversity inclusion work to remain vigilant about one's own exercise of
privilege.

(Melissa) Racism is so isolating. I am so blessed to have a person in
my life who has the permission from our culture to ignore and deny racism, yet she tries to see, to acknowledge. I'm not perfect, and I know that
I haven't always shared my anger, pain, or frustration in ways that have
been as "affirming" as you describe them above. This is where love enters
in. I know that things can get rocky in a society where racism is such a per-
vasive part. I am committed to continue to reach for relationship because I
know that it is not only a way to maintain our friendship, not only because
it provides some support for my stress, but also because it is a powerful form of activism. The impossible relationship you had with Robin is
an example of how racism shuts down the possibilities for authenticity.
Every day we hang on, we embrace the possibility of authentic relationship, and turn our noses on the racism that seeks to alienate us from one
another.

(Shared voices) As we reflected, we realized even more acutely how
brilliant our provost was to select the NCBI model of diversity inclusion.
We are convinced that reaching for one-on-one relationships is the path to
structural change and a source of support for those doing the work. We
know from our NCBI training that creating safe spaces for people to face
inequities, accept their mistakes, and clean up the mess is critical. Indeed,
relationships are the only thing that may work. We need people from all
different walks of life to reach for relationships. The question that remains
is how to motivate them to feel the need to do so when the process is slow
and challenging. Even when institutional change doesn't come quickly or
at all, we are sustained by knowing that we continue to move forward in
a meaningful and nourishing relationship. We hope sharing our story can

be a powerful motivator to propel people out of their comfort zone into authentic relationship.

REFERENCES

Anonymous. (1902). A colored woman, however respectable is lower than the white prostitute. *The Independent, 54*(2807), 2221–2224.

Bell, E., & Nkomo, S. (2001). *Our separate ways: Black and white women and the struggle for professional identity.* Boston, MA: Harvard Business School Press.

Brondolo, E., Brady, N., Pencille, M., Beatty, D., & Contrada, R. (2012). Coping with racism: A selective review of the literature and a theoretical and methodological critique. *Journal of Behavioral Medicine, 32*(1), 64–88.

Brown, C. R., Mazza, G. J., & The National Coalition Building Institute. (2005). *Leading diverse communities: A how-to guide for moving from healing into action.* San Francisco, CA: Jossey-Bass.

Carty, D. C., Kruger, D. J., Turner, T. M., Campbell, B., DeLoney, E. H., & Lewis, E. Y. (2011). Racism, health status, and birth outcomes: Results of a participatory community-based intervention and health survey. *Journal of Urban Health, 88*(1), 84–97.

Chavez, K., & Griffin, C. (2009). Power, feminisms, and coalitional agency: Inviting and enacting difficult dialogues. *Women's Studies in Communication, 32*(1), 2–11.

Fellows, M., & Razack, S. (1998). The race to innocence: Confronting hierarchical relations among women. *Journal of Gender, Race and Justice, 1*(2), 335–352.

Frankenberg, R. (1993). *White women, race matters: The social construction of whiteness.* Minneapolis, MN: University of Minnesota Press.

Hurtado, A. (1989). Relating to privilege: Seduction and rejection in the subordination of white women and women of color. *Signs: Journal of Women in Culture and Society 14*, 833–855.

Lerner, G. (Ed.). (1973). *Black women in white America: A documentary history.* New York, NY: Vintage Books.

Lorde, A. (1997). The uses of anger. *Women's Studies Quarterly, 25*(1/2), 278–285. Reprinted from a speech presented to the National Women's Studies Association, 1981.

Lugones, M. C., & Spelman, E. V. (1983). Have we got a theory for you! Feminist theory, cultural imperialism and the demand for 'the woman's voice.' *Women's Studies International Forum, 6*(6), 573–581.

Marshall, J. M., & Theoharis, G. (2007). Moving beyond being nice: Teaching and learning about social justice in a predominantly white educational leadership program. *Journal of Research on Leadership Education, 2*(2), 1–31.

McIntosh, P. (1988). *White privilege and male privilege: A personal account of coming to see correspondences through work in women's studies.* Working Paper No. 189. Wellesley, MA: Wellesley Centers for Women.

NCBI (National Coalition Building Institute). (n.d.). Retrieved from http://ncbi. org

Srivastava, S. (2005). "You're calling me a racist?" The moral and emotional regulation of antiracism and feminism. *Signs, 31*(1), 29–62.

Srivastava, S. (2006). Tears, fears and careers: Anti-racism and emotion in social movement organizations. *Canadian Journal of Sociology, 31*(1), 55–90.

Sue, D. W. (Ed.). (2010). *Microaggressions and marginality: Manifestation, dynamics, and impact.* Hoboken, NJ: Wiley.

Terrell, M. C. (1904). Lynching from a Negro's point of view. *North American Review, 178* (571), 853–868.

Valverde, M. (1992). "When the mother of the race is free": Race, reproduction and sexuality in first-wave feminism. In F. Iacovetta & M. Valverde (Eds.), *Gender conflicts: New essays in women's history* (pp. 3–26). Toronto, ON: University of Toronto Press.

Chapter 8

Where Do I Belong?: The Formation of a Destabilized Identity

Brandelyn Tosolt

AUGUST 2008

When I arrived on my undergraduate institution's campus, I finally felt like I belonged somewhere. I was looking forward to putting behind my previous lifetime of never quite fitting in, glad to lose myself in the sea of what I knew would be public intellectuals engaged in debating the perils of modern society long into the early morning. Moving my things into my first dorm room, I met my resident assistant, Tonya. She was shorter than me, with pressed hair, dark skin, and a friendly smile. We chatted for a minute and one of Tonya's friends, another Black woman, walked up. She didn't realize that I lived on Tonya's floor. She asked me, "Where do you stay?"

Stay? I don't stay anywhere. I move. I go places. I am heading downstairs right now.

My confusion must have shown on my face, because Tonya looked at me gently, reached out to touch my arm, and said, "She means 'Where do you live?' honey." Then, Tonya turned to her friend and said, "She's just moving onto my floor."

My cheeks burned, and I was immediately thrown back into a familiar isolation; I missed the day when all the girls went from being kids to being pretty. I missed the day when girls realized they needed to go to the bathroom in groups and boys learned to occupy vast quantities of space, their limbs overspilling their desks. I missed the day when high schoolers were taught to start blowing off school and curfew and enjoy their last few years of being a kid. And now, I realized that I must have missed the day when . . . what? When we were taught how to speak to one another? *I don't belong here*, I thought. *I will never belong anywhere.*

In this moment, I knew that these two women were part of something I was not. I held no illusions that I might be able to join them in their group, but I did feel my lack of belonging in any group. I was destabilized, again.

MAY 2014

I can look back now and see how unusual it was that in that moment, I didn't retract in fear. I have now interacted with hundreds of under-graduates, most of them white, many of them interacting with ideas about race explicitly for the first time. The most common response I witness is my students shying away from difference, afraid that they will violate unknown rules governing interactions between people of two different races. Tatum (1992) argues that white students experience reactions "that range from guilt and shame to anger and despair" (p. 2). I don't know precisely why it was that I didn't respond similarly; McAllister and Irvine (2002) found that teachers who were able to reflect on their own experiences with discrimination and oppression were more able to empathize with their students' experiences. I'm unsure of what drove me to using my lived experiences as generative as opposed to avoiding those same lived experiences. It would have been easier, more common perhaps, to simply push away these feelings of discomfort, avoid situations in which I was unnerved, and just go about my life. Broido (2000) found that undergrad-uates who were developing into social justice allies possessed a strong sense of confidence; I would never describe myself that way, particularly as a young adult. Perhaps, had I been more confident, I would have been more likely to ascribe the problem to Tonya and her friend's expressive rather than my own receptive communication. In any case, the interaction, reflected upon more than 15 years later, serves as a powerful moment of destabilization (Bailey, 1998).

MAY 2014 CONTINUED

Othering is the practice of dichotomizing the world into *us* and *them*, and through the construction of *them* gaining insight into who *we* are (Said, 1978). This dichotomous relationship preserves power differentials, grant-ing privilege to *us* and limiting access to power for *them*. Kaplan (2013) explores the experiences of "Miss Annes," white women who chose to live in majority-Black environments during the Harlem Renaissance. Among Kaplan's theses is the idea that when white women chose to cross racialized lines, they gave up the ability to fit into society. No longer were they welcome in white social circles, nor did they ever entirely belong in Black ones. I identify with the Miss Annes of the past; while I do not feel that I've lost membership in white social circles, I believe my experiences have destabilized what it means to be white within white social circles.

As one who speaks about racism, sexism, homophobia, and other intersecting forms of oppression, particularly with white, cisgender, heterosexual, and other majority group members, I destabilize my "insider status by challenging and resisting the usual assumptions held by most white people (such as the belief that white privilege is earned, inevitable, or natural)" (Bailey, 1998, p. 32). I feel destabilization has both internal and external components. The internal aspects prompt a question to myself: "Where do I belong?" I choose the internal destabilization, using it as a tool to better understand my place in the world. In contrast, external forces attempt to destabilize me, divorcing me from my own demographic group in order to police my behavior. Others point out, "You're not what you're supposed to be."

I know I have tremendous advantages in my life because of the demographic groups into which I was born. I could not have been born into a better time to be a woman wanting to pursue a career. I was on the job market for a tenure-track job before the Great Recession. I have to spend little cognitive energy on my gender identity or expression. While I had to take out student loans to do so, I was able to be educated at excellent institutions and emerge with a doctoral degree in hand. And I was born white in the United States. All of these identities build on each other to create a vast array of choices from which I am able to select. I recognize the demographic lottery and my relative winning ticket. In all of these ways, I am tremendously privileged.

My privilege, though, does not fit as comfortably as others suggest it ought. "One of the major advantages of privilege is the sense of absolute belonging and importance" (Hurtado & Stewart, 2004, p. 320). On the one hand, Hurtado and Stewart are referring to the centrality and representation that come from identity in a dominant category. On this point, I agree. There can be no denying the relative frequency with which I see people who look like me represented in a broad range of media and narratives. On the other hand, Hurtado and Stewart are suggesting a sense of internal consonance by their phrase "absolute belonging and importance." I do not feel a sense of absolute belonging among other white people; instead, my internal destabilization serves to create a question. "Where do I belong?" Because I've moved from the center of my privilege, I cannot have "absolute belonging and importance." I continue to occupy a central space in society, for my skin has not changed color. Instead, I have destabilized my own center.

OCTOBER 2003

I am 23 years old, teaching elementary school in Detroit, Michigan. I am on my lunch hour and, as a first-year teacher, I am never caught up. The learning curve is steep and I constantly worry: about failing 34 sixth graders, about missing deadlines, about next week's lessons, about last week's conversations. To prepare for the afternoon, I am writing my agenda on the whiteboard at the front of the room. From my position, I can see into the hallway. As I am writing, two of my girls, Destiny and Shanelle, burst into my room.

"Miss Tosolt! Miss Tosolt! They takin' off they earrings!" Destiny is breathless, her eyes wide, and her hands begging me to understand.

I stand, marker in my hand, and attempt to make sense of her words. *They're taking off their earrings? Why on earth would they be doing that? Are they having an allergic reaction? Are they trading earrings with one another?*

Destiny looks at me and repeats herself, this time slower and with greater emphasis. "They TAKIN' off they EARrings!"

I continue to stand dumbly, not able to attach meaning to her words.

Shanelle pushes in front of Destiny and delivers a message to us both: "She don't know what you're saying. They're gonna fight!"

Oh! I spring into action, dropping my marker, and heading to the phone on my desk to call security.

MAY 2014

"Where do I belong?"

According to my academic institution, I belonged at the front of a classroom. While I was still early in my professional socialization, I had constructed an identity as an educator. I took pleasure in being an urban teacher, delighting in being asked where I taught and I being able to reply, "Detroit." I taught all African American students, all low-income students. I loved my work and my students, though I left school each day either numb or sad. The work felt similar to my work with the LGBTQ community as a staff member of a statewide nonprofit. Even thought my work was tremendously satisfying to me, though, as the above moment shows, I remained destabilized.

I might have felt fully a member of my school community, but my inability to be truly bicultural exposed my lack of centrality. Had I been a teacher of minoritized identity in a school of majority students, I would have walked in to the first day of school year already possessing my double consciousness, my ability to think as from the center and from the outside of society (Du Bois, 1903/1994). My double consciousness would have been a tool for survival developed implicitly through many socializing experiences as well as explicitly through the guidance of my family and significant others in my life. Instead, I was able to reach adulthood without having to learn others' ways of being.

Being a member of a minoritized group by definition removes one from the center of society's power; this lack of central power creates a need for double consciousness. A member of the dominant group occupies the center. However, a member of the dominant group who destabilizes the center occupies a space between, lacking the social power of the center but also lacking the coping skill developed by the Other.

"Where do I belong?"

I desperately wanted to belong in my school, but was regularly reminded that I was an Other. My privilege in the broader society did not privilege me as an insider in my school setting, as the daily lived culture of my school operated outside of my white norms. My internal destabilization, privileged without belonging in the majority, rendered me an outsider, even among members of minoritized groups who were themselves not allowed insider status in broader society, even as they were the majority in the school.

In my discussion of both of the prior critical moments, I focused on my own feelings of destabilization. In both cases, I felt acutely my destabilization, but I don't think that Tonya, her friend, Destiny, or Shanelle intended to create that feeling. I turn now to moments of external destabilization, or those incidents that caused others to state, "You're not who you're supposed to be." While these next incidents still caused me to question, "Where do I belong?," I believe it will become clear that the other participants in these moments did intend to destabilize me.

APRIL 2009

It's the second-to-last class of the semester, and I've brought a panel of teachers in to speak to my students. The panelists include former students and local teachers, one of whom is my husband. The course is for preservice teachers, is focused on diversity (side note: I might wish it focused on inclusion and equity for social justice, but I didn't design it), and serves as the students' sole course that explicitly contains content related to forces of oppression in schooling. My students have been grappling with questions of practicality, not yet trusting themselves to think flexibly and compassionately as their teaching lives unfold. Halfway through class, we take a break, both to allow everyone to stretch their legs and to allow my students to process what they've heard.

Krista slinks over to me and whispers, as if confiding a secret. "Wow. Your husband is not what I expected him to be!"

I reply quickly. "Really? How was he different than what you expected?"

Looking around quickly, Krista stammers through her response. "Well, I don't know . . . I expected him to be, you know. Taller? And Black?" As her words pour out, her face flushes red. It's like she doesn't want me to think less of her for thinking this, but she had to air her confusion.

As Krista stands there, obviously uncomfortable and waiting for me to remove that feeling, my internal processing begins. *What would have made this college student expect my husband to be Black? In this course, I've shared a number of things about him, as he's a current classroom teacher. I've shared with them that he has 15 years in public education, all of it in high-poverty schools, most of it in Detroit, Michigan. I have shared with them pictures of our students and classrooms. I've shared stories of successes and failures we've both had in our classrooms. I know that I've talked about how, in our combined experiences in the Detroit Public Schools, we had a total of three white students. But still, I wonder why Krista would have expected him to be Black.*

And taller? I can't even begin to make sense of this.

In a moment, I decide to simply address my question to her, rather than engaging in an elaborate guessing game. "I'm surprised, Krista. Can you tell me more about why you expected him to be taller and Black?"

More blushing. *I've really done it now. I've worked all semester to create a safe space in which my students feel comfortable asking tough, embarrassing questions. Now I've completely undone that work for Krista.*

Except, as I'm beating myself up, Krista begins to answer. Her words begin slowly, quietly, and gradually become more confident. "Well," she begins, "I can tell how much you love your students. I can tell how much he loves his students. And all of your students were Black. I guess . . ." here, she pauses, then decides to finish her thoughts. "I guess I wondered why you would care so much about Black kids unless you were married to a Black man. I mean, there's so many kids like us to care about. Why choose them?"

MAY 2014

And there it is: ugly and bold. Two issues are revealed to me: one about what I do, one about who I am.

Have I taught them nothing? This is the end of the semester! Why choose "them?" Why not choose them? Why do you feel they're not worth caring about? Why does it seem extraordinary to you to care about someone who's not like you? What happens when you have a student of color in your classroom? Are you admitting that you won't be as committed to that student as you are to the students "like us"? And what do I do with that, as a teacher educator?

Of course, this is the easier piece of the puzzle. For a majority of my students, as for Krista, my course is the first experience they've had speaking explicitly about race. They react in predictable ways, including defensiveness, claiming colorblindness, dismissal, use of extraordinary others as disconfirming proof, and denial of privilege (for more detail on these and other common responses, please see Case & Hemmings, 2005; Locke, 2005;

Lowenstein, 2009; Milner, 2010; Sleeter, 2001; Tatum, 1992). Krista's comment tells me that I need to be more explicit in creating opportunities for students to connect personally to the work. In the coming semesters, I will work with my peers to construct experiences that engage and empower majority students through poetry, the use of accessible texts, structuring the course from white-ness through poverty and into race, and requiring them to plunge into life as an Other for a period of time (Tosolt, Love, & Harte, 2013). This is, of course, the easier component to resolve, as it is about what I do and not who I am.

"You're not what you're supposed to be."

MAY 2014 CONTINUED

Much is known about the isolating and demoralizing experiences of faculty of color teaching about race (Cao, 2011; Stanley, 2006; Tuitt, Hanna, Martinez, Salazar, & Griffin, 2009; Turner, González, & Wood, 2008) including feelings of isolation, shouldering a disproportionate mentoring and service load, and negative teaching evaluations from students encountering their first authority figure of color. This body of research is critical. The lack of access to tenure-track faculty positions for aspiring faculty of color, combined with the uneven support offered to those faculty of color who are offered positions as well as the extra burdens they bear, create an indefensible situation of underrepresentation.

Understanding the pushback that faculty of color face from majority students when openly discussing race teaches us a great deal. The questioning of the authority of the faculty of color on the part of the majority students (Perry, Moore, Edwards, Acosta, & Frey, 2009) serves as an indicator of just how far our society still has to go in addressing persistent racism.

However, understanding the pushback that majority faculty face from majority students when openly discussing race also teaches us a great deal.

Anecdotally, I know that my voice carries more weight with many of my students than does the voice of a faculty of color. My students question the legitimacy of the information when a faculty member of color talks about race in a way they don't when I share the same information. And yet, my identity as a majority member teaching primarily majority students about issues of oppression creates cognitive dissonance for my students, which they express back as a statement meant to destabilize me: "You're not who you're supposed to be." They are revoking my privilege, and while I might remain demographically one of them, their statements serve as notice that they no longer identify me with the group. It is this revocation of my "sameness" that is the big lesson here, and this refusal to identify with me says quite a bit about just how far our society still has to go in addressing persistent racism.

NOVEMBER 2007

Nervously, I submit applications to dozens of tenure-track faculty openings across the country. My field is saturated and multicultural work is not sexy. STEM's the current focus, and I don't do STEM. Instead, I dutifully list my journal articles in process on my vita, double check for spelling errors, and ensure the right cover letter goes in the right envelope. I send off the envelopes and wait for the next week's *Chronicle of Higher Education* to come out. I circle more jobs, repeat the process. My advisors get sick of writing letters of reference for me. I feel guilty, but continue asking. The cycle repeats itself. Finally, my work begins to pay off. I make the cut for lots of phone interviews and eventually find a rhythm to them. I get a couple of nibbles, some on-campus interviews. I'm on one of those on-campus interviews now, waiting to meet the person who would be my chair were I hired.

She emerges from her office, looks at me, seated in the reception area, pauses a moment, then extends her hand. I reach out, shake hers, and walk into her office. A very nice interview ensues. There's good back and forth, she asks insightful questions that probe my prior experience and help me argue my alignment with the department's mission and vision, and I gain confidence. Overall, I feel the interview's going well. As the conversation begins to reach a natural conclusion, she pauses, then says, "You know, I was really surprised to see you."

I pause, unsure of how to address this response. She was surprised to see me? Did my escort from the search committee drop me off at the wrong time? Did I do something wrong? I instinctively feel like apologizing, but I'm not sure what to apologize for.

"I really expected you to show up Black. I mean, from your research interest, your teaching experience, you know . . . I thought you were a diversity hire!"

"A diversity hire." Yes, I definitely feel like I need to apologize. For not being Black? For being white? For misleading her somehow with my vita? I attended to all sorts of tricks when I went on the job market—removing my wedding ring before on-campus interviews so as to not make employers question whether or not I'd quickly utilize FMLA leave. Using heavier stock paper to make my application appear literally more weighty. Following up phone interviews with e-mails to all members of the search committees in which I spoke specifically to something they'd said was an issue for their department and how I thought I might address that need. But the marketing of my race? Or rather, the mismarketing of my race? I hadn't considered that.

MAY 2014

As a white woman, I see myself reflected in the research literature in incomplete ways. I find, as Burns (2004) writes, "much social justice work has been historically focused on . . . ridding the oppressed of their 'false consciousness'" (p. 376). While the emphasis on unlearning racism is certainly warranted, what happens after the false consciousness has been addressed? What happens for those who choose to destabilize themselves and choose to do so publicly? What are the experiences of those majority group members disrupting what Hurtado (1997) calls the unwritten rules of privilege?

As the incident with my prospective chair made clear, the response to publicly destabilizing oneself is clear: "You're not who you're supposed to be."

Where do I belong? I'm not who I'm supposed to be.

The charges and questions get old. When I feel the frustration rising, when I feel myself getting ready to use a sharp tongue to cut a retort, I move into an internal dialogue.

You're tired of this? You're tired of having these same conversations over and over again? Really? You're white. You're educated. You're perceived to be heterosexual and cisgender. Your gender is fully acceptable in the field of education. There are so few ways in which your life could be any easier. Shut up and do the work.

My frustrations are a mere inkling of what my colleagues of color face, of the lived reality of people of color. And so, my destabilizing returns, a familiar tool. White but not center. Conscious but not minoritized. Frustrated but still privileged. Did the prospective chair think and say some really inappropriate things? Absolutely. Did I still get a tenure-track job and recently, tenure? I sure did. These frustrations are just that for me: frustrations. They are the thoughts I live with while making my way through the world.

Or are they merely frustrations?

Goodman (2000) discusses the strengths and challenges presented by three reasons individuals from privileged social groups are motivated toward social justice: empathy, spiritual or moral values, and/or self-interest. It is clear to me that my frustrations with destabilization are a source of great empathy. It is through these incidents that I am able to catch a brief glimpse of another's reality. And while this empathy is important for its own sake, it's also important because of the action to which it calls me.

I occupy a tremendously central role in terms of social power. While I destabilize myself, this ability to choose to be centered or not is another expression of my privilege. While my world view calls me to destabilize myself, I can choose to hide my destabilization as needed. If I truly am a social justice ally, or a member "of dominant social groups . . . who [is] working to end the system of oppression that gives [me] greater privilege and power based on [my] social-group membership" (Broido, 2000, p. 3), perhaps my frustrations are a source of more than just empathy.

Perhaps these experiences, instead, provide the common experience between majority and minority that can lead to change. Bell writes, "The interest of blacks in achieving racial equality will be accommodated only when it converges with the interests of whites" (1980, p. 523). Perhaps I've been using the wrong construct all along. I've been viewing destabilizing as a movement away from the center and, in some ways, toward the margins. This movement has felt isolating, as if I am neither part of one group nor the other. Interest convergence shifts my thinking, though. Rather than feeling isolated between two groups, I instead need to conceptualize myself as a bridge between them.

MAY 2014 CONTINUED

I typically use racial identity models in my courses, using Helms (1990) as a tool to help my students think about their own journey in thinking about race and Gay (1985) as a device for educators on understanding the educational implications of the models. Both models present a view of racial identity development from a time of "innocence" through a series of encounters that reveal the sociological importance of race while attempting to grapple with its meaning, to a (hopefully) reunified identity that includes a healthy racial consciousness. As I revisit my sources each semester to ensure that I'm choosing the most effective materials, I've begun to consider the question of bi- or multiracial identity development. A common rebuttal to Helms and Gay is the age of their work; some of my students argue that surely we're in a postracial society today. After all, "we have a Black President now." Also, the increasing presence of bi- or multiracial individuals makes them question the saliency of race.

I disagree with this charge from a teaching perspective. I view this critique more as a tool of denial than a genuine reflection of the sociological realities of today. Were my students interested in understanding Helms and Gay and adding to their analysis, I would be more amenable to changes.

In any case, however, this critique sends me into the literature, as I realize I am not current in my understanding of bi- or multiracial identity development. The more I read, the more the wheels begin to turn. Let me be clear: I know that I am white. I have no illusions that "some of my best friends being Black" changes anything about my race. However, I find myself drawn to the work challenging multiracial identity as static (Renn, 2008). Instead, the identity of a multiracial individual may be "stable, but different elements are more salient in some contexts than in others" (p. 17). In situations where identifying with the majority was required, these multiracial students positioned themselves as majority. When among minoritized students, they embraced a minoritized identity. Rather than possessing a unified identity they maintained regardless of context, these students were chameleons, shifting to fit the needs of a particular situation.

I wonder: does the experience of being an insider, an outsider, and a destabilized insider parallel some aspects of multiracial identity development? Or, to ask a more useful question, might some of the strategies employed by multiracial individuals in navigating the complex territory of multiple demographic groups be applicable to my life and work? How might concepts like code-switching and cultural frame-switching inform my work? Renn speaks to "participation in legitimizing activities" (2000, p. 407) as providing a sense of belonging. What are my "legitimizing activities," both within the majority and minority communities?

APRIL 2014

I attend Ujima, a night of celebration in which incoming African American students are feted and African American faculty and students are recognized for their achievements. It is a night featuring music, poetry, and soul food.

I love attending this celebration, watching this community on a majority-white campus. I love the looks on the family members[1] faces as their students are called by name to be welcomed by the entire community. I love the pride of current students as their names are revealed as having been recognized for their academic achievement and cocurricular leadership. The entire evening brings tears to my eyes at various moments.

Through no fault of the emcee, presenters, or award winners, the ceremony begins to get long. It's 12 hours since I arrived on campus that morning, and I have to admit, I'm starting to drift a bit. Rounds of applause continue and I look longingly at the desserts, wishing for a brief second I wasn't vegan so I could partake in the chocolate cake.

It's time for the Friend of African American Programs & Services award, one presented to an individual for support and service to the office and its initiatives in the prior year. I sit as the name is called and begin to applaud. One clap in and I realize that the name is quite familiar: it is my own. I am thrilled, of course, to have been recognized as a supporter of this office.

Destabilized, I think, as I walk up to the stage. *Majority, but not of the majority*, I think, as I ascend the stairs. *Minority, but not of the minority*, I think, as I shake hands and hug. *The only white individual recognized tonight*, I think, as I head back to my seat, accepting congratulations, handshakes, and hugs on the way.

REFERENCES

Bailey, A. (1998). Locating traitorous identities: Toward a view of privilege-cognization white character. *Hypatia, 13*(1), 27–42. doi:10.1111/j.1527-2001.1998.tb01368.x

Bell, D. A. (1980). *Brown v. Board of Education* and the interest-convergence dilemma. *Harvard Law Review, 93*(3), 518–534.

Broido, E. M. (2000). The development of social justice allies during college: A phenomenological investigation. *Journal of College Student Development, 41*(1), 3–18.

Burns, A. (2004). The racing of capability and culpability in desegregated schools. In M. Fine, L. Weis, L. P. Pruitt, & A. Burns (Eds.), *Off White: Readings on power, privilege, and resistance* (2d ed.) (pp. 373–394). New York, NY: Routledge.

Cao, W. (2011). An inconvenient identity: Paradox, complexity, and strategies in a social foundations classroom. *Education and Urban Society, 43*(4), 517–532. doi:10.1177/0013124510380719

Case, K. A., & Hemmings, A. (2005). Distancing strategies: White women preservice teachers and antiracist curriculum. *Urban Education, 40*(6), 606–626. doi:10.1177/0042085905281396

Du Bois, W. E. B. (1994). *The souls of Black folk.* New York, NY: Gramercy Books. (Original work published 1903)

Gay, G. (1985). Implications of selected models of ethnic identity development for educators. *Journal of Negro Education, 54*(1), 43–55. doi: 10.2307/2294899

Goodman, D. J. (2000). Motivating people from privileged groups to support social justice. *Teachers College Record, 102*(6), 1061–1085.

Helms, J. E. (1990). *Black and white racial identity: Theory, research, and practice.* Santa Barbara, CA: Praeger.

Hurtado, A. (1997). *The color of privilege: Three blasphemies on race and feminism.* Ann Arbor, MI: University of Michigan Press.

Hurtado, A., & Stewart, A. J. (2004). Through the looking glass: Implications of studying whiteness for feminist methods. In M. Fine, L. Weis, L. P. Pruitt, & A. Burns (Eds.), *Off White: Readings on power, privilege, and resistance* (2nd ed.) (pp. 315–330). New York, NY: Routledge.

Kaplan, C. (2013). *Miss Anne in Harlem: The white women of the black renaissance.* New York, NY: HarperCollins.

Locke, S. (2005). Institutional social and cultural influences on the multicultural perspectives of preservice teachers. *Multicultural Perspectives, 7*(2), 20–28. doi:10.1207/s15327892mcp0702_4

Lowenstein, K. L. (2009). The work of multicultural teacher education: Reconceptualizing white teacher candidates as learners. *Review of Educational Research, 79*(1), 163–196. doi:10.3102/0034654308326161

McAllister, G., & Irvine, J. J. (2002). The role of empathy in teaching culturally diverse students: A qualitative study of teachers' beliefs. *Journal of Teacher Education, 53*(5), 433–443. doi:10.1177/002248702237397

Milner, H. R., IV. (2010). What does teacher education have to do with teaching? Implications for diversity studies. *Journal of Teacher Education, 61*(1–2), 118–131. doi:10.1177/0022487109347670

Perry, G., Moore, H. A., Edwards, C., Acosta, K., & Frey, C. (2009). Maintaining credibility and authority as an instructor of color in diversity-education classrooms: A qualitative inquiry. *The Journal of Higher Education, 80*(1), 80–105. doi:10.1353/jhe.0.0030

Renn, K. A. (2000). Patterns of situational identity among biracial and multiracial college students. *The Review of Higher Education, 23*(4), 399–420. doi:10.1353/rhe.2000.0019

Renn, K. A. (2008). Research on biracial and multiracial identity development: Overview and synthesis. *New Directions for Student Services, 123*(Fall), 13–21. doi:10.1002/ss.282

Said, E. (1978). *Orientalism.* New York, NY: Random House.

Sleeter, C. E. (2001). Preparing teachers for culturally diverse schools: Research and the overwhelming presence of whiteness. *Journal of Teacher Education, 52*(2), 94–106. doi:10.1177/0022487101052002002

Stanley, C. A. (2006). Coloring the academic landscape: Faculty of color breaking the silence in predominantly white colleges and universities. *American Educational Research Journal, 43*(4), 701–736. doi:10.3102/00028312043004701

Tatum, B. D. (1992). Talking about race, learning about racism: The application of racial identity development theory in the classroom. *Harvard Educational Review, 62*(1), 1–24.

Tosolt, B., Love, B. L., & Harte, H. (2013, April-May). *Pedagogical practices that engage and empower white pre-service teachers in multicultural education courses.* Paper presented at the Annual Meeting of the American Educational Research Association, San Francisco, CA.

Tuitt, F., Hanna, M., Martinez, L. M., Salazar, M. de Carmen, & Griffin, R. (2009). Teaching in the line of fire: Faculty of color in the academy. *Thought and Action, 25*(Fall), 65–74.

Turner, C. S. V., González, J. C., & Wood, J. L. (2008). Faculty of color in academe: What 20 years of literature tells us. *Journal of Diversity in Higher Education, 1*(3), 139–168. doi:10.1037/a0012837

Part II

Battles Still to Be Waged

Chapter 9

"Yes, I *Am* Smart!": Battling Microaggressions as Women of Color Doctoral Students

Jessica C. Harris, Jasmine M. Haywood,
Samantha M. Ivery, and Johari R. Shuck

INTRODUCTION

This chapter explores and exposes the racial microaggressions that we, four Women of Color,[1] have encountered while pursuing PhDs in education at a predominantly white institution (PWI) in the Midwest. Accordingly, we detail the ways in which we respond to and cope with these aggressions. Racial microaggressions (RMAs) refer to "subtle, stunning, often automatic, and 'non-verbal' exchanges which are 'put downs' of blacks by offenders" (Pierce, Carew, Pierce-Gonzalez, & Wills, 1978, p. 66). Pierce (1969) asserts that RMAs are "offensive mechanisms" (p. 303) that control and exert energy from people of color and contributes to self-degradation. Sue et al. (2007) categorized racial microaggressions as microinvalidations (expressions that undermine or belittle the experience of being a person of color), microinsults

---

[1]The term "Women of Color" refers to women of non-white racial heritage. We deliberately capitalize this term to uplift this population in an attempt to achieve racial and social justice.

(rude, inconsiderate, patronizing expressions), and microassaults (overt, explicit assaults). RMAs have been found to contribute to hostile environments for graduate students of color and hinder degree completion (Felder & Barker, 2013; Gildersleeve, Croom & Vasquez, 2011; Ingram, 2013; Solorzano, 1998; Truong & Museus, 2012; Williams & Nichols, 2012).

As Women of Color enrolled in a doctoral program at a PWI, we encounter RMAs on a daily basis. Trudging through the white-dominated battlefield of education unavoidably brings RMAs, which then lead to racial battle fatigue (Smith, Allen, & Danley, 2007). To lessen the potential of detrimental outcomes of our racialized experiences, we have employed several coping mechanisms to manage the racial battle fatigue we experience as we confront racism and sexism within the academy. Our stories illuminate how four Women of Color experience and cope with RMAs as PhD students. The implications and discussion that stem from our narrative may help to enhance the academy's ability to cultivate a more inclusive atmosphere that ensures the successes of Women of Color graduate students.

THEORETICAL FRAMEWORKS

Critical Race Theory (CRT) and Critical Race Feminism (CRF) are the theoretical frameworks that shaped this inquiry. While CRT accounts for the realities of race and racism in U.S. society and education (Ladson-Billings & Tate, 1995), CRF focuses on the interlocking systems of oppression that Women of Color encounter on a daily basis. CRF addresses sexism, racism, and other forms of oppressions that impede and impact the lives of Women of Color (Wing, 2003). Taken together, these frameworks allow for a critique and deconstruction of systemic oppression, specifically racism and sexism that impact our experiences as Women of Color doctoral students navigating a PWI.

CRT and CRF focus on the voices and experiential knowledge of people of color to gain understanding and agency (Yosso, 2006). Therefore, we used the methodological tool of composite narratives to divulge "experiences with and responses to racism" (Solorzano & Yosso, 2002, p. 33). Patton and Catching (2009) explain, "Composite characters are created and contextually located to allow the participants' experiences with racism and other intersecting identities to be foregrounded" (p. 716). We composited our own stories, as Women of Color, to write a counterstory that exposes the oppressive structures in the academy, and detail how we experience and cope with institutionalized racism that act as barriers to our success.

LEARNING AND COPING AS WOMEN OF COLOR DOCTORAL STUDENTS

Alex had been excited to meet other Women of Color enrolled in the Higher Education doctoral program since she'd received Bianca's invitation to the Sister Circle meeting a month prior. Bianca had explained in her invitation that Sister Circle, started by Black women in the Higher Education program, was organized to provide a private safe space for Women of Color in the program to support each other personally and academically. Alex had anticipated the gathering since she was new to town. She hoped this group of sistahs would give her a source of support as she continued to pursue her PhD at the University of Middle American (UMA) after relocating and transferring with her mentor, Dr. Lewis.

Alex pulled into the cul-de-sac of Bianca's neighborhood and thought to herself *this is cute*. With hummus and pita chips in hand, she rang the doorbell. Bianca's husband greeted her warmly on his way out, *Hi, you must be Alex. Go on inside and enjoy your first Sister Circle!* He smiled warmly as he walked out the door with his mini-me-child attached to his hip.

Bianca met Alex in the foyer and exclaimed, *Alex I'm so glad you were able to make it! Let me take your dish and follow me, I'll introduce you to the other ladies, we were just catching up. It's been a while since we've had a chance to get together. You know we got us some lives up here in the big city. Sometimes other priorities come before all this.* The two entered the living room of women and interrupted, *Ladies, this is Alex.* The group gave warm welcomes, *Hi Alex! Heeey gurl! Come in sit down.* Alex was in awe of all of the beautiful brown faces in the room, representing a spectrum of identities and experiences. She didn't think this many Women of Color would be at UMA, and found herself pleasantly surprised.

As Alex surveyed the room, she noted young children, teenagers, toddlers, and even one newborn winning the affection of all the sistahs. Alex also recognized some faculty in the room, including Dr. Lewis and two other scholars she was hoping to meet, Dr. Kay and Dr. Griffiths. She instantly felt like she was at a family reunion. Monica, another second-year doctoral student, approached Alex with a warm hug. *Welcome, Alex, I was just in the middle of a story, I'll continue in a second, but I wanted to let you know I am so happy you are on the campus "in the city" with these scholar sistahs, because the white folks take over "down south" . . . on a regular basis!*

Alex had heard that the program, which enrolled students and functioned on two different campuses, felt different in each space. Namely, the cohorts were much more diverse, racially and otherwise, on the urban campus. In response to Monica, Alex nervously chuckled and turned her attention to Monica, who began to continue her story. *As I was saying, there was one particular instance where a white woman in my cohort approached me after class, the one where I am the only brown body of 20 or so whites, to talk about how she felt that there was racial divide between white and Black students in our cohort and that she did not want to be seen as a racist. Her comments were subtle, but also aggravating and problematic.*

Bianca interjected, *"Racial divide" really?*

Monica continued, *As soon as I got back to my office and took a minute to think about what she said to me I immediately wrote an e-mail to the Women of Color in my program. For the rest of the afternoon we exchanged e-mails about the overwhelming racist and sexist foolishness and all-around disregard we feel from our white peers in the program and the academy in general. The e-mails were very cathartic. They helped me process and release some of the frustration I had. We confirmed for each other that we are not going crazy. We aren't the only ones. We're just in the minority and so we're made to feel that we are going crazy simply because our narratives are hidden by the dominant white narrative.*

Monica was obviously upset in telling this story as she reflected on her experiences being marginally accepted by the white members of the program. Someone asked her about the rest of her first year and she recalled, *The first year at UMA was not bad; at least I thought it was not while going through it. Hoowevvver,* (she says real slow for effect, and sits back on the couch) *when I look back on that year, it's clear it may have been the most harmful to my psyche and to my identity as a woman of color scholar trying to deconstruct systems of white supremacy.*

Patriarchy! Jewel exclaimed.

Homogeneity! Bianca chimed in.

Monica continued, *Yes. And yes. I remember it being an odd sort of beginning because the white students were always in my face. Asking me why I did not hang out with them. Something about it just didn't feel genuine. It seemed borderline obsessive and intrusive. Later, I came to find out there was a reason they wanted me to be around . . . to assuage some white guilt.*

Anyway, when I did decide to hang out with them I would experience the most destabilizing microaggressions. "I don't see color . . . though I know I'm supposed to or something according to you." "I want my little babies to look like you . . . and they probably will because I'll most likely marry a Black man" relayed a white woman. And this one annoys me most, when I made any move or success that was before or perhaps better than a white person's I was questioned. Like, "How did you write that so fast?" "How did you get that grant?" "Why do you need to be ahead of everyone?" As if there needed to be an explanation for my drive and intelligence.

Bianca interjected abruptly. *Hold up, hold up y'all! Monica's story of what I'll call intellectual condescension, by these white peers really hits home. That sounds like some mess that Kyle, one of the white men in our cohort, would say. Listen, one day, I got to class a little early. As I sat waiting for class to start, two white guys, Cody and Kyle, were talking. Cody asked Kyle about the requirements for our literature review assignment. Kyle responded with, "Oh I'm not sure. Ask Bianca I'm sure she knows; she's the smart one!" I quickly gave Kyle a look of confusion, then chose not to respond to his comment . . .*

Bianca took a hesitant pause and continued, *Later we had to divide into groups to do an exercise about proper citation. As we were making our groups, Kyle remarked, "I want to be in Bianca's group, she's smart!" I took note of his second microinsult, and continued to ignore him. Once class finished I packed up my bag as other students began to talk. As I headed out Kyle took that opportunity to say, "Well I'm sure Bianca has her presentation all together because . . ." I cut him off before he could finish and said, Because I'm smart? Yes, I am smart. Thank you for the compliment. Y'all have a good night. Furious, I picked up my bag and left. Ya know, why is it white folks in our program feel compelled to comment on the intelligence of people of color? It's as if they expected me to be an idiot, so not meeting their expectations, they had to call out as the abnormality—the woman of color who actually has some smarts.*

The room of women erupted into laughter. *Why am I not surprised?* Jewel said while laughing. *I hated being in class with him and the others who clearly could not understand, nor cared about our experiences as Women of Color in the academy are. Bianca, do you remember when Cody asked a friend of ours why the Black women in the cohort were so angry?*

Alex interrupted, *"Black women?" So, he didn't have the nerve to call names?*

Bianca responded, *That's because we're the only ones in the cohort!*

The room filled with laughter and affirming nods signaling the other women understood the common scenario of Women of Color being misunderstood, pejoratively categorized, and then questioned about their very existence, and of course their intelligence. As the room settled, Jewel continued with a more serious tone, *You know something? At times, dealing with the white faculty can also result in the same inconsiderate racist behavior.*

Monica whispered, *Racism from students and faculty? Now that sounds like a recipe for serious racial battle fatigue!*

Jewel continued, *When they teach classes, you have to go in with your armor on every week! One semester, John Davidson had Women of Color in his class, and he didn't bother to learn to tell us apart. Even though we couldn't look more different from each other! Please believe racial battle fatigue was real.*

Monica asked, *Jewel what about when you took that class with Dr. Richards?*

Bianca answered, *That man is easily the most arrogant, condescending . . .*

Jewel responded with slow, deliberate speech as if she were reliving the incident again. She recounted, *His exact words on feedback on one of my papers was, "You really need to stop over reaching on language. Using big words actually detracts from the value of what you are saying and makes it seem like you are trying to seem smart without being smart."*

Alex interjected, *Help me Lord! What am I getting into?*

Jewel, now more animated continued . . . *oh that's not all he said, he continued with "You are smart so do what smart people do, use the simplest language possible to communicate clearly." I don't know what pissed me off more, his condescending tone, his assumption that I don't use "big words" in my everyday vernacular, or his pompous presumption that I give a damn about his pseudovalidation of my intelligence. Looking back, I find it interesting that he failed to make mention of word use in a paper I coauthored with a white classmate. And I word-smithed that paper alone!*

Jewel finished her story, *it's a shame we have to deal with this type of thing from faculty who claim to be so supportive of our research.* Jewel, now looking in Alex's direction and realizing how scary it may be for her to hear about the realities of racism in the program on her first visit to Sister Circle, says, *Girl, I'm so rude! Alex, I'm glad you got to join us today. We've all been looking forward to meeting you. I've heard a lot about you, now that you have heard us vent, tell us how your transition has been.*

No worries, this has been great, Alex replied, *My previous institution also had faculty who were less than warm towards me, and other Women of Color doctoral students. Since we're sharing stories, perhaps you all can help me understand this interaction I had with Dr. Carr, a full professor, white woman. One morning I was heating up my breakfast when this Dr. Carr walked in to get coffee. She and I shared the usual morning pleasantries, that is until I said, I'm heating up my breakfast. The rest of the exchange went something like this, "Breakfast?! It's a little late for breakfast isn't it? I've been up since 6 a.m. Idle hands." I was shocked and offended. First of all, what time I eat has nothing to do with anything other than when I feel like eating. The snide comment and implication that I had "idle hands" is a Christian reference that connotes that idle hands are the devil's playground. The implication was not only hurtful, as I identify as a Christian woman, but also blatantly racist and stereotoytpical. She knew I worked as a TA on the floor. How did Dr. Carr get the impression that I was idle? I thought perhaps I was just overreacting, until she did it again.*

Uh Oh, Monica murmured.

Alex continued, *One day, after class, I was sitting at my cubicle on the department floor discussing with two white colleagues. Suddenly, out of nowhere Dr. Carr enters. She leans over the cubicle, looks directly at me and only me, and says, "I can hear you all the way in my office and I'm trying to work. Perhaps you should take this discussion elsewhere."*

Jewel and Bianca shouted, *No she did NOT!* And the room breaks out in laughter.

Alex finished, *She didn't even address the two white students. I was stunned. I wasn't talking, who she heard were my white colleagues. Why did she choose to only address me (the Black student) and ignore the two white students who she saw talking as she approached the desk? My question is why was Dr. Carr intent on silencing me and making me feel like an outsider? I was just so hurt, angry, and overall tired.*

Dr. Kay chimed in, *Well, that's understandable Alex. Over time the result of these microaggressions you all are describing requires you to spend time, energy, and emotions unpacking the experiences and convincing yourself and each other that you are not the problem. Racism and white supremacy and patriarchy, amongst others, are the problems.*

Alex responded, *It's a tough place to negotiate. One moment I'm trying to study and dismantle this stuff in the academy and the next moment my very existence in doing so reveals the myriad ways white supremacy and racism work to invalidate my experience. But what I'm really interested in knowing is how you all are coping with these experiences here at UMA.*

Well, I can tell you how I coped, Monica offered. *I coped by shutting down. I completely isolated myself from the situation, from the white people in the program, regardless of how they treated me—because in the end, they had strength and privilege in numbers. In my eyes they were all a product and contributor to the same system. And they would never give up their privileges to support me and be associated with me.*

Bianca, *Wow. It must be lonely to isolate yourself to maintain your sanity in an all-white environment.*

Monica continued, *Yeah. I went into spaces when I knew they, the whole gang, would not be around. I started driving the hour to the city to be in our virtual classrooms with other Women of Color. Ironically, when I did run into white students down south they would ask me "what's wrong with you?" I thought it interesting, privileging, that they could pretend that something was wrong with me and my reaction to racism. As if they were not a part of the problem. I was the one who was crazy. I was the one that was being overly sensitive to their micro- and macroaggressions. When I could not isolate myself, when I had to sit in meet- ings or class with these people I coped by reaching out to my "scholar sisters" most of whom were hours away.*

Monica finished with tears in her eyes, *I am so very thankful for the brown women in this room who support me in becoming my best self, personally and professionally. Thank you.*

Bianca responded, *Girl. We got you. I coped by venting to my sister scholars too, as well as to my father and my husband about the incidents. This group of women is my support system and my counterspace. I can go to one or all of you when I experience these kinds of racial microaggressions. Also, if I didn't have a great advisor/mentor of color, I would have lost it!*

Jewel also added her experiences with her microaggressions and how her advisor/mentor helped her cope, *One day, I'd reached my limits with the white privilege and close-mindedness I was forced to deal with, weekly. I was tired of white students projecting their insecurities onto me, cloaked in microaggressive comments like, "Wow, the Women of Color in our program seem to really have their act together"; this was a comment received from a white woman the day we shared our progress on our dissertations.*

After class, I called Dr. Griffiths and she told me to just pick my battles. Don't offer feedback to those who won't appreciate it. Just don't say anything, to pro- tect your own peace of mind. So that is how I coped. I talked to my advisor and learned to tune out my classmates. Although I find it sad and alarming that our white classmates, who strive to be faculty and leaders in higher education are so close-minded and refuse to learn about the experiences of marginalized people, I've learned that it is not my issue. You can't get through to everybody.

I share this story, because despite what white colleagues and faculty think we must remember that we do have our acts together. And I f you can't remember, reach out to our Sister Circle.

The room was nearly still for a few moments before Dr. Kay, who had been silent until this point, spoke up and shifted the mood. *This is why I am so happy that this group has organically formed. This is loving and powerful relationship-building at work. You are beautiful brown women! I am so pleased to know you are supporting and caring for each other in real and authentic ways. Don't hesitate to let me know when I can be supportive. From the bottom of my heart, I deeply appreciate each and every one of you.*

The group continued sharing stories and giving advice about how to negotiate the persistent racist and sexist attitudes and behaviors of both classmates and faculty. After a couple of hours the group began to slowly leave and head back to home, work, and the busy lives they lead as doctoral students, wives, teachers, daughters, and so on. After many of the women left, Bianca, Jewel, and Monica cleaned up and chatted about how cathartic Sister Circle had been.

Bianca, *I'm so glad we've still got this going.*

Jewel, *Indeed, and I'm also glad Alex joined us. I think she needed to know she wouldn't be alone here.*

Monica, *Yeah, these stories are always so empowering and encouraging. They keep me focused on the goal. You know something else, we should write about all of this some day. It could be great for us, but maybe it is a way to actually get through to someone . . .*

Bianca and Jewel, *Indeed.*

DISCUSSION AND IMPLICATIONS

The racialized experiences of four Women of Color doctoral students and the ways in which they cope with RMAs while enrolled at a PWI are captured in the above narrative. These women encountered microinvalidations, microassaults, and microinsults regularly. One of the most common microaggressions encountered by these women was the questioning of their intelligence. White peers and faculty often drew attention to and questioned their academic abilities asking, "How did you get this far this fast?" and stating, "Wow, all the Women of Color seem to have their stuff together!" These microinsults expose the dominant ideology and stereotypes rife in the academy. The mere presence of these Women of Color in an academy built for white men destabilizes the status quo and disrupts the dominant narrative that Women of Color are unintelligent.

The RMAs detailed in our narrative elucidate the endemic nature of racism that complicates efforts to address and redress the racist acts that become normal and commonplace in the academy. The embeddedness of racism also complicates attempts to point out and/or explain RMAs to those that perpetrate them. As a result, Women of Color question their own sanity. For instance, Alex asked herself is *she* was the one going crazy after she experienced RMAs. White peers asked another woman what was wrong with *her* when she began to cope via isolation.

CRF enhances our understanding of this narrative and exposes interlocking systems of oppression that extend beyond racism. For instance, the intersections of patriarchy and whiteness are exposed when examining the comment "Why [are] the Black women in the cohort angry?" This questioning, by a white male, reinforces controlling images that white society has created to racialize and define Women of Color (Collins, 2009). The "angry Black woman" is one such controlling image. Moreover, this statement essentializes our experiences in the academy. The white male assumed that all the Women of Color in the cohort identified as Black (not true), and that all of them were angry. This essentialism silences and makes invisible the intricacies of our lives and experiences, relegating us to the margins of the academy.

The way in which we coped with our dehumanizing experiences were manifold. Our coping mechanisms aligned with Truong and Museus' (2012) model of internal, controlled, and external coping styles. Internally, we utilized one another, family members, and community members to handle with the deleterious experiences we faced encountered. We wrote e-mails to one another, participated in Sister Circles, vented to our partners, and leaned on our advisors/mentors. Controlled responses included isolation from students and faculty that harmed us, avoiding spaces certain colleagues frequented, and removing ourselves from toxic environments (i.e., the classroom). Externally, we respond with our research and scholarship. CRT and CRF call for a focus on the voices of Students of Color so that they may gain visibility in an academy that does not often see them.

There is no doubt that RMAs and the impact they have on Women of Color pursuing terminal degrees is damaging. The structures that give rise to this racism must be addressed in order to support and ensure the success of these students. More Women of Color must be recruited and retained in the academy. While we four have found a counterspace, Sister Circle, in which we may cope and care for one another, our experiences are unique to the many Women of Color who remain "the only one" in their cohorts and programs. In order to feel visible and heard, there must be a stronger representation of Women of Color in the academy. This representation not only rewrites the dominant narrative that the academy is made of and for white men, but it also allows for the increase of female professors of color.

Recruitment and retention through counterspaces is only the beginning of what institutions, administrators, and faculty can do to support Women of Color through doctoral journeys. There must be a systemic commitment to the well-being of these women who currently exist on the margins. Moreover, white students and faculty must be held accountable for the microaggressions they commit. Ignorance can no longer be an excuse. Therefore, it is critical for institutions to address the dominant culture of whiteness and patriarchy that is the lifeblood to many institutions. Curriculum and pedagogy are important places to start when rooting out this culture and subsequently racism and sexism. Pedagogy and curriculum must move away from the white norms of the academy toward a more inclusive environment that supports success for those not in the majority and allows for a rearticulation of knowledge that actualizes and affirms all experiences and identities (Ladson-Billings, 1995). It is only when our voices, and those of every other Woman of Color in the academy, are accounted for and heard that we will fully succeed and soar in the academy and beyond.

REFERENCES

Collins, P. H. (2009). *Black feminist thought: Knowledge, consciousness and the politics of empowerment*. (2nd ed.) London, UK: Routledge.

Felder, P. P., & Barker, M. J. (2013). Extending Bell's concept of interest convergence: A framework for understanding the African American doctoral student experience. *International Journal of Doctoral Studies, 8*, 1–20.

Gildersleeve, R. E., Croom, N. N., & Vasquez, P. L. (2011). "Am I going crazy?!" A critical race analysis of doctoral education. *Equity and Excellence in Education, 44*(1), 93–114.

Ingram, T. N. (2013). Fighting F.A.I.R. (feelings of alienation, isolation, and racism): Using critical race theory to deconstruct the experiences of African American male doctoral students. *Journal of Progressive Policy and Practice, 1*(1), 1–18.

Ladson-Billings, G. (1995). Toward a theory of culturally relevant pedagogy. *American Educational Research Journal, 32*(3), 465–491.

Ladson-Billings, G., & Tate, W. G. (1995). Toward a critical race theory of education. *Teachers College Record, 97*(1), 47–68.

Patton, L. D., & Catching, C. (2009). "Teaching while black": Narratives of African American students affairs faculty. *International Journal of Qualitative Studies, 22*(6), 713–728.

Pierce, C. M. (1969). Is bigotry the basis of the medical problems of the ghetto? In J. C. Norman (Ed.), *Medicine in the ghetto* (pp. 301–312). New York, NY: Meredith.

Pierce, C. M., Carew, J., Pierce-Gonzalez, D., & Willis, D. (1978). An experiment in racism: TV commercials. In C. Pierce (Ed.), *Television and education* (pp. 62–88). Beverly Hills, CA: Sage.

Smith, W. A., Allen, W. R., & Danley, L. L. (2007). "Assume the position . . . you fit the description": Psychosocial experiences and racial battle fatigue among African American male college students. *American Behavioral Scientist, 51*(4), 551–578.

Solorzano, D. G. (1998). Critical race theory, race and gender microaggressions, and the experience of Chicana and Chicano scholars. *International Journal of Qualitative Studies in Education, 11*(1), 121–136.

Solorzano, D. G., & Yosso, T. J. (2002). Critical race methodology: Counter-storytelling as an analytical framework for education research. *Qualitative Inquiry, 8*(1), 23–44.

Sue, D. W., Capodilupo, C. M., Torino, G. C., Bucceri, J. M., Holder, A. M. B., Nadal, K. L., & Esquilin, M. (2007). Racial microaggressions in everyday life: Implications for clinical practice. *American Psychologist, 62*, 271–286.

Truong, K. A., & Museus, S. D. (2012). Responding to racism and racial trauma in doctoral study: An inventory for coping and mediating relationships. *Harvard Educational Review, 82*(2), 226–255.

Williams, J. L., & Nichols, T. M. (2012). Black women's experiences with racial microaggressions in college: Making meaning at the crossroads of race and gender. In C. R. Chambers & R. V. Sharpe (Eds.), *Diversity in higher education, volume 12: Black American female undergraduates on campus: Success and challenges* (pp. 75–96). New York, NY: Emerald Group.

Wing, A. K. (2003). Introduction. In A. K. Wing (Ed.), *Critical race feminism: A reader* (pp. 1–19). New York, NY: New York University Press.

Yosso, T. J. (2006). Critical race counterstories across the Chicana/Chicano educational pipeline. New York, NY: Routledge.

Chapter 10

"Black Sheep" in the Ivory Tower: Academics of Color Explore Racial Battle Fatigue and Microaggressions in "Postracial America"

Crystal Shelby-Caffey, Lavern Byfield, and Edwin Úbeda

Elementary teachers filled an auditorium awaiting the guest speaker for the Migrant Council Conference. The director introduced the speaker as a faculty member at a major institution who would be sharing his expertise regarding English Learners and their families. From the moment the speaker took the stage, something was notably different. Through conversations, it was evident that his dark hair and olive skin caught the attention of teachers as they were accustomed to hearing from white presenters. He offered assurances regarding his qualifications and commonalities with the teachers. At one point, he exited the stage and walked through the crowd, where he gave the remainder of his presentation. This was peculiar as no other presenter had ever attempted to convince the teachers that: (a) they were qualified to present on the topic, and (b) they were "one of them." The presenter was Dr. Martinez (a pseudonym), a Mexican American associate professor, and the oddities within his delivery served as a prologue to a subsequent encounter. It was during a conference that conversation ensued between Dr. Martinez and two of the authors in which they exchanged stories of macro- and microaggressions. This discussion fueled reflection that signaled coherence in his seemingly odd lecture at the Migrant Conference. Not only were there uncanny intersections in our narratives, it became evident that, as academics of color, our lives were overloaded with emotional, psychological, and physical stressors triggered by the constant requirement to justify our presence in the cloistered white spaces of the ivory tower. Each instance of aggression elicits symptoms of racial battle fatigue (RBF) as the implications are that, as academics of color, we lack the requisite knowledge, skills, and capital regardless of our credentials.

INTRODUCTION

With the election of Barack Obama, many people are of the opinion that we are now in a postracial society. In multicultural classes, many students have declared that white privilege does not exist today. With this statement, the claim is made that the racial tensions of the 1960s are no longer evident in cross-cultural interactions and there is no preferential treatment of whites (Brown et al., 2003). However, with the continuous changing demographic landscape of the United States, many minority groups feel tensions as debates "which ought to involve thoughtful negotiation, turn[s] angry and acrimonious" (Lessow-Hurley, 2013, p. 1). Contrary to popular beliefs of a postracial society, the aggressions encountered by minorities, particularly those working in predominantly white institutions (PWIs), is still a matter of concern (Smith, Allen, & Danley, 2007; Solorzano, 1998, 2002).

DOES RACE STILL MATTER IN THE 21ST CENTURY?

Given the historical, sociopolitical, and cultural milieu of the United States, several scholars have articulated ways that racism emerges in contemporary society (Carter & Goodwin, 1994; Cowhey, 2006; Lessow-Hurley, 2013; McIntosh, 1998; Roberts, Bell, & Murphy, 2008; Rogers & Mosley, 2008; Rogers, Mosley, & Kramer, 2009; Smitherman, 2006). McIntosh (1998) alludes to the benefits of being white in a supposedly postracial society. She argues that oppression (gender or racial) is unconscious, and many individuals are oblivious to their unearned privileges. McIntosh (1990) further asserts that such mindful ignorance regarding privilege is perpetuated within white families and societal teachings.

The systemic nature of oblivion toward unearned privilege is evident in academia. Discussions about the realities of race in academia are seen as taboo while perceptions of unearned privileges of whites, such as the privileging of white interests over those of others, prevail (Harper &

Hurtado, 2007). College administrators (even those of color) concede an apprehension to intervene, as there is concern about the possibility of negative repercussions, mainly job loss (Harper & Hurtado, 2007). The reluctance to identify the unearned privilege of whites is even evident in how disparities that are attributable to racial factors that privilege whites are discussed in academic literature. Harper (2012) highlights the tendency for scholars to attribute such findings to anything other than race, even when it seems clear that "racism and racist institutional norms [are] plausible reasons for racial differences" (p. 9). Attempts of scholars and institutions to employ colorblind means of discussing race is consistent with Bonilla-Silva's (2003) claims that this practice permits Americans to disregard racial inequities. Within the United States, there is a tendency to acknowledge racial differences while ignoring and even rejecting the social ills that accompany those differences (Bell & Hartmann, 2007).

NARRATIVES AS AUTOETHNOGRAPHY

In this autoethnographic piece, we draw on critical race theory (CRT) to frame the discussion of microaggressions and RBF as we dispel the myth of a postracial society. Aligned with the traditions of CRT, we offer narratives or counterstories (Roberts et al., 2008) as a means to explore the experiences of three academics of color (African American, Jamaican, Latino). The use of narratives provides a platform for discussing the aggressions in terrains that are supposedly "colorblind" and highlighting systemic racism as is deeply ingrained within the ivory tower and rooted in American culture.

We bring varied yet conjoined experiences that illustrate the impact of RBF. Our narratives have been compiled over several years, and they collectively portray our lived experiences with microaggressions at PWIs and the resulting RBF. Our personal narratives are presented as interwoven vignettes and are intentionally masked without reference to the specific party involved. Autoethnography allows the prospect for each of us to be the vessels through which these particular narratives are shared and requires an element of "self-conscious reflexivity" (Ellis & Bochner, 1996) as we provide critical analysis. Further, we explore efforts that are currently underway in our classrooms and professional lives that, while serving to tap into social justice pedagogy, also fuels occurrences of microaggressions. Finally, we share the various strategies that we have used in efforts to minimize the effects of RBF.

CRT as a Lens for Reflection

On college campuses, there exist divergent views regarding affirmative action as scholars try to come to a consensus about providing equal opportunities for all regardless of race, nationality, language ability, sexual orientation, religion, and so on. There are those who assert that affirmative action levels the playing field, if there is any leveling after centuries of enslavement of Blacks, mistreatment, and displacement of Native Americans, and decades of Jim Crow laws. However, this leveling is controversial and may soon become an issue of the past (Garces, 2012; Harvey, 2005). CRT provides a lens through which the myth of a postracial America is deconstructed (Bell, 1987; Crenshaw, 1995; Delgado & Stefancic, 2013) along with the belief that race and color are irrelevant in the United States. CRT takes into account the intersection of race, power, and privilege as well as the impact of these on minorities in a predominantly white society with deep-seated racism.

The salience of race in discussions regarding African Americans who enter academia are well documented in the literature surrounding microaggressions and RBF (Smith, 2004). However, there is slight deception in the established and accepted explications of these phenomena; one that relegates their use solely to describing the experiences of African Americans while generally failing to reference other persons of color. The culture that cultivates inequity is a ubiquitous meme that is nourished by aggressions against the other; the other taking on various forms (race, sex, language ability, sexual orientation, religion, beliefs, etc.) depending on one's environment. In our experiences and those of colleagues at PWIs, microaggressions are commonly enacted on faculty and students of color regardless of race and nationality. While our discussion herein centers on microaggressions and RBF experienced by three academics of color who actively promote social justice pedagogy, we acknowledge that such instances are not limited to our respective groups. Through this cathartic process of sharing our stories, it is our intent to give voice and validation to each author and to provide insight that may prove beneficial to others with similar experiences.

DIVERGENT ACADEMICS, CONVERGENT NARRATIVES

Within circles of doctoral students, time spent interviewing for faculty positions is often lauded and applauded as yet another milestone that demarcates accomplishments of an already relatively small portion of society. Newly minted academics begin this process with a zeal for growing as scholars within their chosen field and contributing to the education of future generations. This is where reality diverges for academics of color. Our entry into academia is fraught with microaggressions that surface during the interview process and intensify once we have accepted our dream job. "No matter what, don't you ever let anyone here tell you that you were a 'minority hire!' You are qualified and you deserve to be here." This counsel was bestowed while one author interviewed for a position at a PWI. The context surrounding the statement was seemingly benevolent.

However, this minor insertion should have served as a premonition for what it would be like, as a person of color, to work at a PWI; the flashing light that serves to let a driver know that there is ice on the bridge; or the gate being lowered with bells whistling and lights flashing that warns of an oncoming train. Much like these drivers, many academics of color enter the ivory tower and find themselves at risk of sliding tragically across unfamiliar, tumultuous terrain or being hit head on at full speed with both aggressions from students, colleagues, and administrators.

There are tensions experienced by academics of color who study and work at PWIs. At either end of the spectrum, one attempts to find his/her way through a department of scholars and professionals with years of experience. Admittedly, there is an esteem and privilege that accompanies an advanced degree or securing a coveted faculty position. However, for academics of color, this privilege is jointly tied to marginalization, silencing, and invisibility. It is common for both students and faculty members of color to be ignored by colleagues or mistaken for support staff or a student athlete (Orelus, 2013).

THE MYTH OF A POSTRACIAL SOCIETY

Smith (2004) contends that white students are primed, through a process of socialization, to view African Americans and others in stereotypical ways. White positionality is viewed as transparently normative while other perspectives are simultaneously exoticised and undervalued. In accordance, conversations about the systemic nature of racism are suppressed and blame ascribed to minorities as white students and colleagues seek to preserve their position while basking in the normalcy of whiteness.

As teacher educators, with an interest in language instruction for culturally and linguistically diverse students, it has become more evident that many preservice and in-service teachers are of the opinion that race is no longer relevant in contemporary society. Our courses are specifically designed to sensitize teachers to the needs of diverse student populations, including language minority students. Such preparation demands that the teachers who take our courses draw on literature that subscribes to a critical stance and social justice framework. Materials are selected for the courses that bring awareness to the historical context of schooling within the United States as well as an examination of contemporary classrooms. Topics explored in the courses include pre-civil rights era education for language minority students, the impact of *Brown v. Board of Education,* and the changing landscape of education for traditionally underrepresented groups. Evidence of the effects of racial priming is noticeable when our students overtly and covertly refute the notion of accommodating learners from diverse backgrounds, discount the literature that supports native language instruction, and interact with us in ways that make their biases evident.

MATTERS OF RACE IN THE CLASSROOM

Students argue that it is rather uncomfortable engaging in conversations about race. An undergraduate who stopped by our office attested that race was relevant in the 1960s but today there is no need to talk about these issues. She later accused the instructor of giving her a "B" in the course because of her conversation, yet was unwilling to discuss her performance on a shoddily done final project. Another student explained how it was difficult to talk about topics related to race, which indeed it is; however, according to Watkins, Lewis, and Chou (2001), race is entangled with every sphere of life. Scholars (Hilliard, 1999; Wells et al., 2005) have argued that to ignore sociohistorical and sociocultural influences on students' lived experiences and differential achievement may further marginalize traditionally underrepresented groups. When faculty members of color must defend grading practices, provide a rationale for having students participate in a national event honoring African American authors, or are admonished that "teaching about English learners doesn't just include Spanish speakers," one begins to simultaneously see how enmeshed race is in our daily lives and how it is difficult for some students to broach race-based discussions.

Pittman (2012) found that faculty members of color reported experiencing both microinvalidations and microinsults when interacting with colleagues and students. We have encountered microinvalidations and microinsults that encompass students' uncertainty of our ability to select course materials or evaluate student work, as well as inquiries as to "what should we call you?" and queries from colleagues as to whether we "only read books about [a particular ethnicity]." We recount instances in which, as doctoral students, we were mistaken for an undergrad, a nontraditional student, someone working on a master's; anything but a doctoral student. Imagine for a moment one's surprise when one goes to sign his/her work agreement and on looking at the signed paperwork and seeing that the graduate student status is checked, the older white female responsible for preparing the contract hesitates for a moment and says, "Oh, you are a graduate student? You decided to return to work on your master's?" Slightly embarrassed and insulted, you aptly inform her that you are a doctoral student. In another instance, a school administrator accompanies a group of visiting international teachers as they tour a facility that you staff. You engage the visiting teachers in conversation about the program. During the first break in conversation, the administrator strategically positions him/herself as a barrier between you and the teachers. On another occasion, you decide to attend a departmental function though it is likely you will be the only person of color in attendance. While there, you strike up a conversation with a colleague. A senior faculty member takes a seat and proceeds to slide between you and the colleague with whom you were talking. With her back turned to you, the senior colleague introduces the other faculty member to guests while physically excluding you out of the conversation.

We have also discovered that though we are the instructor in charge of any given course, students challenge our authority. There is an assumption that our mostly white students are the experts in our respective field of study and that our credentials are insufficient qualifiers for our roles. The onus is then placed on us to "soften up" and "tell them about [our] qualifications and experience." When receiving such advice one cannot help but wonder if white colleagues, especially those endeared colleagues who rank lower than you, have ever been urged to do the same. The underlying assumption is that, in sharing our qualifications with students, we will somehow engender them to develop empathy and see us as human. Such faulty reasoning aligns with CRT's notion of empathic fallacy and shifts the attention from the aggressor to the faculty member of color who must master the art of self-promotion.

We maintain that Smith's (2004) conception of racial priming as well as the general dis-ease that accompanies race and culture based dialogue cuts across racial lines and manifests in a myriad of ways: students who rebuff engaging with multicultural literature; students levying complaints that portray their instructor as "harsh," "unfair," "difficult to understand" (though the instructor is native English-speaking), "unresponsive to students," and "unprepared"; undergraduates who request a meeting with a college administrator to implicate their instructor (a person of color) in possibly altering course evaluations before they had even been scored and then justifying their presuppositions by explaining that their concern stemmed from the fact that the instructor "was the only one left in the building and had access to the forms." We argue that Smith's proposition overlooks the implication of subliminal messages that all students receive about race and culture. These impact students of color in that they too are primed regarding expectations of and "appropriate" responses to colleagues and instructors from various races and cultures, including their own. It has been extremely disheartening and distressing when, at times, our primary aggressors have been students of color; their allegations were welcomed and encouraged by an administration that created an environment in which it was acceptable to deride faculty of color. Each time, administrators validated the students' perspective, thereby further perpetuating stereotypical ideology about persons of color.

LIVING AT AN INTERSECTION

Admittedly, there are times when it is unclear whether the mircroaggressions are due to race, gender, or a combination of the two. Stereotypical narratives persist about both sexes of our respective ethnicities.

Consider the following comments from a colleague that occurred just days after one of the authors made a request with another colleague for a later course time: "I'm tired of hearing students say they can't make it to class at 8:00 a.m. because they don't have a babysitter. I tell them to go to church and make friends (to babysit). This is the real world and real people have to be at work at 8 a.m." Should the victim take offense because the microaggression alludes to the stereotypical narrative that members of her ethnic group are lazy and don't want to work? Perhaps the real affront lies in the fact the victim requested the change in course schedule because of family responsibilities. It was unclear if this microaggression was due to the fact that the victim was female, or if it served to reify stereotypes about the victim's race.

The intersection of race, class, nationality, gender, and sexual orientation has the potential to further muddy any possible claims of discrimination as they make it difficult pinpoint the perpetrator's particular bias (Delgado & Stefancic, 2012). Imagine a female of color who, when standing before her students for the very first time, senses an overall tension in the air. Students' general apprehensions are eclipsed only by the indignation and vitriol revealed through the responses from white males. Despite the faculty member's attempts to connect with the students, the negative responses increase as the semester continues. Each response relays the message of "I'm not going to let her tell me what to do." It is unclear to the faculty member if the male students respond this way because she is female, a person of color, or a muddled combination of the two. This example illustrates the complexity that faculty members of color often face when they "operate at an intersection of recognized sites of oppression" (Delgado & Stefancic, 2012, p. 57).

THE NEUTRALITY OF EDUCATION

Discussions surrounding the importance of creating environments that are welcoming for all faculty, students, and families often reflect the white experience as many white educators cannot fathom instances in which colleagues, students, or families would feel unwelcome. Many also consider schools and the act of educating others as a neutral endeavor while disregarding the impact of social, cultural, and political variables. Somehow, the responsibility lies with the "others" to maintain the connection despite historical narratives that continue to undergird incidents involving persons of color. CRT holds that life events are markedly dissimilar for people of different races. Coupling this viewpoint with disparate perceptions of respective groups leads one to consider interest convergence, the assertion that "people believe what benefits them" (Delgado & Stefancic, 2012, p. 47). In each of the previous examples, there was something to be gained by the adoption of narratives that highlight the "otherness" of persons of color and by relegating our experiences to a comparison to white norms.

We argue that the inclination to defend and simultaneously understate the normalization of whiteness while subscribing to stereotypical views of minorities serves to underscore the salience of race in the 21st century. It is commonplace for white faculty to encourage a colleague of color to, "please, don't hesitate to tell me if I say or do something that's offensive, because I don't mean to be. I'm not racist. I'm just ignorant to some things." The same faculty members allow adopted stereotypical narratives to prevail and will collude with others in doubting and questioning colleagues of color when complaints are levied. It is clear that white colleagues' interests are served by reliance on stereotypical narratives when they query, "So, how do you prepare students for that assignment?" or an administrator approaches a graduate student to disclose, "I heard that you're having problems with your advisor and that you don't like working with her" or notifies you that "A parent called and said that you haven't been doing office hours." Acts such as these serve to reify stereotypes of "otherness" while reinforcing the normalcy of whiteness. That is, each illustration depicts faculty and students of color as unequipped to handle courses, lazy, antagonistic, and noncollegial while the tacit comparison is to knowledgeable, dependable, and collegial white colleagues.

THE IMPACT OF MICROAGGRESSIONS

Over time, there is a compounding effect of the macro- and microaggressions that one endures. When the physiological effects of RBF surface, one can feel as if they are suffering from posttraumatic stress disorder, yet such claims would seem baseless. You begin to wonder what implications your work life is having on your home life and your health. You have been working with your family doctor to reduce your intake of medications. But, each time your medications are reduced, an incident occurs at work that causes your doctor to increase the dosage. Though it seems that you are losing the battle to be medication free, you shrug it off and ignore the reality that your job is contributing to your illness. It becomes all too real when you go in for your annual eye exam and the ophthalmologist explains that the unusual curvature in the blood vessels behind one eye is of concern and requests that you see your family doctor as soon as possible. You agree, and leave the office planning to keep your regular appointment that is several weeks away. Even still, you are baffled when you get home and the ophthalmologist has left a message stating that she went ahead and booked your appointment to see your family doctor and an eye specialist the following day. During your visit with the specialist, she discloses the scary truth; she is concerned that you may lose vision in one eye due to a condition that can be stress induced.

You decide to share your health scare with a trusted colleague. But, you are hesitant because you wonder if s/he will be compassionate. As you openly reflect on multiple encounters that could have contributed, you can tell that this is all too unbelievable for your colleague. You realize, in mid-sentence, that it may be best to remain silent lest you seem paranoid and delusional. Who wants to appear mentally unstable among peers? Could colleagues sense that you were always waiting for the other shoe to drop? You can't help but wonder how often you were so consumed with "putting out all the little fires" so much that it affected your home life, your ability to be productive, or to sleep? Was it enough to redesign the courses each semester? Did you do or say something to set all of this in motion?

CONCLUSION

But if racism is embedded in our thought processes and social structures as deeply as many crits believe, then the "ordinary business" of society—the routines, practices, and institutions that we rely on to do the world's work—will keep minorities in subordinate positions. Only aggressive, color-conscious efforts to change the way things are will do much to ameliorate misery. (Delgado & Stefancic, 2012, p. 27)

We realize that our racial and ethnic identities combined with the marginalization of many academics of color at PWIs may impact our efforts in promoting social justice within our courses. However, in order to dismantle the status quo, the onus is on individuals, regardless of race, nationality, or creed to use various strategies to promote an inclusive environment and minimize the effects of RBF. Though we have chosen a steadfast approach of engaging our students and colleagues in discussions that examine systems that covertly and overtly marginalize and oppress "others," our efforts were largely met with aggressions that increased in severity and included damage to personal property. We must acknowledge that, consistent with Delgado and Stefancic's (2012) claim, small improvements tend to be overshadowed by deeply entrenched racism and major upheaval does more to disrupt oppressive structures. Drastic changes pierce the stagnancy that allows "isms" to thrive and afford opportunities for counternarratives to emerge.

Collectively, our experiences in the academy speak to the notion that, while on the one hand, racism and discrimination are conveyed through a "system of images, words, attitudes, unconscious feelings, scripts, and social teachings" (Delgado & Stefancic, 2012, p. 21), they nonetheless expose the legacies of a system that was never intended to embrace students nor faculty of color. Such inequities are deeply ingrained within society as a whole and are therefore replicated within every level of the educational system. In sharing our narratives, we have provided a window through which readers may view the lived experiences of three persons of color who have encountered microaggressions at PWIs. Each vignette provides a snapshot that debunks the myth of America as a postracial society and demonstrates the salience of race for students and faculty of color at PWIs, those of us who are made to feel like "black sheep" in the ivory tower.

REFERENCES

Bell, D. A. (1987). *And we are not saved : The elusive quest for racial justice.* New York, NY: Basic Books.

Bell, J. M., & Hartmann, D. (2007). Diversity in everyday discourse: The cultural ambiguities and consequences of "happy talk." *American Sociological Review, 72*(6), 895–914.

Bonilla-Silva, E. (2003). *Racism without racists: Color-blind racism and the persistence of racial inequality in the United States.* Lanham, MD: Rowman & Littlefield.

Brown, M. K., Carnoy, M., Currie, E., Duster, T., Oppenheimer, D. B., Schultz, M. M., et al. (2003). *Whitewashing race: The myth of a colorblind society.* Berkeley:, CA: University of California Press.

Carter, R., & Goodwin, A. L. (1994). Racial identity and education. *Review of Research in Education, 20,* 291–336.

Cowhey, M. (2006). *Black ants and Buddhists: Thinking critically and teaching differently in the primary grades.* Portland, ME: Stenhouse.

Crenshaw, K. (1995). *Critical race theory: The key writings that formed the movement.* New York, NY: New Press.

Delgado, R., & Stefancic, J. (2012). *Critical race theory: An introduction.* New York, NY: New York University Press.

Delgado, R., & Stefancic, J. (Eds.). (2013). *Critical race theory: The cutting edge* (3rd ed.). Philadelphia, PA: Temple University Press.

Ellis, C., & Bochner, A. P. (1996). *Composing ethnography: Alternative forms of qualitative writing.* Walnut Creek, CA: AltaMira.

Garces, L. M. (2012). The impact of affirmative action bans in graduate education. Los Angeles, CA: University of California, Los Angeles.

Harper, S. R. (2012). Race without racism: How higher education researchers minimize racist institutional norms. *Review of Higher Education, 36*(1), 9–29.

Harper, S. R., & Hurtado, S. (2007). Nine themes in campus racial climates and implications for institutional transformation. *New Directions for Student Services, 120,* 7–24.

Harvey, J. C. (2005). Affirmative action and equal opportunity for blacks in higher education and the University of Michigan cases. *Race, Gender & Class, 12*(3/4), 47–55.

Hilliard, A. (1999). What do we need to know now? "Race," identity, hegemony, and education. *Rethinking Schools, 14*(2), 4.

Lessow-Hurley, J. (2013). *The foundations of dual language instruction* (6th ed.). Boston, MA: Pearson.

McIntosh, P. (1990). White privilege: Unpacking the invisible knapsack. *Independent School, 49*(2), 31.

McIntosh, P. (1998). *White privilege and male privilege: A personal account of coming to see correspondences through work in women's study.* Wellesley, MA: Wellesley College Center for Research on Women.

Orelus, P. W. (2013). The institutional cost of being a professor of color: Unveiling microaggression, racial [in]visibility, and racial profiling through the lens of critical race theory. *Current Issues in Education, 16*(2), 1–10.

Pittman, C. T. (2012). Racial microaggressions: The narratives of African American faculty at a predominantly white university. *Journal of Negro Education, 81*(1), 82–92.

Roberts, R. A., Bell, L. A., & Murphy, B. (2008). Flipping the script: Analyzing youth talk about race and racism. *Anthropology & Education Quarterly, 39*(3), 334–354.

Rogers, R., & Mosley, M. (2008). A critical discourse analysis of racial literacy in teacher education. *Linguistics and Education: An International Research Journal, 19*(2), 107–131.

Rogers, R., Mosley, M., & Kramer, M. (2009). *Designing socially just learning communities: Critical literacy education across the lifespan.* New York, NY: Routledge.

Smith, W. A. (2004). Black faculty coping with racial battle fatigue: The campus racial climate in a post–civil rights era. In D. Cleveland (Ed.), *A long way to go: Conversations about race by African American faculty and graduate students at predominately white institutions* (pp. 171–190). New York, NY: Peter Lang.

Smith, W. A., Allen, W. R., & Danley, L. L. (2007). "Assume the position . . . You fit the description": Psychosocial experiences and racial battle fatigue among African American male college students. *American Behavioral Scientist, 51*(4), 551–578.

Smitherman, G. (2006). *Word from the mother: Language and African Americans.* New York, NY: Routledge.

Solorzano, D. (1998). Critical race theory, race and gender microaggressions, and the experience of Chicana and Chicano scholars. *International Journal of Qualitative Studies in Education (QSE), 11*(1), 121.

Solorzano, D. (2002). Keeping race in place: Racial microaggressions and campus racial climate at the University of California, Berkeley. *Chicano-Latino Law Review, 23*, 15.

Watkins, W. H., Lewis, J. H., & Chou, V. (Eds.). (2001). *Race and education: The roles of history and society in educating African American students.* Boston, MA: Allyn and Bacon.

Wells, A. S., Holme, J. J., Revilla, A. T., Atanda, A. K., Braddock, J., & Walker, V. S. (2005). How society failed school desegregation policy: Looking past the schools to understand them. *Review of Research in Education, 28*, 47–100.

Chapter 11

"They Shouldn't Get Any Credit for It!": Mexican American Studies, Mexican Heritage People, Racial Microaggressions, and Racial Battle Fatigue

Richard Orozco

In the course of conducting research for a manuscript, I was writing in 2011 concerning Arizona's HB 2281, the bill eventually resulting in the termination of Mexican American Studies (MAS) in the Tucson Unified School District (TUSD), and I came across many statements that caused within me great consternation. While none of the statements were directed at me, they were, nevertheless, antagonistic toward Mexican heritage people and impacted me as a Mexican American. Specifically, the statements produced feelings of anxiety and anger. The statements were made by those in Arizona's state government and by citizens of Arizona. Unfortunately, the consternation I felt in 2011 was not new. I felt similarly years before as a consequence of comparable statements made by colleagues during the years I taught high school MAS at a different district in Tucson. In all cases, whether during the process of researching for my manuscript or during my years teaching MAS, there was a rejection of the validity and importance of all that was MAS: the program itself, its teachers, and its students. This rejection and invalidation took the form of racial slights and verbal attacks referred to as *racial microaggressions* that were emotionally draining to me. As a result of these racial microaggressions, I felt stress and its consequence, *racial battle fatigue.*

Stressful is, perhaps, the best way to describe the work I attempted to do in a public high school for 15 years. To be sure, most teachers feel stress as a result of teaching. It is, after all, a position with a great many responsibilities and expectations. Yet, the antagonistic remarks to teaching courses that many colleagues and administrators reject as valid adds a layer of stress felt by few other teachers. This antagonism regarding the courses, unfortunately, also found its way toward me, individually, as well as the students who were in my courses. As I note above, these same antagonisms were played out on a larger scale when governmental leaders in the state of Arizona made MAS in TUSD the target of legislation. In this chapter, I attempt to link the actions and discourses I experienced in my work as a high school MAS teacher (micro-level discourse) with those that took place years later during both legislative and social debates, and during state activities regarding MAS (macro-level discourse). I then attempt to describe the racial battle fatigue I experienced as one invested greatly in MAS. This description includes two different forms of racial battle fatigue: chronic and acute. I then discuss efforts at dealing with racial battle fatigue. However, before describing my experiences any further, allow me to offer the context within which my experiences as a high school educator took place.

During my 15 years as a teacher, I taught social studies in an urban, segregated high school in Tucson, Arizona, located less than a one-hour drive from the U.S.-Mexican border. It was a school with a Mexican heritage student population consistently above 90 percent. As is the case with most segregated urban schools, the academic achievement rate at the school was low and the *push-out*[1] rate was high. While an overwhelming amount of the students were of Mexican heritage, nearly two-thirds of the faculty was white. Although the numerical discrepancy in the racial/ethnic make-up between students and teachers is important, it must be clear that the antagonistic discourses I experienced were not brought on solely by whites. Teachers of Mexican heritage also engaged in discourses that contributed to the racial battle fatigue I describe in this chapter. Thus, the experiences I share are not about white people, but about the discourses of whiteness that all people, including people of color, can and frequently do engage (Leonardo, 2002).

---

[1] I use *push-out* rather than dropout to reflect the role of schooling institutions in failing to serve Mexican heritage students.

RACIAL MICROAGGRESSIONS AND RACIAL BATTLE FATIGUE

The episodes I detail in this chapter are racial microaggressions. It is from these microaggressions that ultimately racial battle fatigue is created. Sue and colleagues (2007) describe racial microaggressions as "brief and commonplace daily verbal, behavioral, or environmental indignities, whether intentional or unintentional, that communicate hostile, derogatory, or negative racial slights and insults toward people of color" (p. 271). Specifically, racial microaggressions can occur in three different forms:

1. microinvalidations—exclusion or denial of a person of color's "thoughts, feelings, or experiential reality" (Sue, 2010, p. 29)
2. microassaults—verbal, nonverbal, or environmental attacks against ones race/ethnicity
3. microinsults—rude and insensitive communications that put down ones race/ethnicity

A consequence of racial microggressions, racial battle fatigue is "the physiological and psychological strain . . . and the amount of energy lost dedicated to coping with racial microaggressions" (Smith, Allen, & Danley, 2007, p. 555). Among the physiological symptoms of racial battle fatigue are headaches, elevated heart rate, upset stomach, and fatigue. The list of psychological symptoms includes anxiety, frustration, anger, and hopelessness. While I list these symptoms separately here, they are connected by their microaggressive source. I propose that racial battle fatigue has both chronic and acute dimensions. Ultimately, the cumulative effects of racial microaggressions and racial battle fatigue can work to adversely "affect the biological, emotional, cognitive, and behavioral well-being of marginalized groups" (Sue, 2010, p. 106). Unfortunately, attempts by people of color to call attention to racial microaggressions and their consequences are often silenced with "you're just playing the race card," or "you need to not be so sensitive," and "just get over it" as common replies. There is a discounting of the narrative of the oppressions experienced by people of color. As Sue (2010) explains, "When the oppressed are not allowed to express their thoughts and outrage, when their concerns are minimized, and when they are punished for expressing ideas at odds with the dominant group, their voices are effectively silenced" (p. 112). In such instances, dominant groups attempt to exercise greater power and authority over racial realities. The racial realities of people of color are invalidated and their integrity assailed (Sue, 2013). This chapter, then, is my attempt to highlight oppressive discourses and their effects on me. Some discourses were directed at me; others were not. Yet all were racial microaggressions that resulted in my own racial battle fatigue. Before describing specific racial microaggressive discourses I have encountered,

I briefly review Arizona's activities aimed at eliminating MAS as a course of study in K–12 schools.

GOVERNMENTAL ACTIVITY AGAINST MAS IN ARIZONA

Initial calls for the dismantling of MAS started in 2007 with a letter written to the citizens of Tucson by then Superintendent of Public Instruction (SPI), Tom Horne. In the letter, after describing MAS as divisive, hostile, and ethnically chauvinistic (Orozco, 2011), Horne (2007) implores the citizens of Tucson to vote out of office TUSD school board members who supported MAS in their district. However, despite Horne's pleas, not only were TUSD board members kept in place, MAS was expanded. In response, Horne obtained the assistance of law makers in the writing of legislation that would effectively end MAS in TUSD. The initial bill aimed at eliminating MAS, Arizona SB 1108, died before going to a vote in 2009. Likewise, a second iteration, SB 1069, also never made it to a vote. Finally, HB 2281 was written, voted on, passed, and signed into law in 2010. While the law did not explicitly call for an end to MAS, both Horne and the author of the bill, Steve Montenegro, discussed at length during legislative debates that the target of the legislation was TUSD's MAS. Included in the law's prohibitions were courses that:

- promote the overthrow of the United States government
- promote resentment toward a race or class of people
- are designed primarily for pupils of a particular ethnic group
- advocate ethnic solidarity instead of the treatment of pupils as individuals

To secure the demise of MAS, the new law allowed the state board of education and the SPI to determine whether or not any K–12 course in Arizona was in violation. Predictably and in spite of findings by a neutral auditing team, in 2011, new SPI and Horne colleague, John Huppenthal, deemed TUSDs MAS in violation of the law and ordered dismantling of MAS under threat of the district losing its state funding. In January 2012, some five years after Tom Horne's open letter to the citizens of Tucson, TUSD dismantled MAS.

RACIAL MICROAGGRESSIVE DISCOURSES

Discourses I describe here took place at different times and often by different people. Despite these differentiations, the discourses all engaged in some form of racial microaggression. In the field of linguistics, this similarity of content across a variety of times and persons is part of the notion of *intertextuality*; the idea that "one spoken or written text alludes to, quotes, or otherwise relates to, another one" (Gee, 2005, p. 21). The importance of intertextuality is that it is a mechanism "whereby discourses have an effect on individuals as social subjects" (Mills, 2004, p. 137). Thus, I present racial microaggressive discourses that were (1) directed at either me, my students, or our class during my time teaching high school MAS from 1995 to 2009; (2) made during state activities concerning MAS (its teachers and students, as well as the program itself) in Arizona from 2007 to 2010; and (3) published in newspaper accounts of the MAS controversy starting in 2007. The attacks I describe below (in italics) crossed lines from a more localized, micro-level (at the high school where I taught) to a larger macro-level (legislative debates, community responses to newspaper stories) microaggressive discourse and are primarily divided by the type of microaggression (microinvalidation, microassault, microinsult).

MICROINVALIDATION AT THE MICRO-LEVEL (THE HIGH SCHOOL)

After the Social Studies Department meeting adjourned, a colleague asked me to give her a description of the content of the Introduction to MAS course I was teaching as an elective. I described the course as a historical survey that spanned from pre-Columbian Mexico to present analyses of the Chicana/o experience in the United States. She then asked if it was a history class. I responded that it was historical but also included contemporary social analyses. To this she declared, "Well, whatever the content, they shouldn't get any credit for it!"

In this situation, my colleague invalidates MAS as a course worthy of credit. Her dismissal of the course content is an invalidation of the study of the history and social experiences of Mexican Americans.

A student who had completed a course of study in MAS agitatedly came into my classroom and restlessly proclaimed, "I am so mad! I need to talk to you!" Her angry tone caught me somewhat by surprise because of her usual jovial disposition. "My English teacher assigned us a paper. We need to write a biography about a civil rights leader. We had to let him know which leader we chose to write about. I told him mine is about 'Corky' Gonzalez and he told me I had to pick a real civil rights leader or that he wouldn't accept it! I told him who 'Corky' was and he asked where I learned about him. I told him in Mexican American Studies, but he said that choosing 'Corky' doesn't count because he doesn't know what's taught in the class. I can't believe he said that! I'm so mad! I don't know if I want to do the assignment."

The English teacher's unfamiliarity with Mexican American civil rights leaders resulted in the invalidation not just of Rodolfo "Corky" Gonzalez, the civil rights leader himself, but also in the invalidation of the MAS coursework wherein the student learned of him. Unfortunately, this racial microaggression resulted not only in my racial battle fatigue, but likewise for the student as expressed by her sense of anger.

MICROINVALIDATION AT THE MACRO-LEVEL (STATE ACTIVITY)

In legislative hearings for SB 1069 in 2009, Arizona State Senator Ken Cheuvront and SPI Tom Horne engaged in the following regarding the bill's prohibition of courses designed primarily for pupils of a particular ethnic group:

Cheuvront: Say we have Western Civilization, we learn about Greek and Roman history. That, to me, if there was a course just based on Western Civilization, would also be prohibited from being taught because that is one ethnic group.

Horne: It would not be prohibited under the language of this bill because it would not be aimed at the students of a particular ethnic group. The teachings of the Greeks are universal for all of us.

Horne's response that teaching of "the Greeks" is "universal" and allowable as a course of study in school, while teachings of Mexican Americans is not invalidates the historical contributions of Mexican Americans as legitimate academic content.

MICROINVALIDATION AT THE MACRO-LEVEL (COMMUNITY RESPONSE)

As a response to an article in Tucson's newspaper regarding the signing into law of Arizona HB 2281, the following was posted as a comment: "If the culture of one's ethnicity is so important to an individual(s) [sic], then it should be taught at home by the parents or extended family. History is what should be taught at school." (Howard Fischer Capitol Media Services, 2010)

In these comments, Mexican American history, as part of Mexican American culture as well as the larger U.S. cultural make-up, is invalidated as a topic worthy of study in schools. Indeed, the commenter alludes that the history of Mexican Americans be exempted from any academic study in history courses.

MICROASSAULT AT THE MICRO-LEVEL (THE HIGH SCHOOL)

Over several years, students in my MAS classes had painted murals on the walls of the classroom where I taught for 14 of my 15 years. Depictions on the murals included images of Mexican and Mexican American icons. In my final year, I was assigned to a different room. On the first day of that final year, I stepped into what had previously been my classroom and immediately noticed the murals had been whitewashed over. I soon understood that the new teacher in the room had done this. In explaining his reason for doing so, he stated, "I'm not into murals." My response was that it was student work and they deserved to be consulted, to which he replied, "Not everyone is into it. Not every student here is a Chicano and the murals just weren't that important. The murals didn't represent what these kids should be about."

This teacher, a Mexican American, who painted over the student murals in the classroom engaged in a microassault in the form of an environmental attack against Mexican heritage representations. This microassault is compounded by his comment regarding the Mexican icons not being "what these kids should be about."

MICROASSAULT AT THE MACRO-LEVEL (STATE ACTIVITY)

In his "An Open Letter to the Citizens of Tucson," SPI Horne (2007) writes the following about the behavior of students and teachers in the MAS program whom he throughout the letter makes clear are Mexican American: "I've never seen students act rudely and in defiance of authority, except in this one unhappy case. I believe the students did not learn this rudeness at home, but from their Raza teachers." Then, later in the same letter, Horne remarks that the students "are creating a hostile atmosphere in the school for the other students, who were not born into their 'race.'"

Because Horne indubitably refers to Mexican Americans as the teachers and students in the MAS program, they become the subjects of his writing. Thus, the above passages are racial microassaults insofar as Mexican Americans are depicted wickedly (rude, hostile) in these comments (Orozco, 2012).

MICROASSAULT AT THE MACRO-LEVEL (COMMUNITY RESPONSE)

In December 2011, an administrative law judge upheld the SPIs decision that TUSDs MAS program violated HB 2281 and that grounds existed for the state to withhold funding to the district. In public response to a

Tucson newspaper article regarding the decision, the following comments were made:

"There should not be ethnic studies of any kind . . . You don't like what we teach here than [sic] go back to where you came from or where your family came from."

As a racial microassault, this comment attacks at once the MAS program and Mexican heritage people. In it, the commenter attaches MAS as a program of study to people deemed as un-American and unworthy of being present in the United States. The comment positions a nativist whiteness, or what "we teach here" versus a nonwhite, "ethnic studies of any kind."

MICROINSULTS AT THE MICRO-LEVEL (HIGH SCHOOL)

During a conversation with a Mexican American colleague who taught math, we discussed the academic achievement gap between Mexican Americans and their white peers in the context of mathematics. When referring to Mexican American students, this teacher remarked, "They don't get it, and they never will. They don't have what it takes." After challenging his claim as unfounded, he attempted clarification by stating, "No one in their families can help them. That's what they lack."

Despite the unsuccessful attempt to save face by describing familial deficiencies, itself a microaggression, the initial microinsult is this Mexican American math teacher's ironic perception that Mexican Americans lack capacity to perform mathematical tasks. This prejudicial position includes not just current capacities, but is extended by a second microinsult that prognosticates future failure due to some genetic deficiency since "no one in their families can help them."

MICROINSULT AT THE MACRO-LEVEL (STATE ACTIVITY)

John Huppenthal, then a member of the Arizona State Legislature, who later while running for SPI in Arizona proclaimed that he would put an end to "La Raza," visited a TUSD MAS class. In his comments regarding the Mexican American teacher of the class, Huppenthal states, "The teacher himself, he is . . . perfectly groomed. He's wearing a long-sleeve, white shirt. He's wearing a tie. So from that standpoint . . . he's presenting classic American values. Now again, was that on show for me?" (McGinnis & Palos, 2011)

Huppenthal's comments are revealed as microinsults through his use of both the *reciprocal determination* of nationality and race/ethnicity (Balibar, 2005) and as an *inference-triggering device* (Quasthoff, 1973; as cited in

Wodak & Reisigl, 1999). In the former, Huppenthal reciprocally invokes nationality (American) and ethnicity (white) by invoking a fictively unified national culture (whiteness) in his declaration that the teacher demonstrates "classic American values." This suggests that the Mexican American teacher is not really American or white, but simply "presenting" these arbitrarily determined *classic American values*. In the latter, the inference-triggering device is his question, "Now again, was that on show for me?" In this way, Huppenthal infers that the Mexican American teacher's appearance is not what is normally observed in Mexican Americans, but an exception made for his visit.

MICROINSULT AT THE MACRO-LEVEL (COMMUNITY RESPONSE)

From the same 2011 newspaper article described above wherein an administrative law judge upheld the SPIs decision that TUSDs MAS program violated HB 2281 and that grounds existed for the state to withhold funding to the district, the following response appeared: "You really don't need MAS anyway just have a current events class [sic]. Study the everyday events in Mexico. Murders, rapes, hangings from bridges, beheadings, etc. That should be enough cultural awareness for . . . La Raza."

Making reference to myths of crimes committed along the border in Mexico, this microinsult equates crime and criminality with Mexican culture. This characterization is one that has been used historically to describe Mexican Americans (Acuña, 2004) and has been the basis of discriminatory activity.

RACIAL BATTLE FATIGUE

In a line from the film *Separate but Equal* (Margulies & Stevens, 1991), Sidney Poitier, playing the role of NAACP attorney Thurgood Marshall and his work in the *Brown v. Board of Education* case, states the following after losing a lower court decision to end segregation and being subjected to negative racial discourse from a white man, "I get very weary trying to save the white man's soul." Besides demonstrating the commonplace rejection of those involved in the work of social justice, in this line, the effect of racial battle fatigue is clearly shared. It communicates the weariness that results when engaging in the strenuous mental activity of working for racial justice. However, weariness was not the only effect I felt from the racial microaggressions I share in this chapter. Weariness did not set in for me until after I experienced several other psychological and physiological effects. That is, the weariness I felt was the result of the extended psychological and physiological effects of the racial microaggressions. Most notably, in all of my encounters with racial microaggressions, I have felt the psychological responses of anxiety and anger. It is more the case that I feel anxiety with each microaggressive event I encounter. The anger I experience is more the result of the continued feelings of anxiety I must endure. Thus, I suffer anxiety during each microaggressive event with eventual anger setting in as a result of the anxiety. In any case, all of this is followed very soon by physiological signs such as heart palpitations and stomach upset. While these physiological signs are reduced with time, they present themselves again when the anxiety and anger associated with the next microaggression takes place.

In carefully considering both the psychological and physiological effects of racial microaggressions, the racial battle fatigue that results takes on two forms: acute and chronic. With each microaggression encountered there is a renewed sense of anxiety and the appearance of the symptoms I described previously. Depending on the microaggression, the symptoms can be more or less severe. That is, while all microaggressive events I experience create some anxiety, some events have greater impact than others. For example, those microaggressive events that are directed at me and about me personally create greater anxiety and anger. Still, with all racial microaggressions, whether or not they are personal, there is, without failure, the resultant appearance of psychological and physiological symptoms. Before long these symptoms diminish; the palpitations slow and the upset stomach settles. This transience is, therefore, characteristic of acute racial battle fatigue. However, the cumulative effects of racial microaggressions are longer lasting; they create a more chronic racial battle fatigue. By this I mean that, in this form, the symptoms persist. In chronic racial battle fatigue, a general weariness is experienced along with profound frustration. This chronic racial battle fatigue is obstinate, and there is no need for new racial microaggressions to reintroduce the weariness. While the weariness may become latent, it endures and is quite perceptible even in simple conversations about the work that I perform now.

ESCAPING RACIAL BATTLE FATIGUE

Attempts to deal with racial battle fatigue are difficult. Racial microaggressions often occur quicker than one can stop them; they are unveiled in an instant. Thus, the onset of acute racial battle fatigue is similarly sudden. Meanwhile, because of the persistent, deep-rooted nature of the chronic form of racial battle fatigue, its appearance is always imminent. Yet, most people involved in the project of attempting to create racial and social justice continue in their work in spite of racial battle fatigue. Why? Why would one continue this work and position oneself to deal with such discomforts? For me, there are two answers: (1) I can't stop, and (2) I don't want to stop. The former involves a response that is compelling; the latter, a response that is altruistic. Alleviation of the racial battle fatigue I have shared here has been suggested. The suggestion involves avoiding racial battle fatigue by just stopping my engagement with the racial and social justice work I started as a high school teacher. This proposition is futile since doing so would involve not just disregarding injustice, but not seeing it in the first place. Furthermore, not seeing injustice would require a dysconsciousness (King, 1991) characterized by "limited and distorted understandings" (p. 134) of racial and social injustice. In the context of this discussion, once one becomes *aware* of the workings of racial microaggressions as unjust activities, once its understanding is not limited and is clear, one cannot be *unaware* of them. This awareness is compelling in the sense that racial microaggressions and other forms of injustice cannot be controlled by voluntary cognitive blindness. It cannot be unseen. Thus, I can't stop being aware of them. Even if I or anyone could stop being aware of them, would there be a desire to do so? For me the answer is no because of the prospect of racial and social equity.

I have often stated to family and friends that I wonder if the work I do in trying to move racial/ethnic justice is ever going to make a difference. Such doubt is typical but transient and thus a symptom of acute racial battle fatigue. The doubt subsides and is replaced by new-found energy to continue. I find myself in this mental roller coaster of fatigue and energy; I am fatigued by the battles and energized by the prospect of racial and social equity. It is this energy that fuels a desire to continue the work. Here then, the work is altruistic. It continues based on a belief that the work is needed and will ultimately benefit all. Still, the work continues under caution because as this short-term doubt becomes recurrent and more profound, hopelessness, a symptom of chronic racial battle fatigue (Smith, Allen, & Danley, 2007), is periodically generated.

WORKING THROUGH ATTACKS ON MAS AND RACIAL BATTLE FATIGUE

In consideration of the negative comments that were made about MAS, the program itself, its teachers, and its students, there is little doubt that some of the commenters feel strongly about their positions. The conviction of their voices, lost in any written account, is strong. At the same time, however, there is quite a bit of other discourse that does not sound aggressive. Such discourses are more polite, but effectively deliver the same force. Perhaps this adds to the morbidity of microaggressive discourse and the racial battle fatigue it creates. Whether aggressive or not, it becomes clear to the victims that for the perpetrators of racial microaggressions, racial equity and equality are threatening. Yet, it is precisely this conviction to maintain unequal and inequitable racial arrangements by the architects of racial microaggressions that produces much of the energy to continue the work against such convictions.

Along with important academic reasons, the project of MAS was created to address the kind of social injustice characterized by inequality and inequity. It serves as a port through which analyses of social conditions can be taken up and through which solutions to inequities and injustices can be sent out. Opposition is certainly forthcoming to this project; history in Arizona and other places has made this evident. This opposition will include the use of racial microaggressions, and those involved in MAS or any other racial justice movement will experience racial battle fatigue. However, it is the common, everyday use of racial microaggressions and its accompanying racial battle fatigue that is a reminder that the work of Mexican American Studies and all other social and racial justice projects are necessary and need to continue.

REFERENCES

Acuña, R. (2004). *Occupied America: A history of Chicanos*. New York, NY: Pearson Longman.

Balibar, E. (2005). Racism and nationalism. In P. Spencer & H. Vollman (Eds.), *Nations and nationalism* (pp. 163–172). New Brunswick, NJ: Rutgers University Press.

Gee, J. (2005). *An introduction to discourse analysis: Theory and method* (2nd ed.). New York, NY: Routledge.

Horne, T. (2007, June 11). An open letter to the citizens of Tucson. Retrieved November 2, 2009, from http://nau.edu/uploadedFiles/Academic/CAL/Philosophy/Forms/An%20Open%20Letter%20to%20Citizens%20of%20Tucson.pdf

Howard Fischer Capitol Media Services. (2010, May 12). Brewer signs law on ethnic studies. *Arizona Daily Star*. Retrieved January 1, 2014, from http://azstarnet.com/news/local/education/precollegiate/article_10fb594b-cca6-5a3f-a65e-9689f1e963bb.html?mode=story

King, J. (1991). Dysconscious racism: Ideology, identity, and the miseducation of teachers. *The Journal of Negro Education, 60*(2), 133–146.

Leonardo, Z. (2002). The souls of white folk: Critical pedagogy, whiteness studies, and globalization discourse. *Race, Ethnicity, and Education, 5*(1), 29–50.

McGinnis, E. (Producer), & Palos, A. (Director). (2011). *Precious knowledge: Arizona's battle over ethnic studies* [Motion picture]. Available from www.dosvatos.com

Margulies, S., & Stevens, G. (Producers), & Stevens, G. (Director). (1991). *Separate but equal* [Motion picture]. United States: New Liberty Films.

Mills, S. (2004). *Discourse: The new critical idiom*. New York, NY: Routledge.

Orozco, R. (2011). "It is certainly strange . . .": Attacks on ethnic studies and whiteness as property. *Journal of Education Policy, 26*(6), 819–838.

Orozco, R. (2012). Racism and power: Arizona politicians' use of the discourse of anti- Americanism against Mexican American Studies. *Hispanic Journal of Behavioral Sciences, 34*(1), 43–60.

Smith, W., Allen, W., & Danley, L. (2007). "Assume the position . . . you fit the description": Psychosocial experiences and racial battle fatigue among African American male college students. *American Behavioral Scientist, 51*(4), 551–578.

Sue, D. (2010). *Microaggressions in everyday life: Race, gender, and sexual orientation.* Hoboken, NJ: Wiley.

Sue, D. (2013). Race talk: The psychology of racial dialogues. *American Psychologist, 68*(8), 663–672.

Sue, D., Capodilupo, C., Torino, G., Bucceri, J., Holder, A., Nadal, K., & Esquilin, M. (2007). Racial microaggressions in everyday life: Implications for clinical practice. *American Psychologist, 62*(4), 271–286.

Wodak, R., & Reisigl, M. (1999). Discourse and racism: European perspectives. *Annual Review of Anthropology, 28,* 175–199.

Chapter 12

Weathering Through: How a Doctoral Candidate with White Male Privilege Succumbed to Racial Battle Fatigue

Steven Funk

Prior to beginning my doctoral program, I had heard the horror stories about students who struggled to write dissertations while committee chairs took sabbaticals with little notice, leaving them in a state of academic limbo. Other students recalled how their committees argued endlessly with one another over minutiae and asked them repeatedly to rewrite entire chapters of their dissertations. This is not my story. This story is not even my own.

The adversity I faced while trying to write a dissertation was not directed at me, but at the populations whom I chose to study. Moreover, perceived among faculty as a white, heterosexual male, I was endowed with privileges many scholars cannot claim. I was keenly aware that I was seen as a member of the dominant group among faculty. Perhaps it is for this reason that I met resistance when I tried to design a study addressing LGBTQIA education at the medical school of an elite research university. Perhaps this is why, after abandoning that study and completing another, I was admonished to write my findings in such a way that they would buttress the university's claim to excellence in research and education for social justice. This story is about how I paradoxically benefited from white male privilege while succumbing to racial battle fatigue.

Navigating my way through a social science doctoral program at one of the nation's largest research universities, I felt as though I were on my way to becoming, as Anna Yezierska (2003) simply put it, "a person" (p. 66). Drunk on the nectar of everything the scientific method had to offer, I reveled at the prospect of conducting empirical research that cultivated equity in education. I no longer, however, say that I "earned" my doctorate; "navigated" is more appropriate, because rather than focusing on how to conduct research and scholarly inquiry within my field, I spent the bulk of my program predicting emotional weather patterns of faculty. I needed to forecast what topics and terms might initiate a storm among advisors or committee members. While earning my doctorate, I learned more about the pitfalls of meritocracy (Yosso et al., 2004; Brennan & Naidoo, 2008) than I did about my own discipline. It was not so much hard work that earned me more initials behind my last name as it was a willingness to abide by unwritten rules. My graduation was more of a celebration at having sailed through the waters of subtle biases and privilege than having conducted ethical progressive scholarship.

After completing the preliminary coursework in my program, I initially proposed to study how medical students learned about serving the LGBT-QIA population and whether an educational intervention might improve care and/or interactions between medical staff and people identifying as LGBTQIA. Like any pragmatic new scholar, I wanted to work where my passion lay and where there was a need. After conducting several interviews, I found that the university's medical students had little to no sensitivity training for working with gender nonconforming or queer patients. A comparable research university had integrated a unit on LGBTQIA concerns and sensitivities into its medical students' curriculum. This program found that it improved its graduates' bedside manner and level of care, and offered to collaborate with me on the project. Faculty from the medical school and leaders of the campus LBGTQIA alliance wanted to see my research project set sail. I had designed a study that would make a difference and my next challenge was to find faculty willing to sit on my dissertation committee.

I met with nearly every faculty member within (and some outside of) my department during the following academic year. None would chair my research. One advisor warned me to remember that my dissertation would "follow me everywhere" and possibly limit my "employment horizons." I left his office feeling as though my dissertation had the potential of trailing me like a criminal record. He asked me to reflect on how important this line of inquiry really was to me, considering that it might well define me as a scholar and "reveal my priorities."

Never before this endeavor had I thought that by working toward social justice for LGBTQIA individuals, I might limit my "marketability" as a scholar. In fact, because I had already taught as an adjunct for close to a decade, I did not see the short-term benefits of writing a dissertation at all. Considering the tenure-track job market dwindling at most universities, and "publish or perish" becoming more a maxim than a cliché, I knew I could not use merely a dissertation as a springboard to full-time work as an academic. As Bell (1995), has argued, I thought that the satisfaction should not come from some potential opportunity or award, but from the work itself. I intended to use my dissertation to learn how to conduct research and to offer findings to the literature on a topic that would promote social justice. Instead, I was bombarded with questions concerning my personal motivations to conduct a study in this field. I seemed to offend the white, cisgender, heterosexual faculty who could not understand why I, someone who seemingly reflected their identities, chose this topic. Moreover, the LGBTQIA faculty treated me like an outsider with ulterior, not altruistic, motives.

During meetings with faculty and campus leaders, I was asked questions that violated my rights under the Federal Educational Right to Privacy Act (FERPA), and I tired at the strain of repeatedly defending my scholarship. Smith, Yosso, and Solorzano (2006), call this bombardment of personal questions a form of microaggression. Naive at the time, however, I believed the faculty and advisors were protecting my best interests. While they ostensibly warned me of the potential "pitfalls" of conducting a multicultural sensitivities study in the guise of mentoring me, faculty echoed the wishes of so many well-meaning, yet heterosexist, parents who wish their gay kids were heterosexual (or their transgender children were cisgender), so that life might be easier for them.

While my dissertation had unfortunately not grown in months, my tuition bill had. I saw self-identified gay colleagues initiate research in queer studies and Latino colleagues begin researching Latino/a Critical Race Theory (LatCrit). While some of my colleagues began writing their proposals for their preliminary orals, I began brainstorming for an entirely new study—one that would explore critical pedagogy and social justice issues in higher education, but one that faculty would (hopefully) not find incendiary.

Any doctoral candidate knows the phrase, "A good dissertation is a done dissertation." I became a believer. Having shifted my topic from LGBTQIA education to critical pedagogy, I found faculty members open and receptive to working with me. Through this process, I learned that overt heterosexism and white male privilege, which blocked my initial research, are easier to withstand than covert racial microaggressions. Although my doctorate was almost finished, my education had only begun.

My dissertation progressed smoothly through the various stages. I described the problem: there was a dearth of data reporting how university faculty members taught critical pedagogy and experienced pedagogical struggles while doing so. I reviewed the literature: critical pedagogy is a field so mired in theory that empirical research is needed to describe how critical pedagogues translate theory into praxis. Passionate about my topic, I quickly cruised through my preliminary oral exam. Only after collecting data did I see once again the insidious nature of discrimination.

Having reviewed the literature in order to perform the study, I was steeped in critical pedagogy and critical race theory. Because of this, I decided to reflect the diversity of my participant pool in my data and findings. During my research, I read hundreds of qualitative studies that named their participants "David," "Peter," "Michael," "Mary," "Samantha," or "Jennifer." What I could deduce from my reading was that either little research had been conducted with ethnic minority participants, or that essentially every researcher thought it an acceptable practice to choose participants' names randomly from a white Anglo-Saxon baby-naming book. White was the default. Much of the literature on critical pedagogy emphasizes the need for educators to enable students to see how "normalcy" is constructed and perpetuated. Some of my participants (all of whom were males who held advanced degrees) had ethnic (nonwhite) names, and I realized that by naming them "Peter" or "Paul" I would only contribute to the research literature that characterizes whiteness as normal and white people more worthy of study or examination than members of other cultures or ethnicities.

By using names that represented, yet protected, the participants' ethnic backgrounds, I hoped to fulfill my commitment as an ethical researcher to my institution's review board (IRB) while maintaining the ethnic integrity of my participants, many of whom had overcome adversity integrally tied to their identities as ethnic minorities. I also wanted to ensure that my research did not propagate the myth of colorblindness, which, Giroux (2006) argues, has rendered ethnic minorities "invisible, utterly disposable, and heir to that army of socially homeless that allegedly no longer exist in color-blind America" (p. 175). Names are loaded with cultural and political implications that researchers should not ignore.

Recent research has indicated a correlation between names perceived as representative of ethnic minorities (and genders) and discrimination (Bertrand & Mullainathan, 2004; Aura & Hess, 2010). Considering the content of my study, I felt obligated to honor my participants' cultural capital (Bourdieu & Passerson, 1990; Sullivan, 2002) and, in my own small way, to further social justice. Because ethnic and racial discrimination are cultural norms, and because my research studied how educators task their students to challenge cultural norms, I believed that the way in which my study reported its findings should likewise challenge normative research practices. I also had to adhere to strict confidentiality protocols as mandated by the institution's IRB.

Evans (2004) argues that IRB protocols, particularly those regarding qualitative research involving adults performed in the social sciences, have adversely affected some of the participants they originally sought to protect. "In qualitative branches [of research] . . . anonymity can obscure community authority and voice, and the intent of [confidentiality] is undone. In fact, misplaced confidentiality can "disappear" people and communities" (Evans, 2004, p. 72). My most significant data were mined from ethnic minority intellectuals, and I refused to whitewash their names. Maschke (2008) argues that justice and cultural representation reflected in research practices, in some instances, may be more important than confidentiality:

> The principle of beneficence means that the potential harm from research participation should be minimized and that the potential benefits should outweigh it. Justice means that potential benefits and harms of research should be shared by everyone, rather than falling disproportionately to people of a certain race, ancestry, economic status, or educational attainment. (Harm in these principles can be physical, psychological, and "dignitary," as when a participant's religious or cultural traditions are violated.) (p. 20)

Names, for many, are strong links to cultural traditions, and I did not want to trivialize that; however, as a fledgling researcher, I knew that I did not have the scholarly reputation to insist on conducting completely transparent research in the name of protecting cultural capital. As Svalastog and Erikssond (2010) contend, I decided that the best course of action would be to discuss the issue of naming my participants with the participants themselves.

The participants whom I interviewed were excited to choose their pseudonyms. Among the initial names created or chosen were Farooq, Miguel, Alejandro, Michael, and Lee. These names not only represented the cultural backgrounds of the participants, but also their voices. Participants chose names that they believed reflected their cultural identities without breaching their confidentiality.

The theoretical framework of the study was undergirded by critical pedagogy, poststructuralism, and constructivism. It was through these perspectives that the study was designed and these perspectives that the study sought to advocate. This research grounded itself in the assumptions that education must promote humanization, not dehumanization (Freire, 1970); that a progressive political philosophy should support modern acts of critique and inquiry (Butler, 2001; Foucault, 2007); and that human knowledge is never without its biases, rather it is constructed and therefore fallible (Phillips, 1995; Piaget, 1980). I knew that every decision I made as a researcher reflected an ideological framework and contributed to what my participants and reading audience would consider "normal."

Naming was important to me and to my participants, who all expressed appreciation for being allowed to choose their own alias.

As I transcribed interview transcripts, I carefully "coded," "dumped," "combed" my data. I then employed a second reader to verify the accuracy of my qualitative methods. My dissertation progressed smoothly. I had avoided choosing committee members known to have acrimonious relationships with one another, and I was on schedule to defend my dissertation early enough to file it and participate in my graduation ceremony only three years after having begun.

Just prior to scheduling a date for my oral defense, I met with an advisor. He was one of the faculty members who warned me that a study on an LGB-TIA educational intervention might limit my future employment opportunities. An elderly white male with tenure who had served the university for decades, he beamed with pride at learning of my speedy progress through the dissertation and said he could see me working in his capacity one day. Then he shook my hand as a politician: first by shaking my hand, and then by cupping his free hand around both of our hands as they were locked together. This physical domination of me did not conclude until he looked into my eyes and said, "I'm glad you're graduating soon because I know you've got a family you've got to support." The sexism (and heterosexism alike) rang in my ears as I exited his office. What began as a meeting to celebrate my progress had devolved into a "good ol' boys" meeting.

While the new tack I was sailing had saved me tuition money and time, the price I paid, in terms of my dignity and identity as a feminist, was steep. I felt as though I were living in Conrad's (1982) *The Secret Sharer*. My advisor had convinced himself that I did not possess a "mysterious similitude to the young fellow he had distrusted and disliked from the first" (Conrad, 1982, p. 149). He saw in me a reflection of himself. Unsure as to whether I played the role of the captain or Leggatt, his cryptic doppelganger, I sailed onward.

After setting a date for my oral defense, I began preparing the full manuscripts of my dissertation for my committee to read, critique, and annotate. Within hours of delivering the manuscripts, I received feedback from two committee members. Initially, I was pleased by their quick response time. Reflecting now, however, I can only estimate that their immediacy resulted from seeing in my draft an emergency to be handled. That emergency was the naming of my study's interview participants. One member commented on the names by inserting notes adjacent to them. They read, "Why this name?" and, "Is this name significant in some way?" I did not anticipate the storm on the horizon.

One night while an advisor chatted online with me about my draft, she asked if I would accept her phone call, saying, "It would just be faster to talk." She began the conversation by asking why I had chosen names so "out of the norm." I told her that during my preliminary oral, I expressed concern about the ways in which many research studies seem to paint their participants with a broad Aryan brush and that I wanted the diverse voices of my participants to shine. After an awkward pause and a long sigh, she suggested that I use "less unique" names for my participants. She prodded me to know which name was the pseudonym for which instructor, which would have breached confidentiality. She was not the faculty advisor sponsoring my research through the IRB and I knew that by answering her question, I would violate the confidentiality of the research subjects. Conversely, I felt pressured to answer her question because of the authority her academic title carried. I assured her that in some instances, the participants created their pseudonyms and in others, they chose one from a list. Moreover, I reminded her, the participants all regarded naming as a significant process and expressed gratitude at my including their consideration. She was not satisfied. She wanted to conclude the phone conversation and meet with me personally.

Days later, my advisor was more direct. She said that by choosing these "less common" names, I had run the risk of "alienating" some readers. Her remarks seemed well intentioned. She said she wanted to see me succeed and graduate. She was also a professor at an esteemed research university who aligned herself with the social justice focus of its program. For Sue (2010), however, her good intentions and progressive philosophies do not preclude her from harboring racially biased views and committing microaggressions. Sue (2010) argues that:

> It is not the White supremacists, Klansmen, or Skinheads, for example, who pose the greatest threat to the people of color, but rather well intentioned people, who are strongly motivated by egalitarian values, who believe in their own morality, and who experience themselves as fair-minded and decent people who would never consciously discriminate. (p. 23)

Likely speaking at the behest of one (or more) of my committee members, my advisor told me that unless I chose participant names that were "less unique," I might set myself up for "some difficulty" during my defense. She contended that by using these ethnic names, I could alienate the majority of my readership, who was likely white. With my final oral defense only weeks away, I spoke frequently with multiple advisors who suggested that I choose less "controversial names," names that were "more common" and "perhaps less unique." I acquiesced, though not completely. I named the participants with letters of the alphabet. This maintained their confidentiality while ensuring that my study would not contribute to majoritarian sentiments or ethnic stereotypes. The names of my participant pool, however, were not the only element of my research project receiving heavy critique.

During this time, I also met with a prominent researcher in my department who advised me, much to my chagrin, to change the gender of several of my participants. This was problematic, as the narrow representation of gender among the faculty participants was one of my key findings. She confided that she had been shocked to discover that the university employed not one female in the department being studied, considering that the majority of the department's students were female (indicated by data collected in the study). Essentially, she realized there was miniscule diversity within the department. After I reminded her of my key finding (the need for more gender diversity was described by students in the study), she retreated. She said I did not need to change their genders and that she had merely been trying to "help" me protect my participants' "confidentiality." This surprised me, as I had neither expressed concern about their confidentiality, nor received criticism from the IRB concerning my methods for protecting confidentiality. Reflecting now, I see that she wanted to protect the reputation of the department, one that had historically been dominated by men, yet espousing its educational philosophy as deeply rooted in social justice pedagogy. Having come to this program from graduate studies in Literature, I was hoping to find "truth" in empirical research; however, I learned that sometimes research is as narrativized as any fiction.

Not only did I discover how little control I had over the direction of my own study, but I also gained a deeper appreciation for the ways in which "invisibilized groups and their interests are . . . removed from the educational arena" (Swartz, 2009). The nectar of empirical research had soured. My research process taught me how marginalized groups are not merely underrepresented at institutions of higher education by virtue of their lack of physical presence among faculty and students, but how they can be actively erased from the public's view through empirical research practices.

By contextualizing my own experience within the literature of critical race theory (CRT), I hope to unveil an issue that is often whispered about by doctoral candidates, but seldom researched (Bryan, Wilson, Lewis, & Willis, 2012; Ong, Fuller-Rowell, & Burrow, 2009). History has proven that, in the face of discrimination, "Inaction is the most troubling" (Hernandez, 2013). Indeed, my own action of writing this narrative may "follow me," or limit my "employment horizons," yet I know that no good will come of my research unless what I learned while conducting the research is offered up for others to consider.

An eager, hopeful idealist, I began a doctoral program to conduct provocative empirical research that made a difference. I had hoped that by heightening healthcare practitioners' awareness surrounding LGBTQIA patients, I could chart a course that would positively influence society on a broad scale. Instead, I contributed to a small niche of research that will likely be read by few and considered significant to even fewer. Like

Yezierska (2003), I "want[ed] to learn something. I want[ed] to do something" (p. 66). What I learned, however, was not the program's intended learning outcome.

I now have three initials behind my last name that carry with them a weighty responsibility. This is now the wind in my sail. I am no longer propelled by complicity to an ignorance claimed by so many do-gooders. Instead, I have seen the sexist, racist underbelly of an academy too concerned with protecting its reputation to publish meaningful and honest research. The heterosexism I encountered early in my program was easy to identify. My advisors explicitly warned me that either I would fail to finish a study on LGBTQIA medical education or that I would pay more tuition while struggling to complete it and graduate. The racism I witnessed during the process of writing my dissertation on critical pedagogy, however, was subtle. It manifested itself through comments and suggestions made by people who seemed to have my best interests in mind. This constant barrage of attacks and insinuations exhausted me. I understand that this story may not represent even a fraction of scholars in higher education, but working for equity is not the same as working for equality. Scholars today who convince themselves that the academy is impartial or fair to people who have suffered centuries of psychological and physical abuses (especially those sanctioned by law), need to pay attention to the "little things"—the oblique glances, the body language, the phrases said in hushed tones in the privacy of faculty offices.

According to Juarez, Smith, and Hayes (2008), "Social justice means just us white people" (p. 20). Until scholars, my colleagues and I, begin to reflect on the ways in which our willful ignorance can obliterate the voices of once-silenced perspectives, we will continue to alienate ethnic and cultural minorities, proving research to be nothing more than a narrative more fictional than fiction itself. This story is mine. As long as this story belongs to anyone (or any one), I claim it as my own.

REFERENCES

Aura, S., & Hess, G. (2010). What's in a name? *Economic Inquiry, 48*(1), 214–227. doi:10.1111/j.1465-7295.2008.00171

Bell, D. (1995). Who's afraid of critical race theory? *University of Illinois Law Review, 1994*(4), 893–910.

Bertrand, M., & Mullainathan, S. (2004). Are Emily and Greg more employable than Lakisha and Jamal? A field experiment on labor market discrimination. *American Economic Review, 94,* 991–1013.

Bourdieu, P., & Passerson, J. (1990). *Reproduction in education, society and culture.* Thousand Oaks, CA: Sage.

Brennan, J., & Naidoo, R. (2008). Higher education and the achievement (and/or prevention) of equity and social justice. *Higher Education, 56*(3), 287–302. doi:10.1007/s10734-008-9127-3

Bryan, M., Wilson, B., Lewis, A., & Willis, L. (2012). Exploring the impact of "race talk" in the education classroom: Doctoral student reflections. *Journal of Diversity in Higher Education, 5*(3), 123–137. doi:10.1037/a0029489

Butler, J. (2001). *What is critique? An essay on Foucault's virtue.* Presented at the Raymond Williams Lecture at Cambridge University, University of California, Berkeley.

Conrad, J. (1982). *The Secret Sharer.* New York, NY: Bantam Dell.

Delgado, R., & Stefancic, J. (1993). Critical race theory: An annotated bibliography. *Virginia Law Review, 79*, 461–516.

Evans, M. (2004). Ethics, anonymity, and authorship in community centred research or anonymity and the Island Cache. *Pimatisiwin: A Journal of Aboriginal and Indigenous Community Health, 2*(1), 59–75.

Freire, P. (1970). *Pedagogy of the oppressed.* New York, NY: Continuum.

Foucault, M. (2007). What is critique? In S. Lotringer (Ed.), *The politics of truth,* L. Hochroth (Trans.). Los Angeles, CA: Semiotext(e).

Hernandez, A. (2013, March 1). *Christopher Dorner and racial battle fatigue.* Retrieved from http://www.huffingtonpost.com/angelica-v-hernandez/christopher-dorner-and-ra-battle-fatigue_b_2744000.html

Juarez, B., Smith, D., & Hayes, C. (2008). Social justice means just us white people: The diversity paradox in teacher education. *Democracy and Education, 17*(3), 20–25.

Maschke, K. J. (2008). Human research protections: Time for regulatory reform? *Hastings Center Report, 38*(2), 19–22.

Ong, A., Fuller-Rowell, T., & Burrow, A. (2009). Racial discrimination and the stress process. *Journal of Personality and Social Psychology, 96*(6), 1259–1271. doi:10.1037/a0015335

Phillips, D. (1995). The good, the bad and the ugly: The many faces of constructivism. *Educational Researcher, 24* (7), 5–12.

Piaget, J. (1980). The psychogenesis of knowledge and its epistemological significance. In P. Palmarini (Ed.), *Language and learning.* Cambridge, MA: Harvard University Press.

Smith, W., Yosso, T., & Solorzano, D. (2006). Challenging racial battle fatigue on historically white campuses: A critical race examination of race-related stress. In C. Stanley (Ed.), *Faculty of color teaching in predominantly white colleges and universities.* Boston, MA: Anchor.

Sue, D. W. (2010). *Microaggressions in everyday life: Race, gender, and sexual orientation.* Hoboken, NJ: Wiley.

Svalastog, A., & Erikssond, S. (2010). You can use my name; You don't have to steal my story—A critique of anonymity in indigenous studies. *Developing World Bioethics, 10*(2), 104–110. doi:10.1111/j.1471-8847.2010.00276

Swartz, E. (2009). Diversity: Gatekeeping knowledge and maintaining inequities. *American Educational Research Association, 79*(2), 1044–1083. doi:10.3102/0034654309332560

Yezierska, A. (2003). *Bread Givers.* New York, NY: Persea Books.

Yosso, T. J., Parker, L., Solorzano, D. G., & Lynn, M. (2004). From Jim Crow to affirmative action and back again: A critical race discussion of racialized rationales and access to higher education. In R. Flodden (Ed.), *Review of Research in Education, 28,* 1–25. http://rre.sagepub.com/content/28/1/1.full.pdf+html

Chapter 13

A Critical Eulogy for Joaquin Luna: Mindful Racial Realism as an Intervention to End Racial Battle Fatigue

Antonio Tomas De La Garza

As Critical Race Theory (CRT) scholars have suggested for some time, the right words have the potential to wound or heal (Matsuda, Lawrence, Delgado, & Crenshaw, 1993) and yet the pain caused by wounding words is often brushed off, rarely fully considered, and often treated as secondary to structural violence. However, one need only feel the sting of a racial slur, or burn with resentment from a memory of being subordinated in order to be known that, despite the materiality (the physical and the structural dimensions) of white supremacy, race is a political phenomenon and thus is maintained, reproduced, and activated discursively. The U.S./Mexico borderlands are one of the most powerful and enduring symbols of the racial order in the United States. As a cultural construct the borderlands are the material manifestation of ideology that figures immigrants as pollutants, parasites, and invaders (Cisneros, 2008; Dechaine, 2009). Because the border can be crossed and even trespassed, it suggests to our entire society the disruptive and dangerous potential of those who do not belong, of those who are not white, of the Other.

The escalating militarization of the U.S./Mexico border coincides with increasingly panicked depictions (brought to us by members of both the media and this country's political and economic elite) of a "flood of illegal immigrants" (Ono & Sloop, 2002, p. 54) hell bent on "stealing jobs," unable or unwilling to "assimilate," and intent on no less than the "Reconquista" of the land that was stolen from them so long ago.[1] Yet, as juvenile and patently manipulative as these depictions may be they are persuasive appeals to the fears of the majority that help justify the subordination and exploitation of immigrants.

Representations mainly of Latinas/Latinos and the border operate in ways similar to Orientalist discourse as described by Edward Said (1979, 1994) in that they deploy the intellectual and cultural resources of a society to justify and then obscure violence in the name of economic prosperity. However, as I will show discourse can do more than justify or mask violence. Drawing from the work of critical race scholarship on "racial battle fatigue" (Smith, Hung, & Franklin, 2011; Smith, Yosso, & Solorzano, 2006), I argue that rhetoric used to justify the marginalization of immigrants not only facilitates violence but is itself a form of violence. I make this argument by writing what I call a "critical eulogy" of a man who committed suicide after the DREAM Act failed to pass in Texas. In particular I discuss the discursive and cultural conditions and contexts that existed that ultimately helped end suicide Joaquin Luna's life. After describing the violence done to Joaquin by the anti-immigrant movement, I offer a way to intervene against violence, especially racial battle fatigue. I call this intervention "Mindful Racial Realism" (MRR), which is the merging of the therapeutic practices of mindfulness with the identity reclaiming politics of Racial Realism (Bell, 1992). It is my hope that this essay will provide insight not only into the ways that racist speech does violence but also into ways that people of color and their allies can combat, or at least survive, the disempowering narratives that assail them.

This chapter will proceed in three parts. First, I articulate the relationships among racial battle fatigue, mindfulness, and discourse in order to show the interplay between the physical and the discursive and how that can affect an individual's physical health. Second, I provide a critical eulogy of Joaquin Luna in order to demonstrate the lethal power of immigration discourse. Third, I review clinical research on chronic stress and the therapeutic benefits of mindfulness. Finally, I advance a theory Mindful Racial Realism (MRR) as a tactical communicative intervention that aids those struggling against white supremacy and can potentially

---

[1]For a more complete analysis of the discourse used to describe immigrants, see Ono and Sloop, *Shifting Borders*.

save lives. People of color live in a constant state of distress because of white supremacy . . . and it is killing us. It is time for scholars of color to lend their resources to finding better ways to fight back.

THEORIES FOR CHANGE

Studying the interplay between the representational and the material dimensions of power allows us to understand the effects that communication can have on the body. At the most abstract levels we can see that discourse, which can be understood as a constellation of thought and communication practices that structure the meaning of a particular concept or idea (Foucault, 1972), influences how meaning is ascribed to bodies. In the case of the immigration debate in the United States *discourse* is inclusive of communication by the dominant media (including both fictional and nonfictional portrayals of immigrants), politicians, scholars, lawyers, judges, activists, and immigrants themselves. However, this is not to say that all parties have equal access to speak. Discourse also constructs the conventions, relationships, and rules that determine who can say what, when, where, and to whom. The means of cultural production tend to be controlled by those with cultural hegemony (Gramsci, 1971). This means that those in power will have more space to be heard, that their voice will carry more weight, and that their perspective will more closely reflect the "common sense" of a society (Bourdieu, 1990). Thus, while immigrants themselves are the most afflicted by mainstream immigration discourse, because they are cultural outsiders (Ono & Sloop, 2002) they are the least likely to be heard.

Contemporary communication (Björkvall & Karlsson, 2011; Bost & Greene, 2011; Cloud, 2000) scholarship has taken this notion of discourse and, with it, has begun to explore the ways that discourse can influence the body. Discourse structures the relationship between subjects and the society, but more proximally, discourse can affect a subject, influencing its emotional, mental, and physical state. Racial battle fatigue adds another layer to this analysis by explaining how the cumulative effect of structural, discursive, and aversive racism damages the bodies of people of color. Racial battle fatigue theory develops as an extension of theories of racial microaggression, which are defined as

1. subtle verbal and nonverbal insults directed at people of color, often automatically or unconsciously;
2. layered insults, based on one's race, gender, class, sexuality, language, immigration status, phenotype, accent, or surname; and
3. cumulative insults, which cause unnecessary stress to people of color while privileging whites. (Smith et al., 2006, p. 300)

Racism puts the body experiencing it under a kind of stress similar to that of experienced during a physical attack. White supremacy, which is the ideological justification for the unequal distribution of social, political, and economic privileges afforded "white citizens"[2] (Olson, 2004, p. XIX) of the United States, is a constant presence in the lives of people of color in the United States. As a result, people suffering from racial battle fatigue are more likely to experience feelings of alienation, strain, injustice, and frustration. Racial microaggression "activates a stress-response system, originally evolved for responding to acute physical and emotional emergencies" (Smith et al., 2006, p. 300). The chronic stress induced by living in a racist society could explain why people of color are more prone to illnesses such as hypertension, heart disease, diabetes, and depression than their white counterparts.[3] Despite the important contribution such a theory makes to an understanding of racism, the focus on the discrete and cumulative effects of racism within the theory means there is little research on racial battle fatigue that specifically examines how culture and discourse function as part of racial battle fatigue. My analysis extends the theory of racial battle fatigue by exploring the ways that immigration discourse can harm the bodies of undocumented immigrants.

EULOGIZING JOAQUIN

In order to show how racist discourse can harm and even kill people of color, I engage in a "critical eulogy" for Joaquin Luna. Though there have been other scholarly attempts to discuss someone's death while also addressing social issues,[4] there has, as of yet, been no attempt to articulate critical eulogy as a method of social and political critique. Critical Eulogy is rhetorical intervention in the construction of memories of loss and trauma whereby the scholar interprets the loss of a life as a rupture in the social world, the meaning of which is imbricated with power and will be contested. Thus, it is not a question if a high-profile (visible) death will be framed, reimagined, reinterpreted, and politicized. Rather, the question

---

[2]Olson's book *The Abolition of White Democracy* provides a thorough discussion of the ways that whiteness, as a political category is a foundational component of American democracy. He addresses the notion of a "white citizenship" as a form of political identity that consists of a "cross class" alliance between white workers and white elites. In return for maintaining the racial and economic order white workers are beneficiaries of (increasingly untenable) unearned advantages as demonstrated "in nearly every social indicator from life expectancy to unemployment rates to net financial assets to incarceration rates to SAT scores" (Olsen, 2004, p. XXI).

[3]Even when other demographics are controlled for (Smith, Allen, & Danley, 2007).

[4]The last chapter of Lisa Cacho's book *Social Death* provides a beautiful illustration of how eulogizing rhetoric can be a form of knowledge production and social critique.

is whether or not there will be a singular, banal, trite lesson, or if the event will be contested if its meanings can avoid being foreclosed on. It's not a question of having the "right" interpretation but of searching for answers while sincerely grieving.

"Critical eulogy" is a rhetoric for those who can no longer speak. The rhetorician tells the story of the life and death of a person in order to make sense of the social conditions that made their death possible. Whereas most forms of eulogy are designed to help the survivors move back to a place of normalcy, critical eulogy attempts to intervene against the normative by transforming a personal crisis (the loss of a child, sibling, friend, and community member) into an opportunity for reflection and a call for change on a societywide level. In doing so, scholars attempt to keep open the breach created by social crisis (Turner, 1982) in order to intervene. The eulogy is praxis; it blends epistemic speech with political critique.

Joaquin Luna was born in Reynosa, Mexico, but like many "illegal" immigrants he was brought into the United States as a baby. Joaquin grew up in Mission, Texas, a rural town located in the heart of one of the most impoverished counties in the United States, where more than 35 percent of the population lives in poverty (Fernandez, 2011). Despite the negative influences that accompany systemic poverty (crime, drugs, alienation from school), Joaquin strove to succeed. He played guitar in his church (Llenas, 2011), worked odd jobs to help his family make ends meet, had a solid GPA in high school, and had aspirations for a college education. Joaquin also had a passion and talent for architecture and engineering. In his room you could find sketches and blueprints (Fernandez, 2011) of buildings he hoped to create. He even drafted the blueprints that became the foundation for his mother's home. Joaquin was respected by his teachers, loved by his family, and hoped to make a positive contribution to his community. On November 25, 2010, Joaquin put on a suit and tie, apologized to his mother for failing to become the person he had aspired to be, said goodbye to his family members, walked into the bathroom, put a loaded gun in his mouth, and pulled the trigger (Barrera, 2013).

His family claims that Joaquin killed himself because he could not cope with being unable to go to college. In one of the letters he left behind, he wrote, "Jesus, I've realized that I have no chance in becoming a civil engineer the way I've always dreamed of here . . . so I'm planning on going to you and helping you construct the new temple in heaven" (Fernandez, 2011, para. 2). On the door to his bedroom, a small hand drawing of an angel accompanied by the caption, "To go to heaven you don't need papers" (Cabrera, 2011) also suggests that the issue of "illegality" weighed heavily on Joaquin's spirit. It did not take long for the press to publicize Joaquin's suicide. Almost as quickly, whether from sincere outrage or political convenience, Joaquin's death became an allegory, yet another example of the urgent need for immigration reform (Llenas, 2011).

The arguments made by both sides of the immigration debate about the causes of Joaquin Luna's suicide shift from the political to the ethical. To take a tragedy and spin it in order to advance a political agenda is (perhaps rightly) seen as unethical and opportunistic by many. That someone as young and talented as Joaquin would choose to end his own life saddens and angers me, and yet to depoliticize his death is also wrong because to do so ignores the ways that racist discourse influences the lives of people of color in the United States. Regardless of what is *right* when a tragedy like this enters the public arena it is always already political. Social meaning will be created from this event, but the critical eulogy I offer ensures that more than one meaning is made; it keeps the discussion from ossifying and demands accountability.

Joaquin was articulated across constellations of ideology, production, and discourse that influence the way that U.S. citizens understand immigration. Complex networks of commodities and desires tie citizens to immigrants; for instance, we buy products from maquiladoras and farms that rely on immigrant labor, and we participate in the system of capital that exploits their labor. Our taxes support a government that intentionally destabilizes the governments and economies of the developing world in order to create and produce positive profit margins (Hardt & Negri, 2005). U.S. lifestyles are subsidized by the poverty and instability those policies create. Keeping people poor, desperate, and wanting ensures a ready and willing labor pool, which is an essential component of a "needs-based economy." We are part of a public that frames "illegals" as security threats, criminals, and victims (Ono & Sloop, 2002). Our border kills hundreds of people each year. Whether or not Joaquin's suicide was actually motivated by the failure of the DREAM Act is not the issue. What matters is that we acknowledge our complicity with his death, that we apologize, that we mourn.

Joaquin's life was constrained by ideological and social relations that are products of a weaponized rhetoric. As DeChaine (2009) argues, the border's primary "function is to designate, produce, and/or regulate the space of difference" (p. 44): the difference between the United States and Mexico, the difference between being a citizen of one state and an "illegal" within that very same state, and the difference between the value of one state and another. The regulation of difference produces a host of stressors and obstacles that literally make it harder to live. As an "illegal" Joaquin would struggle to go to college, and as an "illegal" he would struggle to find a job. As an "illegal" he would live in fear of deportation, of being exiled from his home. Surrounded by a figurative border (Ono, 2012) composed of surveillance and control tactics that keep immigrants in a heightened state of stress and anxiety about identity and belongingness in addition to value and futurity, Joaquin experienced a world that is more hostile, more dangerous, and more precarious than the world that citizens experience. Enforcement through attrition policies, racial profiling, detention camps, and raids are the material manifestation of a militarized border culture. Depression, stress, anxiety, and anger are the psychic manifestations of that culture. Butler (1997) argues that illocutionary speech can perform the violence it describes, meaning that Joaquin was *made* illegal in the presence of anti-immigrant discourse.

Structural, aversive, and discursive racism were all realities of Joaquin's life. As an "illegal" Joaquin felt his opportunity to get an education slip away as DREAM Act failed to garner legislative support. According to Joaquin's brother Diyer Mendoza:

> Every time he would put in an application, the first thing that would pop up was "Are you a U.S. citizen?" No. "Resident?" No. "Social Security number?" No. It was all just mounting and mounting on top of him. I truly believe that if that DREAM Act would have already passed, he would still be here today. (Fernandez, 2011, para. 16)

The statement by Joaquin's brother expresses a frustration at the limitations imposed on immigrants by structural forms of discrimination. Despite his abilities and his work ethic, Joaquin's status was a barrier. It surrounded him, defining and limiting his opportunities. Constantly surrounded by borders, Joaquin was feeling pressure, feeling constrained. Joaquin "didn't (see) any other way or no other option" (Barrera, 2013, para. 7). The publicity surrounding Joaquin's death makes his story a public act of memory. The story cannot be told without referencing the border, Joaquin's status, and the DREAM Act. Regardless of the "truth" behind the motivations for Joaquin's suicide, his family and countless others who identify with him will *feel* like the border killed him. The border between the United States and Mexico, the border between him and acceptance, and the border between "the good life" and "a bare life" evinces a particular form of vital power. The violence committed against Joaquin can be transferred; the brutality of border he experienced is vicariously and virtually loss and trauma for those of us who identify with him.

MINDFUL RACIAL REALISM

In *Depression: A Public Feeling*, Ann Cvetokovich applies critical theory and a cultural studies approach to the subject of depression. Rather than treating depression as a personal medical problem, the author argues for studying depression as social phenomena influenced by material factors such as the economy and social factors like discourse and culture. Viewing depression as a public feeling means that our discourse can aggravate or remediate cultural factors linked to depression. This insight suggests that racial battle fatigue, a syndrome arising from socially produced inequality, can also be influenced by discourse. Perhaps more importantly the social nature of depression means that communicative interventions may be developed to help combat racial battle fatigue.

So far, most of the published research on racial battle fatigue is limited to describing and defining the scope and symptoms of the disorder. Thus, there is very little research at the moment on the communicative aspects of the syndrome. Racist power relationships are activated by representational processes (this includes everything from the creation of racially discriminatory laws to the slurs and slights that people of color may experience in their everyday lives). This section will describe the study of racial battle fatigue and will suggest some possible steps people of color can take to heal and resist the damage done to them by weaponized border rhetorics. In order to bridge the representational and the corporeal I include clinical research on the effects of stress within the field of political theory. By merging mindfulness with the theory of racial realism I am able to suggest communicative strategies that may have material effects. CRT research demonstrates that people of color can view racism as a direct threat (Smith et al., 2006). Like any other form of threat, they trigger the body's fight-or-flight response, altering a person's physical state even when that person may not be consciously aware of his or her own response. The invisibility of racism as a stressor diminishes people's ability to cope because they may not be aware that they are suffering.

This section focuses on literature that describes a relationship between psychosocial stress and the functioning of the immune system. Based on Segerstrom and Miller's (2004) meta-analysis of more than 300 empirical articles, the effects of stress on the immune system can be divided into two types: acute stress and chronic stress. *Acute stress* is an intense stress lasting minutes. In some of these experiments research participants were told they were going to have to give a public speech (Bassett, Marshall, & Spillane, 1987). Even though there was a suppression of cellular immunity, humoral immunity is preserved. Humoral immunity is the part of the immune system that is influenced by macromolecules that are found in bodily fluids within which cells exist. These extracellular fluids, blood, saliva, and bile are composed of secreted antibodies, complementary proteins, and some antimicrobial peptides. At the conclusion of a stressful event the cellular immune function recovers, so there is no long-term harm done by acute stress. This form of stress is shown to have a positive effect on the body and on the attitude of the person experiencing the stress. People who experience acute stressors also experience an adaptive response. Acute stress has been shown to harden the body and psyche of the individual to a given stressor, reducing even the short-term negative effects of similar stressors. Acute stress functions as an inoculation, better preparing a person for dealing with stress.

The second form of stress is *chronic stress*. Though there are differences between the ways that the stress is manifested depending on the causes of stress (trauma affects the body and mind differently than loss), chronic stressors suppress both cellular and humoral immunity. The effects of this form of stress are much longer lasting and have not been shown to bring about an adaptive response. Instead, Creswell et al. (2012) have demonstrated a relationship between chronic stressors such as loneliness that contribute to an increase of protean markers. These markers are associated with inflammation that plays a role in the development and progression of diseases that can be drivers of late-life morbidity and mortality. Additional research has shown that people exposed to chronic stressors are more likely to suffer from low self-esteem and depression, are more likely to experience intense physical pain from injury, and are less likely to recover from illnesses than are those not exposed to chronic stressors.

This research is laying the groundwork for ways to combat the damage that racial battle fatigue does to the bodies and minds of people of color. One study on loneliness is very promising. According to the research, "feeling lonely is a significant risk factor for morbidity and mortality in older adults. For example, lonely older adults have increased risk for cardiovascular disease, Alzheimer's disease, and all-cause mortality" (Creswell et al., 2012, p. 1095). Based on bioinformatic analysis or "the study of information processes in biotic systems" (Hogeweg, 2011), signaling pathways that regulate gene expression suggest that loneliness may activate biological defensive programming (Cole et al., 2007). This chronic state of biological defensiveness closely resembles the experiences of people of color who operate within a set of social relations that diverge between a person's desired and actual social standing.

In response to the well-established relationship between stress and health, John Kabat-Zinn (2006) developed a program to help people cope better with their stress. Mindfulness meditation-based stress reduction (MBSR) is an intensive program designed to help people deal more effectively with chronic stress. Incorporating this technique with the theory of racial realism could help develop mindful awareness of racist actions. Mindfulness is characterized by nonevaluative, sustained immanent awareness of mental states and processes (2006). Nonevaluative means that the subject is abstaining from judging whether or not the sensation is good or bad but instead seeks awareness of the connection between the affective and the physical. This includes continuous, immediate awareness of physical sensations, perceptions, affective states, thoughts, and imagery. Mindfulness is nondeliberative: It merely implies sustained attention paid to ongoing mental content without thinking about, comparing, or in other ways evaluating the ongoing mental phenomena that arise during periods of practice. Thus, mindfulness may be seen as a form of naturalistic observation, or participant-observation, in which the subject makes oneself aware of affective and physiological experiences during waking consciousness (Grossman, Niemann, Schmidt, & Walach, 2004). However, these theories have not been developed with a political lens in mind. What is needed is a form of mindfulness that redresses politically induced stressors.

A politics of mindfulness would fuse the stress reduction tactics of mindfulness with political practices that dismantle racist discourses. Toward that end I suggest that people of color and their allies engage in a praxis of "mindful racial realism." Mindful racial realism is an intentional and focused effort to live a life that combats racist oppression. The first premise of this approach is to recognize the inevitability of racist oppression. As Bell (1992) argues, white supremacy is a permanent feature of American culture. When people of color place their hope on achieving racial equality they are deferring their ability to cope to a transcendent future in which racial oppression no longer exists. This is problematic. Bell explains that striving for racial equality is destined to fail, and in failing burn out activists, and leads to feelings of failure and despondence. Instead, people of color should abandon racial equality as a goal and focus instead on resistive action. Resistance brings dignity to those who struggle. More to the point, making resistance the *telos* of an antiracist movement does not *defer* success to some transcendent future. Instead, a resistance grounded racial realism would reframe the locus of the struggle on the proximal and the immediate. People of color need to find ways to resist oppression as they live their lives, wherever they are, whenever they can. This form of resistance should in no way abandon the possibility of structural change. Resisting oppression can lead to changes in policy, but a politics of mindful racial realism sees that change as an ancillary benefit but not the reason for the struggle.

This brings me to the second premise of my theory: confrontation. Organizing and activism place people of color in direct confrontation with racist institutions and actors that justify and enforce inequality, including the legal system and the police. Confronting the police, speaking up and out, building community support and solidarity, and doing the work of challenging racial supremacy places the body and psyche under stress. Prior to the lunch counter sit-ins in Birmingham, Alabama, activists were subjected to rigorous training in nonviolent resistance. These activists would role play the sit-in and be exposed to racist, demeaning, and threatening discourse. Furthermore, civil rights activists were taught how to interact with law enforcement, including how to resist arrest without "resisting arrest." These exercises train people how to respond in the moment, while also hardening their bodies and minds to the stressful reality of what it takes to confront white supremacy.

Finally, MRR draws on the lessons of mindfulness: being present, aware, and in control of stress as a way for people of color to remediate the damage that racial battle fatigue does to their bodies and minds. As clinical research has shown, cultivating mindfulness as a practice increases self-esteem, decreases feelings of loneliness, and enhances engaged, positive, affirming action. People who practice mindfulness are less likely to suffer from the biological effects of stress and stress-related illness. They feel less pain and they heal more quickly from their wounds.

Activists employing mindful defiance accomplish the dual tasks of resisting white supremacy and inoculating themselves against the stress induced by racist discourses. Taken together, these three premises represent what I hope will become a core component of future antiracist efforts: an intentionally cultivated politics of immanent self-aware resistance. In the opening lines of *Souls of Black Folk*, W. E. B. DuBois (2007) refers to a question unasked but persistent among his interactions with the white world. The question: how does it feel to be a problem? For people like Joaquin Luna, the answer can include feelings of isolation, hopelessness, and depression. However, when merely existing becomes a criminal act, surviving can become a form of resistance. Critical scholarship on immigration points to the emancipatory potential of outlaw, hybrid, and immanent performances of belonging. I suggest that by combining critical theory with clinical research we can cultivate ontologies of defiance. Furthermore, the discipline of communication is uniquely positioned to take the lead in developing techniques of resistance, providing tools that help people like Joaquin, people like us, find a better way to fight.

REFERENCES

Barrera, D. (2013). Student commits suicide, letters reveal worries over immigration status. *Valley Central News*. Retrieved from http://www.valleycentral.com/news/story.aspx?id=690993

Bassett, J. R., Marshall, P. M., & Spillane, R. (1987). The physiological measurement of acute stress (public speaking) in bank employees. *International Journal of Psychophysiology, 5*(4), 265–273. doi:10.1016/0167-8760(87)90058-4

Bell, D. (1992). Racial realism. *Connecticut Law Review, 24*(2), 363–379.

Björkvall, A., & Karlsson, A.-M. (2011). The materiality of discourses and the semiotics of materials: A social perspective on the meaning potentials of written texts and furniture. *Semiotica, 2011*, 141. doi:10.1515/semi.2011.068

Bost, M., & Greene, R. W. (2011). Affirming rhetorical materialism: Enfolding the virtual and the actual. *Western Journal of Communication, 75*(4), 440–444.

Bourdieu, P. (1990). *The logic of practice*. Stanford, CA: Stanford University Press.

Butler, J. (1997). *Excitable speech: a politics of the performative*. New York, NY: Routledge.

Cabrera, J.-M. (2011, December 1). Joaquin Luna's Unfinished Blueprint. *Huffington Post*. Retrieved from http://www.huffingtonpost.com/jorgemario-cabrera/joaquin-lunas-unfinished-_b_1122183.html

Cacho, L. M. (2012). *Social death racialized rightlessness and the criminalization of the unprotected*. New York, NY: New York University Press.

Cisneros, J. D. (2008). Contaminated communities: The metaphor of" immigrant as pollutant" in media representations of immigration. *Rhetoric & Public Affairs, 11*(4), 569–601.

Cloud, D. (2000). Materiality and discourse in social change: Some reflections for feminist studies. *Women and Language, 23*(1), 43.

Cole, S. W., Hawkley, L. C., Arevalo, J. M., Sung, C. Y., Rose, R. M., & Cacioppo, J. T. (2007). Social regulation of gene expression in human leukocytes. *Genome Biology, 8*(9), R189. doi:10.1186/gb-2007-8-9-r189

Creswell, J. D., Irwin, M. R., Burklund, L. J., Lieberman, M. D., Arevalo, J. M. G., Ma, J., . . . Cole, S. W. (2012). Mindfulness-based stress reduction training reduces loneliness and pro-inflammatory gene expression in older adults: A small randomized controlled trial. *Brain, Behavior, and Immunity, 26*(7), 1095–1101. doi:10.1016/j.bbi.2012.07.006

Dechaine, D. R. (2009). Bordering the civic imaginary: Alienization, fence logic, and the Minuteman Civil Defense Corps. *Quarterly Journal of Speech, 95*(1), 43–65. doi:10.1080/00335630802621078

Du Bois, W. E. B. (2007). *The souls of black folk*. UK: Filiquarian Pub., LLC.

Fernandez, M. (2011, December 10). Joaquin Luna Jr.'s Suicide Touches Off Immigration Debate. *The New York Times*. Retrieved from http://www.nytimes.com/2011/12/11/us/joaquin-luna-jrs-suicide-touches-off-immigration-debate.html

Foucault, M. (1972). *The archaeology of knowledge & the discourse on language*. New York, NY: Pantheon Books.

Gramsci, A. (1971). *Prison notebooks*. New York, NY: International Publishers.

Grossman, P., Niemann, L., Schmidt, S., & Walach, H. (2004). Mindfulness-based stress reduction and health benefits: A meta-analysis. *Journal of Psychosomatic Research, 57*(1), 35–43.

Hardt, M., & Negri, A. (2005). *Multitude: War and democracy in the age of Empire*. New York, NY: Penguin Books.

Hogeweg, P. (2011). The roots of bioinformatics in theoretical biology. *PLoS Computational Biology, 7*(3), e1002021. doi:10.1371/journal.pcbi.1002021

Kabat-Zinn, J. (2006). Mindfulness-based interventions in context: Past, present, and future. *Clinical Psychology: Science and Practice, 10*(2), 144–156. doi:10.1093/clipsy.bpg016

Llenas, B. (2011, November 28). Family Hopes Teen's Suicide Pushes Passage of DREAM Act. *Fox News Latino*. Text. Article. Retrieved April 28, 2013, from http://latino.foxnews.com/latino/news/2011/11/28/family-hopes-teens-suicide-pushes-passage-dream-act/

Matsuda, M. J., Lawrence, C., Delgado, R., & Crenshaw, K. (1993). *Words that wound: Critical race theory, assaultive speech, and the first amendment*. Boulder, CO: Westview Press.

Olson, J. (2004). *The abolition of white democracy*. Minneapolis, MN: University of Minnesota Press.

Ono, K. A. (2012). Borders that travel: Matters of the figural border. In R. DeChaine (Ed.), *Border rhetorics: Citizenship and identity on the US–Mexico frontier* (pp. 19–32). Tuscaloosa, AL: University of Alabama Press.

Ono, K. A., & Sloop, J. M. (2002). *Shifting borders: rhetoric, immigration, and California's Proposition 187*. Philadelphia, PA: Temple University Press.

Said, E. W. (1979). *Orientalism*. New York, NY: Vintage Books.

Said, E. W. (1994). *Culture and imperialism*. New York, NY: Vintage Books.

Segerstrom, S. C., & Miller, G. E. (2004). Psychological stress and the human immune system: A meta-analytic study of 30 years of inquiry. *Psychological Bulletin, 130*(4), 601–630. doi:10.1037/0033-2909.130.4.601

Smith, W. A., Allen, W. R., & Danley, L. L. (2007). "Assume the position . . . You fit the description": Psychosocial experiences and racial battle fatigue among African American male college students. *American Behavioral Scientist, 51*(4), 551–578. doi:10.1177/0002764207307742

Smith, W. A., Hung, M., & Franklin, J. D. (2011). Racial battle fatigue and the miseducation of black men: Racial microaggressions, societal problems, and environmental stress. *The Journal of Negro Education, 80*(1), 63–82.

Smith, W. A., Yosso, T. J., & Solorzano, D. (2006). Challenging racial battle fatigue on historically White campuses: A critical race. Examination of race-related stress. In C. A. Stanley (Ed.), *Faculty of color: Teaching in predominantly White colleges and universities*. Bolton, MA: Anker Publishing.

Turner, V. W. (1982). *From ritual to theatre: the human seriousness of play*. New York, NY: Performing Arts Journal Publications.

Chapter 14

Effective Gender Activism: An Exercise in Marginalization

Wendy Murphy

As one of the attorneys and academics leading the fight since the early 1990s for women's safety and equality I've learned to value the marginalization that comes with effective activism. It used to bother me to sit on boards of organizations that wasted time doing busy work when we could have been out changing the world. But while I can appreciate the role of institutions as stabilizing forces in society, it's also true that institutions inhibit people from organizing effectively to generate more effective change. Institutions produce silos and cause people to compete for meager grant dollars that come with strings attached that prohibit advocates from doing *political* things that matter. Change depends on people resisting those forces and fighting to redesign the box even as others struggle to make adjustments within it. It's an activist's job, frankly, to be the bad guy on the outside, and I take pride in being the person on the edge, along with many others, in the fight for women's safety and equality.

That said, it's difficult to function outside the mainstream even though it is extraordinarily disturbing that in the year 2014 women are still explicitly unequal in America and that the U.S. Supreme Court is composed of (some) justices who have no qualms about stating in black letter law that women are *not* equal and that there is no constitutional right to gender equality. This alone should have women marching in the streets—or at least protesting outside the Supreme Court on a regular basis. But energy that could be mobilized has largely been co-opted by factors that dissipate our collective strength.

Even courts vested with the responsibility of ensuring "justice for all" usually function to discourage advocacy that *could* make equality a reality. As an impact litigator and former prosecutor, I have seen firsthand the way our legal system frustrates rather than facilitates women's access to justice. Indeed, the first time I prepared an impact litigation case in 1992 to correct a legal doctrine that undermined rape victims' constitutionally protected privacy rights, I naively thought the court would say, "thank you, Attorney Murphy, for bringing this to our attention. We will act swiftly to correct this injustice." Instead the court went out of its way to hide the fact that I had developed an unprecedented litigation strategy that forced them to overturn a prior ruling allowing accused rapists to obtain unfettered access to victims' irrelevant privileged medical and counseling files—simply for the asking.

The test case I filed challenged the constitutionality of the ruling, and I managed to get the case in front of an appellate court by having a rape counselor refuse to comply with a judge's order. I advised her to be held in contempt, instead, because a contempt judgment would enable me to file an appeal, during which I could ask the court to reverse its earlier decision on the grounds that it violated victims' constitutional rights.

The case captured the public's attention, and I was soon standing before the Massachusetts Supreme Judicial Court, literally asking them to change the law. Supportive amicus briefs had been filed by organizations from all over the country. We had a lot of momentum on our side, and the justices' questions made me feel confident that we had a strong case. A few months later the decision was announced. We won! But the victory I had fought so hard for was announced in *someone else's case* on the very same day that my case was decided in a rescript opinion that ignored the merits of my case on procedural grounds. I was shocked, not because they declined to give me the credit I deserved but because the lawyers in the other case hadn't even briefed the issue, much less asked the Court to change the law! I not only asked the Court to overturn its prior ruling, it was the *only* issue I argued. And though I was correct, the Court gave credit to a lawyer who hadn't even *mentioned* the issue.

That the Court tried to hide what I had done inspired me to focus even more on the systemic injustices endured disproportionately by women victims of violence. I examined closely the ways that law itself produced women's inequality in law and society, and I started designing new test cases using only constitutional and civil rights doctrines to pressure appellate courts to fix the problems.

Most laws and legal doctrines look good at first blush but on careful read, reveal serious inequities. For example, in most states the crime of rape requires proof of nonconsent *plus* force, which means women's autonomy is not protected at all because nonconsensual sex is perfectly legal so long as force isn't used. By contrast, theft crimes require proof only of nonconsent. When force is present, the more serious crime of robbery occurs. In other words, the simple taking of another person's property without consent is a crime whereas the taking of a woman's bodily integrity without consent is not a crime, unless force is used. This alone demonstrates law's structured inequality because human beings are *supposed* to be more valuable than objects, yet the law fails to criminalize the nonconsensual intrusion into women's bodies in the absence of force.

In turn, prosecutors and police can plausibly decline to arrest or file charges against rapists on the grounds that evidence of force "is not strong enough" to prove a case "beyond a reasonable doubt," which is often true in non-stranger rape cases where coercion in a relationship and/or a victim's diminished capacity from drugs or alcohol often play a role in facilitating the crime without need for force.

Even when force is present or the crime occurs in a jurisdiction where force is not required, an irrational prosecutorial decision not to file charges is impossible to challenge or correct because the same lawmakers who design unfair rape laws also enact immunity laws that protect government officials from liability for wrongful failure to prosecute. And because women's and victims' rights groups receive funding that often comes with strings that forbid political activism, organizations that should be speaking out stay silent. They refuse even to take the meager step of mobilizing politically to ensure the election of prosecutors who will prioritize the prosecution of gender-based crimes. In short, the legal system is a virtual fiefdom where the written law incentivizes rape, and enforcement officials have unchecked authority to ignore violence against women with impunity. The general public has little understanding of this reality, largely because the public narrative is controlled by the same people who devalue women's lives in the lawmaking and law-enforcement processes.

These problems in larger society are magnified on college campuses where school officials are even more immune from oversight and accountability. And more so than the government, universities have powerful incentives to hide the truth about violence against women on campus to avoid negative media attention that might diminish a school's reputation. From destroying evidence in rape kits and not conducting blood tests until rape drugs dissipate, to having advisors and "counselors" persuade victims not to call police or file reports on campus, delaying hearings until graduation, and literally punishing victims and employees who dare to speak out, there is apparently no limit to the steps certain schools will take to conceal the fact that women in higher education endure very high rates of sexual violence. Even policy manuals are problematic because they often obfuscate rather than enlighten campus communities about the nature of violence against women as a civil rights problem.

My professional role in the struggle for women's safety and equality has at times led me into contentious legal battles and caused me to suffer significant professional strife. The aggressive steps I took against Harvard in 2002,[1] and Harvard Law School and Princeton in 2010,[2] for example, led to me being disinvited to speak about my work; being removed from campus-based listservs and being shunned by antiviolence organizations. I was even removed from an advisory board for a national nonprofit organization after I publicly criticized a member of Congress for filing the Campus

---

[1]While serving as a Visiting Scholar at Harvard Law School, I prepared an unprecedented Title IX policy complaint with the Office for Civil Rights (OCR) at the Department of Education (DOE) on behalf of women as a class after Harvard's Faculty of Arts and Sciences adopted a new rule requiring sexual assault victims to produce "independent corroboration" for their claims as a mandatory prerequisite to redress. Harvard tried to negotiate a compromise during the investigative process so they could retain some version of the rule, but I refused. They were forced to withdraw the corroboration rule and the policy complaint process soon became commonplace across the country. This significantly increased advocacy on behalf of women's equality on campus because it was no longer necessary to have a particular student suffer a violation of rights and then engage in contentious litigation with her university. The policy complaint process brought about substantial reforms because it allowed people who were not even affiliated with universities to force schools to bring their policies into compliance with federal law.

[2]When Harvard Law School hired me in 2010 to consult on a Title IX matter I told them their Title IX policies were noncompliant and I filed an OCR complaint with the DOE when they refused to bring them into compliance. They owed me a lot of money when I filed and I assumed I would never be paid, but I filed anyway and they did pay me. OCR accepted the complaint and opened its first ever Title IX sexual assault investigation against Harvard Law School in the Fall of 2010. Around the same time, I filed a complaint against Princeton University for many of the same problems I saw at Harvard Law School. I sent both cases to OCR headquarters in Washington, D.C., and asked them to issue some form of global guidance because problems at both schools were systemic in higher education. They agreed and issued that global guidance in the form of a "Dear Colleague Letter" on April 4, 2011. The "Letter" provided excellent guidance on the steps that schools were obligated to take in response to gender-based violence on campus and made clear that Harvard and Princeton were not in compliance. Days later a bill was filed with Congress to overturn the "Letter" and weaken Title IX. The investigations of Harvard and Princeton stayed open while that law, known as the SaVE Act, was making its way through Congress. After the SaVE Act was passed, but before it took effect, Harvard and many other schools changed their policies to incorporate SaVE's weaker provisions. One year later, right before SaVE was to take effect, I filed a federal lawsuit implicating Harvard Law School and the University of Virginia and asking the federal court to enjoin the SaVE Act from being adopted on *any* campus on the grounds that it violated women's equal protection and due process rights. A few weeks later, Harvard changed its policy again and rejected those provisions in SaVE that weakened Title IX. Other schools soon followed suit and properly adopted equitable policies to provide the exact same redress for civil rights violence "on the basis of sex" as were being applied to the redress of civil rights violence "on the basis of" other protected class categories such as race and national origin.

SaVE Act, an offensive federal law that weakened Title IX by, among other things, allowing schools to impose more onerous legal burdens, such as a more burdensome standard of proof, on victims of victims of gender-based civil rights violations compared to victims of civil rights violence based on other protected-class categories such as race and national origin. Advocates, including people affiliated with the "Know Your IX" group and the "Victims' Rights Law Center," along with many naive students across the country, supported and promoted the SaVE Act. Some even testified before Congress. All were apparently lacking in sufficient understanding of constitutional law, and they trusted the wrong legal advisors who lied and told them SaVE was a good thing. Students and groups willing to compromise on women's rights and support SaVE were celebrated at conferences and in the media, while people who spoke out against SaVE and stood firmly in support of women's safety and equality were marginalized and silenced.

Even sophisticated, seemingly feminist advocates who knew SaVE would weaken Title IX refused to speak out, presumably because they preferred to curry favor with certain universities or obtain some of SaVE's proposed funding for "training and education" programs. Advocacy groups that should have criticized SaVE were having victims referred to their organizations for "services," along with the tacit understanding that victims would be encouraged not to file charges and to "put the matter behind them" and "focus on their studies." A few groups that tried to complain went silent when SaVE was attached to the Violence Against Women Reauthorization Act, which is a big funding bill that many groups rely on to keep their doors open.

I couldn't be part of that racket. I saw too many victims quit school or transfer, devastated more by the betrayal of their beloved university than by the sexual assault. I saw too many students with 4.0 GPAs start to fail classes and to lose confidence in their self-worth and abilities. I saw young women in pain struggling to make sense of why a crime the U.S. Supreme Court says is the most severe harm to the self "short of homicide" was treated like a night of "bad sex" by campus officials.

Watching this horrifying mistreatment of women made me think a lot about the way civil rights laws had inspired people of all genders, colors, and stripes to stand proudly together against discrimination in education based on race, religion, and national origin. Why was there no similar collective pride on behalf of discrimination in education based on sex? The answer appeared to be that, from a legal and political perspective, women were simply not "worth" as much as other "types" of people. On campus, for example, punishing one valuable male athlete at a Division I school could cause a university to lose significant advertising revenue. Punishing a legacy student at an elite university could mean the loss of tuition and alumni dollars from an offender's family. Not punishing an offender would generally be less costly because women usually have less value in terms of athletics and legacy donations. Indeed, women have only recently even been admitted into some of the most elite schools. Moreover, by siding with offenders, schools deter victims from reporting, which prevents public scandals and bad press. Plus, schools' lawyers and risk management folks know that it's easier for offenders to sue in civil court for wrongful punishment than it is for victims to sue when their civil rights are violated.

Violence against women on campus was not even widely understood as a civil rights issue until a few years ago—some 40 years *after* Title IX was enacted! The first time the idea was made known in published form was in a law review article I wrote in connection with a complaint I filed against Harvard in 2002. I was also the first to publicize the idea in mainstream media in my capacity as a contributing editor for Women's eNews. While I was glad to be an original writer on these important ideas, I was mystified by the fact that it took 30 years before *someone* stated in writing that gender-based violence on campus was the same type of civil rights harm as race-based violence. Racist harassment and violence was instantly understood as a civil rights issue the moment the Civil Rights Act was passed in 1964. But it took decades for people to understand the civil rights nature of sexist harassment and violence, not because the point wasn't obvious in 1972 when Title IX was enacted, but because Title IX was propagandized in society as a sports equity rule. That women failed to express outrage at the framing of sex discrimination as a sports equity problem is perplexing. Imagine the public's reaction if, in response to the problem of ethnic harassment of Jews, schools offered Jewish students their own basketball team?

I've written and lectured widely on the topic of sexual assault as a Title IX/civil rights issue since the mid-1990s, and I've filed lots of test cases against colleges and universities, starting with Harvard in 2002, to pressure all schools to bring their policies into compliance with civil rights laws. By far the most depressing aspect of this work has been the refusal of women's rights groups to help or even acknowledge the issue. Indeed, it was not until 2010, after complaints I filed against Harvard Law School and Princeton University led to both schools being subjected to unprecedented Title IX investigations by the Office for Civil Rights (OCR) at the Department of Education (DOE) that women's groups and others started paying attention.

The Harvard and Princeton cases started when Harvard Law School hired me in 2010 to consult on a Title IX matter, in connection with which I told them their policies were noncompliant with federal law. When they refused to change them, I filed a complaint with OCR. Around the same time, in the fall of 2010, I filed a similar OCR case against Princeton University, and I sent both cases to the Washington, D.C., headquarters of the DOE along with a request that they issue some form of "global guidance" because problems at both schools were systemic in higher education. The DOE agreed, and on April 4, 2011, a "Dear Colleague Letter" (DCL) was released in which it was made clear that both schools' policies were non-compliant. While the DCL was obviously written in response to my cases against Harvard and Princeton, no mention was made of me, or of either school, when the DCL was released. Reminiscent of the way the Supreme Judicial Court in Massachusetts ruled in my favor in someone else's case years earlier, I took it on the chin and decided that I'd rather win and not be recognized than lose and have a parade in my honor. But even that major, if silent, victory was short lived as only days later the Campus SaVE Act was submitted to Congress for the purpose of overturning the DCL and significantly weakening Title IX. My cases against Harvard and Princeton then languished for years even though OCR investigations are almost always resolved within 180 days. The Harvard and Princeton cases remained open while SaVE was making its way through Congress with the help of significant lobbying dollars. If the investigations remained open until SaVE took effect in 2014 both schools could credibly claim their policies were compliant with federal law even though they were noncompliant when the investigations were opened in 2010.

While SaVE was becoming law I wrote many articles for my regular column at the Patriot Ledger and Women's eNews about how dangerous SaVE was, and how shocking it was that decades after Title IX's enactment, a law could be proposed to make Title IX *weaker*. Problems with the law were disturbing and obvious but not a single women's rights group said a word. Even the National Women's Law Center (NWLC) stayed quiet despite its reputation for being fiercely independent. I was stunned, though I soon learned that the NWLC had done very little about violence against women, on campus or in larger society, and had no record of treating violence against women on campus as a Title IX issue. In fact, in a major speech in 2009, the Director of the Center talked about the history of Title IX without once mentioning its applicability to gender-based violence.

There was literally nobody in any organized women's rights group willing to speak out against SaVE. Thus, it was no surprise that SaVE sailed through Congress and was signed into law without controversy—except for the articles I was writing. After SaVE was enacted but before it took effect in March 2014, schools across the country, including Harvard, amended their policies to take advantage of SaVE's weaker standards. Determined not to let any school so blatantly discriminate against women I decided to file a federal lawsuit to stop SaVE on the grounds that it violated women's equal protection and due process rights because it allowed civil rights violence against women to be addressed under less protective standards compared to the redress of all other forms of civil rights violence on campus based on categories such as race and national origin.

I asked many women's rights groups to become involved in the lawsuit, and I invited self-proclaimed Title IX experts to help, but they all declined, with one important exception.

The "Godmother of Title IX," Dr. Bernice Sandler, agreed to read the law carefully, at my request. She was there when Title IX was first enacted, and she had spent much of her life fighting for its effective enforcement. After reading the SaVE Act, Dr. Sandler was outraged, not only because of its offensive language but also because people she trusted had told her SaVE was "good" for women.

Dr. Sandler then volunteered months of her time helping me prepare a federal lawsuit to stop SaVE. I asked her at one point what she would do when the inevitable call came asking her to stop working with me and to back away from criticizing SaVE. Lucky for me she replied, "Wendy, I'm in my mid-80s; I fought hard to get Congress to enact Title IX in 1972 and I will not sit by and watch Congress make it weaker all these years later. I'm too old to give a damn about politics. No matter who calls me, I'm not backing down."

Dr. Sandler spent a lot of time with me explaining the politics behind the enactment of Title IX, and I helped her understand the equal protection doctrine. Together we prepared a powerful lawsuit that laid out in detail why certain provisions in SaVE were unconstitutional and could not lawfully be enforced on any campus. As we worked to develop a brief on the issues, women's groups were inexplicably working against us. Even Ms. Magazine published a piece declaring SaVE a "good" law for women. Days before we filed suit, Dr. Sandler said, "I may be the Godmother of Title IX, Wendy, but you are most certainly the Goddaughter. Nobody else had the guts *and* the legal expertise to do what you did. This is a very important lawsuit."

We filed suit in February 2014, two weeks before SaVE was to take effect on March 7, 2014. We implicated Harvard Law School and the University of Virginia in our claims because open OCR investigations against both schools would be affected by SaVE. At the end of the day on March 6, 2014, our lawsuit was approved by the court to proceed. Several weeks later, Harvard amended its policy to reject SaVE's unconstitutional provisions. Among other things, Harvard agreed to lower the burden of proof on victims reporting gender-based violence to a mere "preponderance of the evidence," and it adopted civil rights definitions such that offenses were established by proof of "unwelcomeness" and "offensiveness" instated of the far more burdensome criminal law definitions required by SaVE such as "sexual assault" and "force." Harvard also added a guarantee of "equity" even though SaVE authorized schools to provide women with less than "equitable" redress.

Because change in higher education trickles down not up, Harvard's move will lead to improved policies on campuses nationwide, though few people will understand that Harvard was forced to change its policies because of the federal lawsuit Dr. Sandler and I wrote. As with so much of my work, the lawsuit received little attention.

Nor will I win prizes for changing the law in larger society through similarly aggressive and creative litigation strategies, even though other lawyers who do the same kind of work on behalf of other marginalized groups are regularly lauded by bar associations and lawyers groups and others. I've grown used to watching my work be ignored and even punished until my ideas become more mainstream and establishment groups start doing the same work.

The first time I tried to change the law was in my capacity as a young prosecutor specializing in child abuse and sex crimes. Victimized women and children were routinely subjected to intrusive court orders and violations of personal rights compared to victims of other types of crimes. I would speak up to judges and say things like "I understand the court's ruling but it makes no sense. This court has never granted a man charged with theft access to his victim's therapy file, why would the court issue such an order in a rape case?" By pointing out such obviously disparate treatment, I expected judges to say "Thank you for pointing that out, Attorney Murphy, I'll revise my ruling." But that never happened. Instead, judges would say, "Ms. Murphy, you are the government. Your job is to state the law, not complain about it. If you want to change the law, you need to get a different job."

So I did.

When I left the prosecutor's office and decided to use the skills I had as a litigator and appellate attorney to change the law and make things fairer for victimized women and children, I expected the systemic response to be as responsive as it was when defense attorneys fought to change the law to the benefit of accused criminals or when the ACLU fought to change the law to help convicted sex offenders. I sincerely believed that lawyers were *supposed* to shine a light on injustice because "justice" is a fundamental concept around which society is organized, and it is *supposed* to matter when laws and legal doctrines devalue certain people's lives because of who they are in society.

I thought I was doing something noble when I told victims their rights were being violated and that a judge's order was illegal. But time and again I was punished, shunned, or criticized for doing what other lawyers were celebrated for doing in the same courtroom, in front of the same judge, just *not* on behalf of victimized women and children.

In one such case involving a rape victim at the U.S. Air Force Academy, a military judge in a court-martial rape case ordered the victim's *civilian* rape counselor to turn over the victim's treatment file. I instructed the therapist not to comply on the grounds that the military judge had no power to order her to do anything, much less turn over a privileged file.

I submitted a brief and flew to Texas to explain to the judge that he had no authority to compel the release of the victim's file. The judge didn't care. He ruled against us and threatened to have the therapist arrested.

I advised my client to persist in her refusal to comply, in response to which the judge sent federal law enforcement officers to my client's home to take her into custody. I dared them to arrest her and promised a swift and expensive lawsuit if they touched her. A bunch of government and military lawyers had an emergency meeting in Washington and told the federal marshal I was right. The officers were instructed to stand down. When the military judge in Texas learned that federal officials refused to enforce his arrest warrant, he put them on speakerphone in his courtroom and berated them for disobeying his order. He was later reassigned. My case led to the well-known "Air Force Academy" rape scandal, and I was invited to give a talk in Washington, D.C., but that invitation was soon withdrawn. I was told that people in Washington didn't want me "inspiring" advocates to follow my lead and oppose military judges' orders in other cases.

In a similar nonmilitary case in Massachusetts, the lawyer for a man named Manuel Valverde, who had been charged with rape, insisted that the court allow him full access to the victim's rape counseling file. Though openly conceding he had no idea what was in there or why he needed it, he demanded that the judge hand him the entire file. The lawyer found out about the file's existence after sending a private investigator, paid for by public tax dollars, to pester the victim's grandmother (her legal guardian at the time) with probing questions about personal issues like whether the victim had ever been abused as a child, and whether the grandmother had ever been charged with a crime or received assistance from social services.

The grandmother resisted the investigator initially, but on an occasion when she was sick in bed, the investigator showed up again—and she relented, telling the investigator the victim sought counseling at a local rape crisis center. The defense wasted no time sending a subpoena for the file.

I advised the crisis center to resist the subpoena because it was illegal. I told the judge the defense had no right to the file, and I insisted the attorney be punished for harassing the victim's grandmother. I explained how the grandmother started crying when she learned her statements to the investigator were helping the defense violate her granddaughter's rights.

Rather than punishing the defense, the judge, a former public defender, threatened the center with contempt and imposed a fine of $500 per day until they turned over the file. The crisis center couldn't afford the electric bill much less a $500 fine for a single day, so I filed an emergency motion with the appellate court to put a hold on the fine long enough for us to appeal the contempt judgment. The New York Times was covering the case, thankfully, and the public was outraged that a judge would not only order disclosure of a confidential file without *any* cause, but also punish an impoverished crisis center with a $500 per day fine for lodging a legitimate objection to a clearly unconstitutional court order.

With the help of a nonprofit organization called "Stop Family Violence," I started a petition drive and got 500 people to agree to spend one night in jail, each, in lieu of the $500 fine. I attached the list of 500 protestors to my appellate brief. While it's technically improper to "protest" in a courthouse, and my list was akin to a protest, I argued that it was important evidence the court should consider on the value of the privacy interests at stake. It should matter to the court, I argued, that complete strangers were willing to go to jail to stop an injustice.

It worked for a while, and we won an initial stay of the fine, but when the public protest died down months later, the court ruled against us. This was not unexpected because lots of judges just don't like it when victims stand up for their rights and file appeals. It's an important lesson, however, in the value of public protest. When people make a lot of noise about injustice, judges do pay attention.

In another case where I should have won an award but instead was sanctioned I filed a very creative federal lawsuit against a West Virginia judge who ordered a child rape victim to submit to a forced genital examination so her rapist could conduct "discovery" inside her vagina. The prosecutor tried to appeal but West Virginia's highest court shockingly upheld the order on the grounds that it was no big deal because women get gynecological exams all the time. It's embarrassing that *all* the justices thought nothing of the *court-ordered* rape of a child. When the state's highest court makes such a wildly inappropriate decision, the victim's only recourse is to file an action in federal court, so I filed a petition for certiorari with the U.S. Supreme Court, and when that was unsuccessful I filed suit in federal court to stop the state court judge from enforcing his barbaric order. My lawsuit was unprecedented but would have been successful except that someone contacted the victim without my knowledge or consent and "persuaded" her to submit to the exam, thus causing a mootness problem with my case. It's unethical in the extreme that anyone would speak to my client without my permission, but the court didn't care and the case was dismissed as moot because the victim complied with the very order she had been challenging. A few years later I tried filing a class-action lawsuit to overturn the decision on behalf of all women in West Virginia but the court dismissed that suit on the grounds that nobody had filed such a lawsuit before. The court also decided that I should be sanctioned, even though I had an opinion letter from a former federal judge supporting what I'd filed and opining that the lawsuit was proper. I decided the sanction was worth paying (an organization volunteered to pay the few-hundred-dollar fine for me) because the fact that I had proved a victim *could* sue in federal court, and that I was watching the state closely, meant no judge would dare enforce that horrifying decision in the future for fear I'd show up again and file another federal lawsuit on behalf of a real victim.

In another case, I sued a Nebraska judge in federal court after he ordered a rape victim not to use the words "rape" or "sexual assault" during her trial testimony. He actually gave her a long list of forbidden words and phrases and threatened to throw her in jail if she didn't comply. I flew to Nebraska and filed a brief explaining that the judge had *no authority* to censor a victim's descriptive trial testimony. I cited cases proving that the victim had a First Amendment right to use any words she wanted to describe what happened to *her* body. When the judge realized I was right, he ignored me. He knew I was from Boston and had five young children. He knew I couldn't stay in Nebraska forever, so he waited me out. When I was literally on my way to the airport after days of being ignored, he ordered my client to appear in court without me. Luckily, I'd prepped her for the court's predictable strategy, and she handled the judge beautifully. He put her under oath and asked if she understood his order and intended to obey him. She replied, "Your Honor, when I raise my hand and swear to tell the truth, the whole truth and nothing but the truth, that's exactly what I intend to do." The judge was furious and he had no comeback. He dismissed the case in a fit of frustration, then issued a public statement the next day saying I'd left town because I was afraid of being prosecuted for practicing law without a license. In fact, I had complied with all pro hac vice rules and had two local lawyers sponsor my appearance. But the judge was so embarrassed by the bad press he received for issuing such an outrageous order, he stooped to lying about me to cover for his own shame. Later that year, the judge won the ignoble "Jeffersonian Muzzle Award" from a prestigious First Amendment organization in Washington, D.C., which is given to government officials who blatantly violate citizens' Free Speech rights.

In the meantime, the prosecutor filed the case again, which gave me time to file a lawsuit in federal court before the next trial date. I asked the federal court to order the state court judge not to violate my client's federal constitutional rights by forbidding her to use certain words, such as "rape," at the next trial. Nobody had filed such a lawsuit before so the federal judge was not exactly warm to my case, but I'd done all the research and the case was proper. I was simply asking the federal court to do its job and stop a Nebraska state official from violating the federal constitution.

The federal judge didn't see it my way, and he criticized me for being a "woman lawyer from Boston" who showed up in his court do what he called "gender politics." I thought I was "doing" the First Amendment but he clearly noticed my gender more than the legal issues. While I was waiting for the federal court to rule, a Nebraska state senator filed a lawsuit against God, then went on a national news programs to denounce the case I had filed as audacious. He literally said at a press conference, "If a rape victim can sue a judge, then I can sue God." I'm still wondering how he planned to serve the complaint or take God's deposition, or why he thought God would appreciate being equated to a lowly judge.

I eventually lost the federal case in a snippy, poorly written decision that ignored relevant case law. But while the judge ruled against us, he also noted in a well-placed footnote that it was disturbing for a state court judge to order a rape victim not to use the word "rape" during a rape trial. He said the decision was the kind of thing that happens in countries where women wear burkas. So we lost the battle but won the war because comparing a state court judge to a radical Islamist ensured that no judge would ever do something so stupid again to any rape victim in Nebraska. More rape victims should file federal lawsuits when their constitutional rights are violated, but few victims' lawyers know how to file federal lawsuits against state court judges and fewer still have the guts to do it. More lawsuits would at least make judges more mindful when ruling on issues that could affect victims' fundamental rights, which would reduce the number of victims who decline to report crimes or walk away from justice to avoid unfair tactics.

Because victims are not parties to criminal cases, they can't object or file appeals the way prosecutors and criminal defendants can. A criminal case is between the government and the accused. The victim is but a witness for the prosecution. This means that when women as a class suffer harm to their rights in a criminal appellate decision, there is no seat at the table for the problem of gender discrimination, no way for women's objections to be known or their constitutional rights to be represented. Prosecutors are usually on the victim's "side" but they cannot ethically advocate for the personal rights of crime victims because they speak for society as a whole, which includes protecting the rights of the accused.

Many judges assume that because a victim is not a party to a criminal case, she has no right to be heard. But one need not be a formal "party" to a case to have a right to be heard as a matter of due process. Judges who deny victims a right to be heard on the grounds that they are not "parties" to criminal cases don't understand that victims would not be asking for a right to be heard if judges were not wrongly imposing the power of the government, in the form of court orders, into victims' personal space. Or as I like to say to the judges in these cases, "If my client has no right to be heard, Your Honor, then you have no authority to act—because her right to be heard is the flip side of the authority coin." Put another way, victims aren't *asking* to be heard when *they shouldn't* be, they are *forced* to object because a judge has asserted the government's power where *it shouldn't*.

When judges must, constitutionally, listen to my clients but they refuse, I instruct my clients to disobey the judge and be held in contempt, not as a form of protest but because being held in contempt enables me to file an appeal. The first time I did this was in the early 1990s in a case where a judge had ordered a rape crisis center to turn over a victim's treatment file. It was a high-profile case and the public was on our side. Gloria Steinem even came to Boston to headline a legal fundraiser. It soon became clear not only that we were likely to win our appeal but also that our case would change the law to better protect privacy rights for all victims. But before the appellate court had a chance to issue its decision, the defense lawyer in the case had her client plead guilty. He was sent to state prison for eight to ten years; a tough punishment for a guy who'd never been behind bars. Then the defense attorney demanded that my appeal be dismissed as moot.

Here's what's interesting about this. The perpetrator was a free man, out on very low bail at the time he pleaded guilty. He would have stayed out of jail for at least another year while our appeal was being decided. Yet his lawyer had him plead guilty and go to prison for *eight to ten years* so that my appeal would become moot. The perpetrator's lawyer originally told the judge her client couldn't get a fair trial unless she could examine the contents of the victim's counseling file. But when we were on the verge of winning our appeal and changing the law, the defense lawyer abandoned her request and had her client go to prison without seeing the records and without even giving her client a fair trial. I considered filing an ethical complaint because as much as I didn't give a damn about the rapist, the guy was entitled to a fair trial and his lawyer was sending him down the river for strategic gain in my appellate case. To this day, I don't think the guy has a clue why he was advised to plead guilty.

But the strategy failed. I found an obscure case that said appeals from contempt judgments do not become moot when the underlying case is resolved because the "stigma of contempt" deserves its own resolution. My appeal was allowed to proceed, and we won a landmark decision that changed the law and improved privacy rights for victims.

Over the next 20 years, I filed numerous procedurally similar cases in state and federal courts around the country, using constitutional doctrines and civil rights laws and rarely used devices like "writs of mandamus" and "equitable" remedies to get my foot in an appellate court's door.

The unapologetic purpose of my work is to irritate the system and make people uncomfortable with how the law works when victims suffer needless indignities and violations of fundamental rights. While I win most of the time I'm careful about which cases I file because I respect the law and I want to work within it to make it better. After decades of creative lawyering as an "activist academic," I've become bolder because I've learned that I can't be effective if I'm worried about offending people.

It would be easier if lawyers could work together to identify problem areas in the law and craft strategic lawsuits in the right jurisdictions to highlight and repair defects. Lawsuits rooted in constitutional and civil rights laws can serve as a kind of quality-control device—one that naturally elevates the conversation about violence against women to a higher plane of civi and constitutional rights while inspiring all judges to be more mindful of the impact of their rulings on the safety and equality of women as a class.

People will not long respect a legal system that incentivizes violence against women and produces inequality in the name of *justice*, but fixing the problem is not easy. For me, it's been like climbing a mountain of ice while wearing plastic slippers. It's cold, I don't get much traction, and the surface is solid and relentlessly unforgiving. But I keep climbing because it takes persistence to tackle such a big problem. The more of us who climb the mountain, the faster we will melt the ice and see benefits emerge—like fewer incidents of gender-based harassment, violence, and discrimination; better institutional oversight and accountability; and ultimately, more human kindness.

BIBLIOGRAPHY

Martin, J. L., Kearl, H., & Murphy, W. J. (2013). Bullying and harassment in schools: Analysis of legislation and policy. In M. A. Paludi (Ed.), *Women and management: Global issues and promising solutions. Volume 2: Signs of Solutions* (pp. 29–51). Santa Barbara, CA: Praeger.

Murphy, W. (1997, June). Gender bias in the criminal justice system. *Harvard Women's Law Journal*.

Murphy, W. (1998). Minimizing the likelihood of discovery of victims' counseling records and other personal information in criminal cases: Massachusetts gives a nod to a constitutional right to confidentiality. *New England Law Review, 32*(4) (recognized in "Worth Reading," *National Law Journal*).

Murphy, W. (2001). The victim advocacy and research group: Serving a growing need to provide rape victims with personal legal representation to protect privacy rights and fight gender bias in the criminal justice system, *Journal of Social Distress and the Homeless, 11*(1), 123.

Murphy, W. (2003, April). *OCR issues ruling in Harvard "corroboration rule" case.* National Sexual Violence Resource Center/Security on Campus.

Murphy, W. (2005). "Federalizing" victims' rights to hold state courts accountable. *Lewis and Clark Law Review, 9*, 647.

Murphy, W. (2006). Using Title IX's "prompt and equitable" hearing requirements to force schools to provide fair judicial proceedings to redress sexual assault on campus. *New England Law Review, 40*(4), 1007–1022.

Murphy, W. (2011). Privacy rights in mental health counseling: Constitutional confusion and the voicelessness of third parties in criminal cases. *Journal of the American Academy of Psychiatry and Law, 39*, 387–395.

Murphy, W. (2011). Sexual harassment and Title IX: What's bullying got to do with it? *New England Journal on Criminal and Civil Confinement, 37*, 305–324.

Murphy, W. (2012). Unpacking the rights of third parties in criminal cases. *Family and Intimate Partner Violence Quarterly, 5*(1).

Murphy, W. (2013). *Book review: Addressing rape reform in law and practice* (Caringella). Sexual Assault Report, Civic Research Institute (May/June) (pp. 67–68).

OTHER RESOURCES

Berry v. Chi. Transit Auth., 618 F.3d 688 (7th Cir. 2010).

Chadwick, D. L., Giardino, A. P., Alexander, R., & Thackeray, J. D. (2014). *Chadwick's child maltreatment, volume 2: Sexual abuse and psychological maltreatment*. St. Louis, MO: STM Learning.

Davis v. Monroe County Bd. of Ed., 526 U.S. 629 (1999).

Dennerlein, L. (2014). Study: Females lost self-confidence throughout college. *USA Today*, September 26.

Franklin v. Gwinnett County Public Schools, 503 U.S. 60 (1992).

Heldman & Dirks. (2014). One in five women students on college campuses will experience sexual assault. *Ms. Magazine*.

Humphrey, J., & White, J. (2000). Women's vulnerability to sexual assault from adolescence to young adulthood. *Journal of Adolescent Health, 27*, 419–424.

Kilpatrick, D. (2007). *Drug-facilitated, incapacitated, and forcible rape: A national study*. Retrieved from https://www.ncjrs.gov/pdffiles1/nij/grants/219181.pdf

Kintz, P. (1996). Drug testing in addicts: A comparison between urine, sweat, and hair. *Therapeutic Drug Monitoring, 18*, 450–455.

Kintz, P., Cirimele, V., Tracqui, A., & Mangin, P. (1995). Simultaneous determination of amphetamine, methamphetamine, 3,4-methylenedioxyamphetamine and 3,4-methylenedioxymethamphetamine in human hair by gas chromatography—mass spectrometry. *Journal of Chromatography, 670*, 162–166.

Kintz, P., & Samyn, N. (1999). Determination of "Ecstasy" components in alternative biological specimens. *Journal of Chromatography, 733*, 137–143.

Krebs, C. P., Linquist, C. H., Warner, T. D., Fisher, B. S., & Martin, S. L. (2009). College women's experiences with physically forced, alcohol or other drug-enabled, and drug-facilitated sexual assault before and since entering college. *Journal of American College Health, 57*(6), 639–647.

Lisak, D., & Miller, P. M. (2002). Repeat rape and multiple offending among undetected rapists. *Violence and Victims, 17*, 73–84.

Martinez, A. (1998). *A statistical analysis of the deterrence effects of the military services' drug testing policies*. Master's Thesis, Naval Postgraduate School, Monterey, CA.

McCloskey, L. (1997). The continuum of harm: Girls and women at risk for sexual abuse across the lifespan. In D. Cicchetti & S. L. Toth (Eds.), *Developmental perspectives on trauma: Theory, research, and intervention* (pp. 553–578). Rochester, NY: University of Rochester Press.

McKinnis v. Crescent Guardian, Inc., 189 F. Appx. 307 (5th Cir. 2006).

Perez-Pena, R. (2013). *College groups connect to fight sexual assault*. Retrieved from http://www.nytimes.com/2013/03/20/education/activists-at-colleges-network-to-fight-sexual-assault.html?pagewanted=all&_r=0

Rand Report. (1977). *Rand objective analysis. Effective solutions*. Retrieved from http://www.rand.org/content/dam/rand/pubs/reports/2008/R2136 pdf (examining disparities in programs and activities aimed at enforcing Title IX compared to programs and activities aimed at enforcing Title IV and noting that both statutes are equally designed to promote "sex desegregation" and "race desegregation").

Rennison, C. M. (2002, August). *Rape and sexual assault: Reporting to police and medical attention, 1992–2000*. Washington, DC: U.S. Department of Justice, Bureau of Justice Statistics, NCJ 194530.

Sandler, B. (1997). *Too strong for a woman*. Retrieved from http://www.bernicesandler.com/id44.htm

Smith, C., & Freyd, J. (2013). Dangerous safe havens: Institutional betrayal exacerbates sexual trauma. *Journal of Traumatic Stress, 26*, 119–124.

Stefan, S. (1994). The protection racket: Rape trauma syndrome, psychiatric labeling, and law. *Northwestern University Law Review, 88*(Summer), 1271.

Testa et al. (2010). *Journal of Consulting and Clinical Psychology, 78*(2), 249–259.

Turner v. Saloon, Ltd., 595 F.3d 679 (7th Cir. 2010).

U.S. Commission on Civil Rights. (2013). *Sexual assault in the military*. Retrieved from www.usccr.gov

Valentin, I. (1997). *Title IX: A brief history*. Education Development Center. http://www2.edc.org/WomensEquity/pdffiles/t9digest.pdf

GENERAL RESOURCES

Campus SaVE Act, §3,(6)-(8)(B)(v)(I)(aa), govtrack.us, available at https://www.govtrack.us/congress/bills/112/hr2016/text (last visited Jan. 30, 2014).

Civil Rights Restoration Act of 1987 (clarifying that substantive standards from Title VI apply with equal force to Title IX, 20 U.S.C. §1687; 29 U.S.C. §794, 42 U.S.C. §2000d-4a, and 42 U.S.C. §6101).

Decker, J., & Baroni, P. (2012). "No" still means "yes": The failure of the non-consent reform movement in American rape and sexual assault law. *Journal of Criminal Law and Criminology, 101*(4), 1081 (noting the wide variety of definitions of non-consent among the states and that in some states lack of affirmative consent is enough, while in others, the lack of affirmative consent is not sufficient in the absence of force).

Federal Bureau of Investigation. (2013). *Criminal Justice Information Services (CJIS) Division Uniform Crime Reporting (UCR) Program* (last visited Jan. 30, 2014). http://www.fbi.gov/about-us/cjis/ucr/recent-program-updates/reporting-rape-in-2013

Sexual harassment: It's not academic. Retrieved from http://www2.ed.gov/about/offices/list/ocr/docs/ocrshpam.html ("A student's submission to the conduct or failure to complain does not always mean that the conduct was welcome").

U.S. Department of Education. (2011). *OCR, Dear colleague letter* (April 4), 34 CFR §106.71.

U.S. Department of Education. (2012). *Title VI enforcement highlights office for civil rights* (last visited Jan. 30, 2014). http://www2.ed.gov/documents/press-releases/title-vi-enforcement.pdf (repeatedly noting that Title VI requires schools to apply standard of "equity").

U.S. Department of Education's Office of Civil Rights. (2005). *Annual Report to Congress: Fiscal Year 2004*, available at http://www2.ed.gov/about/reports/annual/ocr/annrpt2004/report.html (OCR's fiscal year 2004 report states that it resolved 91 percent of the complaints it received within 180 days, which exceeded its goal of 80 percent).

U.S. Department of Justice. (2001). *Title IX legal manual* (last visited Jan. 30, 2014). http://www.justice.gov/crt/about/cor/coord/ixlegal.php (noting that "Congress consciously modeled Title IX on Title VI" and citing *Alexander v. Choate*, 469 U.S. 287, 294 (1985) (noting that because Title IX and Title VI contain parallel language, the same analytic framework should apply in the context of administrative redress proceedings because both statutes were enacted to prevent unlawful discrimination and to provide remedies for the effects of past discrimination)).

U.S. Department of Justice. (2012). *Justice department announces investigations of the handling of sexual assault allegations by the University of Montana, the Missoula, Mont., Police Department and the Missoula County Attorney's Office* (May 1). Retrieved from http://www.justice.gov/opa/pr/2012/May/12-crt-561. html (announcing Title IX compliance review and Title IV investigation of the University of Montana and noting, "Title IX of the Education Amendments of 1972 and Title IV of the Civil Rights Act of 1964 each prohibit sex discrimination, including sexual assault and sexual harassment in education programs").

University of Montana-Missoula, the U.S. Department of Justice, Civil Rights Division, Educational Opportunities Section, and the U.S. Department of Education, Office for Civil Rights. (2013). *Resolution agreement.* http://www. justice.gov/crt/about/edu/documents/montanaagree.pdf (announcing resolution agreement with the University of Montana and noting that Title IV, Title VI, and Title IX are subject to the same regulations to ensure enforcement of rights regarding discrimination, harassment, and violence in education "on the basis of sex." 28 C.F.R. Part 54 and 34 C.F.R. Part 106).

42 U.S.C. §2000d-7 (requiring equal treatment on behalf of all protected class categories and in a section labeled "Civil rights remedies equalization," the statute provides that "(1) A State shall not be immune under the Eleventh Amendment of the Constitution of the United States from suit in Federal court for a violation of §504 of the Rehabilitation Act of 1973 [29 U.S.C. 794], Title IX of the Education Amendments of 1972 [20 U.S.C. 1681 et seq.], the Age Discrimination Act of 1975 [42 U.S.C. 6101 et seq.], Title VI of the Civil Rights Act of 1964 [42 U.S.C. 2000d et seq.], or the provisions of any other Federal statute prohibiting discrimination by recipients of Federal financial assistance." This "Civil rights remedies equalization" mandate further states that "(2) In a suit against a State for a violation of a statute referred to in paragraph (1), remedies (including remedies both at law and in equity) are available for such a violation *to the same extent* as such remedies are available for such a violation in the suit against any public or private entity other than a State." (emphasis added)).

Violence against Women Reauthorization Act of 2013, Pub. L. No. 113-4, 127 Stat. 89 (2013).

Chapter 15

Black Women in Academia: The Invisible Life

Jenelle S. Pitt, Mya Vaughn, Aisha Shamburger-Rousseau, and LaKeisha L. Harris

What does it mean to be invisible in the academy? "Women of color are rendered invisible by virtue of our femaleness and race" (Rodriguez & Boahene, 2012, p. 453). The double consciousness of actively navigating race and gender in academe and being held "hostage" as our lived experiences play out in the ivory tower is an everyday battle. Women of color engage in *shifting,* as a way of surviving the structures embedded in academia that largely privilege "white, male profiles and career paths" (Essed, 2000, p. 889). There are many narratives that cut across dimensions of teaching, research, and service, which highlight marginalization experiences for women faculty of color (Gutiérrez y Muhs, Niemann, González, & Harris, 2012). Although women of color are making great strides in educational attainment as evidenced by 65 percent of all doctoral degrees for 2009–2010 being awarded to Black women, 55 percent being awarded to Hispanic women, 56 percent being awarded to Asian/Pacific Islander women, and 54 percent being awarded to American Indian/ Alaska Native women (U.S. Department of Education, National Center for Education Statistics, 2012), women, in general, are still not largely represented in university spaces.

According to the 2012–2013 Annual Report on the Economic Status of the Profession, 44 percent of women are in non-tenure track positions as compared to 33 percent of men (Curtis & Thornton, 2013), which is problematic for institutions, as opportunities for advancement and organizational engagement are vastly diminished (Harper, Baldwin, Gansneder, & Chronister, 2001). In 2007, women of color accounted for 7.5 percent of the entire positions that were occupied by full-time faculty (Ryu, 2010). Not only do women faculty of color have lower base salaries at the time of hire than that of male colleagues, which affect movement along the career trajectory (Renzulli, Grant, & Kathuria, 2006), but they also experience tenure and promotion at decreased rates (Lee, 2011). When examining women faculty of color who were seeking during the year 2009–2010, 9 percent were Asian American, 8 percent were African American, 4 percent were Hispanic, and less than 1 percent were Native American (*Chronicle of Higher Education*, 2010), suggesting that the academy should demonstrate more accountability in addressing pipeline considerations.

While the authors posit that universities need "women of color intellectuals to challenge unicultural perspectives" (Essed, 2000, p. 889), this particular chapter will focus on the concerns of *Black* female professors in institutions of higher education, as we account for 2.9 percent of all full-time teaching faculty (*Chronicle of Higher Education*, 2010), and only 3.9 percent of those having associate or full professorship (Ryu, 2010), thus underscoring the context of physical loneliness and magnifying the need for support. Not only are Black women underrepresented, but we also embody unique world views based on our experiences related to the simultaneous overlap of interlocking systems of power such as race and gender (Crenshaw, 1989; Hill Collins, 2000).

Assaults on our scholarship and professorial competence, frequent requests for a "diverse" perspective on service assignments, and differential treatment relative to pay and promotion are explicit reminders of how others see our worth. Black women largely exist in the margins as "part of the whole but outside the main body" (hooks, 1990, p. 149). For example, one of the present authors remembers sitting in a faculty meeting where a student was being reviewed and being the only one asked, "Do you think she's a good role model?" With everyone waiting for her to provide a response and no one serving as her ally in the room, she remembers pausing, and thinking, "not again." Instead of answering with, "I'm getting tired of this shit," she chose to offer the following in a soft tone accompanied by a curious facial expression and her head tilted to one side: "What do you mean? Is she a good role model for Black students, or is she a good role model in general?" At that point, the tenured faculty member who initially asked the question turned and began speaking to the other tenured faculty member about the student as if nothing had ever occurred. Though, she was raging inside, she was also smiling for having had the courage, in the moment, to not let offenders "slide." This chapter will offer some of our lived experiences of racial battle fatigue (Smith, 2004) and instances of surviving in hostile workplaces, which exposes us to mundane extreme environmental stress (MEES) (Pierce, 1975; Carroll, 1998). As a whole, we deliver our stories through the lens of "one of the present authors" to maintain anonymity. Living on the margins can be used as spaces of resistance and intervention; yet, too often academe fortifies structures that cause Black women to feel invisible and isolated (Henderson, Hunter, & Hildreth, 2010, resulting in silenced experiences.

SILENCED EXPERIENCES OF MOTHERHOOD

One of the present authors remembers an incident before becoming a faculty member that she calls a "foreshadowing" for what to expect as a Black single mother in academia. A white professor suggested that the author and her child clean a woman's house, who happened to be the professor's friend, in exchange for editing her dissertation. Mothering in the academy is complicated. The push and pull of choosing to or timing when to become a parent while serving as a female faculty member can be replete with stress, especially as women go to extreme measures to hide the fact that they have children or want to have children as doctoral students, while interviewing, and/or after arriving in the academy (Thompson & Dey, 1998; Lewis, 2013). For Black female faculty, "pregnancy, like race, announces the body as present, disobedient, and sexualized" (Nzinga-Johnson, 2013, p. 96), thus forcing our invisibility to become uncloaked. The decision to have children can become even more complicated when it involves nontraditional forms of parenting (e.g., single parenting, same-sex parenting) (Dugger, 1996; Marr, 2013). Hill Collins (2000) affirms that motherhood is contradictory, and hence, experienced in a myriad of ways. While experiences of Black female faculty who are also mothers are being discussed (Nzinga-Johnson, 2013), there seems to be an absence of narratives being widely published and a lack of institutional mechanisms in place to ensure discussion is brought to the forefront. Are these experiences silenced, ignored, or unreported?

One of the most stigmatized parenting experiences for Black women (faculty) is that of being a single mother (Brown & Davis, 2000). In an environment where our competency is challenged, and our race and gender are always on display, adding offspring to the equation not only exacerbates visibility, but also raises questions of perceived commitment to the institution while evoking a layered experience of devaluation (Nzinga-Johnson, 2013). One of the present authors remembers being told by a senior mentor in administration that, "Being a person of color [Black], who's a single mother, especially in [name of city withheld]—as it is pretty conservative, will not go over well for promotion and tenure." According to

Hill Collins (2000), "[many] U.S. Black women who find themselves maintaining families by themselves often feel that they have done something wrong" (p. 84). These feelings tend to be rooted in historical symbols of Black women. In the example above, some may perceive a well-intentioned mentor as providing *feedback* and helping a new faculty member to hedge off experiences that may have been on the horizon. Others may discern that the individual was relating to the author as a Jezebel (whore), a Welfare Mother ("bad" mother, no morals, and diminished work ethic), or a Matriarch (too aggressive, perceived "destroyer" of the Black family). While the situation can be analyzed from multiple lenses, it is not uncommon for many Black female faculty to experience stereotypical images and to encounter colleagues who relate to them through these frames while navigating the treacherous terrain otherwise known as academia (Bryant et al., 2005; Harley, 2008).

Surviving in the academy for Black female faculty who are single mothers may also mean wearing masked smiles and demonstrating forced engagement after incessant questioning arises from students, colleagues, and administrators regarding how the woman's partner (or lack thereof) feels about what's going on, "when are you two getting married," and whether he is "moving to be closer to you" (Stanley, 2005). One of the present authors recalls a colleague asking her if her husband was going to obtain employment in the same town where the university was located. After becoming mentally exhausted from finding ways to dodge questions, she finally answered, "I'm not sure." The only thing she kept thinking is number one, "I'm not married," and number two, "I guess people think this is the only way that children can be raised if you work in academia." That was an "I'm keeping my door closed" kind of day as a way of temporarily coping with the MEES. A counternarrative to the detrimental stereotypical images of Black single mothers in academe involves "othermothering" and/or "community mothering." James (1993) refers to othermothering as the informal or formal accepting of responsibility for another's child(ren), while community mothering also encompasses the notion of taking care of the *whole*, which can be traced to African ancestry and ideals of interdependence, and social/political activism evidenced by service to the community and ethics of caring (Gilkes, 1980; Hill Collins, 2000). Visibility can be heightened when Black women, in particular, engage in forms of mothering (i.e., othermothering and community mothering) that are juxtaposed with white traditional two-parent, heterosexual households, which has been touted as "good," "right," or "ideal." However, it is these very counter-forms of mothering that serve to empower Black women and Black parenthood, while at the same time offering ways of resisting (Hill Collins, 2000; O'Reilly, 2004).

Valuing the continuum of mothering arrangements that Black women engage in and publicly supporting these ways of being would go far in helping to minimize the tension headaches, stress, and inauthentic experiences that many Black female faculty face within the ivory tower. Until then, rather than say what one really feels, Black women will continue to find spaces within written published works, develop trusting relationships among sister scholars, and leverage established networks such as the Faculty Women of Color in the Academy National Conference sponsored by the University of Illinois Urbana-Champaign and Research Boot Camp sponsored by Sisters of the Academy Institute, where disclosure is acceptable and support is received in planning and executing strategies as well as in the next steps (Gregory, 2001; Davis, Reynolds, & Jones, 2011).

SILENCED EXPERIENCES IN THE CLASSROOM

For Black women, our mere embodiment often defies what students believe professors should look like (Smith & Womble, 2000). "Given the scarcity of women in the academic ranks, students are not accustomed to seeing [us] as sources of knowledge, let alone as people who generate or produce that knowledge" (Johnson-Bailey & Lee, 2005, p. 114). A research participant in Harlow's (2003) study of race stated, "students do not usually see [Black] people in positions of power, especially [Black] women. As a result, they may doubt [Black] women's academic and leadership capabilities" (p. 353). Simply, informing students that one's name is Dr. _____ and should be addressed as such is met with strong resistance (Pittman, 2010). One of the present authors recalls receiving an e-mail from a student in which the author was addressed by the use of her first name while the student, in the same e-mail, referred to the author's colleagues, one who was a white male and another who was an Asian female, as "Dr. _____." She felt disappointed, as the student seemed to know enough to call the other professors by their title. So she responded to the e-mail and signed off as "Dr. _____." In another example, a student reported one of the authors to a superior, as she had informed the student that she was welcome to refer to her as "Dr. _____." The person above the author tried to *coach* her through what she had done wrong. The author was angry because of the pettiness of the situation, that she would not only have to encounter the student but the administrator as well, who did not understand the microaggression that had occurred, and thus, could not serve as an ally.

What we choose to teach also influences students' perception of our academic and leadership ability. Teaching courses that focus on diversity, multiculturalism, cultural competence, and intersectionality of different lived experiences such as disability, race, and class or gender and sexuality, comes at a high price (Orelus, 2013). Black women who teach these courses are described as intimidating, "bitter . . . [and] putting forth a political agenda" (Ladson-Billings, 1996, p. 79). One of the present authors, as a

Black professor in classrooms where 99 percent of the students are white, suggests that teaching sessions on white privilege and issues regarding people of color is uncomfortable. She states:

> I know that as counselors-in-training, students need to increase their self-awareness regarding racial identity development, stereotypes and assumptions about others based on privilege, I just wish I wasn't the one that had to teach these parts of the class. They are important conversations to have, but I feel like students think that I am only saying these things because I am Black and they do not have to take it seriously or pay attention. I see students rolling their eyes or proclaiming, 'I have a problem with immigrants coming over here and taking all the resources . . .' I want to respond to these comments, but I fear students will file complaints against me or I will be viewed as militant and potentially lose my job. Since students' outward responses on immigration and other like subjects, I have made regular appointments with my therapist to cope with the anxiety I experience from teaching this material.

Black women faculty also risk having cultural-specific courses assessed as "too narrow" and "unnecessary," as students ask, "Why is it important for me to learn this?" It is not atypical for Black women to receive low teaching evaluations (Bradley, 2005; Pittman, 2010; Smith & Johnson-Bailey, 2011) and for students to express their dissatisfaction in powerful ways. One of the current authors arrived at the office to find an evaluation underneath her door. A student had written all over the evaluation form with a Sharpie, expressing her displeasure that "too much time was spent on counseling skills and not enough time was spent teaching [her] how to get a job." Afraid of what other students thought, the author avoided reading the remaining evaluations. Another one of the authors remembers the first time she received student evaluations that ranged from comments on her style of dress (e.g., "needs to dress more professional"), performance (e.g., "she should not receive tenure"), and course content (e.g., "too much emphasis on cultural issues"). Now, her stomach drops every time she has to hand out course evaluations. In reflecting on those experiences, we found that while our course ratings are significantly above the departmental average and have been since our first year, we quickly glance at the overall scores to ensure we are in good standing and then shove the entire envelope in our file drawers in an attempt to contain the craziness that is potentially waiting and to physically exert some control over the situation. We only look more intently at the entire evaluations when it is time to develop our binder for promotion and tenure after we have created a degree of emotional distance from the situation, which could be an entire year later.

Smith and Johnson-Bailey (2011) described student ratings of teaching effectiveness for women faculty and found that "non-White female faculty's evaluation scores were lower than White female faculty and of the non-White female faculty, Black female faculty scores were lowest" (p. 128). As student evaluations impact tenure and promotion, Black female faculty may not feel comfortable sharing these experiences with colleagues or administration. Even when shared, sometimes, the response is not supportive. Negative teaching evaluations send the message that Black women do not belong and are perceived as less competent (Lazos, 2012). Regarding level of competency, 54 percent of Black women felt they had to prove their competence or intelligence, and 23 percent received inappropriate student challenges to intellectual authority (Harlow, 2003). Some challenges have to do with race, gender, and age simultaneously. For instance, Black female professors tend to experience greater challenges with younger white female students if they are 35 or younger and greater challenges with nontraditional students if they are 40 and older (McGowan, 2000). Our sense of belonging and levels of competence are assaulted in the classroom and manifest through micro-aggressions (Rockquemore & Laszloffy, 2008) tied to aggressively challenging course assignments, class structure, and content (Harris, 2007), which tend to emerge in the form of verbal attacks, such as "I don't mean to be rude, but . . ." and "Professor So-and-So didn't make us do that."

Navigating classroom hostility and the flat-out disrespect that spills over into e-mails, hallways, or our office leaves us drained, as we are constantly balancing multiple experiences of being a woman and a person of color, while fighting off "stereotypes of [being a nurturer] . . . or the bitch" (Pittman, 2010, p. 186). One of the present authors recalls a classroom experience in which a student spent a large part of the first class explaining how "Dr. X set his syllabus up this way . . . I'll show you a copy of his syllabus, so you can learn how to do one." The author felt disrespected and humiliated, as her ability to teach a course and develop a syllabus was doubted. Being compared to male professors or white professors is insulting. The relationship between the student and the author was strained throughout the entire semester, with the student constantly challenging the author and *Google*-ing concepts to try to argue that she was either wrong or erroneous in delivering information. She dreaded that class, lost her appetite before and after each session, and had nightmares when she imagined confronting the student. When she discussed these issues with administration, she was told that it was a classroom-management issue. Feeling unsupported, she left each class exhausted and questioned whether a university was the best place to work.

Black female faculty may often feel conflicted regarding how best to respond to students who challenge our embodiment. Will our responses be perceived as the Sapphire or the Mammy archetype (Bryant et al., 2005)? "These stereotypes, which evolved during slavery, continued to exist after the end of slavery and still contribute to the unique harassment experiences of [Black] women today" (Yarbrough & Bennett, 2000, para. 12). However, these are not the experiences that are discussed among nonwhite faculty at the lunch table or at the new faculty orientations. There is power in the willingness to acknowledge "something just ain't right," as it serves as a critical catalyst in birthing conversations and implementing strategies focused on deep structural change. Black women, as part of our socialization into the ivory tower must "resist the internalization of marginalization within the academy and fully embrace the belief that we have earned the right to be in the academy" (Henderson et al., 2010, p. 36). Finding ways to resist and cope with the spiritual and mental strain working in the academy brings is crucial for us.

Working in the academy is stressful enough without having to be concerned with battling judgmental comments about marital status, parenting choices, and dealing with unsavory students who behave in negative ways in the classroom, then "turn right around" and request a letter of recommendation. Having to decline writing letters, as the recommendation would be unfavorable, creates more disgruntled students, and the cycle continues. Racial battles occur in and out of the classroom and often lead to fatigue that manifests in the form of headaches, loss of sleep, decreased appetite, and to a great extent, withdrawal and isolation. Coworkers attacking personal choices and students doubting our capabilities to perform the job is compounded by colleagues who are sexually inappropriate and/or engage in bullying tactics in response to the intersection of our race and gender.

SILENCED EXPERIENCES OF SEXUAL HARASSMENT AND WORKPLACE BULLYING

The Equal Employment Opportunity Commission (1980) defines sexual harassment as:

Unwelcome sexual advances, requests for sexual favors, and other verbal or physical conduct of a sexual nature when (1) submission to such conduct is made either explicitly or implicitly a term or condition of an individual's employment, (2) submission to or rejection of such conduct by an individual is used as the basis for employment decisions affecting such individual or (3) such conduct has the purpose or effect of unreasonably interfering with an individual's work performance or creating an intimidating, hostile or offensive working environment. (pp. 74676–74677)

Sexual harassment is inclusive of gender harassment (e.g., hostile or misogynistic attitudes usually directed toward women), unwanted sexual attention (e.g., unsolicited sexualized comments, gestures, or contact), and sexual coercion (e.g., job-related threats or benefits to induce sexual cooperation; Fitzgerald, 1996). A meta-analysis of 86,000 respondents across multiple work sectors found that sexual harassment is more likely to occur in organizations with large power differentials between levels of the organization; however, reported incidents were notably lower in the academic sector (Ilies, Hauserman, Schwochau, & Stibal, 2003). The theory of double jeopardy posits individuals of multiple devalued social groups, such as Black women, are at greater risk to be targets of workplace sexual harassment (Beal, 1970). Berdahl and Moore (2006) tested this theory, with results indicating that minority women were significantly harassed more than minority men, white men, and white women.

Entering the academy, we are aware that while minority women are more likely to be harassed (Dey, Korn, & Sax, 1996), it is not unusual for incidents of sexual harassment to go unreported (Firestone & Harris, 2003). Rather than disclose incidents of sexual harassment out of fear of retribution, retaliation, beliefs that the harasser will go unpunished, risk of being ostracized or labeled a *troublemaker*, or being viewed as a *victim*, Black women often deal with the issue of sexual harassment in silence, by leaving the organization, or tolerating the behaviors (McDonald, 2012). Studies suggest that these aforementioned fears or reservations to report incidents of sexual harassment are not unfounded. Although "silence means that sexual harassment at the office may go on and on" (Jones & Shorter-Gooden, 2003, p. 39), weighing the decision to break one's silence is made more complex, as it is not uncommon for outcomes to remain the same or possibly worsen for those who choose to report experiences of sexual harassment (Bergman, Langhout, Palmieri, Cortina, & Fitzgerald, 2002; Lee, Heilmann, & Near, 2004).

One of the authors shared that she silently endures unwelcomed comments about her physicality and continually seeks ways to fend off unwanted invitations to fraternize outside of work by a tenured colleague, while attempting to maintain decorum and professional collegiality with him because he sits on the committee for promotion and tenure. She stated, "I hate going anywhere in the building where I may run into him, especially if I'm alone." She also mentioned experiencing anxiety and stomach problems. The fear of a lack of professional and personal support as well as minimization of the situation has caused her not to report his actions to administrators. Short- and long-term effects of sexual harassment can be far-reaching. Empirical research suggests that women who have experienced sexual harassment have increased negative mental, emotional, and health outcomes such as depression, anxiety, fear, eating disorders, sleep disturbances, and stress-related illnesses, as well as decreased productivity and concentration and lower rates of life satisfaction (Lampman, Phelps, Bancroft, & Beneke, 2009; Munson, Hulin, & Drasgow, 2000; Nydegger, Paludi, DeSouza, & Paludi, 2006; Rederstorff,

Buchanan, & Settles, 2007). While sexual harassment has become a widely discussed issue in the media, bullying still remains a silenced and toxic experience for Black women in academia.

Bullying in the academy has received little attention in comparison with many other issues that arise among professionals working in higher education. While there is no one true recognized definition for workplace bullying (Lewis & Orford, 2005), it has been defined as excessive negative attention or harassment directed toward an employee who has a fear of defending her or himself (Einarsen, Hoel, Zapf, & Cooper, 2011). Workplace bullying has been identified as a major source of stress in the workplace for both genders; however, for women, bullying in the workplace tends to have even more detrimental effects because of its impact on health, self-esteem, work performance, and increased impairment in social relationships (Lewis, 2006; MacIntosh, Wuest, Gray, & Aldous, 2010). Additional consequences of bullying in academia include high occurrences of sickness and fatigue leading to an increase in the frequency of sick leave taken among women (Keashly & Neuman, 2010), which greatly exacerbate the situation if conditions remain the same upon the woman's return to work (O'Donnell, MacIntosh, & Wuest, 2010). The authors acknowledge that white women in academia experience workplace bullying, yet the intersection of race and gender creates a differentiated experience for Black women, who are more often likely to report feelings of marginalization and powerlessness (Harley, 2008).

As bullying in academia is often related to power struggles between a faculty member and administrator or someone in a position of authority, many instances of bullying go unreported out of fear of negative consequences (Keashly & Neuman, 2010). Bullying can take place in several ways including, but not limited to, denial of resources, obligating excessive amounts of work, and unfair evaluations (Raineri, Frear, & Edmonds, 2011). One of the present authors recalls:

> Over the years, my department chair became increasingly demeaning in the way in which he spoke to me, and the demands he made seemed to intensify. Although I considered myself to be a hard worker, I began to realize that a lot of work was being dumped on me because I was the newest and youngest African-American faculty member. I was hesitant to say anything because I had not yet gained tenure, and I was afraid of being denied, although, my teaching, research, and service went above and beyond the standards set. As a Black Woman working in a White male-dominated atmosphere, it was difficult to ascertain if my concerns would be heard or if I would just be regarded as another "angry Black woman." His condescending behavior and attitude did not extend to the non-minority faculty and it was my perception that minority women bared the harshest

forms of bullying. The anxiety I experienced at the thought of walking into this White man's office to tell him that I was unhappy frightened me to my core because I knew that if I failed in this attempt, the next person in the chain of command looked exactly like my supervisor. The thought of this manifested itself in headaches and other physical symptoms such as sweating and chest palpitations. In the end, it wasn't until the semester after I was granted tenure that I actually felt empowered enough to have a conversation with him about his behavior—a full six years after it began.

CONCLUSION

The lived experiences of Black women in academia are ones that have often gone overlooked or untold. Despite the legitimate and expert power bestowed on professors, Black female professors struggle with referent power. "Black women in the academy is a place of privilege and challenge simultaneously" (Henderson et al., 2010, p. 37). While the decision to work in academia has been made, managing manifestations of racial battle fatigue and employing methods to cope with MEES is no easy feat and is, at times, downright draining. The authors expound on instances of double consciousness and intersectionality as experienced by Black women who have been faced with the difficult decision of keeping silent about experiences related to motherhood, incidents in the classroom, sexual harassment, and workplace bullying.

Black women in academia need a safe space to break the silence regarding our experiences. Providing more financial support to attend conferences that focus on Black women in higher education, as an example of a safe space, is only one step in that direction. The Association of Black Women in Higher Education and the American Association of Blacks in Higher Education are organizations that Black women in academia could turn to for support and validation. We charge institutions to not only remain committed to supporting safe spaces abroad (e.g., conferences), but to also act with intentionality and diligence in establishing safe spaces in "their own backyard." Doing so is vital in demonstrating congruence and establishing trust that silenced experiences can be shared.

REFERENCES

Beal, F. (1970). *Double jeopardy: To be black and female*. Detroit, MI: Radical Education Project.

Berdahl, J., & Moore, C. (2006). Workplace harassment: Double jeopardy for minority women. *Journal of Applied Psychology*, *91*(2), 426.

Bergman, M., Langhout, R., Palmieri, P., Cortina, M., & Fitzgerald, L. (2002). The (un)reasonableness of reporting: antecedents and consequences of reporting sexual harassment. *Journal of Applied Psychology*, *87*(2), 230.

Bradley, C. (2005). The career experiences of African American women faculty: Implications for counselor education programs. *College Student Journal, 39*(3), 518–527.

Brown, C., & Davis, J. (Eds.). (2000). *Black sons to mother: Compliments, critiques, and challenges for cultural workers in education.* New York, NY: Peter Lang.

Bryant, R., Coker, A., Durodoye, B., McCollum, V. J, Pack-Brown, S., Constantine, M., & O'Bryant, B. (2005). Having our say: African American women, diversity, and counseling. *Journal of Counseling and Development, 83*(3), 313–319.

Carroll, G. (1998). *Environmental stress and African Americans: The other side of the moon.* Westport, CT: Praeger.

Chronicle of Higher Education. (2010). *Almanac of higher education 2009–10.* Retrieved from http://chronicle.com/section/Almanac-of-Higher-Education/141

Crenshaw, K. (1989). Demarginalizing the intersection of race and sex: A black feminist critique of antidiscrimination doctrine, feminist theory, and antiracist politics. *University of Chicago Legal Forum,* 139–167.

Curtis, J., & Thornton, S. (2013). The annual report on the economic status of the profession 2012–2013. *Academe,* 4–19.

Davis, D., Reynolds, R., & Jones, T. (2011). Promoting the inclusion of tenure earning black women in academe: Lessons for leaders in education. *Florida Journal of Educational Administration and Policy, 5*(1), 28–41.

Dey, E., Korn, J., & Sax, L. (1996). Betrayed by the academy: The sexual harassment of women college faculty. *The Journal of Higher Education, 67*(2), 149–173.

Dugger, K. (1996). Social location and gender-roles attitudes: A comparison of black and white women. In E. N. Chow, D. Wilkinson, & M. Baca Zinn (Eds.), *Race, class, and gender: Common bonds, different voices* (pp. 32–51). Thousand Oaks, CA: Sage.

Einarsen, S., Hoel, H., Zapf, D., & Cooper, C. L. (2011). The concept of bullying and harassment at work: The European tradition. In S. Einarsen, H. Hoel, D. Zapf, & C. L. Cooper (Eds.), *Bullying and harassment in the workplace: Developments in theory, research, and practice* (pp. 3–26). Boca Raton, FL: CRC Press.

Equal Employment Opportunity Commission. (1980). Guidelines on discrimination because of sex (Sect. 1604.11). *Federal Register, 45,* 74676–74677.

Essed, P. (2000). Dilemmas in leadership: Women of colour in the academy. *Ethnic and Racial Studies, 23*(5), 888–904.

Firestone, J., & Harris, R. (2003). Perceptions of effectiveness of responses to sexual harassment in the US military, 1988 and 1995. *Gender, Work and Organization, 10,* 42–64.

Fitzgerald, L. F. (1996). Sexual harassment: The definition and measurement of a construct. In M. A. Paludi (Ed.), *Sexual harassment on college campuses: Abusing the ivory power* (pp. 21–44). Albany, NY: University of New York Press.

Gilkes, C. (1980). Holding back the ocean with a broom: Black women and community work. In L. Rodgers-Rose (Ed.), *The black woman* (pp. 217–232). London, UK: Sage.

Gregory, S. (2001). Black faculty women in the academy: History, status, and future. *Journal of Negro Education, 70*(3), 124–138.

Gutiérrez y Muhs, G., Niemann, Y., González, C., & Harris, A. (Eds.). (2012). *Presumed incompetent: The intersections of race and class for women in academia.* Boulder, CO: University Press of Colorado.

Harley, D. (2008). Maids of academe: African American women faculty at predominantly white institutions. *Journal of African American Studies, 12*(1), 19–36.

Harlow, R. (2003). "Race doesn't matter, but . . .": The effect of race on professors' experiences and emotion management in the undergraduate college classroom. *Social Psychology Quarterly, 66*(4), 348–363.

Harper, E., Baldwin, R., Gansneder, B., & Chronister, J. (2001). Full-time women faculty off the tenure track: Profile and practice. *The Review of Higher Education, 24*(3), 237–257.

Harris, T. (2007). Black feminist thought and cultural contracts: Understanding the intersection and negotiation of racial, gendered, and professional identities in the academy. *New Directions of Teaching and Learning, 2007*(110), 55–64.

Henderson, T., Hunter, A., & Hildreth, G. (2010). Outsiders within the academy: Strategies for resistance and mentoring African American women. *Michigan Family Review, 14*(1), 28–41.

Hill Collins, P. (2000). *Black feminist thought: Knowledge, consciousness, and the politics of empowerment* (2nd ed.). New York, NY: Routledge.

hooks, b. (1990). Marginality as site of resistance. In R. Ferguson, M. Gever, T. Minh-ha, & C. West (Eds.), *Out there: Marginalization and contemporary cultures* (pp. 341–343). Cambridge, MA: MIT Press.

Ilies, R., Hauserman, N., Schwochau, S., & Stibal, J. (2003). Reported incidence rates of work-related sexual harassment in the United States: Using meta-analysis to explain reported rate disparities. *Personnel Psychology, 56*(3), 607–631.

James, S. (1993). Mothering: A possible black feminist link to social transformation? In S. James and A. Busia (Eds.), *Theorizing black feminisms: The visionary pragmatism of black women* (pp. 44–54). London, UK: Routledge.

Johnson-Bailey, J., & Lee, M. (2005). Women of color in the academy? Where's our authority in the classroom? *Feminist Teacher, 15*(2), 111–122.

Jones, C., & Shorter-Gooden, K. (2003). *Shifting: The double lives of black women in America*. New York, NY: HarperCollins.

Keashly, L., & Neuman, J. (2010). Faculty experiences with bullying in higher education: Causes, consequences and management. *Administrative Theory and Praxis, 32*(1), 48–70.

Ladson-Billings, G. (1996).Silence as weapons: Challenges of a black professor teaching white students. *Theory into Practice, 35*(2), 79–85.

Lampman, C., Phelps, A., Bancroft, S., & Beneke, M. (2009). Contrapower harassment in academia: A survey of faculty experience with student incivility, bullying, and sexual attention. *Sex Roles, 60*(5-6), 331–346.

Lazos, S. (2012). Are student teaching evaluations holding back women and minorities? The perils of "doing" gender and race in the classroom. In G. Gutiérrez y Muhs, Y. Niemann, C. González, & A. Harris (Eds.), *Presumed incompetent: The intersections of race and class for women in academia* (pp. 164–197). Boulder, CO: University Press of Colorado.

Lee, J. (2011). Does universalism hold in academia? Focusing on women and racial minority faculty. *The Journal of the Professoriate, 6*(1), 48–66.

Lee, J. Y., Heilmann, S. G., & Near, J. P. (2004). Blowing the whistle on sexual harassment: Test of a model of predictors and outcomes. *Human Relations, 57*(3), 297–322.

Lewis, S. (2006). Recognition of workplace bullying: A qualitative study of women targets in the public sector. *Journal of Community and Applied Social Psychology, 16*, 119–135.

Lewis, S., & Orford, J. (2005). Women's experiences of workplace bullying: Changes in social relationships. *Journal of Community and Applied Social Psychology, 15*, 29–47.

Lewis, V. (2013). To tell or not to tell: Single motherhood and the academic job market. In M. Castaneda & K. Isgro (Eds.), *Mothers in academia* (pp. 57–65). New York, NY: Columbia University Press.

MacIntosh, J., Wuest, J., Gray, M. M., & Aldous, S. (2010). Effects of workplace bullying on how women work. *Western Journal of Nursing Research, 32*(7), 910–931.

Marr, V. (2013). Teaching for change: Notes from a broke queer hustling mama. In S. Nzinga-Johnson (Ed.), *Laboring positions: Black women, mothering and the academy* (pp. 58–74). Bradford, ON: Demeter Press.

McDonald, P. (2012). Workplace sexual harassment 30 years on: A review of the literature. *International Journal of Management Reviews, 14*(1), 1–17.

McGowan, J. (2000). Multicultural teaching: African-American faculty classroom teaching experiences in predominantly white colleges and universities. *Multicultural Education, 8*(2), pp. 19–22.

Munson, L. J., Hulin, C., & Drasgow, F. (2000). Longitudinal analysis of dispositional influences and sexual harassment: Effects on job and psychological outcomes. *Personnel Psychology, 53,* 21–46.

Nydegger, R., Paludi, M., DeSouza, E. R., & Paludi, C. A. (2006). Incivility, sexual harassment, and violence in the workplace. *Gender, race, and ethnicity in the workplace: Issues and challenges for today's organizations, 2*, 51–81.

Nzinga-Johnson, S. (2013). *Laboring positions: Black women, mothering and the academy.* Bradford, ON: Demeter Press.

O'Donnell, S., MacIntosh, J., & Wuest, J. (2010). A theoretical understanding of sickness absence among women who have experienced workplace bullying. *Qualitative Health Research, 20*, 439–452.

O'Reilly, A. (2004). *Mother outlaws: Theories and practices of empowered mothering.* Toronto, ON: Women's Press.

Orelus, P. W. (2013). The institutional cost of being a professor of color: Unveiling micro-aggression, racial [in]visibility, and racial profiling through the lens of critical race theory. *Current Issues in Education, 16*(2), 1–10.

Pierce, C. (1975). The mundane extreme environment and its effect on teaming. In S. G. Brainard (Ed.), *Learning disabilities: Issues and recommendations for research* (pp. 111–119). Washington DC: National Institute of Education, Department of Health, Education, and Welfare.

Pittman, C. (2010). Race and gender oppression in the classroom: The experiences of women faculty of color with white male students. *Teaching Sociology, 38*(3), 183–196.

Raineri, E. M., Frear, D. F., & Edmonds, J. J. (2011). An examination of the academic reach of faculty and administrator bullying. *International Journal of Business and Social Science, 2*(12), 22–35.

Rederstorff, J., Buchanan, N., & Settles, I. (2007). The moderating roles of race and gender-role attitudes in the relationship between sexual harassment and psychological well-being. *Psychology of Women Quarterly, 31*(1), 50–61.

Renzulli, L., Grant, L., & Kathuria, S. (2006). Race, gender, and the wage gap: Comparing faculty salaries in predominately white and historically black colleges and universities. *Gender and Society, 20*(4), 491–510.

Rockquemore, K., & Laszloffy, T. (2008). *The black academic's guide to winning tenure without losing your soul*. Boulder, CO: Lynne Rienner.

Rodriguez, D., & Boahene, A. (2012). The politics of rage: Empowering women of color in the academy. *Cultural Studies ↔ Cultural Methodologies, 12*(5), 450–458.

Ryu, M. (2010). *Minorities in higher education 2010 status report*. Washington, DC: American Council on Education.

Smith, W. (2004). Black faculty coping with racial battle fatigue: The campus racial climate in a post-civil rights era. In D. Cleveland (Ed.), *A long way to go: Conversations about race by African American faculty and graduate students* (pp. 171–190). New York, NY: Peter Lang.

Smith, B., & Johnson-Bailey, J. (2011). Student ratings of teaching effectiveness: Implications for non-white women in the academy. *The Negro Educational Review, 62*(1-4), 115–140.

Smith, B., & Womble, M. (2000). African American women: effective teaching in the academy. *Research Association of Minority Professors Journal, 4*(1), 29–47.

Stanley, T. (2005). The one with the baby: Single-mothering in academia. In R. Bassett (Ed.), *Parenting and professing: Balancing family work with an academic career* (pp. 82–88). Nashville, TN: Vanderbilt University Press.

Thompson, C., & Dey, E. (1998). Pushed to the margins: Sources of stress for African American college and university faculty. *Journal of Higher Education, 69*(3), 324–345.

U.S. Department of Education, National Center for Education Statistics. (2012). *The condition of education 2012 (NCES 2012-045), Indicator 47*. Retrieved from http://nces.ed.gov/fastfacts/display.asp?id=72

Yarbrough, M., & Bennett, C. (2000). Cassandra and the "Sistahs": The peculiar treatment of African American women in the myth of women as liars. *Journal of Gender, Race and Justice, 626–657*. Retrieved from http://academic.udayton.edu/race/05intersection/gender/AAWomen01a.htm

Chapter 16

At the Margins of Social Justice: The Moral Debate on Special Education and the Other Latino

Bernardo E. Pohl, Jr.

AMERICAN MISMATCHED FAITH IN EDUCATION

As a national institution, public education holds a very privileged and important place in our country. It is the democratic, cultural, and social compass of our nation, which must mold young people in this country into productive citizens. As David Purpel (1989) argues, it is in the schools where students must learn how to read and write, do math, succeed in sports, be poets and artists, learn to cook and sew, and be dreamers and realistic achievers. We expect our schools to be safe, comfortable places where students decipher their deepest questions regarding sex, health, rituals, friendship, love, and hate. In this country, we are firm in our conviction that everyone must benefit from a formal education, believing that such education is the giant umbrella that holds everyone together as the big social equalizer. In short, America has a great amount of faith in our public education system.

Unfortunately, it is sad to realize that public education, as a national institution, is under attack. It is suffering from a mountainous barrage of assaults from a disgruntled public in the form of angry taxpayers, disappointed parents, homeschooling advocates, magnet school proponents, private school supporters, disingenuous business leaders, opportunistic journalists, and religious groups (Miller, 1990; Purpel, 1989). Moreover, special interest factions (e.g., parents, lawyers, business leaders, religious groups, and others) have hijacked the public school system in order to promote their political agendas. Surprisingly, however, these groups tend to share the common belief that our public schools must promote, sustain, and protect some basic democratic values—values rooted on a economic apparatus based on capitalism, patriotic convictions rooted on Puritanism, and concepts of individual freedom grounded on rigid Protestant traditions (Miller, 1990). In that regard, there seems to be very little disagreement in what this nation expects from our public schools.

SPECIAL EDUCATION IN CRISIS

Today, 10–12 percent of the population suffers from a disability (Jones, 2007); and in the primary and secondary schools, there are over 6 million students enrolled in some form of federally funded program that supports the special needs population. To put it in simpler terms, one out of eight students in this nation officially qualifies for special education services (Valentine, 2007). Unfortunately, the education of the disabled is also in crisis. It is safe to say that we are at the end of road, and there is nowhere else to turn. As Joe Valentine (2007) argues, we—those working with the disabled—find ourselves in a constant state of professional schizophrenia (p. 127) as we deal with the riddles, tensions, demands, and contradictions of the profession. Sadly, the result is that we find ourselves unable to figure out how society's most pressing matters affect the disabled: economical, social, political, and cultural.

For years, academics have addressed the most pressing social and cultural issues regarding general education (Freire, 1970; Kincheloe, 2004; Miller, 1990; Purpel, 1989). Therefore, in the second decade of the twenty-first century, we should be able to say that there is a well-established field of disability research in that context. Unfortunately, the sad truth is that we cannot (Valentine, 2007). There is minimal research that investigates how these forces affect the disabled (Artiles, Harris-Murri, & Rostenberg, 2006)—especially research that explores how these factors impact disabled individuals who are also ethnic minorities (Artiles, Trent, & Kuan, 1997). Examples are rare of emancipatory and liberating pedagogies on disability education (Goldstein, 1995; Poplin, 1995). Furthermore, narrative inquiry and ethnographic studies of exceptional students continue to be unexplored (Clandinin & Raymond, 2006). When it comes to narrative, as Jones (2007) states, they—the disabled—continue to be the silenced voice (p. 32). In conclusion, as Valentine (2007) argues, there is a culture of silence when it comes to social justice and education of the disabled in academia (p. 128).

If this is not enough to make us pause, consider the fact that special education must confront three major dilemmas. The first dilemma involves the inclusion movement, which has been gaining popularity over the last couple of decades (Blanchet, Brantlinger, & Shealey, 2005). The key concept of inclusion is to educate the disabled student within the general school population. This is referred as *the least restrictive environment*. Inclusion, however, comes with its own bag of problems, including lack of training, funds, and teacher support. However, the major problem with inclusion continues to be a problem of attitude by parents, teachers, and administrators. The main reason for this is because special education no longer includes a small portion of the student population with very specific medical challenges and severe disabilities (Dorries & Haller, 2001). Today, there are 13 main categories for special education services, which include milder and less severe conditions, ranging from hearing impairment and blindness to emotional disturbance and learning disability. Within these categories, there are plenty of subcategories, making the entire situation overwhelming. In addition, inclusion comes with the tensions and raw feelings from professionals working in a system that continually demands more from teachers, parents, and administrators—a system that offers very few guidelines on how to go about implementing a better learning experience for those with special needs.

The second dilemma is the overrepresentation of linguistic and racial minorities' students in special education (Valentine, 2007). Latinos, African Americans, and Native Americans are particularly affected by this trend, especially in the urban schooling settings where the disability labeling has become the new tool for segregation. What makes this particularly disturbing is the social acceptance of this form of disability-based apartheid (Ferri & Connor, 2005; Kauffman & Hallahan, 1995). Sadly, it is safe to say that discrimination based on disability does not spark the same social outcry that other forms of discrimination generate (Ferri & Connor, 2005; Pohl, 2013). Contrary to what we might tend to believe, issues of race, linguistic, and ethnicity are not at the front-and-center of the disability and education discourse (Slee, 2001), while class and socioeconomics do play a very big role in determining whether or not a student receives special services (Valentine, 2007).

The third dilemma is the apparent silence—the disregard from the academic setting to truly comprehend the disabled. The current research and discourse in disability education continue to be driven by scientific demands and constraints of academia (Gallagher, 2001). For the last four decades, the medical and social models have been the two main dominant forces in disability research (Baglieri & Knopf, 2004; Barnes, 1997; Reiser, 2006). The medical model looks at disability as a biological problem, which needs to be fixed (Ong-Dean, 2005); the social model proposes that the limitation the disabled encounters are social barriers (Oliver & Zarb, 1989; Stiker, 1999). Generally, however, disability research continues to be data driven, numerical in nature, and scientifically rationalized (Pohl, 2013)—research that rarely explores the human, lived experience of the disabled (Jones, 2007). The result is an endless supply of technically jargonized literature, which is hardly ever utilized by professionals in the trenches (Valentine, 2007).

THE URGENCY OF OUR TIMES

In the first decade of the 21st century, we cannot ignore the urgent troubles of our times: permanent unemployment, terrorism, the resurgence of the Cold War, and economic uncertainty. Yet, it seems that in special education there are other issues at the forefront of the discourse deemed more important: evaluation, diagnostic, placement, budget, inclusion, and tracking. In this new millennium, we are now witnessing a serious decline in the government's concerns for human welfare, ignoring the profound social effects of massive layoffs, salary stagnation, serious international competition, a state of apprehension for challenging the status quo, the revival of political fear and intolerance, and the erosion of labor rights. As more fervent calls are made to include the disabled student in the mainstream classroom, while some profess to the benefits of including the disabled in the standardized testing craze (Hehir, 2005), it is rather appalling to see how society ignores these social issues in regards to the disabled.

NARRATIVE, DISABILITY, AND CITIZENSHIP

As we can see, the problems faced by education—regular or special—are many; and by now it is clear that we are in need of a pedagogy of consciousness for the disabled. This means having a society where its members work together for a common good, while attaining their own individualism (Erevelles, 2002). Nevertheless, even within the disability studies community, people appear to be at odds about what constitutes citizenship for the disabled. There might be many explanations for this, and we cannot list all of them; however, the answer might be in our apparent lack of self-narrative and examination, which deprives us from ontological spaces where we can explore our state of *being*.

Narrative has the benefit of providing the chance for the individual to be critical and frank about the struggle between society, justice, and power (Freire, 1970; Kincheloe, 2002). It is a dialectic mode where a profound self-conversation can occur, where the individual becomes aware of the dominating social forces surrounding him or her. It is a process that encourages examination of society's relationship, self-critiquing the factors limiting self-growth (Valentine, 2007). Narrative, as an inquiry, produces the critical *self* who explores the social, political, ideological, economic, and cultural problems of our times (McLaren & Kincheloe, 2007).

In this form, narrative becomes a desire to address moral issues in education within the increasingly normalized (Gur-Ze'ev, 2002), technically rationalized (Eisner, 2001), and objective based pedagogy demanded by those advocating for the official knowledge (Apple, 1993), indicating a profound personal transformation and pedagogical self-construction (Ellis, 1997). Believing that education is but one aspect of human transformation, the teacher becomes a researcher, embracing the understanding of the human experience of teaching and learning (see Aoki, 1983; Aoki, 1989/1990). As a result, there is a greater awareness of the educator's role; therefore, education is no longer the dispensing of facts (Freire, 1970), but a lived experience (Aoki, 1983). In the end, the promise of this inner transformation becomes attainable; and this self-awareness becomes an invaluable effect, helping one to cope with the promises and challenges of educating our youth.

Self-narrative inquiry establishes the opportunity for teacher reflection (McNiff & Whitehead, 2002) and action research (Schön, 1991). Narrative is a powerful tool for understanding teaching as a human experience (Craig, 2001), which promotes the livelihood and fluidity of inquiry (Schwab, 1982), helping us reflect on processes and practices (Schön, 1982). Action research promotes empirical questions (McNiff, 2007; Whitehead, 1989). This study, as such, explores the various scenarios necessary for addressing moral issues in special education through research, narrative, and self-inquiry.

MY LIFE: THE DISABLED AT THE MARGINS AND THE OTHER LATINO

As a child, I looked at my life in very paradoxical terms. I grew up in a multicultural, multiethnic South American family. My mom is from Chile, and my dad is from Argentina. She has deep Spanish-Chilean roots, while he has a strong German-Argentine heritage. However, I did not acquire a strong cultural mark from either side. I spent my childhood constantly traveling South America, living with my family in different countries because of my dad's work in the oil business. I was born in Argentina, but I never spent any significant time in that country to consider myself a true Argentine. By the time I was five, we had lived in Brazil and Peru for two years. When I was six, my family returned to Argentina to spend a year with our grandparents so that my dad could go to work at the offshore oilfields of Scotland and Nigeria. When I was seven, we moved to Venezuela, where I lived the rest of my childhood and my early teens at an American company oil compound.

In Venezuela, my life quickly evolved around street baseball, salsa music, and tropical nature. Venezuela was so different from Euro-centric Argentina and the cold-crisp Patagonian plains. However, it had an instantaneous hold on my soul, which I never let go. In the oil company compound, I was quickly inducted into English from the Venezuelan Americans, who acted more like American than Venezuelan, pretending that they did not understand a word of Spanish. Eventually, English would become our semiofficial language.

However, growing up in different places left me asking many questions regarding my identity, sparking my curiosity about our family's true heritage and culture, wondering why it always felt as if we were the outsiders who never have had a place that we could truly call our own—a place where we could actually belong. In many ways, my life has many parallels with *West Side Story*, had Maria and Tony been able to marry, properly live as husband and wife, and have kids. The color of the skin, economic status, and a privileged education did help tremendously in preventing what otherwise would had been total marginalization from all possible sides. After all, for my maternal grandmother, he was not Chilean, but another cold-hearted German boy from upper Buenos Aires in search of an innocent southern girl. For my paternal grandfather, she was not German, but another darky from the Patagonian south in search of a better life in the big city. For her friends, he was not one of the boys from the neighborhood, but another geophysicist venturing outside the compound. For her sisters and aunties, he was only having fun while he was in town for the drilling season. For his brothers, the family's German heritage would be lost. Later, as the years went on, for our Argentine friends, we were the deserters who were traveling the world. For the Americans and Europeans in the compound in Venezuela, we were the Argies who were not supposed to live there; and once in Houston, we were the wets who crossed the river, and the Argentina and oil company story was just a lie. For the Mexican and Cubans in school, we were the arrogant Argentines. So much left me wondering, nevertheless, how I survived this experience without any major trauma. In my early years, I wanted to seek those answers to my questions; it just seemed, however, that I was never able to find proper spaces where I could do just that. Many of these questions would be unanswered until I went to graduate school.

Living among Americans, Canadians, and Europeans, the compound had an Anglo-Saxon-American feeling to it. Inside the compound, one was in suburban small-town USA; and in many ways, it truly was a different world from tropical Venezuela. Halloween, Thanksgiving, Sunday crab-boils, and college bowls replaced soccer, Maté tea, and Argentinean empanadas. Soon, the Spanish-Italian-Euro-centric culture of Argentina and Chile faded in memory. Mom, however, refused to send us to the American school. According to her, we needed to keep our heritage, so we attended the local private Catholic school. Therefore, we grew up in this weird, mixed environment of the American-Anglonized culture inside the company's compound and the flare of Venezuela's Caribbean life at school. Eventually, we would move to suburban Houston; and for me, the "burbs" were just like the oil compound, only on steroids.

During most of the 1970s, Mom practically raised us by herself. Dad was constantly being deployed around the world due to his work. Quickly, Mom asserted herself as the stronghold and pillar of the family. She was the relegated stepdaughter who was thrown out of the house and left to survive on her own since the age of 11 or 12; therefore, she did not waste any time in imposing her no-nonsense, pull-no-punches, and take-no-garbage personality. Dad was the family's teddy bear, showing us his tenderness and love every time he was at home. From Mom, we got our faithfulness and strong obedience to Catholicism, desire to make good grades, and determination to succeed. Forced to fight for her mere survival since she was a little girl, she never accepted or tolerated weakness or defeat. Under her wing, one must fight, be strong, be the hardest worker, swallow your tears, and never let your guard down. From Dad, we got our love for books, painting, music, reading, and studying. Under his wing, we learned to pursue our passion for education.

Education has always been important in my life. For Dad, who grew up in a family of teachers and educators, education was essential. He showed the tender, loving side of learning, encouraging us to do our homework and make good grades. For Mom, growing up in a family where the concept of education was almost nonexistent, she was the strong-willed person, determined to make sure we did our very best in school and became productive members of society. She always said that we were not going to end up like her good-for-nothing brothers and cousins, while she praised my dad and his father for having so many degrees and so much education. As I grew older, education became more than simply doing homework and making good grades; it emerged as the avenue where I could indulge my curiosity of exploring all these crossing languages and cultures, fueling my life and spirit.

I was born prematurely with cerebral palsy due to labor complications. When my mom was pregnant and on vacation, she had an accident while crossing a snowy street at a ski resort in Chile. I turned upside down inside my mother's womb. A military medic, who was also on vacation, helped my mom survive the critical first 48 hours, as she had convulsions and high fever, and almost lost me. Once my parents were back in Argentina, doctors suggested an abortion. My mom insisted on giving birth. During a routine check, an inexperienced resident broke the amniotic sac, causing my mom to go into premature labor. In the commotion, I lost oxygen to the brain during the drug-induced and forced labor. Once I was born, nurses were unable to detect whether I was breathing, so they literally started to punch me. After they stopped beating me, I was officially declared dead. As the hospital's nun and chaplain on duty were performing my last rites, they discovered that I was alive. My dad decided to place his glasses on my nose, and they saw that I was breathing. I was so small that they kept me in an incubator for three months.

I was paralyzed from the neck down until I was two; I could not use my legs until I was four. Doctors told my parents that I was going to be a complete vegetable, a useless human being. My mother decided that things were going to be different, so she taught herself how to perform physical therapy. In order to relax my stiff muscles, she gave me intensive massage sessions; eventually, I was able to move my head, neck, and arms. When I was three, she took the initiative to make me walk. She achieved this by filling an entire room with balloons, placed me in the floor, and let me play. Since I wanted to grab the balloons, I started to move around on the floor. Soon, I was able to move my legs. By the time I was six, I was running and jumping.

Despite my disability, I do not remember that I became truly aware of my disability until I was a teenager. My childhood was consumed with playing cops and robbers, recreating Maradona's World Cup moves with my brother, and dreaming of working on the oilfield like my dad. It was not until I became a teenager that the reality of the laughs, mockery, and limitations started to have an effect on me. Mom also had a lot to do with this. All of us had to grow up under her strong-willed command, and there was no space for feeling sorry or defeated. We never had a time to think about it. If things went wrong, tough it up and keep on going.

Elementary and middle school were fun—lots of playing without too much regard for making good grades. It was in high school, however, where my life took a sudden turn. It hit me very hard to see my brother and two sisters excel effortless in everything they did. Actually, it was not effortless. It was the result of very hard and arduous work, but I did not see it that way. During my tenth grade, I finally decided to be like them. I was going to make the grade, be on the honor roll, and excel just like them. By the time I graduated from high school, I was making straight As, was a regular in the honor roll list, and moved from 610th to 205th place in the class ranking.

Not everything in secondary school was a success story. I was placed officially in special needs services in eighth grade. With that came all of the stigmas of being placed in a totally separate category, without truly understanding why. Suddenly, I found myself in different classes, away from my brother. This was different from Venezuela, where my disability was a mere physical inconvenience, but I was part of the regular class, and everyone helped me in that regard. Peers helped me with homework, notes, and projects. Teachers provided me with the support and the extra time that I needed. In sports, I was the goalie, umpire, or server, and I was part of the action. In the United States, everything was so different; and abruptly, I was labeled, tracked, evaluated, and separated. For somebody capable of hitting a perfect home run or bend it like Beckham, playing chess and shuffleboard in adaptive physical education was so humiliating.

Despite my new reality, my disability was the last thing I had in my mind. Middle school was a struggle in survival. I was just trying to learn the system. Freshly arrived in the United States, learning the ropes of an American middle school was like trying to learn to live on a totally different planet. For me, it was horrible to cope with the bell-to-bell period schedule without time for rest. Gone were the days of long recess, studying periods between classes to do our work, and the lazy lunches under the mango trees.

High school was equally hard for me. Yes, I did make the grades and honor roll. In high school, however, I learned how detrimental and devastating the world of special education can be. Coming from Venezuela, where I attended regular classes, being placed in modified classes with a watered-down curriculum was so detrimental. Counselors and administrators seriously believed that the grades from Venezuela were not a true reflection of my abilities, and they did not hide their belief that I was socially promoted before I arrived in the United States When I started to make nothing but straight As in high school, I requested to be placed in regular courses; however, I was told that I would not survive the demanding curriculum. I always wanted to be in Algebra and regular math like my brother, but my pleas were never heard. I was not allowed to take Algebra I—a freshman-level course—until I was a junior. When I made a perfect one hundred in Algebra I for the year, I requested to take Algebra II in 12th grade. However, the administrators placed me back in Consumer Math during my senior year. They told me that Algebra II was too hard, and I needed a refresher, according to my counselor, Mr. Pears (not his real name). Moreover, he made it clear that my algebra teacher, Mrs. Flower (not her real name), modified my grades to give me a little slack.

My dream was to be an architect. Since I was little, I loved to do drafting, also known as technical drawing. As a little kid, I would sit beside my dad or my godfather in their studies and pretend that I too was designing an oilfield tool. In high school, I fought so hard to take drafting and learn the craft. I was always told no. One day, during my junior year, I showed my drawings to Mr. Pears. He took me to see the drafting teacher, Mr. Orsak (not his real name), who basically told me to not even think about taking his class. He said that he did not have the time for a student like me. In the end, my experience in high school was a constant struggle of proving myself that I could succeed and convincing my counselor that I could make the grade, while dealing with the disillusion of being considered inferior to the rest of my peers.

Unfortunately, during high school, my family also went through serious financial times. It was the late 1980s and the oil bust hit Houston hard.
Oil companies in Houston were terminating jobs as fast as one could
blink. Dad was not terminated from his job, but he had to accept a 60 percent cut in his salary. Soon life stopped in its tracks for all of us. The days
when I could ask for a pair of the most expensive pair of Nike shoes were
over. Suddenly, my family was making the toughest of choices on a daily
basis, such as what bills to pay and whether it was milk or the electric bill.
As soon as we could, my siblings and I started to work. The food was on
us, so Dad would only have to worry about paying the other bills. Mom
would wake up at three o'clock every morning and bake the daily bread.
She figured out that it was cheaper to bake our own bread for lunch than
to buy the bread at the store. During high school, my lunch was homemade baked bread with a thin slice of cheese and ham with a glass of milk.
These were truly the hardest days of my life.

After high school, I financed my way through college with a combination of loans, scholarships, and part-time jobs. My high school transcript
was worthless, so I decided to start all over again at the local community
college. I had to literally do everything from the beginning. Lucky, for me,
I found at the community college instructors and advisors who supported
and encouraged me. I took the basic courses again, and after two years,
I applied to the architecture program at the University of Houston. The
acceptance letter made me jump three feet up in the air. In 1997, at the age
of 26, I received my architecture degree.

Soon after graduating from college, I had what I dreamed all my life—
a Bachelor's Degree in Architecture. I was ready to conquer the world.
Things, however, did not go well for me. A mediocre portfolio, average
grades, and a deflated job market in the construction industry did not
help me in my hunt for a job. Soon, I returned to work at the grocery store
where I had worked as a teenager. In a sudden turn of fate, one day a
friend of mine recommended I join him at the school where he worked. He
offered to start me as a substitute teacher. The offer was very attractive—I
was going to make in a day what I made in a week at the grocery store.
It did not take long to earn the reputation of being the good, efficient sub
who followed the teachers' lesson plans. After the last day of school, I
decided to put in my application for my teaching certification.

I started to work as a special education teacher 12 years ago. In addition to teaching, I was also a tracking academic manager. My functions,
however, were mostly clerical—as a coteacher, I often did what the content teacher told me to do; and as a tracking academic manager, I find
myself following the administrative decisions from the top. It was at that
time that I soon discovered that there was very little teaching involved
in my teachings—mainly I was just a deskilled professional following
the cookie-cutter curriculum. Unfortunately, it did not take long to find

myself in trouble as I challenged and questioned many of the accepted practices in my department—mostly, why the teachers' input mattered so little to administrators when it came to special needs services. Trying to find the space where I could escape the daily demands of the job, I decided to enroll in graduate school. My plan was to go as far as I could. I eventually earned a Doctorate in Education.

My decision to enter graduate school was an important event in my life, which opened new doors to finding a new perspective for understanding my reality. It was in the academy where I became acquainted with supportive professors and colleagues who challenged me to engage in the praxis of pursuing new visions of what education was supposed to be. The experience was liberating, allowing me to understand the inequities that marginalized me. For me, graduate school was the place that harbored those who resisted the dominant ideology of school and society. Graduate school was my symbol of hope.

I worked for nine years in a suburban school with students of all abilities (general and special education) in all-inclusive classrooms. I currently work with future special education teachers at a local university's teacher education program. In understanding my life, I have learned to visualize my social situation, which allows me to help my students understand a system that is set for failure and oppression. My lived experiences allow me to relate to them. Because of my background, I can look at them in the eye, telling it to them *as it is* because I know what it is to be in their shoes. My empathy allows me to guide them in a direction of hope—a hope that they can help us make it real.

REFERENCES

Aoki, T. (1983). Experiencing ethnicity as a Japanese Canadian teacher: Reflections on a personal curriculum. *Curriculum Inquiry, 13*, 321–335.

Aoki, T. (1989/1990). Beyond the half-life of curriculum and pedagogy. *One World, 27*, 3–10.

Apple, M. W. (1993). *Official knowledge*. New York, NY: Routledge.

Artiles, A., Harris-Murri, N., & Rostenberg, D. (2006). Inclusion as social justice: Critical notes on discourses, assumptions, and the road ahead. *Theory into Practice, 45*(3), 260–268.

Artiles, A., Trent, S. C., & Kuan, L.-A. (1997). Learning disabilities empirical research on ethnic minority students: An analysis of 22 years of studies published in selected referred journals. *Learning Disabilities Reasearch and Practice, 12*, 82–91.

Baglieri, S., & Knopf, J. (2004). Normalizing differences in inclusive teaching. *Journal of Learning Disabilities, 37*, 525–529.

Barnes, C. (1997). Disability studies: Past, present and future. In L. Barton & M. Oliver (Eds.), *A legacy of oppression: A history of disability in Western culture*. Leeds, UK: Disability Press.

Blanchet, W. J., Brantlinger, E., & Shealey, M. W. (2005). Brown 50 years later—exclusion, segregation and inclusion. *Remedial and Special Education, 26,* 66–69.

Clandinin, D. J., & Raymond, H. (2006). Note on narrating disability. *Equity and Excellence in Education, 39,* 101–114.

Craig, C. J. (2001). The relationship between and among teachers' narrative knowledge, communities of knowing, and school reform: A case of "the Monkey's Paw." *Curriculum Inquiry, 31,* 303–331.

Dorries, B., & Haller, B. (2001). The news of inclusive education: A narrative analysis. *Disability and Society, 16,* 871–891.

Eisner, E. (2001). *The educational imagination.* New York, NY: Prentice Hall.

Ellis, C. (1997). Evocative autoethnography: Writing emotionally about our lives. In W. G. Tierney & Y. S. Lincoln (Eds.), *Representation and text: Reframing the narrative voice* (pp. 115–139). Albany, NY: State University of New York.

Ferri, B., & Connor, D. (2005). Tools of exclusion: Race, disability and (re)segregated education. *Teachers College Record, 107,* 453–474.

Freire, P. (1970). *Pedagogy of the oppressed.* New York, NY: Herder & Herder.

Gallagher, D. J. (2001). Neutrality as a moral standpoint: Conceptual confusion and the full inclusion debate. *Disability and Society, 16,* 637–654.

Goldstein, B. S. C. (1995). Critical pedagogy in a bilingual special education classroom. *Journal of Learning Disabilities, 28,* 463–475.

Gur-Ze'ev, I. (2002). Martin Heidegger, transcendence, and the possibility of counter-education. In M. Peters (Ed.), *Heidegger, education, and modernity.* Lanham, MD: Rowman & Littlefield Publisher.

Jones, M. (2007). An ethnographic exploration of narrative methodologies to promote the voice of students with disabilities. *Journal of Ethnographic and Qualitative Research, 2*(1), 32–40.

Kauffman, J., & Hallahan, D. (1995). *The illusion of full inclusion: A comprehensive critique of a current special education bandwagon.* Austin, TX: Pro-Ed.

Kincheloe, J. L. (2002). *Getting beyond the facts: Teaching social studies/social sciences in the twenty-first century* (2nd ed.). New York, NY: Peter Lang.

Kincheloe, J. L. (2004). *Critical pedagogy primer.* New York, NY: Peter Lang.

McLaren, P., & Kincheloe, J. L. (2007). *Critical pedagogy: Where are we now?* New York, NY: Peter Lang.

McNiff, J. (2007). The significance of "I" in educational research and the responsibility of intellectuals. Presented at the New Horizons for Quality in Higher Education and Training. Retrieved from www.jeanmcniff.com/thesignificnaceofi.html

McNiff, J., & Whitehead, J. (2002). *Action research: Principles and practice* (2nd ed.). London, UK: RoutledgeFalmer. Retrieved January 1, 2014, from http://www.loc.gov/catdir/enhancements/fy0650/2001031911-d.html

Miller, R. (1990). *What schools are for: Holistic education in American culture.* Brandon, VT: Holistic Education Press. (Originally published in 1990)

Oliver, M., & Zarb, G. (1989). The politics of disability: A new approach. *Disability, Handicap and Society, 4,* 221–239.

Ong-Dean, C. (2005). Reconsidering the social location of the medical model: An examination of disability in parenting literature. *Journal of Medical Humanities, 26*(2/3), 141–158.

Pohl, B. (2013). *The moral debate on special education.* New York, NY: Peter Lang.

Poplin, M. S. (1995). Looking through other lenses and listening to other voices: Stretching the boundaries of learning disabilities. *Journal of Learning Disabilities, 28,* 392–398.

Purpel, D. E. (1989). *The moral & spiritual crisis in education: A curriculum for justice and compassion in education.* Granby, MA: Bergin & Garvey.

Reiser, R. (2006). Inclusive education or special educational needs: Meeting the challenge of disability discrimination in schools. In M. Cole (Ed.), *Education, equality and human rights: Issues of gender, race, sexuality, disability, and social class* (pp. 157–179). London, UK: Routledge.

Schön, D. A. (1984). *The reflective practioner.* New York, NY: Basic Books.

Schön, D. A. (1991). *The reflective practioner: Case studies in and on educational practice.* New York, NY: Basic Books.

Schwab, J. (1982). *Science, curriculum, and liberal education.* Chicago, IL: University of Chicago Press.

Slee, R. (2001). Driven to the margins: disabled students, inclusive schooling and the politics of possibility. *Cambridge Journal of Education, 31*(3), 385–397.

Stiker, H. (1999). *A history of disability.* (W. Sayers, Trans.). Ann Arbor, MI: The University of Michigan Press.

Valentine, J. (2007). How can we transgress in the field of disabilities in urban education? In S. R. Steinberg & J. L. Kincheloe (Eds.), *19 urban questions: Teaching in the city* (pp. 127–142). New York, NY: Peter Lang.

Whitehead, J. (1989). Creating a living educational theory from questions of the kind, How do I improve my practice? *Cambridge Journal of Education, 19*(1), 41–52.

Part III

Pedagogy and Practice

Chapter 17

Reflections on Feminism in the Classroom: A "Life Raft" for Students

Michele Paludi

Any woman who chooses to behave like a full human being should be warned that the armies of the status quo will treat her as something of a dirty joke . . . She will need her sisterhood.

—Gloria Steinem

In 2002, for the front cover of my book, *Psychology of Women*, I asked my editor to use an image of a quilt because I wanted to highlight Margaret Gentry's (1989) metaphor of feminism. According to Gentry, each contribution by feminists joins with other contributions just as each piece of a quilt joins with other pieces to form the completed work. No one part of the quilt is more important than another. Each individual uses different stitching on their pieces of the quilt. We need all pieces if we are to complete the quilt that is feminism. According to Gentry (1989):

Feminist psychology and feminism in general seem to be at the point of trying to piece together the individual parts of a quilt. The overall pattern of the quilt that we want is still emerging. No one knows what equality in post-patriarchal world will look like. We are beginning to piece the separate parts together—to explore the kinds of

stitching to use in connecting the pieces and how to place the separate pieces into the pattern. But we have not stopped questioning the
process of quilting itself. (p. 5)

I have used this metaphor of feminism as a quilt in my teaching courses
on the psychology of women, gender violence, and women and management. In each of my courses I discuss individual, organizational, and
societal changes for valuing women and men. I have found this metaphor to be useful since not all students want to work for social justice
on an organizational or societal level but may want to value feminism
in their friendships and relationships, especially their romantic relationships. I explain that individual change is equally important and discuss
how being feminist also means leaving an abusive relationship, taking
care of one's health, taking responsibility for one's sexuality, and valuing
all women, including oneself. I have provided students suggestions for
working for gender justice. Some of these suggestions are presented in
Table 17.1. Additional recommendations may be found in Martin (2008);
Chrisler and Segrest (2008); Paludi, Denmark, and DeFour (2008); and
Paludi (1996).

Table 17.1
Suggestions for Working for Gender Justice

Write articles for your campus newspaper about feminism and gender justice.

Vote for political candidates who will value women and men in education, healthcare,
and the workplace.

Avoid harming your body in order to meet some unrealistic image of women or men
perpetuated by the media.

Write letters to newspaper, television, and movie executives regarding the anti-woman
messages presented in advertisements, rock music videos, commercials, and motion
pictures.

Volunteer at an organization that is dedicated to assisting victims of gender violence,
(e.g., battered women's shelter, rape crisis center).

Encourage family and friends with children to purchase nonsexist books and toys for
their children and grandchildren.

Inquire about health issues women in your family have faced. Identify how nutrition,
vitamins, and exercise impact these health issues. Share your research with relatives.

Work on improving your communication in your romantic relationships. Identify
your honest feelings about your sexual relationship. Do you believe you are
communicating these honest feelings to your partner? Practice saying what you
want, without making apologies.

Source: Adapted from Paludi (2002).

"QUILTS" AND STAGES OF FEMINIST IDENTITY DEVELOPMENT

I myself have never been able to find out precisely what feminism is: I only know that people call me a feminist whenever I express senti-ments that differentiate me from a doormat.

—Rebecca West

I discuss the "quilt" metaphor at each of the stages of feminist identity development that most students experience (Downing & Rousch, 1985): passive acceptance, revelation, embeddedness/emanation, synthesis, and active commitment. At the passive acceptance stage students frequently state that discrimination is no longer present in economics, education, politics, or the workplace. The topics with which I typically begin the course (e.g., in the psychology of women: heritage of women in the field of psychology, research methodologies, theories of women's personality) begin the process of students questioning their long-held assumptions.

A common transition occurs from the passive acceptance stage to revelation. Students discuss their memories of ways they have experienced discrimination because of their sex, sexual orientation, race, and/or religion. I ask students to bring in magazine advertisements and music videos that objectify women. During this stage I notice students becoming angry with themselves about why they either didn't notice these advertisements before or why they were silent about what they observed.

Sharing anger is important in a feminist course. This assists with students connecting with others, sharing their experiences, and sharing ways of responding to discrimination. This is the embeddedness/emanation stage. I facilitate this stage by having small-group exercises so students can share their experiences. Guest speakers who represent each of the four generations currently in the workforce (i.e., veterans, baby boomers, Generation X, and Millennials) join our class to discuss their ways of dealing with discriminatory treatment, including sexism and the intersectionality of racism and sexism, and homophobia. Young women who identify themselves as feminists or third-world feminists often identify themselves and their feminism in opposition to the previous generation of feminists (Enns & Sinacore, 2005). Zucker and Stewart (2007) reported that feminism is internalized quite differently depending on the developmental stage in our lives. Women guest professors are at different stages in life, in their career, and in relationships, and yet they are bound with the students in my class by shared stories.

I also have invited students to contribute brief "thought pieces" to books I'm editing (e.g., on work-life integration for women). My books thus have provided a multigenerational view of women's feminist voices. I owe this change in my own writing to my listening to students resolve feminist issues in their own lives.

The embeddedness/emanation stage is replaced by synthesis, in which statements about women and men as individuals, not as members of sex categories, are offered. Finally, students who are in the active commitment stage report wanting to take more feminist courses, conduct feminist research, volunteer at a battered women's shelter or rape crisis center, and pursue careers in which they can assist women (e.g., attorney, therapist, physician, dean of students).

These stages of feminist identity development are discussed throughout the course; students are asked to identify transitions in their thinking about the topics of the course. At the end of each class, I "data collect" aloud: Students share the transitions they were experiencing as a result of the course. These include challenging relationships they were in with men and/or women who did not welcome their taking a feminist course. The feminist classroom may be the only place where students can feel safe to express their concerns.

RESISTANCE REVISITED

Resistance from students is common in feminist classes, including anger, denial, defensiveness, disagreement over feminist pedagogy, lack of empathy, engaging in contrapower harassment by providing poor teaching evaluations, and victim blaming (Kimmell, 1999; Paludi, 2012). I have found the following responses to students' resistance helpful: encouraging students to share their life experiences and turning the challenging questions back on the questioner after I have answered their questions. I have also learned that students' resistance develops when they perceive that feminist ideas are being imposed on them (also see Crawford & Suckle, 1999). Feminist courses challenge students' long-standing beliefs and perceptions about science, truth, and the construction of knowledge (Markowitz, 2005; Paludi, 2012). Certainly, collaborative teaching and learning processes encourage students to become participants in the development of meaning and reduce resistance to the experience of imposed knowledge.

TEACHING-LEARNING MODEL USED: FEMINIST CONTENT AND PEDAGOGY

> *To reflect feminist values in teaching is to teach progressively, democratically and with feeling.*
> —Nancy Schniedewind

Feminist pedagogy can only be liberatory if it is truly revolutionary because the mechanisms of appropriation within white supremacist, capitalist patriarchy are able to co-opt with tremendous ease that which merely appears radical or subversive.

—bell hooks

My courses implement assumptions consistent with learning objectives, of how learning occurs, and the philosophy of women's and men's optimal development (Lord, 1982; Paludi et al., 2008). These assumptions include:

1. The course is a laboratory of feminist principles.
2. The traditional patriarchal teaching-learning model is dysfunctional in the development of healthy women and men.
3. Every individual in the class is a potential teaching resource.
4. Integration is imperative for the development of healthy, whole individuals. Therefore, the course should foster mind/body integration as well as the integration of ideas and behavior and thoughts and feelings.
5. The subjective, personal experience of women and men is valid and important.
6. The student should assume responsibility for her or his own learning and growth.
7. Cooperation among students pursuing learning objectives creates a more positive learning climate than does competition; cooperative learning is fostered through the use of criterion-referenced rather than a norm-referenced evaluation system.
8. The course should provide vehicles outside the class through which students can deal with personal feelings and frustrations such as journals and dyads.

I incorporate the following feminist pedagogical strategies in my courses (also see Paludi, 2012).

Nonhierarchical Seating Arrangement. Students sit around a conference table or in a circle in order to facilitate communication. The flow of communication is thus not just from me to students only. I view and treat each student as a teaching resource.

Critical Thinking. I strive to encourage confidence in students and a positive sense of self (Paludi, 1996; Paludi et al., 2008). I thus set up critical-thinking opportunities to permit students to see themselves as capable of critical analysis, to incorporate statistical methodologies in their analyses, and to possess sufficient knowledge and perspective to engage in substantive critical analyses (see Paludi, 2012). In addition, critical thinking requires an opportunity for students to talk in the first person, to place faith and value in their opinions and analyses. To foster critical thinking, students are asked to integrate the readings, lectures, and discussions in answering take-home essay exam questions. I also ask them to critique a journal article, noting biased assumptions, inaccurate statistical analyses, and faulty interpretations of the data (see Paludi, 1996). I have found this approach empowering for students, especially for reentry women who may have been silenced in their life experiences as well as in other courses.

Furthermore, feminist classes challenge students' long-standing beliefs and perceptions. Our content and pedagogy ask that students question fundamental beliefs about science and truth. We teach our students that knowledge is constructed and to question scientific methods, claims, and received knowledge. This questioning has consequences for students; they may become disheartened and discouraged as their self-protective illusions are shattered (Stake & Hoffman, 2000). In addition, their questioning may not be welcome by some faculty.

Integration of Knowledge. I foster class discussions so that students can integrate the course material into their lives. Students are given an opportunity to accomplish this by interviewing a woman researcher, advocate, manager, or leader in order to determine the perspective of this woman's role in the organization and to foster networking among the students and interviewees. Interviews are conducted via e-mail, telephone, or in person. This technique has also been important for fostering discussions of graduate training and mentoring for students.

In addition, students are required to write a five-page "reaction paper" on a topic of their choice related to the course content. This requirement encourages students to express their own thoughts and feelings about topics we have discussed, including opportunities for students to disagree with the perspectives shared in the readings and in the lectures.

I have also asked students to prepare a portfolio. For this assignment students collect popular press information that is relevant to our course. This is an opportunity for students to apply theories, laws, and empirical research discussed in our class and texts to real-world events and information. Students' portfolios may be comprise newspaper articles, magazine articles, advertisements, advice columns, or anything else pertaining to our course topics. For their portfolio, students must include the original source and a typed, double-spaced explanation of the concept being illustrated and the way in which the item relates to the concept. Students are asked to illustrate five different course concepts. Our final class is devoted to a "mini-conference" at which students present and discuss their portfolios.

I also distribute resources for each class in order to assist students in integrating the material from the course. These resources include websites, scholarly articles and books, lists of organizations, and networking sites. Furthermore, I distribute outlines for each class in order to facilitate students' preparation for class.

Shared Leadership. Students are invited to lead the discussion at the beginning of each class. Topics included television programs, newspaper articles, and other popular media accounts of topics that are part of the class content.

Experiential Exercises. Students are engaged in class in discussing experiential exercises dealing with their own experiences with mentors, leadership skills they use, ways to integrate work and family roles, and women they admire the most. These exercises serve as another vehicle through which students could develop and refine their skills in critical thinking. The exercises also require integration of theories, research findings, and practical experience from several sources that necessitate a critical reflection of ideas. Furthermore, this pedagogical technique provides students with an opportunity to reflect a broad range of knowledge and the need to define, qualify, and dispute commonly heard overgeneralizations about women and men. Sample experiential exercises are presented in Table 17.2. Additional exercises may be found in Paludi (1996).

Table 17.2
Sample Experiential Exercises

Exercise: Personal Entitlement

Pretend you are an undergraduate student who has been invited to work as a research assistant with Dr. Johnson, who is a professor of psychology. You will be working with Dr. Johnson all summer, entering data that Dr. Johnson collected for a major research project. What hourly salary do you believe would be appropriate for you for doing this work for Dr. Johnson?
　Modifications: Provide sex of Dr. Johnson

Adapted from: Byslama and Major (1992); Hogue and Yoder (2003); Matlin, M. (2012).

Exercise: Attitudes toward Victim Blame with Respect to Sexual Harassment

Do you agree or disagree? Or, are you unsure?

1. Women often claim sexual harassment to protect their reputations.
2. Sexually experienced women are not really damaged by sexual harassment.
3. It would do some women good to be sexually harassed.
4. Many women claim sexual harassment if they have consented to sexual relations but have later changed their minds.
5. Women put themselves in situations in which they are likely to be sexually harassed because they have an unconscious wish to be harassed.

Adapted from: Paludi (2002).

(continued)

Table 17.2
Sample Experiential Exercises   (*continued*)

Exercise: Attitudes about Body Size

How would you answer the following questions:
   Never
   Sometimes
   Unsure
   Often
   Frequently

   1. I comment about my own weight to people.
   2. I compliment other people if they seem to have lost weight.
   3. If someone has gained weight, I avoid commenting about this.
   4. When someone makes a joke about fat people, I express my disapproval.
   5. When looking at a magazine I'm concerned that the photographs may be encouraging eating disorders.
   6. I eat relatively little food so that I can keep thinner than average.
   7. I make jokes about women who are overweight.
   8. I encourage people to feel good about their bodies, even if they do not meet the cultural norms for being slender.

Adapted from: Berg (2000); Matlin (2012).

Exercise: Assigning Responsibility for Rape

Who is responsible for each of the following occurrences? Use 50%/50%; 100%/0%; 75%/25%, etc.
John and Jane are college students.

   1. Jane is walking back to her dorm from the campus library at 10 p.m. She takes a route that everyone considers safe. As she passes a dorm, John jumps in front of her, drags her to an unlit area and rapes her.
   2. Jane is at a friend's party. She is wearing a short skirt. She meets a pleasant-looking man, John. After they dance for a while, he suggests they go outside. John attempts to rape Jane until another student sees what's happening and intervenes.
   3. Jane is at a friend's party. She meets a pleasant-looking man, John. After they dance for a while, he suggests they go outside. John attempts to rape Jane until another student sees what's happening and intervenes.

Adapted from: Matlin (2012).

Multicultural Learning. The goal of multicultural learning in my classes involves a complex set of intellectual and personal traits. In order to learn about other cultures, students needed to be able to draw connecting links between their own experiences and the experiences of others; to comprehend cultural differences; to deal with "culture shock"; and to clear away subjective obstacles to multicultural learning such as sexism, racism, heterosexism, and ethnocentrism. Thus, I structure my courses to present a more inclusive course. Rather than discuss culture at the end of the course, topics each week include a discussion of cultural similarities and differences. I begin most classes by addressing cultural issues and research findings. This ensures keeping multiculturalism central, not marginal, to the course. In addition, I address issues of privilege and oppression. I also incorporate scholarship by women from marginalized groups. Students are tested on articles authored by women of color and lesbians.

I have found that these feminist pedagogies can assist students in overcoming their resistance to dealing with discrimination and oppression (Markowitz, 2005). Participation in feminist courses is also positively correlated with more progressive gender role and racial attitudes (e.g., Vedovato & Vaughter, 1980). Students are more likely to work toward feminist causes following a course in women's studies (Harris, Melaas, & Rodacker, 1999). Recently, Kernahan and Davis (2007) reported that students' awareness of and attitudes toward racism shift positively during a course on the psychology of diversity. In addition, students also increase their interaction with peers of other races. Stake and Hoffman (2000) noted students' ratings of positive class impact were significantly higher for courses in women's studies that implemented feminist pedagogies than in non-women's studies courses.

VALUING FEMINISM

Over the course of my career I have learned that I need to operationally define feminism for students. Research has suggested for some time that most people reject the term "feminist" when describing themselves but support feminist principles (e.g., equal pay for equal work). Goldner's (1994) study noted that when women who hold feminist beliefs anticipate a negative reaction from their peers to the label "feminist," they will avoid using the term to describe themselves. Goldner indicated that media is a primary source of negative images of feminists. It is common to see photos of women identified as feminists having clenched fists. These images are not representative of feminists.

More recent research by Rudman and Fairchild (2007) found that the stereotype that feminists are unattractive still persists. Considering the fact that young adult women are still buying into the belief they need to adhere to traditional gender roles in order to be considered popular as potential dates and mates, discussing this view of feminism is imperative if we want the next generation of women to adopt feminist principles and work for change on one or more levels.

To facilitate this discussion of what feminism means and to have students identify their own biases, I use a pedagogical technique introduced to me by Sue Rosenberg Zalk (personal communication, 1986).

This technique involves asking students to discuss ways in which either a self-identified feminist or nonfeminist is viewed by women and men. Here is one version of the case:

> You are at a social gathering talking to a small group of people you have just met. They all appear fairly informed and articulate. After some small talk about New York City's urban plight, the conversation turns to the accusations about gang rapes and the growing realization that such incidents may be more common than previously thought.
>
> Everyone in the group agreed that it was scandalous although different motivations and explanations were attributed to the men's behavior. Finally, one of the men in the group laughed softly and stated, "I know feminists will have a field day with this, but we can hardly generalize from the misdirected behavior of some boys trying to prove they are men, to the entire society."
>
> The nods to his comment were interrupted by the voice of one of the women. She announced: "I am a feminist and you are greatly underestimating the social meaning and impact of their behavior." She proceeded to explain her position. A few other women added comments, but you were most impressed with how articulate she was and the thoughtfulness of her argument.

Students are then asked a series of questions about this case:

1. How closely do you think men listened to the woman's statement?
   Very   Unsure   Not at all

2. How seriously do you think she was taken by the men?
   Very   Unsure   Not at all

3. How closely do you think women listened to the woman's statement?
   Very   Unsure   Not at all

4. How seriously do you think she was taken by the women?
   Very   Unsure   Not at all

5. How assertive do you think the men thought she was?
   Very   Unsure   Not at all

6. How assertive do you think women thought she was?
   Very   Unsure   Not at all

7. Do you think it mattered that she began with the words "I am a feminist?"

Yes   Unsure   No

8. Why do you believe she began her statement this way?

This case is modified in the following ways: (1) the woman states "I am not a feminist," a man states "I am a feminist," or a man states "I am not a feminist."

I do not tell students at the beginning of this exercise that four different versions of the case were distributed in class. I list the descriptive statistics obtained for each version and ask students to offer an explanation for the results. When I inform them of the different versions of the case, they are now ready to discuss biases toward women and men who identify as feminists. At this point in our discussion I have found Anderson's findings on perceptions of feminism helpful. Anderson (see Kanner & Anderson, 2010) reports that the myth of the "man-hating" feminist denies the reality that feminists are not critical of men just because they are men. I also discuss Paludi, Paludi, and DeFour's (2004) work that suggests individuals reject the label feminist because they view themselves as in control, as powerful rather than as victims of gender inequality. Thus, they perceive the term "feminist" to imply a powerless position, which they reject (Rhode, 1977).

FEMINISM AS "LIFE RAFT"

> *Feminism is a transformational force, an individual and social force. It is a way of looking at the world—a questioning of power/domination issues, an affirmation of women's energy.*
>
> —Charlotte Bunch

The following incident has occurred numerous times over my 34-year career as a feminist professor when I am teaching about gender violence. I make concluding comments about the topic we discussed that day and wish students well until we meet again. However, many students do not leave the classroom. They remain silent. Their eyes are filled with tears. Their heads are lowered. In fact, the number of students in class on the days we discuss gender violence is fewer than for other topics. I make sure I announce the topics verbally as well as on the syllabus. I prepare them a week in advance. I also distribute a copy of the campus' sexual harassment and sexual assault policy and have the campus's Title IX coordinator join the class as a guest speaker. I also provide a list of support services on campus (e.g., counseling center, women's center, Title IX coordinator, dean of students). I discuss gender violence late in the semester. Students have had an opportunity to get to know each other and me, and we have fostered a sense of trust among us.

The impact of discussing legal terms, incidence rates, and impact of gender violence on women and men is significant. If there is no class in the room after our class I remain there with students who want to join me. Otherwise, my office has standing-room only with students who want to talk with me about that day's topic. I notify counselors in the counseling center about my teaching a unit on gender violence and have asked them to be available for consultations immediately following my class discussions.

I will postpone moving on to the next topic until we as a class deal with the issues and feelings raised on the first day of the discussion of gender violence. That may necessitate my changing take-home-exam due dates. That also may necessitate informing students via e-mail that the discussion will continue at the next class period. Since all students receive the essay exams the first day of class, no student is at a disadvantage if they miss a particular class.

I believe our feminist courses must serve as a "life raft" (Klonis, Endo, Crosby, & Worell, 1997) for our students, especially those in the Millennial and younger generations. For me, this value gets translated to stopping my own agenda and assisting our students with ways to resolve feminist issues with which they are currently dealing. Research has suggested the effectiveness of feminist pedagogies (e.g., Falk-Rafael, Chinn, Anderson, Laschinger, & Rubotzky, 2004) has indicated improvements in students' self-esteem and self-concept, increased student participation in courses, and empowerment of students in the classroom and in their personal lives.

A few years ago, while tutoring a nine-year-old girl, Andrea, she asked me what I do when I teach college students. I described some of the content and pedagogy of my course on the psychology of women. Shortly before the end of the term I asked Andrea, "What do you think I should say to my students at the end of our course?" Andrea's response to my question sums up why we must continue to teach in feminist ways to complete the quilt. Andrea replied: "Tell them not to forget us little girls."

REFERENCES

Berg, F. (2000). *Women afraid to eat: Breaking free in today's weight-obsessed world.* Hettinger, ND: Health Weight Network.

Byslama, W., & Major, B. (1992). Two routes to eliminating gender differences in personal entitlement: Social comparisons and performance evaluations. *Psychology of Women Quarterly, 16,* 193–200.

Chrisler, J., & Segrest, M. (2008). "A" is for activism: Classroom-based approaches to preventing campus violence. In M. Paludi (Ed.), *Understanding and preventing campus violence* (pp. 95–98). Westport, CT: Praeger.

Crawford, M., & Suckle, J. (1999). Overcoming resistance to feminism in the classroom. In S. Davis, M. Crawford, & J. Sebrechts (Eds.), *Coming into her own: Educational success in girls and women* (pp. 155–170). San Francisco, CA: Jossey-Bass.

Downing, N., & Rousch, K. (1985). From passive acceptance to active commitment. *The Counseling Psychologist, 13*, 695–709.

Enns, C., & Sinacore, A. (Eds.). (2005). *Teaching and social justice: Integrating multicultural and feminist theories in the classroom.* Washington, DC: American Psychological Association.

Falk-Rafael, A., Chinn, P., Anderson, M., Laschinger, H., & Rubotzky, A. (2004). The effectiveness of feminist pedagogy in empowering a community of learners. *Journal of Nursing Education, 43*, 107–115.

Gentry, M. (1989). Introduction: Feminist perspectives on gender and thought: Paradox and potential. In M. Crawford & M. Gentry (Eds.), *Gender and thought* (pp. 36–58). New York, NY: Springer-Verlag.

Goldner, M. (1994). *Accounting for race and class variation in the disjuncture between feminist identity and feminist beliefs: The place of negative labels and social movements.* Paper presented at the Annual Meeting of the American Sociological Association, Los Angeles.

Harris, K., Melaas, K., & Rodacker, E. (1999). The impact of women's studies courses on college students of the 1990s. *Sex Roles, 40*, 969–977.

Hogue, M., & Yoder, J. (2003). The role of status in producing depressed entitlement in women's and men's pay allocations. *Psychology of Women Quarterly, 27*, 330–337.

Kanner, M., & Anderson, K. J. (2010). The myth of the man-hating feminist. In M. Paludi (Ed.), *Feminism and women's rights worldwide. Vol. 1: Heritage, roles and issues* (pp. 1–25). Westport, CT: Praeger.

Kernahan, C., & Davis, T. (2007). Changing perspective: How learning about racism influences student awareness and emotion. *Teaching of Psychology, 34*, 49–52.

Kimmel, E. (1999). Feminist teaching, an emergent practice. In S. Davis, M. Crawford, & J. Sebrechts (Eds.), *Coming into her own* (pp. 57–76). San Francisco, CA: Jossey-Bass.

Klonis, S., Endo, J., Crosby, F., & Worell, J. (1997). Feminism as life raft. *Psychology of Women Quarterly, 21*, 333–345.

Lord, S. (1982). Research on teaching the psychology of women. *Psychology of Women Quarterly, 7*, 96–104.

Markowitz, L. (2005). Unmasking moral dichotomies: Can feminist pedagogy overcome student resistance? *Gender and Education, 17*, 39–55.

Martin, J. (2008). Anti-violence pedagogy: Strategies and resources. In M. Paludi (Ed.), *Understanding and preventing campus violence* (pp. 73–94). Westport, CT: Praeger.

Matlin, M. (2012). *The psychology of women.* Belmont, CA: Wadsworth.

Paludi, M. (1996). *Exploring/teaching the psychology of women: A manual of resources* (2nd ed.). Albany, NY: State University of New York Press.

Paludi, M. (2002). *The psychology of women* (2nd ed.). Upper Saddle River, NJ: Prentice Hall.

Paludi, M. (2012, March). *Feminist courses as catalysts for transformational change.* Paper presented at the Southeastern Women's Studies Association Conference, Fairfax, VA.

Paludi, M., Denmark, F., & DeFour, D. (2008). The psychology of women course as a "catalyst for change" for campus violence. In M. Paludi (Ed.), *Understanding and preventing campus violence* (pp. 103–111). Westport, CT: Praeger.

Paludi, M., Dillon, L., Stern, T., Martin, J., DeFour, D., & White, C. (2008). Courses in the psychology of women: Catalysts for change. In F. Denmark & M. Paludi (Eds.), *Psychology of women: A handbook of issues and theories* (pp. 174–201). Westport, CT: Praeger.

Paludi, M., Paludi, C., & DeFour, D. (2004). Introduction: The more things change, the more they stay the same. In M. Paludi (Ed.), *Praeger guide to the psychology of gender* (pp. xi–xxxi). Westport, CT: Praeger.

Rhode, D. (1997). *Speaking of sex.* Cambridge, MA: Harvard University Press.

Rudman, L., & Fairchild, K. (2007). The F word: Is feminism incompatible with beauty and romance? *Psychology of Women Quarterly, 31,* 125–136.

Stake, J., & Hoffman, F. (2000). Putting feminist pedagogy to the test. *Psychology of Women Quarterly, 24,* 30–38.

Vedovato, S., & Vaughter, R. (1980). Psychology of women courses changing sexist and sex-typed attitudes. *Psychology of Women Quarterly, 4,* 587–590.

Zucker, A., & Stewart, A. (2007). Growing up and growing older: Feminism as a context for women's lives. *Psychology of Women Quarterly, 31,* 137–145.

Chapter 18

Teaching Trayvon: Teaching about Racism through Public Pedagogy, Hip Hop, Black Trauma, and Social Media

Bettina L. Love and Regina N. Bradley

INTRODUCTION

Before we begin to discuss what "Teaching Trayvon" means to us, we think it is important to explain why we do the work we do as engaged pedagogues defined by bell hooks. In her book *Teaching to Transgress,* hooks (1994) writes that she strives, "[t]o teach in a manner that respects and cares for the souls of our students [which] is essential if we are to provide the necessary conditions where learning can most deeply and intimately" begin (p. 13). We are, of course, inspired by hooks' words, but we also feel challenged and pushed by this proposition to think about ways we can reach our students beyond the restrictions of the classroom to create what Gutierrez and Stone (2000) call a *third space.* The third space provides teachers and youth with the opportunity to create and traverse authentic interactions in an effort to "shift in the social organization of learning and what counts as knowledge" (Gutierrez, 2008, p. 152). According to Gutierrez and Stone (2000), the third space acts as "a discursive space in which alternative and competing discourses and positionings transform conflict and difference into rich zones of collaboration and learning" (p. 157).

The idea of Teaching Trayvon is found in the third space because it represents the present, and social and cultural history, of our students, as they wrestle with the reality of the murder of Trayvon Martin, racism, trauma, Hip Hop, and social media. It also allows teachers to investigate how the complexities of their identities are tied and tethered to Martin as a symbol of racial injustice in this so-called "postracial" America through the lens of social media. In our work, we examine how youth negotiate these intersections within formal and informal educational settings (cyberspace). Furthermore, we see Teaching Trayvon as a space to expand notions of public pedagogy in conjunction with the Internet as a site of contemporary Black activism and the Internet as a space to mourning. Teaching Trayvon builds on the idea that new social media is a highly accessible multimedia platform of communication and (race) performance accessible across social-economic and cultural discourses. Thus, this chapter seeks to unpack the grounding of Hip Hop and social media as a form of 21st-century public pedagogy. The lynchpin of our argument is the murder of Martin and the protest discourse that arose with youth in contexts both in and out of school. The chapter asks the question: How do we engage youth as critical pedagogues in the historicized discourse of violence endured by Blacks in the 21st century juxtaposed multimodally with platforms like YouTube, Twitter, and Facebook, which provide a space for the Black youth to witness, mourn, and resist aspects of the post–Civil Rights Black experience?

HIP HOP, PUBLIC PEDAGOGY, SOCIAL MEDIA, AND TRAYVON MARTIN

The term public pedagogy is defined as the educational happenings outside of formal schooling, and the positioning of out-of-school contexts (i.e., popular culture, Internet, parks, museums) as sites of pedagogy that can foster both reproduction and resistance (Sandlin, Schultz, & Burdick, 2010). Public pedagogy recognizes that schools are not the "sole sites of teaching, learning, or curricula, and that perhaps they are not even the most influential" (Sandlin et al., 2010, p. 2). We argue, as did Hill (2009) and Williams (2009), that Hip Hop music and culture operate as a site of public pedagogy because rappers' narratives and their listeners' orientations spur the development of cultural knowledge. Furthermore, Hip Hop in the current landscape of social media exemplifies as a public pedagogy space and contains youth literacy practices that signify sites of reproduction and resistance. Hip Hop is a global art form with commercial success that impacts youth across diverse communities. Youth are borrowing, appropriating, adapting, and localizing Hip Hop to generate their own identities (Ballivían & Herrera, 2012; Osumare, 2008). According to Williams (2009), Hip Hop can be a source for raising the critical consciousness of youth because rappers, through their rhymes and commercial personas, are public pedagogues.

However, the predominantly visual space of social media allows Hip Hop consumers to be public pedagogues as well. The commercial, yet organic and messy, marriage of Hip Hop and social media signifies a "semipublic and a counterpublic space of engagement with and resistance to mainstream narratives, policies, and actions" (Banks, 2011, p. 25).

A particularly useful grounding of Hip Hop and social media as a form of 21st-century public pedagogy is the public beating of Rodney King and the aftermath of the trial surrounding his brutal attack. The lynchpin for situating King's beating within Hip Hop and protest discourse is George Holliday's amateur video capturing King's assault. Awakened by screams outside his home, Holliday videotaped police officers beating King. The video arguably ushers in the significance of social media as a contemporary means of disseminating information. Building on that idea, new social media is a highly accessible multimedia platform of communication and (race) performance accessible across social-economic and cultural discourses. Holliday's home video is a form of new social media as it offers a recognizable visual that permanently signifies the police brutality associated with post–Civil Rights minorities. Reading Holliday's video through a Hip Hop sensibility suggests the videotape as a visual vindication of "gangsta rap's" claims of crooked police and their unfair treatment of Blacks. It precedes director John Singleton's debut film *Boyz in the Hood*, the cornerstone film of what would come to be known as the Hip Hop–infused "hood film" genre of the early 1990s. Thus, Holliday's recording of King's beating—grainy, violent, and amateurish—arguably sets precedence as the first "hood film" and parallels the conflicted existence of working-class Blacks in southern California.

It is important to note, however, that Holliday witnessed this violence outside of the working-class communities made notorious in gangsta rap. From this perspective, Holliday's witnessing of King's beating in the suburban San Fernando Valley parallels Americans' fascination with the gangsta rap aesthetic. Holliday's observance of King's beating provides a visual demonstration of understanding police brutality as a working-class normality framed via middle-class sensibilities. Alexander's (1994) analysis of Black bodies in American visual culture suggests it as a communal space of contemporary "witnessing" of Black trauma. Her analysis can be applied to the consideration of the videotape as a predecessor of current social media serving as social commentary. Alexander writes:

> In the 1990s African American bodies on videotape have been the site on which national trauma—sexual harassment, date rape, drug abuse, AIDS, racial and economic urban conflict—has been dramatized . . . Black bodies and their attendant dramas are consumed by the larger populace. White men have been the primary stagers and consumers of the historical spectacles . . . but in one way or another,

Black people also have been looking, forging a traumatized collective historical memory which is reinvoked at contemporary sites of
conflict. (p. 79)

Violence serves as an empathetic lens through which Rodney King's beating and ensuing racially motivated traumas, including Hurricane Katrina;
the "Jena 6;" and the murders of Amadou Diallo, Sean Bell, and Oscar
Grant can be accessed through social media. This space, predominantly
visual, informs Blacks' "collective memory" through "witnessing" the
historicized trauma that Alexander argues is sustained through narratives and storytelling. Yet grounding the multicultural spectatorship of
late-20th-century Black trauma via cultural venues like Hip Hop helps
situate Holliday's videotape as a springboard for thinking about contemporary Black trauma as a messy space of civic responsibility and
commodification.

The most recent form of this messy intellectual discourse takes shape
with the Internet, a digitized space of witnessing framed by the historicized discourse of violence endured by Blacks.[1] Multimodal platforms
like YouTube, Twitter, and Facebook provide Internet users a capability
to create and witness a post–Civil Rights Black experience. Adam Banks
(2011), for example, identifies the possibility of the Internet as a site of
collective Black resistance. Blacks use the Internet as a "highlight [of] African American skepticism of white, western reverence—even worship—of
technology and the fierce determination that Black people have always
had to be free, to assert their own individual and collective humanity in
relationship with technology and in resistance to systems of domination"
(p. 18). Banks' reading of the Internet as a social-political space parallels
the origins of Hip Hop culture as a site of protest and Black empowerment. The popularity of the Internet in tandem with the digitization of
Hip Hop culture—that is, sound production, distribution, and online
Hip Hop periodicals like *AllHipHop*, *RapGenius*, and *HipHopDX*—point
toward a symbiotic relationship between these spaces. The romanticized
understanding of the Internet as an "open" space and its frivolous nature
are best signified by the construction and engagement of racial identities as fictional characters called avatars. Nakamura (2002) theorizes
these digital performances as "cybertypes," the "distinctive ways that
the Internet propagates, disseminates, and commodifies images of race
and racism . . . [it] is the process by which computer/human interfaces,
the dynamics and economics of access, and the means by which users are
able to express themselves online interacts with the 'cultural layer' or ideologies regarding race that they bring with them into cyberspace" (p. 3).

---

[1]See also Houston Baker's discussion of historical cultural memory in *Critical memory: Public
spheres, African American writing, and Black fathers and sons in America* (2001).

Nakamura argues that the context in which these avatars or "cybertypes" exists is one of (white) privilege and entitlement, digitally manifesting the social-political tensions in which America currently exists. The "trickiness" of creating and sustaining a plausible body invested in both cyber and social-cultural discourse is highlighted in the treatment of the Black body. Similarly, Brock (2009) recognizes this messiness of cyber race and identity politics as "a paradox of constructing an embodied identity in a virtual space . . . an ontological [re]consideration of racial identity—that is a social constructed artifact with more to do with social and cultural resources than with skin color" (p. 32). Black bodies' lack of importance in postracial America is heightened within cyberspace. The signifying of cyber and literal violence against Black bodies demands new discourse and critical frameworks to reflect how Blacks' self-definition and calls to action are treated within new social media.

Trayvon Martin's death in February 2012 amplifies the messiness of new media as a cultural and resistant space. Martin's death takes place in a moment where racial trauma is considered nonexistent and mobilization for racial justice is considered irreverent. The Martin case exemplifies these current anxieties. His murder sparked national debate that jarred Americans' investment in an American postracial agenda that worked. He represents the failure of claims of postraciality while simultaneously bolstering the drive to claim a postracial American society. Much of this discourse took place on Internet discussion forums, Twitter, and online periodicals. Martin's death spurred a call for racial justice that bridged the civil rights movement and contemporary calls to action seen in the reaction to Rodney King and Jena 6. Unlike the Jena 6 or King, however, Martin's death stirred a multicultural response embedded in reaction to what was available to people online. In this sense, Martin is likened to Emmett Till, the young Black man lynched in Money, Mississippi, in 1955 for allegedly whistling at a white woman. At the insistence of his mother Mamie Till Mobley, photos of Till's badly beaten and water-bloated body in an open casket were plastered throughout various newspapers and magazines, particularly Black periodical fixtures *Jet* and *Ebony* magazines. Similar to Till, Martin is eulogized through pictures: family photos of a smiling Martin's face in a red American Eagle t-shirt, pictures of Martin with his father Tracy Martin or mother Sybrina Fulton, or a photo of Martin taking a knee in his football jersey with a football in hand. His youth and "innocence" are embodied in his pictorial narrative, making his body valid and the violence against him validated as wrongdoing. And, like Till, Martin's visual narrative is a response to the engrained pathology of Black male bodies imbedded in American culture.

So now more than ever, we feel it necessary again to invoke the work of hooks (1994), who calls on radical pedagogy, which "insist[s] that everyone's presence is acknowledged. It has to be demonstrated through pedagogical practices. . . . There must be an ongoing recognition that everyone influences the classroom dynamic, that everyone contributes. These contributions are resources" (p. 8). Her words here are fundamental to our practices as educators because Black males are being "spirit-murdered" in schools every day. Borrowing from the work of legal scholar, Patricia Williams (1992), Love (2013) defines the term "spirit-murdered" as the "personal, psychological, and spiritual injuries to people of color through the fixed, yet fluid and moldable, structures of racism, privilege, and power. Spirit-murdering denies inclusion, protection, safety, nurturance, and acceptance—all things a person needs to be human and to be educated" (p. 13). Thus Teaching Trayvon is a starting point to repair youths' spirits. Below we illustrate how, in Teaching Trayvon, we strive to recognize our students knowledge, experiences, and fluid identities within the classroom and in cyberspace via Twitter and YouTube.

SO WHAT DOES IT MEAN TO "TEACH TRAYVON"?

Educators are often so concerned with education as a repository of curriculum content, access to resources, and the distribution of 'quality' learning materials in our schools that even with the best intentions they fail to acknowledge the deep syntax of human sociability, the knotting of discourses to social relations that condition the production of knowledge, what we would call the "pedagogical unconscious." (Jaramillo, 2012, pp. 21–22)

Simply stated, youth theorize on a regular basis and construct new knowledge, but often educators do not have the time, space, or understanding to build on their experiences to create classrooms spaces in the physical that allow students' home life, communities, and school to cohabitate. Furthermore, returning to the third space, teachers often are not able to help students create spaces of their own that are deeply rooted within their realities. For example, for many youth of color, "Travyon Martin's death was a visceral counter-narrative to the colorblind world that has been so skillfully and intentionally constructed" (Love, 2014b, p. 19). That tragic event prompted a closer "read[ing] of the word and world" (Freire & Macedo, 1987, p. 36) to find spaces of resistance, alongside individual and collective identities. In that way, Martin's murder impacted the lives of youth of color because it represented the failure of postraciality and provided a discourse for youth to unite.

Therefore, to Teach Trayvon from an educational standpoint is to vehemently reject the notion that youth cannot construct discourses that challenge dominative knowledge production (Lissovoy, 2014). Second, to Teach Trayvon is to honor and affirm youths' capacity for resistance in the aim of creating "materially and epistemologically agentic" (Lissovoy,

2014, p. 546) spaces for antidominative knowledge production. According to Anzaldúa (1987), this method is the work of survival, to move beyond mere facts to produce powerful critical knowledge that is often times painful, and full of gender struggles, yet vital for youths' complex individual and collective identities. In our work as critical pedagogues and cultural workers, Martin's murder provided a lens to utilize the formal school curriculum and cyberspace to confront issues of racism, discrimination, and hate, but, more importantly, it allowed us to position his murder in the sphere of public pedagogy as a site of resistance and a place to construct counternarratives.

WHAT DOES IT MEAN TO TEACH TRAYVON WITH ELEMENTARY-AGED STUDENTS?

The first author is the founder and director of Real Talk: Hip Hop Education for Social Justice. The program is an educational after-school program for elementary-school-aged students aimed at promoting issues of social justice through Hip Hop–based education (HHBE). The rationale for the program rests on a well-researched theory arguing that students learn best when their ways of learning, speaking, and overall world view are a fundamental part of the classroom (Gay, 2000; Ladson-Billings, 1995). Thus, the goal of Real Talk is to create an after-school program rooted in the principles of critical pedagogical frameworks (Kincheloe, 2008) and cultural modeling methods (Lee, 1995) to form a classroom that positions the culture, social context, learning styles, and students' experiences at the center of the curricula.

In the spring of 2013, 17 fifth graders, all Black but one, for 26 weeks engaged in conversations concerning global warming, Black-on-Black crime, shootings, Georgia's high school dropout rate, and the death of Trayvon Martin, all topics generating from students' real lives connected to school curricula. However, the primary goal of the course was to promote issues of social justice with elementary-aged students that were linked to their everyday realities. Additionally, another important goal of Real Talk was to teach students the history and the five elements of Hip Hop (i.e., Rapping, Breakdancing, Graffiti, Deejaying, and Knowledge of Self and Community) with special emphasis on the fifth element: Knowledge of Self.[2] For the final project of the course students addressed an issue of their choosing within their community or society at large using the elements of Hip Hop and utilized a vital space(s) to educate their community beyond the classroom. After little debate, students decided

---

[2]For further details about the project and the five elements of Hip Hop, see Bettina Love's (2014b) work, Urban storytelling: How storyboarding, moviemaking & hip hop–based education can promote students' critical voice. *English Journal, 103*(5), 53–58.

to write a rap, create a mural, and make a short movie, which would be posted to YouTube, that described the night of Trayvon Martin's death and what the students felt could be done to stop the killing of another Black male. The first author was the students' teacher. After the students selected their project topic and media, they were taught how to storyboard, use cameras to create particular shots, such as "wide shot" or "close shot," and work together, as well as independently, to complete the final class project. To view the project, please visit http://www.youtube.com/watch?v=IJWYiGI7uwA.

Since the educational text emerged from students' lives, the final project allowed the students to act as public pedagogues who, along with their teacher, created a third space in the classroom (Love, 2014b). The students researched the facts of the case and interrogated those facts. Ultimately, they determined as a class that, based on their understanding, Martin died because of stereotypes concerning Black males. The final projected created an in-school space for students to create counternarratives (Love, 2014a), build on their multiliteracies (Love, 2014b), and learn how to construct knowledge geared at informing the public through social media about a troubling issue.

The final project also helped students use social media as a site to begin to understand trauma, mourn, and experience racial battle fatigue and the process of healing through arts-based education. Although we employed teaching frameworks such as pubic pedagogy and third space, bell hooks (1994) warns us that, "theory is not inherently healing, liberatory, or revolutionary. It fulfills this function only when we ask that it do so and direct our theorizing towards this end" (p. 61). hooks' warning underlines the importance of digital spaces as youth create discourses that challenge dominative knowledge production, effectively moving theory into practice. The students' YouTube video provided a digital space of healing and remembering in ways that invoked their culture and knowledge production. The video represented their contribution to the echoes of resistance from the chamber of cyber Black activism as 10- and 11-year-old youths. However, their video, rap, and mural are also spaces to mourn.

SO WHAT DOES IT MEAN TO TEACH TRAYVON IN CYBERSPACE?

Using the Internet as a public space of mourning is also a useful pedagogical tool in the college classroom. The second author's use of the hashtag TeachingTrayvon is a means to not only mourn Martin's death but also to map the trajectory of the continued social-cultural impact of Martin's death in digital and offline spaces. For this exercise, students tweet about select readings and responses to Martin's death via a designated Twitter account. This activity is useful in helping students confronting their cultural and academic biases because they interact with others' perspectives and opinions outside of their classroom. TeachingTrayvon in digital spaces allows for the messiness of Trayvon Martin's death to exist as a pushback against the dismissal of race and agency offline.

Because many (desperately?) seek to embrace a postracial society, deaths like Martin's are a painful and constant reminder that race, indeed, does matter. The difference, however, is that the anxieties that are grounded in one's offline experiences are amplified online. The TeachingTrayvon hashtag is a reminder of the angst associated with Americans' negotiation of race, place, and class in contemporary society. Further, continuing discussions about the implications of Martin's death in new media cracks the door for remembering and validating the need to mourn similar deaths like Renisha McBride, Rekia Boyd, and Jordan Davis. Digital media and hashtags like TeachingTrayvon allow for new-media consumers to not only mourn the deaths of young Black boys and girls but also to construct alternative discourses to address shifting representations of race and identity that strangle open dialogue of 21st-century race and identity politics in the United States.

WHO GETS TO MOURN EVEN AS WE RESIST OUTRAGE FATIGUE?

Much of the research concerning racial battle fatigue focuses on college-aged students of color who attend historically white campuses (Smith, Yosso, & Solorzano, 2007), or how racially marginalized groups and individuals deal with daily racial microaggressions (Smith, 2008). Since racism is omnipresent, there are psychosocial stressors and subsequent behavioral responses of fighting racial microaggressions that result in many Blacks feeling frustrated, resentful, fearful, and experiencing physiological stress of headaches, high blood pressure, and insomnia (Smith, Hung, & Franklin, 2011). But what about racial battle fatigue in cyberspace or with elementary-aged students who are doing the work of critical pedagogues? How does the death of Martin add another layer to racial battle fatigue based on the fact that after his death, cyberspace became a site to mourn and acknowledge the trauma of Black bodies for his generation?

However, the space was muddle as a space of mourning because Martin were initially introduced on the Internet with a similar criminal or working-class background. In that way, Martin became a cybertype of the understated racial anxieties and unfamiliarity with the proper treatment of sustained acts of violence against Black bodies. Initial "disembodiment" of Martin's body from the physical realities of pathological discourse surrounding Black men and boys forces the understanding that Martin's death is tragic.

Yet, like in Hip Hop, Martin's Black masculinity problematically collapses him as a Black (man)child into the widely recognized archetype of a thug. David Leonard (2012) highlights the peculiarity of justifying Martin's rowdy behavior as a catalyst for his death: "The focus on his suspension is particularly revealing not only in Trayvon's case, but also in the larger fabric of American racism. For the defenders of [George] Zimmerman and much of the media, the reports of multiple suspensions, of a connection to an 'empty marijuana bag,' are evidence that at best Trayvon was 'complicated' and at worst he was a 'thug' who therefore deserved to be killed." Presenting Martin in gold fronts and highlighting his suspension from school robs him of his humanity—which is then (dis)embodied in the cyber body plastered across the Internet—in the only (digital) space where it existed. Tim Wise (2012) brazenly identifies the correlation between white privilege and the distorted representations of Martin's Black body as dysfunctional:

> If the victim is young, and black, and wearing a hoodie, and has a tattoo (even if it is a tattoo *of his mother's name*), and a partial gold grill, and occasionally poses with macho swagger on a webcam, and has been known to smoke weed. Although none of these are officially listed as penalty enhancement within our nation's justice system, let the word go out from this point forward that they have been elevated to virtual capital offense status on the streets, by a frightened, racially-anxious white public, always seeking to rationalize every death of black men, at the hands of cops, or just folks *pretending* to be cops. (Author's original emphasis)

This "stabilized" sense of white privilege exists in the treatment of Martin's body because it sustains the virulent representations of Black manhood while dismissing the violence against it as deserving. As Entman and Rojecki (2001) argue, "explicitly, media images deny white superiority and the legitimacy of white privilege. In their most obvious dimensions, they promote tolerance, inclusiveness, and (limited) acceptance by whites of Blacks. At the same time, less overt media signals—and equally important, systematic absences from media content—may work against the development of greater interracial empathy and trust" (p. 57). This shift in Martin's cyber image damages Martin's narrative without destabilizing the source of white privilege. In this sense, Nakamura opines, "fluid identities aren't much use to those whose problems exist strictly (or even mostly) in the real world if they lose all their currency in the realm of the real" (p. 11). Maintaining a disconnect between cyber "realness" and actuality pivots on situating white supremacist understandings of Black identity through seemingly harmless racial performance. This disconnect is heightened in part because of the anonymity of online spaces; users' anonymity and open access to the Internet refilters the white supremacy in ways that do not register as offensive.

Trayvon Martin's death provided an opportunity for a(nother) "Kum Bah Yah" moment to manifest across America's cyberscape. What transpired instead is the attempt to maneuver messy dichotomies of racial privilege and identity—voyeurism/witnessing and race performance/race realities. Two years after news of Martin's death first broke across the Internet, we continue to muddle through such efforts. Tragically, Martin's death is not the last of its kind. It instead signifies a racialized Pandora's Box of unexplained/unexplainable deaths of young Black people: Rekia Boyd, Bo Morrison, Chavis Carter, Renisha McBride, Jonathan Ferrell, and Jordan Davis have made national headlines as tragic deaths of similarly "unfortunate circumstances." Yet their cases have not reached the same level of outrage as Martin's death. It has yet to be determined why social media "tuckered out" in the aftermath of these other deaths of young Black men and women and not with Martin. In what ways is America's investment in Trayvon Martin different than similar victims? Indeed, as Charles Blow writes in his essay, "The Curious Case of Trayvon Martin," social media is a register of not only sliding performances of race politics but the currency in which these performances are situated.[3] Are we, as Mychal Denzel Smith asserts, suffering from "outrage fatigue"? Can we be outraged when a victim does not fulfill our idealistic portrayal of an appropriate victim?

Trayvon Martin's case presents the possibilities of the Internet as a site of contemporary Black activism while highlighting its shortcomings as a postracial space. The multiple discourses Martin's death crosses—Hip Hop, race, and class respectability—messily intersect in digital spaces that could not exist offline. Digital fault lines of "idealistic victimization" and activism can be demonstrated while speaking to the physical and cultural trauma that Martin's body represents. In sum, Martin's death publicly clashed and jarred America away from the lull of cyberspace as a postracially harmonious reality.

CONCLUSION

As educators, what do we do with this history within the context of heightened digital spaces? We must teach. Our students' survival depends on their understanding the pathology of Black male bodies in and outside of school walls. According to Ladson-Billings (1995), when Black boys reach school age, they are no longer cute, but are seen as "men" with criminal capabilities. Similarly, Love (2013) argues, "[a]n examination of research concerning teacher beliefs' is disheartening. Research clearly

[3]Please see Charles Blow's essay in the March 16, 2012, *New York Times*.

illustrates that black males' performance of masculinity is misunderstood by teachers, and therefore targeted as oppositional. Black boys are seen as defiant and intimidating by white middle-class teachers" (p. 195). Thus, the murder of Travyon Martin provides a unique lens for youth because his death, and the subsequent not-guilty verdict of George Zimmerman, in particular relation with social media invokes what Bradley (2013) calls Hip Hop sensibilities, a world view that allows Hip Hop to function as a site of "engagement with race and identity—to navigate the social-cultural complexities of what is deemed postracial America" (redclayscholar). It is therefore our duty to assist youth in navigating complex spaces that are sites of public pedagogy, but invoke rage, trauma, and activism, and draw on youth Hip Hop sensibilities to move beyond rhetoric into action.

REFERENCES

Alexander, E. (1994). "Can you be BLACK and look at this?": Reading the Rodney King video(s). *Public Culture, 7*(1), 77–94.

Anzaldúa, G. (1987). *La frontera/borderlands.* San Francisco, CA: Aunt Lute Books.

Ballivían, R. R., & Herrera. L. (2012). Schools of the street: Hip-hop as youth pedagogy in Bolivia. *International Journal of Critical Pedagogy, 4*(1), 172–184.

Banks, A. J. (2011). *Digital griots: African American rhetoric in a multimedia age.* Carbondale, IL: Southern Illinois University Press.

Blow, C. (2012, March 16). The curious case of Trayvon Martin. *New York Times.* Retrieved March 2014 from http://www.nytimes.com/2012/03/17/opinion/blow-the-curious-case-of-trayvon-martin.html?pagewanted=all&_r=0

Bradley, R. N. (2014, February 15–16). Keeping it real? Hip hop and the rhetoric of and the quest for social change. *Hip Hop Literacies Conference.* Columbus, OH.

Brock, A. (2009). "Who do you think you are?": Race, representation, and cultural rhetorics in online spaces. *Poroi 6*(1), 15–35.

Entman, R. M., & Rojecki, A. (2001). *The black image in the white mind: Media and race in America.* Chicago, IL: University of Chicago Press.

Freire, P., & Macedo, D. (1987). *Literacy: Reading the word and the world.* New York, NY: Routledge.

Gay, G. (2000). *Culturally responsive teaching: Theory, research, and practice.* New York, NY: Teachers College Press.

Gutierrez, K., & Stone, L. (2000). Synchronic and diachronic dimensions of social practice: An emerging methodology for cultural-historical perspectives on literacy learning. In C. D. Lee & P. Smagorinsky (Eds.), *Vygotskian perspectives on literacy research: Constructing meaning through collaborative inquiry* (pp. 150–164). New York, NY: Cambridge University Press.

Gutierrez, K. D. (2008). Developing a sociocritical literacy in the Third Space. *Reading Research Quarterly, 43*(2), 148–164.

Hill, M. L. (2009). *Beats, rhymes, and classroom life: Hip-hop pedagogy and the politics of identity,* New York, NY: Teachers College Press.

hooks, b. (1994). *Teaching to transgress: Education as the practice of freedom.* New York, NY: Routledge.

Jaramillo, N. E. (2012). *Immigration and the challenge of education: A social drama analysis in South Central Los Angeles.* New York, NY: Palgrave Macmillan.

Kincheloe, J. L. (2008). *Critical pedagogy primer.* New York, NY: Peter Lang.

Ladson-Billings, G. (1995). Toward a theory of culturally relevant pedagogy. *American Educational Rsearch Journal, 32*(3), 465–491.

Lee, C. D. (1995). Signifying as a scaffold for literary interpretation. *Journal of Black Psychology, 21*(4), 357–381.

Leonard, D. J. (2012). The U.S. school system's criminalization of black youth. *Urban Cusp Magazine.* Retrieved May 24, 2014, from http://www.urbancusp.com/2012/04/on-trayvon-martin-the-u-s-school-systems-criminalization-of-black-youth

Love, B. (2013). "I See Trayvon Martin": What teachers can learn from the tragic death of a young black male. *The Urban Review, 45*(3), 1–15.

Love, B. L. (in-press, 2014a). "Trayvon was standing his ground": Utilizing critical hip hop pedagogy to construct counter-narratives through multiliteracies. *PowerPlay: A Journal of Educational Justice.*

Love. B. L. (2014b). Urban storytelling: How storyboarding, moviemaking & hip hop–based education can promote students' critical voice. *English Journal, 103*(5), 53–58.

Nakamura, L. (2002). *Cybertypes: Race, ethnicity, and identity on the Internet.* New York, NY: Routledge.

Osumare, H. (2008). *The Africanist aesthetic in global hip-hop: Power moves.* New York, NY: Palgrave Macmillan.

Sandlin, J. A., Schultz, B. D., & Burdick, J. (2010). *Handbook of public pedagogy: Education and learning beyond schooling.* New York, NY: Routledge.

Smith, W. A., Hung, M., & Franklin, J. D. (2011). Racial battle fatigue and the miseducation of black men: Racial microaggressions, societal problems, and environmental stress. *Journal of Negro Education, 80*(1), 63–82.

Smith, W. A., Yosso, T. J., & Solorzano, D. G. (2007). Racial primes and black misandry on historically white campuses: Toward critical race accountability in educational administration. *Educational Administration Quarterly, 43*(5), 559–585.

Williams, A. D. (2009). The critical cultural cypher: Remaking Paulo Freire's cultural circles using hip hop culture. *The International Journal of Critical Pedagogy, 2*(1), 1–29.

Wise, T. (2012). Of children and inkblots: Trayvon Martin and the psychopathology of whiteness. Retrieved May 24, 2014, from http://www.timwise.org/2012/05/of-children-and-inkblots-trayvon-martin-and-the-psychopathology-of-whiteness

Chapter 19

Princess Pedagogy: Race, Gender, and the Disney Construct

Christopher Bell

Here, at the outset, I will admit—while this volume is focused specifically on issues of overcoming social justice battle fatigue, this chapter diverges slightly, in that I will not be discussing *overcoming* battle fatigue very much at all. Instead, I would like to offer a possible method for *avoiding* the types of situations that lead to battle fatigue altogether. With my own students, I make extensive use of popular culture to reflect on the state of race and gender relations in contemporary society. It is one of the most useful tools at our disposal in the development of student consciousness surrounding these issues. Anyone that has spent any amount of time teaching students about white privilege (or male privilege, or hetero privilege, or any of the other categories of dominance and oppression in society) understands that going directly at a student's world view is a precarious task. However, using popular culture to demonstrate the ways in which societies are taught the constituent ideologies that construct those world views can oftentimes soften the blow and open students up to a new way of thinking about the issues without so much "skin in the game."

Concepts such as "privilege" can be difficult for students to intellectualize abstractly. Providing them with concrete examples using popular culture references can bring the theoretical into the practical, allowing them to fully understand how the concept operates in the real world. Selecting popular cultural sources with which most, if not all, students have some familiarity allows for a richer discussion of the nature of privilege, as students can examine the impact of the embedded ideologies in their own lives and world views, circumventing some of the factors that can lead to resistance and contribute to racial battle fatigue.

Every semester, I am invited into various Intercultural Communication classrooms to guest lecture on the subject of American popular culture. I always enjoy these guest lectures, primarily because I find the entire concept of intercultural communication incredibly funny. I am always (to the chagrin, perhaps, of the inviting instructor and the students in the room) quick to point out that, in the haste to teach students to learn about and respect the cultures of others, almost no one in the room has done any INTRAcultural communication. That is to say, the vast majority of Americans spend remarkably little time introspectively examining our own culture, yet we are in this rush to understand the cultures of others. Not only does American culture normally go unexamined, but our colloquial parlance is specifically designed to punish those who would ask extended questions about popular culture: "It's just a movie. What are you getting so upset about? It's *only* a movie."

The key to teaching popular culture is convincing students, in stark contrary to the systematic social conditioning to which they have been subjected since birth, that when it comes to culture, nothing is ever *just* anything. This seemingly simply concept, in reality, is incredibly complex. The ability to conceptualize culture as existing on multiple planes is essentially an exercise in the willful suspension of disbelief—it is a choice. In fact, I often begin my courses by presenting students with the same choice Morpheus offers Neo in *The Matrix* (1999): red pill or blue pill? If the student chooses the blue pill, s/he can ignore all evidence I will be presenting over the course of the semester, remain on the surface of popular culture, never examine any deeper or search for any more profound or multilayered reading of cultural artifacts, and not one single person will know or care. The student can live the rest of his/her life in blissful self-imposed ignorance. Or, on the other hand, the student can make the conscious decision to push past the cultural insistence prohibiting more nuanced explanation of culture, and I will manifest the words of Morpheus:

> After this, there is no turning back. You take the blue pill—the story ends, you wake up in your bed and believe whatever you want to believe. You take the red pill—you stay in Wonderland, and I show you how deep the rabbit hole goes. (Wachowski & Wachowski, 1999)

This is a tenuous position for a student made more clear when they are subsequently told a story: Imagine a man—not just any man, though.

A large man. A man who spends most of his time alone, despite the fact that he is fabulously wealthy and owns a very large home. He passes most of his days working out and screaming at his considerable servant staff. Then, one day, he meets a woman to whom he is attracted. He does not know how to talk to her kindly, so instead, he cuts her off from her family and friends. He is verbally abusive, shouts at her all the time, throws things and breaks furniture and punches holes in the walls. For her own part, the woman thinks, "This cannot possibly be the real him. Underneath all of that, he really is a good person. If I just *love* him enough, he will be a better person. If I love him enough, he will *change.*"

This story is a textbook example of a domestic violence relationship (Helpguide.org, n.d.). The relationship is inherently abusive. It is also the story of Belle in Disney's *Beauty and the Beast,* where Beast cuts Belle off from her father, locks her in his estate, and screams things at her like, "If she doesn't eat with me, then she doesn't eat at all!" (Trousdale & Wise, 1991). He throws furniture at Belle on two separate occasions, and breaks objects around his estate out of anger regularly. For her own part, Belle sings, "There's something sweet, and *almost kind*, but he was mean and he was course and unrefined. But now he's dear and so unsure. *I wonder why I didn't see it there before*" (Trousdale & Wise, emphasis mine). Perhaps Belle failed to see the sweet nature and kindness of the Beast because she was busy dodging his daily abusive rage for the first half of the film. *Beauty and the Beast* provides an easy entrée for students into the world of looking past the exterior of a text to the meanings contained within—*Beauty and the Beast* is a film, but it is also so much more than *just* a film. In popular culture, every text is always also something else, and when dealing with American popular culture in particular, the "something else" is typically the same, regardless of the specific text: public pedagogy.

PUBLIC PEDAGOGY

The landscape of work on the concept of public pedagogy is vast and well charted. It would take an entire volume dedicated solely to the concept to unpack it, and that is not my intent here. Hundreds of scholars have examined, recontextualized, reexamined, and examined again the concept of public pedagogy—in a variety of mediums, from radio (Darder, 2011) to photography (Loopmans, Cowell, & Oosterlynck, 2012) to television (Rich, 2011) to the Internet (Hauge, 2010). Public pedagogy has been used to investigate all manner of social justice issues (Chappell, 2011), including race issues (Preston & Chadderton, 2012), dis/ability issues (Christie & Bloustien, 2010), and gender issues (Luttrell, 2011). In fact, because the body of work about public pedagogy is so sizeable and varied, it is important to precisely define the exact version of the term in use for the remainder of this discussion.

Henry Giroux (1994, 1999, 2000, 2004) has been at the epicenter of defining, redefining, and clarifying public pedagogy conceptually. Giroux recognizes "the important implications of tying schooling to the imperatives of radical democracy [and] the significance of extending the meaning of pedagogy into other cultural apparatuses such as the media" (Giroux, 2001, p. xxiii). This phrase is, in essence, made up of two parts: first, the idea that what a student learns directly impacts the manner in which s/he functions in society; second, that school is not the only place where learning happens. It can come as a revelation to students that media are responsible, in large part, for teaching Americans the constituent dominant ideologies that make up this country's "world view." How we learn what we know about other people and about the world is largely dictated by the fact that we live in a nearly 100 percent media-saturated society. There is hardly a single aspect of the modern American human experience that is not in some way mediated, from the clothes that we wear, to the way that we construct relationships, to the jobs that we choose, to the very language we use to form coherent thought. All of it is, in some way, at some point directly influenced by media—either positively or negatively. Often, it is useful to ask students to articulate one single thing in their lives, outside of basic human bodily function, that is free from media influence. Even some of those bodily functions are mediated to some extent—toilet paper brands, the feminine hygiene product industry, or whether to buy an inner-coil mattress or an adjustable pillow-top mattress, for example.

Media, therefore, are some of our first and most lasting sources of meaning making (Aly, 2010; Jonassen, Campbell, & Davidson, 1994; Pahl, 1999; Potter, 2012; Wright, 2010). It is vital that students begin to develop the critical savvy to identify and deconstruct media messages in order to reveal the pedagogical aspects. At the end of the day, the student of popular culture should be able to answer two questions: "What is this text attempting to teach me?"; and "Is this a message I want to consciously choose to believe (or disbelieve)?" This is not so easily accomplished, however, in the current state of media public pedagogy.

In the 1950s, when media wanted to teach the public some sort of ideology, they were fairly straightforward about it. Take this exchange from a 1958 episode of *Leave it to Beaver:*

Wally: You know, Dad, it's funny.
Ward: What's funny?
Wally: Well, whenever we cook inside, Mom always does the cooking. But whenever we cook outside, you always do it. How come?
Ward: Well, it's sort of traditional, I guess. You know, they say a woman's place is in the home, and I suppose as long as she's in the home, she might as well be in the kitchen.

Wally: Well, that explains about Mom, but how come you always do the outside cooking?

Ward: Well, I'll tell you son, women do all right when they have all the modern conveniences. But us men are better at this rugged type of outdoor cooking. Sort of a throwback to caveman days. (JmBartek, n.d.)

The message—"women belong in the kitchen"—could not be more explicitly stated. When presented with this clip, students often react with indignation and disgust: "Clearly, this would never fly in 2013. No one would ever get away with it in modern media." However, they fail to take into account the more adept at concealing public pedagogy to which modern media systems have evolved. For example, a 2007 commercial for Hasbro's "Rose Petal Cottage" toy offers to children (to girls, more specifically, as there are no boys in the commercial) a place of "their own" (mwb1973, n.d.). In this special place, they can play in the kitchen, or in the bedroom, or in the laundry room. There is a toy stove, and a toy bed, and a toy washing machine. Coupled with visuals of happy girls playing with the toys is the song playing in the background, which contains curious lines like, "I love when my laundry gets so clean. Taking care of my home is a dream dream dream" (mwb1973, n.d.).

The message of the commercial (and of the toy itself) is remarkably similar to the message of Ward Cleaver. The joy of the two little girls in the commercial as they rock a baby in a bassinet, fold laundry, and bake muffins could not be mistaken; they are the living embodiment of the Ward Cleaver sentiment. The "Rose Petal Cottage" advertisement illustrates the vastly more nuanced apparatus for public pedagogy media have become.

DISNEY'S PUBLIC PEDAGOGY

For students, there may be no better artifacts for instruction about the nature of public pedagogy than the animated films of the Walt Disney Company. Ask a classroom full of students how many of them have *never* seen a single Disney film, and, barring extreme extenuating circumstances, the response will come up empty. Particularly in the United States, Disney has had a hand in socializing children for a very, very long time. My grandparents were born in the early 1930s; my parents were born in the late 1940s. I was born in the mid-1970s; my daughter was born in the mid-2000s. That is four generations of my family—still alive—that were raised on Disney films. Culturally, we have this enormous emotional attachment to Disney and to Disney products (Doran, 2009; Mollett, 2013). Doran, in particular, takes note of the strong tendency of people to underestimate "the emotional attachment they personally had to the media, and the urge to defend its use with their own families and with the children entrusted to their care" (Doran, 2009, p. 96). In fact, "the multitude not only favors Disney but also often considers as taboo any serious examination—never mind any criticism—of Disney's meaning and impact" (Wasko & Meehan, as quoted in Budd & Kirsch, 2005, p. 2).

Disney perpetuates this attachment (and deflects serious cultural critique) through couching its media products in terms like "innocent" and "magic." Consider the *Time Magazine* (1966) piece, entitled *Walt Disney: Images of Innocence*. For decades, Disney has been known for its "innocent, family-values image" (Budd & Kirsch, 2005, p. 3). This "wholesome family entertainment" approach to media allows for the widest range of cultural consumers: my 8-year-old daughter, my 80-year-old grandmother, and I can all simultaneously have the *same* good time. Disneyland is, by its own branding, "the happiest place on Earth" (Disneyland, n.d.). Disney conducts this campaign of cheer relentlessly. My daughter's first visit to Disneyland happened two summers ago. It was a part of a much larger trip in which she experienced her first plane ride, her first time seeing the ocean, her first time staying at a big resort hotel, and yet, if asked what she did that summer, she will invariably reply, "I went to Disneyland!" Her memories of that trip are virtually *infested* with Disney. Disney intertwines itself around memories of family and friends, the places and people we love. It does so in order to keep the public from thinking about the *reality* of Disney, which is that the Walt Disney Company is a massive transnational media mogul existing solely to garner capital returns. Disney wants to make money, and the company is exceptionally good at it. Pointing out the commercial holdings of the Walt Disney Company to students is often an exercise in watching jaws drop; they are sometimes unaware Disney owns ventures such as ESPN, Marvel Comics, ABC television, the Muppets, and Lucasfilm. It is the perfect opportunity to point out that, since they own radio stations, television networks, film production companies, magazines, theme parks, sports outlets, toy manufacturing, and more, The Walt Disney Company has an incredible amount of control over the types of images people are *allowed* to see every day. It is an excellent entry point to introduce McCombs and Shaw's (1972) agenda-setting theory: Disney does not tell us what to think, but they are pretty good at telling us what to think about.

This matters a great deal; that cannot be understated. If we consider the effects of public pedagogy, and that media are the way in which we first begin to construct our conception of the world beyond the walls of our first home, then who controls that media becomes incredibly important. Their world view can easily become the first basis of our world view. This is due, in large part, to the cumulative effect of media—"water dripping constantly wears away stone" (Noelle-Neumann, 1993, p. 168). Repeated exposure to the same ideology eventually results in an acceptance of the ideology as a normalized truth. Controlling the means of production also controls the ability to imbed ideologies that support the normalized dominance of particular groups, especially the groups currently holding dominant societal positions. It is an elevated version of "my house, my rules." Disney's ideological construct—one that is demonstrably white, heterosexual, male-centered, and anti-poor—is the foundation for its cultural productions, particularly the animated ones. Given the emotional attachment the typical student has to Disney animation, even if s/he cannot recognize or articulate that attachment, Disney films provide a rich context for discussing public pedagogy. Why we think what we think about issues such as race (or gender, or sexual orientation, or, or, or) have been deeply embedded in us by media since we were children—which is why they are so difficult to change as adults. Moving the conversation away from us, as individuals, and toward the texts that taught us to be us can be a much less adversarial proposition.

THE CUMULATIVE EFFECT OF DISNEY—AN EXAMPLE

Let us perform a wholly unscientific experiment: try to describe, in specific detail, what a Disney princess looks like. Not one specific princess, per se, but what characteristics constitute the category "Disney princess." What does one look like? Be precise: describe her hair, eyes, nose, lips, neck, body, limbs, hands, and feet.

If one can effectively navigate this experimental task and create a relatively cohesive list of commonalities, the cumulative effect of media has been successful. In 1937, Disney releases *Snow White,* and Snow becomes what we might term the "protoprincess;" that is to say, she is the first, and all other princesses after her will, in some way, be descendants of her. Snow embodies many of the "princess" characteristics that will become standard: huge eyes, nearly no nose, full lips, tiny hands and feet, tiny waist relative to hip and bust size, relatively long hair, and frail arms and legs. A quick glance at every princess since will reveal those common traits among all of them; Cinderella (1950), Aurora (1959), Ariel (1989), Belle (1991), Jasmine (1992), Megara (1997), Tiana (2009), and Rapunzel (2010) are all drawn nearly identically in terms of their constituent physical characteristics. One can state definitively what a "Disney princess" looks like because Disney has drawn the *exact same woman* for over 70 years, over and over again.

Based on the cumulative effect of media, generations of girls and women (not to mention boys and men) have internalized what a princess looks like, which also presumes what a princess does *not* look like. The problem with this is, nearly *no* girl naturally looks like this, which has profound effects on body image and self-esteem (Do Rozario, 2004; England, Descartes, & Collier-Meek, 2011; Hayes & Tantleff-Dunn, 2010; Hurley, 2005; Wohlwend, 2009). If a little girl does not embody these characteristics, she cannot be the princess. She can be something else. She can be a funny sidekick. She can be an evil witch. But she cannot be the princess, which, up until 1992, explicitly meant *white,* and up until 2009, explicitly meant *not Black*. This gendered version of public pedagogy carries within it intensely powerful hegemonic forces that begin to operate on girls as young as two to three years old.

Couple this physical features public pedagogy with the messages contained within the films about the construction of relationships, and a formidable cocktail of hegemonic pressure reveals itself. It is not simply Belle's domestic violence story that accumulates, but also Snow White's (which tells a girl that if she is beautiful, she must beware that she will incite bitter jealousy in other women—the "mean girls" syndrome (Grant, 2012; Simmons, 2010)), and Aurora's (no agency is required; just wait around for a man to come find you (Hecht, 2011; Sweeney, 2011)), and Ariel's (abandon everyone you have ever known to chase after a man to whom you have never spoken (Lamb & Brown, 2013; Stover, 2013)), and so on and so on. As more and more Disney films are consumed, Disney's version of gender accumulates and accumulates until it becomes naturalized—the very definition of public pedagogy. The constituent ideologies of gender that make up contemporary U.S. society can be found woven throughout Disney's animated films, particularly the princess films.

Consider Ariel for a moment. In *The Little Mermaid* (1989), Ariel is a 16-year-old mermaid girl with a bit of an adventurous spirit. She "falls in love" with Erik (despite, as pointed out earlier, having never even spoken to him) and decides to pursue him to the surface. Everyone, including her best friend, thinks this is a terrible idea. However, being headstrong, she approaches Ursula, the sea witch, to ask for assistance. Ursula agrees to give Ariel legs on one condition: Ariel must give Ursula her voice. Ariel begins to protest that she cannot pursue Erik without her voice. Remember, Ariel is *resistant* to this idea. Then Ursula presents her argument: men aren't "impressed with conversation." In fact, "it's she who holds her tongue who gets her man." Convinced, Ariel *immediately* agrees to the proposition. Ursula's argument literally reduces to, "No one wants to hear what you have to say; just use your body to get what you want." This is the argument that persuades Ariel to hand over her voice. The major problem with this is that Ursula, in the context of the film, is *correct*. Ariel does not, in fact, need to speak a single word in order to get Erik to fall in love with her. The message to girls is clearly that it is fine to give up one's voice in pursuit of a relationship, because it will all work out in the end—a problematic framework, to be certain, considering Ariel was a failure at persuasion when she was outspoken with her father, at the start of the film. Being outspoken, exercising agency—these are liabilities in Ariel's world. Everything Ariel tries to make happen is a failure; everything that happens to Ariel is a success. Passivity is rewarded; agency is punished. And this is the message that is sublimely, under the surface, passed on to the little girls who view *The Little Mermaid*.

However, the "use your body to get what you want" message is not limited to Ariel. In *Hercules* (1997), Megara is instructed by Hades, lord of the underworld, to find a weakness in Hercules so that Hades can defeat him and take over Mount Olympus. He tells her, in no uncertain terms, exactly what he wants her to do:

Megara: I've done my part. Get your little imps . . .
Hades: They couldn't handle him as a baby. I need somebody who can . . . handle him as a man.
Megara: Hey, I've sworn off manhandling.
Hades: Well, you know, that's good because that's what got you into this jam in the first place, isn't it? You sold your soul to me to save your boyfriend's life. And how does this creep thank you? By running off with some babe. He hurt you real bad, didn't he, Meg? Huh?
Megara: Look, I learned my lesson, okay?
Hades: Which is exactly why I got a feelin' you're gonna leap at my new offer. You give me the key to bringing down Wonder Breath, and I give you the thing that you crave most in the entire cosmos: your freedom. (Clements & Musker, 1997)

There are several implications to this exchange: first, Megara has been betrayed by a former love and now owes a debt to Hades; second, that Hades can compel Megara to repay this debt in any way he pleases, including forcing her to seduce Hercules. In very real terms, Hades is operating in this scene as Megara's pimp—"Go get what I want and maybe I'll let you retire from the streets." It is evident that the use of Megara's sexuality is Hades' plan, as in the very next scene, Megara does, in fact, attempt to seduce Hercules. Later, when Megara attempts to withdraw from Hades' plot, he explicitly reminds her:

Hades: Meg, Meg, Meg. My sweet, deluded little minion. Aren't we forgetting one teensy-weeny, but ever-so-crucial little, tiny detail? I OWN YOU! (Clements & Musker, 1997)

In this case, Megara is not even using her body to get what she wants; she is using it to get what someone else wants. This is echoed in Aladdin (1992) as well, as Jasmine seduces the evil sorcerer Jafar so that Aladdin can steal back his magic lamp:

Jasmine: Jafar! I never realized how incredibly handsome you are.
Jafar: That's better. Now, pussycat, tell me more about myself.
Jasmine: You're tall, dark, well dressed . . . and I love those eyebrows, they're so tiny. And I adore those cute little gaps between

> your teeth . . . and your beard is so twisted. You've stolen my
> heart.
>
> Jafar: And the street rat?
> Jasmine: What street rat? (Clements & Musker, 1992)

The entire time she is speaking, she has locked eyes with Jafar so he does not notice her motioning to Aladdin behind Jafar's back. She is literally using her body to get what Aladdin wants—in the moment Jafar notices Aladdin, Jasmine grabs Jafar and kisses him, to the distaste of all of the other characters in the scene (and, presumably, the audience). Jasmine not only uses her body to get what she (or, more specifically, Aladdin) wants, but she is willing to endure the revulsion of the villain in order to accomplish it.

In every case, reducing the female character to her performative sexuality produces superior results to every other kind of agency the character displays. In fact, Ariel is so adept at performative sexuality—without her voice—that it sparks Ursula to have to intervene, sending her minions to capsize Ariel's boat to break up the kiss. Immediately afterward, Ursula monologues:

> Ursula: That was a close one. Too close! The little tramp! She's better
> than I thought. At this rate, he'll be kissing her by sunset for
> sure. (Clements & Musker, 1989)

So, in the end, Ursula tells Ariel to use her body to get what she wants, Ariel does exactly that and succeeds, and Ursula calls her a tramp for it. Students might be encouraged here to think about the ways in which girls in modern society are often encouraged to openly flaunt their sexuality for the benefit of boys and then punished for doing so (Berbary, 2012; Towns & Scott, 2013); "slut shaming" is common practice in the United States (Ringrose & Renold, 2012).

It is worth noting that every one of the Disney princess films was written and directed by men. *The Little Mermaid, Aladdin, Hercules,* and *The Princess and the Frog* were written and directed by the same two men: Ron Clements and John Musker, both of whom are white, heterosexual, and upper-class baby boomers. Those sensibilities pervade the later princess films, revealing the nature of public pedagogy—to secure the dominant positions of those already in power. (For example, we might ask why the first Black princess spends the majority of the film not as a Black princess, but as a green frog—a complete rewrite of the actual fairy tale.) Had any of these films been written or directed by women or people of color, the messaging may have been altered dramatically.

This is not to say that we should indict Clements and Musker (or any other Disney princess writer or director) as somehow malevolent or even intentional in their manner of presentation or in their messaging. However, this is what is more disturbing about the process of public pedagogy. These two men are likely simply acting on their own naturalized world view, one that necessarily casts princesses as white and thin, with flowing hair and giant eyes, and necessarily requires those princesses to use their sexuality rather than their ingenuity to succeed. In real terms, this is what those princesses do because this is what princesses are *supposed* to do, according to our cultural sensibilities. Even when a princess is released from *some* of her princessly obligations, she is not released from them *all*. For example, in *Tangled* (2010), Rapunzel is unambiguously the engine of the story—she is the catalyst for all action for the first three-quarters of the film. Near the end of the film, Rapunzel makes a conscious decision to go with her wicked witch adoptive mother (another of Disney's accumulated messages: step/adoptive parents should be viewed as bad/evil) in exchange for sparing the life of Flynn Ryder, her love interest. She announces this with conviction to both the witch and to Flynn Ryder. The decision is made, Rapunzel has made it, and it is final. However, not five minutes later, Flynn Ryder reverses Rapunzel's decision *for her*, sending the clear message that he, not she, knows what is best. In doing so, he literally physically violates her body (in the form of cutting off her hair) against her will. It is the closest to a rape metaphor Disney has ever produced, and yet, we are encouraged to see it as an act of love and compassion. Without a doubt, this is clearly not the way in which Disney intended this scene to be viewed; nonetheless, the scene can unmistakably be interpreted in this alternate fashion. Whether Disney "did it on purpose" is not really the point.

SO WHAT'S THE POINT?

Presented here is just one example of public pedagogy (specifically about gender) and the way in which popular culture can be used to help teach the concept. Instructors might consider exploring with students the National Football League and the pedagogy of race, or video games and the pedagogy of gender, or *Harry Potter* and the pedagogy of class—choose any text and any ideological construct and combine for discussion. Disney happens to be an easily accessible example, but it certainly is not the only one.

The instructor of popular culture should be prepared for the inevitable "red pill" student, particularly when using a Disney film as the source artifact. The deep emotional ties to Disney that have been inculcated in some students since very early childhood can be difficult to overcome in the span of a few short hours (or weeks, or even a semester). Students should be encouraged to move beyond their standard vocabulary of "It's cool," or "It sucks." This particular type of analysis is not concerned with whether or not the student *likes* the artifact. I very much *like* many Disney films; like most other Americans, I was also raised on Disney. I have my own deep-seated emotional attachments to several Disney films. Liking or not liking is irrelevant; liking something and understanding it are not mutually exclusive endeavors. We can still enjoy popular culture and be aware of its pedagogical aspects at the same time. This is the root of *critical consumption*, which is the goal of media scholarship. Every student may not be willing to traverse the depths of the rabbit hole, but for those who attempt the journey, a brand new way of looking at the world—a more media savvy way—is sure to emerge.

Social justice battle fatigue is the result of "the mundane but extreme stress caused by [microaggressions that] can lead to mental, emotional, and physical strain" (Yosso, Smith, Ceja, & Solorzano, 2009, p. 661). At the risk of perhaps being seen as "blaming the victim," I must admit that as scholars and teachers doing the work of social justice advocacy on the front lines, in classes with students, we often put our own selves in positions that invite microaggressions (and macroaggressions) in the way we approach topics of privilege. The average undergraduate student is neither mentally nor emotionally ready to confront his or her own privilege, despite our deep-rooted, well-intentioned longing for him/her to be. If backed into a corner, the student has very little choice but to fight back, directly, against us. This is a natural response that should not be surprising, yet often, we turn around and blame the student for being "resistant."

Rather than enter into an unrealistic expectation of students that is guaranteed to pile further mental and emotional strain not just on the students, but on ourselves, approaching the concepts of privilege from a more oblique angle can soften the discussion. While this may reflexively rankle some social justice educators, the truth is, concepts such as "privilege," "social justice," or "public pedagogy" can be legitimately difficult for students to intellectualize abstractly. Providing them with concrete examples using popular culture references can bring the theoretical into the practical, allowing them to fully understand how the concept operates in the real world. Selecting popular cultural sources with which most, if not all, students have some familiarity allows for a richer discussion of the nature of privilege and public pedagogy, as students can examine the impact of the embedded ideologies in their own lives and world views.

In many ways, it neutralizes the classic response of, "But I'm not racist!" Instead of having to unpack the tremendously complex minefield that response implies, utilizing popular culture allows the educator to respond, "I understand you don't believe you are racist, so let's look at some of the ways your culture is trying to teach you to be racist, maybe even against your will. Maybe even subconsciously." It diffuses the inherent tension of pointing out a student's privilege without letting him/her off the hook for the privilege being there anyway. We are *all* being taught very specific concepts by our cultural artifacts that inherently are designed to benefit particular groups. We benefit (or do not) regardless of our desire to. Pointing out the ways that privilege is *constructed* by culture can be a much more productive initial conversation that can lead us into a space to discuss students' personal privilege more concretely. In turn, this can help us, as educators, avoid some (not all) battle-fatigue-inducing situations.

REFERENCES

Aly, A. (2010). "Shifting positions to the media discourse on terrorism: Critical points in audience members' meaning-making experiences." *Media International Australia, Incorporating Culture & Policy, 134*, 31.

Berbary, L. A. (2012). "Don't be a whore, that's not ladylike": Discursive discipline and sorority women's gendered subjectivity. *Qualitative Inquiry, 18*(7), 606–625.

Budd, M., & Kirsch, M. H. (Eds.). (2005). *Rethinking Disney: Private control, public dimensions.* Middletown, CT: Wesleyan University Press.

Chappell, S. V. (2011). Utilizing an aesthetics of destabilization to read the public pedagogy in young people's community-based social justice artworks. *Journal of Curriculum Theorizing, 27*(3), 152–170.

Christie, E., & Bloustien, G. (2010). I-cyborg: disability, affect and public pedagogy. *Discourse: Studies in the Cultural Politics of Education, 31*(4), 483–498.

Clements, R., & Musker, J. (1989). *The Little Mermaid* [Motion picture]. USA: Walt Disney Company.

Clements, R., & Musker, J. (1992). *Aladdin* [Motion picture]. USA: Walt Disney Company.

Clements, R., & Musker, J. (1997). *Hercules* [Motion picture]. USA: Walt Disney Company.

Darder, A. (2011). Radio and the art of resistance: A public pedagogy of the airwaves. *Policy Futures in Education, 9*(6), 696–705.

Disneyland. (2013, April 19). Retrieved from http://disneyland.disney.go.com

Doran, R. A. (2009). *Influence of a professional development module focused on the research-based evidence of the culture and gender bias found in Disney animated fairy tales on preprimary early childhood teachers.* Ann Arbor, MI: ProQuest.

Do Rozario, R. A. C. (2004). The princess and the Magic Kingdom: Beyond nostalgia, the function of the Disney princess. *Women's Studies in Communication, 27*(1), 34–59.

England, D. E., Descartes, L., & Collier-Meek, M. A. (2011). Gender role portrayal and the Disney princesses. *Sex roles, 64*(7–8), 555–567.

Giroux, H. A. (1994). *Disturbing pleasures: Learning popular culture.* New York, NY: Routledge.

Giroux, H. A. (1999). *The mouse that roared: Disney and the end of innocence.* Lanham, MD: Rowman & Littlefield.

Giroux, H. A. (2000). Public pedagogy as cultural politics: Stuart Hall and the "crisis" of culture. *Cultural Studies, 14*(2), 341–360.

Giroux, H. A. (Ed.). (2001). *Theory and resistance in education: Towards a pedagogy for the opposition.* Westport, CT: Bergin & Garvey.

Giroux, H. A. (2004). Cultural studies, public pedagogy, and the responsibility of intellectuals. *Communication and Critical/Cultural Studies, 1*(1), 59–79.

Grant, N. P. (2012). Mean girls and boys: The intersection of cyberbullying and privacy law and its social-political implications. *Howard Law Journal, 56,* 169–359.

Hauge, C. (2010). Pasolini's public pedagogy in a YouTube world. *Journal of Curriculum and Pedagogy, 7*(2), 19–21.

Hayes, S., & Tantleff-Dunn, S. (2010). Am I too fat to be a princess? Examining the effects of popular children's media on young girls' body image. *British Journal of Developmental Psychology, 28*(2), 413–426.

Hecht, J. (2011). Happily ever after: Construction of family in Disney princess collection films (Masters thesis). San Jose State University, San Jose, CA. Retrieved from http://scholarworks.sjsu.edu/cgi/viewcontent.cgi?article=5093&context=etd_theses

Helpguide.org. (n.d.). *Domestic violence and abuse.* Retrieved April 19, 2013 from http://www.helpguide.org/mental/domestic_violence_abuse_types_signs_causes_effects.htm

Hurley, D. L. (2005). Seeing white: Children of color and the Disney fairy tale princess. *The Journal of Negro Education, 74*(3), 221–232.

JmBartek. (n.d.). Retrieved April 19, 2013 from http://www.youtube.com/watch?v=tMZZhctPCfQ

Jonassen, D. H., Campbell, J. P., & Davidson, M. E. (1994). Learning with media: Restructuring the debate. *Educational Technology Research and Development, 42*(2), 31–39.

Lamb, S., & Brown, L. M. (2013). Disney's version of girlhood. In M. Hobbs & C. Rice (Eds.), *Gender and women's studies in Canada: Critical terrain* (pp. 336–337). Toronto, Ontario: Women's Press.

Loopmans, M., Cowell, G., & Oosterlynck, S. (2012). Photography, public pedagogy and the politics of place-making in post-industrial areas. *Social and Cultural Geography, 13*(7), 699–718.

Luttrell, W. (2011). Where inequality lives in the body: Teenage pregnancy, public pedagogies and individual lives. *Sport, Education and Society, 16*(3), 295–308.

McCombs, M. E., & Shaw, D. L. (1972). The agenda-setting function of mass media. *Public Opinion Quarterly, 36*(2), 176–187.

Menken, A., & Ashman, H. (1988). Poor unfortunate souls. *The Little Mermaid.* Walt Disney Records.

Mollet, T. (2013). "With a smile and a song . . .": Walt Disney and the birth of the American fairy tale. *Marvels & Tales, 27*(1), 109–124.

mwb1973. (n.d.). Retrieved April 19, 2013, from http://www.youtube.com/watch?v=qVgHrV9H-8k

Noelle-Neumann, E. (1993). *The spiral of silence: Public opinion—Our social skin.* Chicago, IL: University of Chicago Press.

Pahl, K. (1999). *Transformations: Children's meaning making in a nursery.* Stoke-on-Trent, UK: Trentham Books.

Potter, W. J. (2012). The expanding role for media literacy in the age of participatory cultures. In A. Delwiche & J. Henderson (Eds.), *The participatory cultures handbook* (pp. 232–244). New York, NY: Routledge.

Preston, J., & Chadderton, C. (2012). Rediscovering "race traitor": Towards a critical race theory informed public pedagogy. *Race Ethnicity and Education*, *15*(1), 85–100.

Rich, E. (2011). "I see her being obesed!" Public pedagogy, reality media and the obesity crisis. *Health*, *15*(1), 3–21.

Ringrose, J., & Renold, E. (2012). Slut-shaming, girl power and "sexualisation": Thinking through the politics of the international SlutWalks with teen girls. *Gender and Education*, *24*(3), 333–343.

Simmons, G. (2010). Mirrors, make-up and meanings in *Mean Girls*. *Screen Education*, *60*, 132.

Stover, C. (2013). Damsels and heroines: The conundrum of the post-feminist Disney princess. *LUX: A Journal of Transdisciplinary Writing and Research from Claremont Graduate University*, *2*(1), 29.

Sweeney, M. M. (2011). "Where happily ever after happens every day": Disney's official princess website and the commodification of play. *Jeunesse: Young People, Texts, Cultures*, *3*(2), 66–87.

Time. (1966, December 23). *Walt Disney: Images of Innocence*. Retrieved from http://www.time.com/time/magazine/article/0,9171,840796,00.html

Towns, A. J., & Scott, H. (2013). "I couldn't even dress the way I wanted": Young women talk of "ownership" by boyfriends: An opportunity for the prevention of domestic violence? *Feminism and Psychology*, *23*(4), 536–555.

Trousdale, G., & Wise, K. (Directors). (1991). *Beauty and the Beast* [Motion picture]. USA: Walt Disney Studios.

Wachowski, A., & Wachowski, L. (Directors). (1999). *The Matrix* [Motion picture]. USA: Warner Brothers Pictures.

Wohlwend, K. E. (2009). Damsels in discourse: Girls consuming and producing identity texts through Disney princess play. *Reading Research Quarterly*, *44*(1), 57–83.

Wright, S. (2010). *Understanding creativity in early childhood: Meaning-making and children's drawing*. London, UK: Sage.

Yosso, T. J., Smith, W. A., Ceja, M., & Solorzano, D. G. (2009). Critical race theory, racial microaggressions, and campus racial climate for Latina/o undergraduates. *Harvard Educational Review*, *79*(4), 659–691.

About the Editor and Contributors

EDITOR

Jennifer L. Martin, PhD, is an Assistant Professor of Education at the University of Mount Union. Prior to working in higher education, Dr. Martin worked in public education for 17 years, 15 of those as the department chair of English at an urban alternative high school for students labeled at-risk for school failure in metropolitan Detroit. Additionally, she taught graduate and undergraduate courses in Research Methods, Multicultural Education, Educational Leadership, and Women and Gender Studies. Currently, she teaches graduate courses in curriculum and undergraduate courses in multicultural education, gender studies, and content area literacy. Dr. Martin is committed to incorporating diverse texts in all her courses and inspiring culturally responsive pedagogical practices in current and future educators. She is the editor of the two-volume series, *Women as Leaders in Education: Succeeding Despite Inequity, Discrimination, and Other Challenges* (Praeger, 2011), which examines the intersections of class, race, gender, and sexuality for current and aspiring leaders from a variety of perspectives. She has numerous publications on bullying and harassment, educational equity, and issues of social justice. She is currently studying the development of culturally responsive leadership practices.

CONTRIBUTORS

Christopher Bell, PhD, has served as an Assistant Professor of Communication at the University of Colorado, Colorado Springs, since the summer of 2010. He specializes in the study of popular culture, focusing on the ways in which race, class, and gender intersect in different forms of children's and young-adult media, and the ways in which children are taught to be members of society. He serves as the chair of the Southwest Popular/American Culture Association's Harry Potter Studies division. Bell teaches both theory and methodology courses in critical analysis of popular culture, rhetorical theory, representation theory, and mass media. He is a nationally touring speaker on issues of race, class, and gender in the media, and has presented work at regional, national, and international conventions and conferences. In what little spare time is left, Dr. Bell is a competitive gamer, competing on regional and international circuits, and travels with his wife and daughter.

Regina N. Bradley, PhD, is a part-time Assistant Professor of English and Interdisciplinary Studies at Kennesaw State University. She earned her doctorate in African American Literature from Florida State University, a master's degree in African American and African Diaspora Studies from Indiana University-Bloomington, and a bachelor's degree in English from Albany State University (Georgia). Bradley writes about post-Civil Rights African American literature, the contemporary U.S. South, pop culture, race and sound, and Hip Hop. She is also the founder of *Outkasted Conversations*, a critical dialogue series that explores the impact of Hip Hop duo Outkast on popular culture. Bradley's current book project, *Within and Without*, explores how critical Hip Hop (culture) sensibilities can be used to navigate race and identity politics in this supposedly postracial moment of American history. She has published extensively on popular culture and race, including a chapter on Kanye West's sonic cosmopolitanism in *The Cultural Impact of Kanye West* and a forthcoming article titled "Edward P. Jones' *The Known World* and the Hip Hop Imagination" in *Southern Literary Journal*. Bradley's public scholarship has been featured on *For Harriet*, *Ebony*, *AllHipHop*, and *NewsOne*. Also known as Red Clay Scholar, a nod to her Georgia upbringing, Regina maintains a critically acclaimed blog and personal Web site, www.redclayscholar.com

Lavern Byfield, PhD, is an Assistant Professor of Reading and Language Studies in the Department of Curriculum and Instruction, Southern Illinois University-Carbondale. Dr. Byfield teaches literacy methods courses and does research on culturally and linguistically diverse students. She completed teacher training at Shortwood Teachers' College (in 1998) and a bachelor's degree from the University of the West Indies (in 2002), both in Kingston, Jamaica. Having taught at the elementary level in rural Jamaica for five years, she was awarded a scholarship from the Organization of American States (OAS) to pursue a master's degree at the University of Illinois at Urbana-Champaign (UIUC). After earning her degree, she transferred into the doctoral program and completed her PhD in language and literacy studies in the same department.

G. Michelle Collins-Sibley, PhD, joined the faculty at the University of Mount Union (then Mount Union College) in 1994. A Professor of English, she directs the university's Integrative Core (General Education Curriculum) and chairs the newly implemented Department of Interdisciplinary & Liberal Studies. For nearly a decade she served as one of the lead faculty of the annual NEH Summer Seminar, ROOTS: African Dimensions of the History and Culture of the Americas through the Atlantic Slave Trade at the Virginia Foundation for the Humanities in Charlottesville, Virginia. Her teaching and research interests focus on Africana literatures, specifically women writers of the African diaspora, literary theory—womanist/feminist, post-colonial—contemplative and peace pedagogies, and comparative literature.

Antonio Tomas De La Garza is a PhD candidate in the Department of Communication at the University of Utah. He has taught courses in intercultural communication, public speaking, and advanced argumentation courses, and currently teaches in the Ethnic Studies Program. He earned a Master of Arts in Communication and a Bachelor of Science in Political Science from Northern Arizona University, where he received the President's Award for Diversity. While earning his master's degree, De La Garza worked as a Supplemental Lecturer for the Successful Transition and Academic Readiness Program 2010, as well as taught public speaking and college readiness to first-generation, ethnic-minority, and Pell-grant-eligible students. These experiences inspired his primary research interests, which attempt to draw attention to quotidian acts of resistance that counter white supremacy. In order to further explicate this praxis, Antonio's current research examines the ways that immigration and border rhetoric affect the bodies of immigrants. In keeping with his focus on assisting with the success of students of color in the academy, he also examines the types of tactics that students of color employ to successfully navigate their educational experiences.

Sherry L. Deckman, PhD, is an Assistant Professor of Education at Ithaca College in New York, where she teaches social and cultural foundations of education and supervises English Language Arts student-teaching candidates. Her current research explores how undergraduate students from diverse backgrounds negotiate race, class, and gender while participating in culturally focused performing arts groups. She is also interested in how educators are formally prepared to work with students from diverse race and class backgrounds and how educators address issues of race, class, and gender inequity in schools. Deckman's work in education began as a high school teacher in Washington, D.C. She has also been an educator and teacher educator in Fukuoka, Japan, New York City, and Boston and Cambridge, Massachusetts, and a public school volunteer in Philadelphia. Deckman's selected publications include "But What Can I Do? Three Necessary Tensions in Teaching Teachers about Race" (coauthored with Pollock, Mira, and Shalaby, *Journal of Teacher Education*, 2009) and *Humanizing Education: Critical Alternatives to Reform* (coeditor, Harvard Educational Press, 2010).

Steven Funk, PhD, recently graduated as valedictorian with his Doctorate in Education from UCLA, where he received the Alumni Dissertation of the Year Award in addition to the Excellence in Scholarship Award in 2012 and 2013. The American Educational Research Association named him Emerging Scholar in Post-Secondary Education in 2013. He has lectured in English, Literature, and Critical Media Literacy at the university and community-college levels. He is currently authoring a children's book for gender nonconforming children and their parents, as well as essays on non-normative and oppositional readings of media and pop-culture spectacles.

Jessica C. Harris is a doctoral candidate in Higher Education and Student Affairs at Indiana University. Originally from Portland, OR, she received her BA from Occidental College in Los Angeles, CA, and her MEd from the Pennsylvania State University in State College, PA. Her current research interest focuses on utilizing critical qualitative inquiry to explore the racialized experiences of Women of Color in higher education. She has more recently begun to explore and write about using nontraditional qualitative methods to conduct research in education. Jessica is currently a Project Associate with the Faculty Survey of Student Engagement (FSSE).

LaKeisha L. Harris, PhD, CRC, is an Associate Professor at the University of Maryland Eastern Shore, where she has also served as coordinator for the Master of Science Program in Rehabilitation Counseling since 2007. She holds a Doctorate in Rehabilitation Counselor Education from The University of Iowa and holds national certification as a rehabilitation counselor. Harris has published in the areas of counselor development, adjustment to disability, and on offenders with disabilities. She has also been the primary investigator or co-primary investigator on several grants, including a Rehabilitation Services Administration (RSA) grant developed to train graduate rehabilitation counseling students and a grant from the Morehouse School of Medicine to study behavioral health issues among gay and lesbian students. Harris has also served as a board member on the National Rehabilitation Association and the National Association for Multicultural Rehabilitation Concerns. She currently serves on the peer review board for the Rehabilitation Counselors and Educators journal. She has more than 16 years' experience as a rehabilitation counselor and educator.

Jasmine M. Haywood is a doctoral student in the Higher Education and Student Affairs program at Indiana University. She completed her BS at Rensselaer Polytechnic Institute, Troy, New York, and MS at Indiana University, Bloomington. She is currently a graduate research assistant at the Center for Urban and Multicultural Education at Indiana University-Purdue University Indianapolis (IUPUI). Her research and teaching applies a framework of critical race theory to examine inequities in higher education, emphasizing the racialized experiences of students of color.

Samantha M. Ivery is a doctoral student in Higher Education and Student Affairs at Indiana University. She completed her BA from the University of Missouri, Columbia, and her MA.Ed at Western Kentucky University, Bowling Green. Her research and teaching engages critical pedagogies to explore a myriad of social justice topics in higher education with a special focus on race and gender inequity. Ivery is currently a graduate intern at Ivy Tech Community College in the Office of Institutional Research and a graduate assistant in the Division of Student Affairs at Indiana University-Purdue University Indianapolis (IUPUI).

Bettina L. Love, PhD, is an award-winning author and Assistant Professor of Educational Theory and Practice at the University of Georgia. Her research focuses on the ways in which urban youth negotiate Hip Hop music and culture to form social, cultural, and political identities to create new and sustaining ways of thinking about urban education. Her research is focused on transforming urban classrooms through the use of nontraditional educational curricula and classroom structures. Building on that theme, Love also has a passion for studying the school experiences of queer youth, along with race and inequality in education. She is a sought-after public speaker on a range of topics including Hip Hop education, Black girlhood, queer youth, Hip Hop feminism, art-based education to foster youth civic engagement, and issues of diversity. In 2014, she was invited to the White House Research Conference on Girls to discuss her work focused on the lives of Black girls. She is the inaugural recipient of the Michael F. Adams Award (2014) from the University of Georgia. She has provided commentary for various news outlets including NPR and ArtsATL. Dr. Love is one of the founding board members of The Kindezi School, an innovative school focused on small classrooms and art-based education. She conducts workshops/professional development seminars for educators and students for educational entities of all kinds. She is the founder of Real Talk: Hip Hop Education for Social Justice, an after-school initiative aimed at teaching students the history and elements of Hip Hop for social justice aligned with core subjects. She is the author of *Hip Hop's Li'l Sistas Speak: Negotiating Hip Hop Identities and Politics in the New South*. Her work has appeared in numerous books and journals, including the *English Journal, The Urban Review, International Journal of Critical Pedagogy,* and *Journal of LGBT Youth.* Her personal Web site is www.bettinalove.com

H. Richard Milner IV, PhD, is the Helen Faison Endowed Chair of Urban Education, Professor of Education, Professor of Social Work (by courtesy), and Professor of Africana Studies (by courtesy) as well as Director of the Center for Urban Education at the University of Pittsburgh. He is a policy fellow of the National Education Policy Center. His research, teaching, and policy interests concern urban education, teacher education, African American literature, and the sociology of education. In particular, Professor Milner's research examines practices that support teachers for success in urban schools. Professor Milner's work has appeared in numerous journals, and he has authored five books. His book, published in 2010 by Harvard Education Press, *Start Where You Are, But Don't Stay There: Understanding Diversity, Opportunity Gaps, and Teaching in Today's Classrooms,* represents years of research and development effort. Currently, he is Editor-in-chief of *Urban Education* and coeditor of the *Handbook of Urban Education* with Kofi Lomotey, published with Routledge Press in 2014.

Beatriz M. Montilla is currently pursuing her degree in Spanish from Ithaca College. Born and raised in the Bronx, New York, she attended Essex Street Academy for high school. At Ithaca College she is on the executive board of the organization Student2Student, which plans and implements activities for students age 8–12 for several Saturdays out of the semester. Montilla is also a Teacher's Assistant for Spanish 101 as well as a tutor for the AVID program of Ithaca High School. In the fall of 2013, she performed with Ithaca College Teatro in a rendition of *A Proposito de la Duda* for the United Nations' International Human Rights Day.

Wendy Murphy, JD, is Adjunct Professor of Sexual Violence Law at New England Law Boston. She codirects the Women's and Children's Advocacy Project under the school's Center for Law and Social Responsibility. She was a Visiting Scholar at Harvard Law School in 2002–2003, where her work focused on the status of women in their capacity as victims in the criminal justice system. Wendy is a former child abuse and sex crimes prosecutor who now specializes in the representation of crime victims, women, children, and victim service providers. She is an impact litigator and appellate attorney and founded the Victim Advocacy & Research Group, a volunteer legal advocacy organization that has provided free legal services to victims in the criminal justice system since 1992. She has also worked with the U.S. Congress and the White House Women's Office and has served on the faculty of the Poynter Institute in connection with programs related to media and reporting on sexual violence. She is a consultant whose expertise includes constitutional law, legal policy, and litigation strategy regarding victims', children's, and women's rights. Wendy has published numerous law review and pop-culture articles and lectures widely on women's, children's, and victims' rights and criminal justice policy. She has worked for CNN, Fox News, MSNBC, and CBS News as a legal analyst and appears regularly on network and cable television. A columnist for the *Patriot Ledger,* the *Boston Herald,* and *Gatehouse News,* she serves as a contributing editor to Womens' eNews and is the author of several chapters in consortium books. Her first solo-authored book, *And Justice For Some,* was published by Penguin/Sentinel in September 2007 and was revised and released in paperback in 2013.

Richard Orozco, PhD, is an Assistant Professor in the Secondary Teacher Education program at the University of Arizona South. Before completing his PhD in Education with a concentration in Language, Reading, and Culture at the University of Arizona, he taught Mexican American Studies in a segregated high school in Tucson, Arizona. His research interests include investigations of the schooling of Mexican Americans. These investigations include critically analyzing discourses, with particular emphasis on the discourse of whiteness and racial microaggressions in school settings. In addition, Dr. Orozco has studied the effects of state legislation on the schooling experiences of Mexican Americans. His work has been published in *Journal of Education Policy, Hispanic Journal of Behavioral Sciences, Journal of Latinos and Education,* and *Association of Mexican American Educators Journal.*

Michele Paludi, PhD, is President of Human Resources Management Solutions. Paludi, also a series editor for Praeger Publishers, provides human resource management solutions for businesses, K–12, and college/university campuses. Those solutions include performance appraisals, employee handbooks, OSHA regulations, non-discrimination policies, needs assessments, post-training evaluations, communications, disciplining and corrective action, health and safety policies, family and medical leave act policies, and Americans with Disabilities policies. She serves as an expert witness for court proceedings and administrative hearings on sexual harassment and race discrimination. Paludi is the author/editor of 52 college textbooks and more than 200 scholarly articles and conference presentations on sexual harassment, psychology of women, gender, and sexual harassment and victimization. Her book, *Ivory Power: Sexual Harassment on Campus*, received the 1992 Myers Center Award for an Outstanding Book on Human Rights in the United States. Paludi was a Consultant to and a Member of former New York State Governor Mario Cuomo's Task Force on Sexual Harassment. She was also Chair of the U.S. Department of Education's Subpanel on the Prevention of Violence, Sexual Harassment, and Alcohol and Other Drug Problems in Higher Education. Paludi was one of six scholars in the United States to be selected for this subpanel. She has held faculty positions at Franklin & Marshall College, Kent State University, Hunter College (where she earned tenure and a Full Professorship), and Union College. Paludi is the Director of the UGC Certificate Programs in Human Resource Management and in Leadership and Management. She is currently the Equal Opportunity and Employee Relations Specialist/Title IX Coordinator/ADA & Section 504 Coordinator at Siena College.

Melissa Payne is an educator committed to social justice and access in higher education. She is currently a faculty member teaching developmental writing and math at Ellsworth Community College in Iowa Falls, Iowa. She is beginning a faculty role after a career in student affairs focused primarily on assisting students with academic, social, and personal concerns outside of the classroom. She is trained to facilitate diversity inclusion workshops in the National Coalition Building Institute model, and she has experience building community among students from marginalized groups at colleges and universities of various sizes and types. She holds a Bachelor's Degree in German from Truman State University and a Master's Degree in Postsecondary Education/Student Affairs from the University of Northern Iowa.

Dr. Jenelle S. Pitt, PhD, CRC, is an Assistant Professor in the Department of Counselor Education and Rehabilitation at California State University, Fresno. She received a bachelor's degree in Psychology from the University of California, Riverside, a master's degree in Rehabilitation Counseling from Michigan State University, and a doctorate in Rehabilitation Counselor Education from Michigan State University. She has 15 years of experience in working with people with disabilities from marginalized backgrounds across multiple settings including state government, schools, and nonprofit agencies. Pitt's research interests include (a) cultural diversity and multiculturalism, (b) counselor training and preparation, and (c) organizational behavior practices in state vocational rehabilitation programs. Pitt has more than 25 national and state presentations, and 8 invited presentations. Named as the 2014 Rehabilitation Educator of the Year by the National Council on Rehabilitation Education, Pitt has been serving as the President of Researchers and Critical Educators at California State University, Fresno, since 2009, and as Vice Chair for City of Fresno's Disability Advisory Commission since 2011.

Bernardo E. Pohl, Jr., PhD (Doctorate of Education in Curriculum and Instruction from the University of Houston-Main in Texas), has taught secondary social studies and special education for nine years. Currently, he lectures on education methodology at the university level. He is the author of "The Moral Crisis in Special Education: Redefining The Social Model of Disability" in *Journeys in Social Education* (C. S. White, Ed., 2010) and "Voices of Empowerment" (2008) published in *The English Record.*

Linda Prieto, PhD, is the daughter of Mexican immigrants. Growing up poor required that she begin working in the agricultural fields of the central San Joaquin Valley in California with her family at the age of eight. She entered the U.S. public school system a Spanish monolingual, is a single mom of a three-year-old, and was a first-generation college student and only one in her family to have attained a doctorate. She earned her Doctorate in Curriculum and Instruction with an emphasis in Cultural Studies in Education and a Graduate Portfolio in Mexican American Studies from the Center for Mexican American Studies at the University of Texas at Austin. As an Assistant Professor in the Department of Bicultural-Bilingual Studies at The University of Texas at San Antonio, her areas of interest include bilingual education, Latin@ teacher identity, teacher preparation, culturally efficacious teaching, social justice education, supporting early literacy development for native Spanish speakers, and the documentation of attitudes toward and experiences of gay, lesbian, bisexual, transgender Latin@s. She conducts research on teacher formation across the continuum from teacher candidates to teacher educators. She approaches her work from a critical perspective using life her/histories and testimonios informed by Chicana feminist thought.

Victoria Pruin DeFrancisco, PhD, is a Professor of Communication Studies and Women's and Gender Studies at the University of Northern Iowa, where she also coordinates a campuswide program affiliated with the National Coalition Building Institute. DeFrancisco has served on multiple university diversity inclusion committees in her 25 years at UNI, including serving as Director of Women's Studies. She is coauthor of *Gender in Communication: A Critical Introduction* (2014, 2nd ed.) and teaches graduate and undergraduate courses in intercultural and interpersonal communication.

She has also taught in Beijing, China, and Klagenfurt, Austria. She received her PhD from the University of Illinois at Urbana Champaign.

Aisha Shamburger-Rousseau, PhD, is an Assistant Professor in the Department of Disability and Psychoeducational Studies at The University of Arizona. She earned a BA from Spelman College; an MS in Rehabilitation Counseling from the Medical College of Virginia at Virginia Commonwealth University; and a PhD in Health Related Science with a concentration in Rehabilitation Leadership from the School of Allied Health Professions at Virginia Commonwealth University. Shamburger-Rousseau has written and conducted research pertaining to the intersection of disability, gender, and multicultural issues, as well as minority women living with HIV/AIDS. She has a number of peer-reviewed publications in addition to a book chapter. She continues to serve as an invited presenter at the state, national, and international levels. As the first African American doctoral graduate from the Rehabilitation Counseling Department at Virginia Commonwealth University, Shamburger-Rousseau aims to be a voice for underrepresented populations both within and outside of the academy.

M. L. Sharp-Grier is an Assistant Professor of Sociology at an Ohio two-year college. She has a long history of social advocacy and service, having maintained positions in victim advocacy, forensic social work, and criminal justice. Prior to her current position, she served as a Lecturer of Women's Studies at an Ohio four-year institution. Sharp-Grier obtained her Bachelor of Science degree in Criminal Justice/Pre-Law, and a Master of Arts degree in Sociology. She has done postgraduate work in both social work and women's studies, and is a Licensed Social Worker for the State of Ohio. As a public speaker, Sharp-Grier has addressed audiences on the realities of interpersonal violence (IPV). She has provided agency diversity training for nonprofit organizations, and has facilitated statewide and national conversations regarding curriculum design and management, student success, and student engagement. Other professional presentations include discussions of domestic violence, African American women and identity formulation, habitus and cultural standpoint, and race and lesbianism. Sharp-Grier is an honorably discharged member of the U.S. Army Reserve (USAR).

Crystal Shelby-Caffey, PhD, is an Assistant Professor of Reading and Language Studies in the Department of Curriculum and Instruction at Southern Illinois University. She teaches literacy methods courses as well as courses related to diagnosing and correcting difficulties in literacy. Shelby-Caffey's research interests are varied and have included an examination of the intersection between literacy and technology and public school programming for culturally and linguistically diverse students. There is a strong emphasis within her course on multicultural literature, critical literacy, and culturally responsive pedagogy.

Johari R. Shuck, a native of the Chicago area, is a doctoral student in Higher Education and Student Affairs (HESA) at Indiana University, where she also earned an MS in HESA. She completed her undergraduate studies at the University of Michigan-Ann Arbor. Currently, she serves as an associate instructor at Indiana University-Bloomington and a graduate research assistant in the Center for Urban and Multicultural Education (CUME) at Indiana University Purdue University Indianapolis (IUPUI). Her current research is focused on the college and post-college experiences of Black male student athletes and civic engagement in the African American community.

Yukari Takimoto Amos is an Associate Professor in the Department of Language, Literacy, and Special Education at Central Washington University, where she teaches multicultural education and TESL-related classes. Her research interests are immigrant students' English language learning, international students at an American university, and preservice teachers' dispositions toward cultural and linguistic diversity.

Brandelyn Tosolt, PhD, is Associate Professor in Teacher Education at Northern Kentucky University. She completed her undergraduate degree at Michigan State University and began working in the nonprofit sector. After earning her Master's degree in Education from University of Michigan, she taught middle grades in both private and public schools in Detroit, Michigan. She earned her PhD at Oakland University, conducting research on the differences in middle-grades students' perceptions of caring teacher behaviors based on student racial identity. Tosolt's courses promote engagement with ideas of social identity, cultural pluralism, and social justice at the undergraduate, master's, and doctoral levels. She works across divisions on her campus to create a more inclusive, collaborative climate. Her research, which privileges the voices of historically underrepresented groups and seeks to understand perspectives on events in individual lives and the broader society, has been published in a variety of peer-reviewed journals, including *The Journal of Negro Education; Multicultural Perspectives; Race, Gender & Class;* and *International Journal of Multicultural Education.*

Edwin Úbeda is a doctoral student of Reading and Language Studies in the Department of Curriculum and Instruction, at Southern Illinois

University Carbondale. As a doctoral student, Edwin assists in reading methods K–8 grades and preparing preservice in working with English Learners. He was awarded the Smithsonian minority scholarship during his tenure as a Master's student at Western Illinois University. He taught bilingual education at an elementary school in rural Illinois for five years and previously taught adult ESL classes at the local community college. After working five years, he transitioned into the doctoral program and is pursuing a PhD in language and literacy studies.

Mya Vaughn, PhD, is an Assistant Professor in the Department of Rehabilitation Counseling and Services at Maryville University. She earned a BS in Psychology from Southern Illinois University in Edwardsville, an MA in Rehabilitation Counseling from Maryville University, and a PhD in Rehabilitation Counseling Education from Michigan State University. She has been working with people with disabilities since 1998. Dr. Vaughn's experiences with people with disabilities include employment as a researcher in asthma, smoking cessation, Alzheimer's, and Parkinson's disease, counselor for individuals with psychiatric disability, and instructor of psychology and disability studies. Vaughn has written and conducted research pertaining to the intersection of sexuality and disability, multicultural issues, and employment outcomes. Presently, she is a Provisional Licensed Professional Counselor in St. Louis, Missouri, providing home-based counseling services to individuals with various types of disabilities.

Index